Angus q

with mmm ...

from Malcolm

xx

June 2004.

Learning To Talk
Corporate Citizenship and the Development of the UN Global Compact

Edited by Malcolm McIntosh, Sandra Waddock and Georg Kell

I am convinced that a non-violent society can be built only on the foundation of harmony and co-operation, without which society is bound to remain violent. If we argue that this cannot be done it will mean that a non-violent society can never come into being.
In that case our entire culture would be meaningless.

Mahatma Gandhi, at a prayer meeting, October 1941

Quoted in *Passion for Peace: Exercising Power Creatively* by Stuart Rees (Kensington, NSW, Australia: University of New South Wales Press, 2003)

Learning To Talk

CORPORATE CITIZENSHIP AND THE DEVELOPMENT OF THE UN GLOBAL COMPACT

EDITED BY MALCOLM McINTOSH,
SANDRA WADDOCK AND GEORG KELL

Greenleaf
PUBLISHING
2 0 0 4

© 2004 Greenleaf Publishing Limited

Published by Greenleaf Publishing Limited
Aizlewood's Mill
Nursery Street
Sheffield S3 8GG
UK

Printed on paper made from at least 75% post-consumer waste
using TCF and ECF bleaching.
Printed and bound by William Clowes, UK.
Cover by LaliAbril.com.

British Library Cataloguing in Publication Data:
   A catalogue record for this book is available from the British Library.

ISBN 1874719756

Contents

Foreword

Kofi Annan

When I first introduced the Global Compact at the World Economic Forum in Davos in January 1999 I warned that unless more serious consideration were given to social and environmental issues the global economy would grow ever more fragile. I called on business leaders to join a Global Compact as a vehicle for exercising enlightened self-interest: to embrace universal principles in the area of human rights, labour and the environment and to support United Nations goals to contribute to more stable and inclusive markets.

I am delighted to say that business has heeded the call to action. More than 1,200 companies from over 70 countries, as well as dozens of civil-society organisations and global trade unions, are learning how to work together through learning and dialogue. The Compact has inspired a range of new projects on the ground, and many corporations are addressing issues such as human rights for the first time. Business, labour and non-governmental organisations have discovered that co-operation is better than confrontation. And the United Nations itself has learned how to open up its doors and how to work with actors in the private sector.

Processes for change are never free of tension. Indeed, without tension, change may never happen. Nor can it happen without leadership. But let us also remember that behind every leader there are agents of change—individuals who believe in the mission and who have the courage and determination to make change happen, despite the tensions it might entail.

This book offers valuable examples, insights and lessons learned from the Global Compact experience. It also reveals how various expectations have characterised the growth of the initiative. For some, the Compact is primarily a value proposition and an ethical framework. For others, it is a framework for learning how to build alliances with other participants in support of common goals. This variety of perspectives represents a strength, not a weakness. It illustrates that values and principles, projects and initiatives are two sides of the same coin.

Above all, it shows us that the Global Compact is a constant work in progress. I hope this book will help stimulate the debate on how we can best move forward in the years ahead.

Secretary-General
New York, February 2004

Acknowledgements

First and foremost I would like to acknowledge and thank Sandra Waddock at Boston College and Georg Kell at the UN Global Compact for their close collaboration and engagement with work on this book and issues relating to corporate citizenship. Over a number of years and with competing hectic work schedules we have kept in close contact through the production of first a special edition of *The Journal of Corporate Citizenship* (*JCC* 11: Autumn 2003) on the UN Global Compact and now *Learning To Talk: Corporate Citizenship and the Development of the UN Global Compact*. For more than a decade David Murphy has been a close working colleague and I would like to thank him and Rupesh Shah at the New Academy of Business for their help on *JCC* 11. From inception to publication John Stuart, Dean Bargh and their colleagues at Greenleaf Publishing in Sheffield have been sources of strength and encouragement—many thanks.

Second, we would like to thank all those who have written for this book, including those whose work has been published elsewhere previously. We hope that this collection provides insight into the history and development of the Global Compact.

Third, there are some heroes behind the UN Global Compact. The Secretary-General, Kofi Annan, will be recognised for years to come for his great efforts on the complex and sensitive task of developing improved relations between the family of UN agencies and the private sector and civil society. So too will other people on his staff, most particularly Georg Kell, Executive Director of the UN Global Compact Office in New York, who has worked tirelessly in pursuit of the aspirations and aims of the Compact. He has been successful in inspiring many, many people around the world to share the vision of trying to institutionalise human rights, labour standards and environmental protection in global governance through engagement with the Global Compact.

Malcolm McIntosh
Bath, England
April 2004

The UN Global Compact

www.unglobalcompact.org

On 31st January 1999, at the World Economic Forum in Davos, UN Secretary-General Kofi Annan challenged world business leaders to 'embrace and enact' the following set of universal principles within their sphere of influence.

Through the power of collective action, the Global Compact seeks to advance responsible corporate citizenship so that business can be part of the solution to the challenges of globalisation. In this way, the private sector—in partnership with other social actors—can help realise the Secretary-General's vision: a more sustainable and inclusive global economy.

Today, hundreds of companies from all regions of the world, international labour and civil-society organisations are engaged in the Global Compact. The Global Compact is a direct initiative of the Secretary-General; its staff and operations are lean and flexible.

The Global Compact is a voluntary corporate citizenship initiative with two objectives:

a Mainstream the principles in business activities around the world

b Catalyse actions in support of UN goals

To achieve these objectives, the Global Compact offers facilitation and engagement through several mechanisms: Policy Dialogues, Learning, Local Structures and Projects.

The Global Compact is not a regulatory instrument—it does not 'police', enforce or measure the behaviour or actions of companies. Rather, the Global Compact relies on public accountability, transparency and the enlightened self-interest of companies, labour and civil society to initiate and share substantive action in pursuing the principles upon which the Global Compact is based.

The Global Compact is a network. At its core are the Global Compact Office and five UN agencies: the Office of the High Commissioner for Human Rights; the United Nations Environment Programme; the International Labour Organisation; the United Nations Development Programme; and the United Nations Industrial Development Organisation. The Global Compact involves all the relevant social actors: governments, who defined the principles on which the initiative is based;

companies, whose actions it seeks to influence; labour, in whose hands the concrete process of global production takes place; civil-society organisations, representing the wider community of stakeholders; and the United Nations, the world's only truly global political forum, as an authoritative convener and facilitator.

Principle 1
Businesses should support and respect the protection of internationally proclaimed human rights within their sphere of influence.

Principle 2
Businesses should ensure that their own operations are not complicit in human rights abuses.

Principle 3
Businesses should uphold the freedom of association and the effective recognition of the right to collective bargaining.

Principle 4
Businesses should uphold the elimination of all forms of forced and compulsory labour.

Principle 5
Businesses should uphold the effective abolition of child labour.

Principle 6
Businesses should eliminate discrimination in respect of employment and occupation.

Principle 7
Businesses should support a precautionary approach to environmental challenges.

Principle 8
Businesses should undertake initiatives to promote greater environmental responsibility.

Principle 9
Businesses should encourage the development and diffusion of environmentally friendly technologies.

The tenth principle on corruption is expected to be introduced in the second half of 2004:

Principle 10
Businesses should work against corruption in all its forms, including extortion and bribery.

Introduction

Malcolm McIntosh
Independent Commentator

Sandra Waddock
Boston College, USA

Georg Kell
UN Global Compact

The UN Global Compact is an historic experiment in learning and action on corporate citizenship. By promoting the idea that corporations earn their licences to operate not only by being profitable but also by improving practice in line with globally determined core principles and engaging in meaningful dialogue on human rights principles, labour standards and environmental protection, the Global Compact redefines corporate citizenship. Learning to talk productively about these important issues, the framers of the Global Compact believe, will lead not just to talking but also to 'walking the talk'. To be successful, the listening and talking inherent in the operating principles of the Global Compact must lead to real—and responsible—actions, actions that constructively engage stakeholders in all realms of the societies within which companies operate.

This book frames the development of the Global Compact in its first few years, setting the broader context of corporate responsiveness and responsibility, broadly illustrating the evolution of the United Nations and elaborating evolving modes of global governance and new organisational forms. In many ways the Global Compact is at the centre of these efforts to bridge the gap between business as a profit-maximising machine and business as an integral part of society—a part that adds value not just in economic terms but also in societal terms, while not doing harm to nature.

Early in 2003 we invited contributions to a special edition of *The Journal of Corporate Citizenship* to reflect on the origins and developments of the Global Compact. That special edition of the journal has led to this book, the publication of which marks the third anniversary of the launch of the Global Compact by the Secretary-General on 6 July 2001. Almost without exception, each of the contributors to this book has experience in many of the following areas: business, social activism, teaching, writing and journalism, research, management, and broadcasting. Perspectives from researchers and non-researchers, theorists and practitioners, critics and supporters from this wide range of backgrounds and life experiences has produced a rich conversation in itself. None of the views expressed here is necessarily endorsed by the others or by the United Nations but, to misquote Voltaire, 'We defend the right to disagree' within the pages of this book. As the UN Secretary-General Kofi Annan says in his Foreword to this book: 'This variety of perspectives represents a strength, not a weakness. It illustrates that values and principles, projects and initiatives are two sides of the same coin' (page 9).

Learning to Talk provides an opportunity for contributors to take contemplative stock of the first few years of learning from the Global Compact. The Global Compact complements other corporate citizenship initiatives by promoting dialogue on the relationship between business and society. As the only truly global corporate citizenship initiative, it does not provide an auditable standard but rather a set of principles through which businesses and the United Nations can work in partnership for global social development. For some businesses the Global Compact represents simply a codification of their existing policies and management practices, but for many it represents a first engagement in learning about how to talk about—and implement—important universally agreed principles. In that sense, the Global Compact represents both a challenge and an opportunity for businesses to raise their game by aligning profitability with the common good and even to make discussable issues that previously were 'off the table'. For more background information on the Compact please go to www.unglobalcompact.org.

The Global Compact draws its moral authority and global convening power from the UN Secretary-General and its moral and political legitimacy from the United Nations. Within the United Nations, the Global Compact can be viewed as a series of nested networks involving the Secretary-General's Office, the International Labour Organisation (ILO), the United Nations Environment Programme (UNEP), the United Nations High Commission for Human Rights (UNHCHR), the United Nations Development Programme (UNDP), the United Nations Industrial Development Organisation (UNIDO), business, international non-governmental organisations (INGOs) and labour. In its external manifestation, the Global Compact can variously be described as an international learning network, a social network of people and organisations engaged in a global conversation, as a global action network and as a multi-stakeholder dialogue. The greatest success of the Global Compact has been in providing a convening platform for a growing global conversation about social development that engages actors from all important sectors of society and for bringing previously undiscussable issues into the conversation about globalisation.

However the Global Compact is viewed, it is time to reflect on the first tentative steps of an initiative that aims at integrating business into a society that was born in the aftermath of the Cold War, in what some see as the triumph of global economic liberalism and others have seen as the evil of globalisation. In the first few years of the Global Compact the world has experienced the terrorist attacks on the USA on 11 September 2001 ('9/11') and the 2003/4 Iraq War—not forgetting the 40 or so interstate and international wars that are ongoing at this time.

In these early days, whatever is written about the Global Compact will be tentative, but there can be some serious reflection on its aims and origins, and some telling of stories of engagement. There can also be some recognition of how this initiative has quickly become an important reference point in the dialogue on global and corporate governance. The remainder of this introduction looks at the chapters presented in this book and provides a perspective on many of the current discussions in a field that links corporate responsibility, learning theory and global governance.

Learning to Talk: an overview

Part 1: The origins and development of the UN Global Compact

The Secretary-General of the United Nations announced the idea of a global compact in a speech to the World Economic Forum, meeting in Davos, Switzerland, on 31 January 1999. The Global Compact was then officially launched at a high-level meeting in New York in July 2001 chaired by the Secretary-General, Kofi Annan, and attended by senior representatives of business, international civil-society organisations and trade unions as well as representatives of UNEP, the ILO and the UNHCHR. For June 2004 he called a high-level meeting to discuss the progress that was made during the intervening three years. *Learning to Talk* is an account of those first three years.

In calling for a Global Compact between business and society, Kofi Annan put his personal authority and credibility on the line. For him the Compact was a mission that took the United Nations forward by recognising the need for a new world order of social partnerships among business, states and civil society. It was a recognition that multilateral organisations, such as the United Nations, had to find accommodation with other international, global and supraterritorial organisations, whether in business, government, or civil society. Support and legitimacy for this approach was gained at the Millennium Summit held in New York in January 2000 under the banner of 'Renewing the UN': 'Strengthening the UN depends on Governments, and especially on their willingness to work with others—the private sector, non-governmental organisations and multilateral agencies—to find consensus solutions.'[1] Further to this the Secretary-General delivered a report to the General Assembly on co-operation with partners, 'in particular the private sector'.[2]

The Global Compact is the first foray into direct constructive engagement with business by the United Nations. On 31 January 1999, on his third visit to the World

---

1 www.un.org/millennium/sg/report/summ.htm
2 'UN Cooperation between the UN and the Relevant Partners, in Particular the Private Sector', Report of the Secretary-General, 28 August 2001, 01-52342(E): 39.

Economic Forum, Annan spoke of his hopes for a creative partnership between the United Nations and the private sector. He made the point that the everyday work of the United Nations—whether in peacekeeping, setting technical standards, protecting intellectual property or providing much-needed assistance to developing countries—has helped to expand opportunities for business around the world. His hopes were, as is the Global Compact itself, aspirational:

> Our challenge today is to devise a similar compact on the global scale, to underpin the new global economy. If we succeed in that, we would lay the foundation for an age of global prosperity, comparable to that enjoyed by the industrialised countries in the decades after the Second World War (see page 29).

And so the Global Compact was born out of a desire and a necessity to humanise the globalisation process, to build social and environmental pillars in the global temple of commerce. As John Ruggie, a principal architect of the Global Compact, says in this book, '*business* created the single global economic space; business can and must help to sustain it' (page 41).

In contextualising the Global Compact Ruggie reminds us that, while this is not the first time the world has experienced globalisation, this time it is different. The first wave occurred in the 19th century and its unfettered capitalism led to two world wars because it lacked social legitimacy and reflected neither the needs nor the aspirations of the vast majority of ordinary people. Markets need to be embedded in broader frameworks of social values and shared objectives if they and the societies they operate within are to survive and thrive. The difference in the current wave of globalisation is that we have moved from an international world to a global world. We have moved from national economies, engaged in external transactions that governments could mediate at the border by tariffs and exchange rates, to global markets leaving behind national social bargains.

Kell and Levin highlight the need to understand that the Global Compact is but one effort to resolve the deficiencies of global capitalism. Just as the Millennium Summit had highlighted the need to understand new global networks that work alongside international co-operation, so 'the Global Compact is an historic experiment in learning and action' (Kell and Levin, page 65). As an inter-organisational network (see Ruggie, pages 39-40) the Global Compact is a 'global amalgamation of strategic and wide public policy learning networks that cultivates integrative learning' (Kell and Levin, page 47). That it is new, innovative and creative in its origins and processes is a challenge to all actors—not least the UN itself. It is also difficult for many in the corporate responsibility and accountability movement who are rightly looking to measure and report on the social and environmental impact of business. But this UN initiative is different and complements other corporate responsibility initiatives by providing a learning platform for multiple actors to be drawn into the conversation about human rights, labour standards and environmental protection. It is also different because for the first time, the UN is directly (and controversially) engaged with business enterprises.

In opening the United Nations to engagement with the business community for the first time, Kofi Annan recognised that the power of businesses in the modern world needs to be balanced with the interests of the societies of the world and the nations that constitute the United Nations. As Erroll Mendes writes, 'The first major attempt by the United Nations to develop a code of practice for what were termed transnational corporations (TNCs) began in 1977 and a draft code was completed in 1990. Within two years it was dead, killed by the TNCs and Western governments that fiercely opposed it' (page 101). In the vacuum left by the inability of the institutions of global governance to act, a plethora of international and national organisations, non-governmental organisations (NGOs) and business groups have attempted to develop codes of conduct, benchmarks and verification systems applicable to the multinational enterprises (MNEs) globally. As Mendes reports, there are now hundreds of codes that companies can align themselves to.

In this explosion of new initiatives comes the Compact, with an explicit desire to involve the United Nations in forging links between business and society and in bringing the UN machine up to speed with the new globalised world. Cornis van der Lugt, from UNEP (Chapter 8, page 131) refers to this rapprochement between business and the UN based on an understanding by the Secretary-General that sees globalisation as essentially a business-led process. Van der Lugt detects that the UN, through the Global Compact, may have found its own 'third way' and the emergence of a co-regulatory approach. Mendes (Chapter 6, page 101) links the high aspirations of the Global Compact to sustainable human development and human rights.

This shift to active engagement between the UN and business poses the most enormous of challenges to the United Nations, split as it is into a 'family' of organisations with diverse histories, governance procedures and organisational behaviours. According to McIntosh (Chapter 22, page 323), the United Nations and its agencies themselves are on a voyage of discovery to see if they can learn how global business operates. They collectively need to learn how the UN agencies can work together and how to operate to the same standards that the Global Compact demands of business. Further, they need to learn how to manage new social partnerships among corporations, states and civil-society organisations. The outcome of this venture isn't clear as Georg Kell notes when (Chapter 25) questioning the extent to which UN member-states will actually grant the UN an important role in the economic sphere of activity. Success, as he notes, is far from assured at this point.

Nevertheless, as Kell confirms, such criticism of the Global Compact has been instrumental in provoking an ongoing search for the right incentives and methodologies to bring about desired changes while maintaining the integrity of the institution. Georg Kell and David Levin (Chapter 3, page 44) argue that the UN Global Compact must cover two objectives: to help 'lay a foundation of shared values' and to 'promote concrete and sustained action'.

The Global Compact is an experiment, an experiment about the aspirations of humanity in their best sense. One of the major questions is whether the experiment—or a more institutionalised version of it—will continue when Kofi Annan, with whom it is personally identified, is no longer Secretary-General. The issue of experimentation is difficult for all concerned, but especially for an organisation whose members espouse such high principles and set such high targets—as witnessed by the Global Compact's principles and the UN Millennium Development Goals.[3] There is an ambivalence about the Global Compact. On the one hand, it generates a network of concerned companies and relevant others. On the other hand, it is set in the nationally based and bureaucratic context of the numerous agencies of the United Nations, each with its own mandate. On the one hand, it is an experiment in learning, networking and the development of a global conversation about human rights, labour standards and environmental protection. On the other hand, its success will only be accepted by some external critics if it can be shown to have clearly achieved improvements against the Millennium Development Goals or diminish what many perceive to be the problems of globalisation. The longevity of the Global Compact experiment and the idea that the Global Compact may evolve a life of its own, and leave its mother ship—the United Nations—means that ownership could disperse away from the United Nations. Kell and Levin (Chapter 3, page 50) say that:

> The importance of the evolution of these local networks cannot be overstated. It represents a shift towards the decentralisation of the network and the distribution of ownership, both critical to the longevity of the initiative. Besides devolving responsibility to local networks, the Global Compact Office has increasingly empowered 'enablers', such as the World Business Council for Sustainable Development (WBCSD) and Business for Social Responsibility (BSR), to expand the network and to manage issues related to individual companies. Such decentralisation will enhance the potential of the Global Compact to embed markets around the world within a broader consensus of societal needs and concerns.

So, the challenge is that the UN Global Compact should raise the level of conversation about shared global values, particularly in the corporate world, and lead to recognisable actions that result from partnerships between business and the UN which in turn lead to the delivery of the Millennium Targets. In order to do this it must build an inter-organisational network of global change agents, with the UN as the norm entrepreneur.

Part 2: The Global Compact and human rights

By July 2001, 43 companies had committed themselves publicly and in a letter to the Secretary-General to support the Global Compact, and, by the time of the third Learning Forum meeting in Nova Lima in Brazil (in December 2003), this had risen to 1,200. One of the most contentious areas has been the Global Compact principles that refer to human rights. Labour standards and environmental protection codes, conventions and regulation are accepted, if not necessarily adhered to, but human rights is a new field for most businesses.

Klaus Leisinger (Chapter 5, page 73) introduces the links between business and human rights by acknowledging the disquiet about globalisation. He recognises that those who are interested in global development issues point out the over-emphasis on trade and investment at the expense of social issues. But, as Leisinger

3 For more on the Millennium Development Goals, see Appendix A.

says, most signatory companies did not fully realise the implications of what they were committing themselves to and that, furthermore, most have yet to respond to the human rights debate. In addition, for Leisinger, corporate responsibility has three dimensions, or developmental stages of understanding: must, ought to and can—and these stages apply to the emerging understanding of how companies should cope with human rights issues.

Tom Donaldson, in a paper first published in *The Journal of Corporate Citizenship* in July 2003 (reproduced in this volume, Chapter 4), also says that there are three rungs on a 'justificatory ladder' that companies must climb in order to be able to support the Global Compact. These are: 'egoism', 'co-operative egoism' and then 'citizenship'. The idea of the first rung is based on absolute self-centredness. The idea of the second rung is based on Adam Smith's invisible hand (remembering that he never envisaged the size and scope of the modern corporation). Ascendance to the third rung rewrites the role and rules for the company. As Donaldson says (page 70): 'The very name "Global Compact" suggests a hypothetical, implicit, social contract.'

Even if, as Leisinger suggests, companies did not know what they were doing when they signed up to the Global Compact, there is a growing debate on the issues that arise from Principles 1 and 2: namely, those of the corporation's 'sphere of influence' and 'complicity in human rights abuses'. Among enlightened companies this debate has been furthered by the growing numbers of codes, management systems and other reporting mechanisms that have grown up in the past few years around the interface of financial, social and environmental performance measurement, sometimes simplistically referred to as the 'triple bottom line'. Erroll Mendes (Chapter 6, page 104) refers to this growing debate as 'ripples coalescing in the pond of ethical consciousness of the global human family'.

Mendes and Leisinger both argue that the business and human rights debate and the Global Compact consultation process require clarification on these issues, and the more radical argue that the notion of citizenship redefines the company in modern society. As Mendes says (Chapter 6, page 111):

> The problem with taking the non-complicity principle so far is that it would encompass virtually all business operations in virtually all countries, including European and North American countries. The problem is where to draw the line.

Finally, in this section, Mara Hernandez offers both optimism and a reality check in thinking about the potentialities of the Global Compact. She says that (Chapter 7, page 127) the Global Compact might contribute to a new shift in the ' "cognitive framing of quality", from customer satisfaction to stakeholder engagement, building on the "prevent-and-improve" mentality of TQM [total quality management]'.

In Part 2 of the book Donaldson, Leisinger, Mendes and Hernandez analyse the ethical relationship between business and society via the Global Compact's human rights principles. In doing so they speak to the heart of this initiative: namely, that it is an attempt to normalise or institutionalise shared global understandings of human rights, labour standards and environmental protection and provide a normative framework to guide the behaviour of corporations.

Part 3: The evolution of the UN and the UN Global Compact: critical perspectives

The discussion on human rights and the Global Compact redefines the responsibilities of corporations to encompass their day-to-day relationships with a range of internal and external stakeholders. This redefinition leads inexorably to the literature on corporate citizenship and responsibility. Jem Bendell (Chapter 9, page 166) argues that there is a logical progression from definitions that require the company to improve its own internal behaviour and also become involved in the community (McIntosh *et al.* 1998) to corporate citizenship being used to describe a social situation where companies take on the role of providing some of the basic needs and rights of citizens (Crane and Matten 2003).

So, the Global Compact helps redefine the responsibilities of the corporation, going way beyond the 'do good' activities of philanthropy to look at operating practices and strategies and in so doing reinforces recent definitions of corporate citizenship.

Jim Baker, here representing the International Confederation of Free Trade Unions, is not convinced by all this talk of corporate responsibility and citizenship. He says that (Chapter 10, page 169): 'CSR is often rooted . . . in public relations'. Given that Leisinger points out that most companies have not even begun to think about, let alone engage with, human rights issues, Baker may well be right. For most companies the corporate responsibility department is small, under-staffed and not part of mainstream activity or strategic planning. It is akin to a lifeboat being towed aft; it may be pulled on board and its occupants allowed access to the wheelhouse should conditions become difficult for the reputation of the company.

Cornis van der Lugt quotes John Elkington's belief that many business leaders think of corporate responsibility or citizenship as being some 'new form of religion . . . rather than a new form of value which society will demand and which successful businesses will deliver through transformed markets' (Chapter 8, page 141; quoting Elkington 1997: 5). Van der Lugt (page 141) also refers to research that shows that companies fail to exploit the economic advantages of being 'more proactive on environmental issues' because of a range of technical and managerial issues.

Leisinger (Chapter 5), Donaldson (Chapter 4) and Bendell (Chapter 9) all refer to a hierarchy of moral progressions that a company must move through if it is to claim the high moral ground of corporate citizenship. Such movement is worthy in its own right; however, more instrumental—profitability-related—notions can also be served by responsible corporate citizenship, despite some degree of vacuity in arguing that there must always be a 'business case for corporate citizenship'. Despite our belief that there should always be a social case for business action, it is possible, as Claude Fussler (Chapter 19) details, to show that companies that adopt corporate citizenship initiatives, such as the Global Compact, also show better financial performance.

Jem Bendell (Chapter 9) queries the case for the Global Compact when he asks whether the co-regulatory approach might undermine mechanisms for mandatory corporate accountability.

Such scepticism about the misguided virtue of the corporate citizenship movement is echoed by Jim Baker (Chapter 10, page 171), who is concerned that the Global Compact, in trying to be too many things to too many people, may thereby undermine its own relevance and uniqueness. By being vague it may allow the charge of 'blue- or greenwashing' to stick.

Finally Michael Pedersen (Chapter 11), while largely supportive in his analysis of the Global Compact, points out that the primary reason for companies joining the Compact is for reputational and risk management reasons. The challenge is to see how signatory companies change the way in which they do business.

Part 4: action and learning

The complexity of many global systems means that they cannot be completely understood at any single representational level. This reality means that neither a totally holistic nor a totally reductionist approach will help us understand the complexity that is embedded in, but not made explicit by, the simplistic idea of the 'single bottom line' and its recently discovered partner, the 'triple bottom line'.

Chris Tuppen from BT, a first mover in signing up to the Global Compact, says that he has found that the underlying values behind sustainable development are not necessarily useful arguments to be used as the basis for CSR integration in companies (Chapter 12, page 200): 'not because [others in business] do not share some of those values as well, but because the language of pure moral justification does not sit comfortably in the conventional business lexicon'. He says that (page 201) BT has not done anything uniquely specific as a result of signing. BT sees the Global Compact as synergistic and becoming a signatory has helped embed corporate responsibility in the company. Even at its inception, there was no doubt that the Global Compact was going to challenge accepted practice and thinking on the current business model, as elicited in the chapters in this collection, but if we return to the original model proposed by Ruggie in 2000 it may help (Chapter 2, page 33):

> The Global Compact has explicitly adopted a learning approach to inducing corporate change, as opposed to a regulatory approach; and it comprises a network form of organisation, as opposed to the traditional hierarchic/bureaucratic form. These distinctive (and, for the UN, unusual) features lead the Compact's critics seriously to underestimate its potential, while its supporters may hold excessive expectations of what it can deliver.

What the Compact attempts is nothing less than rearranging the moral contract between business and society, which in turn requires new learning and new ways of seeing the world. To accomplish these tasks, we need new language that describes systems at a range of levels of complexity. The overriding feature of high-level systems is the interaction of cross-disciplinary thinking, including consideration of 'hard' technical systems and 'soft' people systems. The acquisition of dependable evidence on the performance of these systems in a common communicable format is one challenge; the production of simulations involving new systems is another. Applying this learning to corporate responsibility is arguably one of the research and learning tasks for this century. It is also the task that many of the contributions to this book begin to tackle by looking at new relationship models and new organisational forms.

Like other contributors to this book (e.g. Ruggie, Chapter 2; Leisinger, Chapter 5; Post and Carroll, Chapter 21; Mendes, Chapter 6; and McIntosh, Chapter 22), Kell, executive head of the Global Compact, and Levin accept the challenge (Chapter 3, pages 50-51):

> The complex structure, diversity of actors and variety of activities within the [Global Compact] network produce a unique context of multiple dialectics in which several types of learning occur. For instance, the Global Compact engenders both network learning and organisational learning. Organisational learning occurs when an organisation institutionalises new structures, routines or strategies that effect changes in action . . . Network learning refers to learning accomplished by organisations as a group, rather than as individuals. At both the network and organisational level, learning may be cognitive, behavioural or both . . . When cognitive and behavioural changes combine and generate repeated, successful implementation, the network learning may be classified as integrative.

It is this integrative aspect requiring a multidisciplinary approach that was at the heart of one of the learning points for Novo Nordisk (McIntosh and Stube, Chapter 18) In the company's investigation of its first-tier supply chain, it was reported that, for one supplier (page 271) the greatest learning came from the cross-functionality of the company's questionnaire.

Given the challenges of joining an effort that has moral, logistical and organisational implications, it is perhaps a wonder that any company joined at all. Yet Pfizer joined—one of the world's largest companies, with a reputation for not being willing to engage with some critics such as NGOs and thus viewed by some NGOs and civil-society organisations as arrogant, unapproachable and incommunicative. In part, companies such as Pfizer joined, according to Nielsen (Chapter 16), because the Global Compact's structure was aspirational—providing a 'positive incentive' rather than a set of rules. Despite the observation that other major US companies had not joined the Global Compact, Pfizer's board unanimously decided to support the Compact. Then the challenge was to introduce, and later embed, across a company with 120,000 employees operating in more than 100 countries.

Despite 'unexpected twists and turns' (page 243) the vision of better healthcare for all was compelling and Pfizer recognised (page 243) the importance of good health in sustaining economic prosperity—and the interdependence of the business community with other important social actors in generating both healthy lives and communities.

Kell and Levin (Chapter 3, page 58) point out that it is the intention of the Global Compact that learning to talk has occurred in multiple ways, not just within companies but also within and between UN agencies. In the UN the Global Compact has, they say, 'enhanced the quality and attractiveness of . . . their workshops around the world' (page 58):

The first phase of the Global Compact Learning Forum was concluded at the Denham conference in England in November 2001. The two most important findings arising from an analysis of the company submissions were that they contain significant information about *outcomes* (what had been achieved) but much less about the *processes* the companies went through to achieve these outcomes and that there is an urgent need to study these processes and to share these stories with other companies. Second, it was felt that there was a need for further research, particularly in-depth, long-term studies of processes (McIntosh *et al.*, Chapter 27).

Sandra Waddock (Chapter 14) reported on the second Learning Forum in Berlin in 2002 and noted that there was 'significant evidence of progress toward understanding what it will take to create a global context in which the principles of the Global Compact become "on-the-ground" reality in companies and in other types of enterprises' (page 230). She points out that driving the principles into practice is the real test of the Global Compact in both multinational corporations and smaller companies. The third meeting of the Global Compact Learning Forum took place in Belo Horizonte, Brazil, in December 2003 and was attended by delegations from business, civil society, multilateral agencies, trade unions and governments from around the world. It is clear that the quality of company case studies is improving as they learn to work with outside researchers and commentators, but the report of this conference says that perhaps the greatest challenge for future conferences should be to help participants envision what the world would look like if the Global Compact principles were to become normalised and institutionalised (McIntosh, Chapter 17).

Finally, in this section of the book, the case study from Novo Nordisk exemplifies points made by many contributors concerning the ethical advancement of companies towards attaining some sense of citizenship. That the company becomes an agent of positive social change, congruent with its ability to survive and remain profitable, is at the heart of the drive, through initiatives such as the Global Compact, to humanise the globalisation process. As Novo Nordisk said in their 2003 report and reiterated in 2004: 'Social responsibility extends beyond the company's grounds. It reaches throughout the supply chain and to the global agenda of sustainable development.'

This section on learning through engagement with the Global Compact exemplifies the learning that has been taking place throughout the world of corporate responsibility. Engagement by companies in the Global Compact is mirrored by a small number of companies that are actively engaging with other corporate responsibility initiatives such as the Global Reporting Initiative, AA1000 and SA8000. There are also a significant number of companies that recognise the necessity to be proactive in understanding their social and environmental impacts and performance and are beginning to report as much. However, this is not the case for the overwhelming majority of companies for whom the day-to-day reality of staying alive, or survivability, looms larger than writing sustainability reports.

Part 5: the unfolding world of the UN Global Compact

One of the preoccupations of business is in asking for the business case for corporate responsibility. Of course, as Jim Baker asks in Chapter 10, if the business case is so obvious, then why aren't all businesses doing it? But there are continuing efforts to link financial performance, the single bottom line, to social and environmental performance, the triple bottom line. One such is presented in this section by Claude Fussler, from the World Business Council for Sustainable Development (WBCSD). Fussler (Chapter 19) found that a business performance index based on a group of 76 signatories of the Global Compact outperformed the Morgan Stanley Capital World Index, concluding that 'Global Compact Signatories . . . create premium shareholder value at acceptable risk levels' (page 282).

This is useful supporting evidence and draws on the sister publication to *Learning to Talk, Raising the Bar: Creating Value with the UN Global Compact* (Fussler *et al.* 2004). But, while it is axiomatic that a business should always remain solvent, there should always be a social case for corporate responsibility. Business is after all licensed to operate by society.

All of these arguments suggest the need for business to engage with global issues. Developing a global systemic vision means attempting to map the relationships between business and society and to have a more coherent understanding of the linkages, connectivities and convivialities because, as Steve Waddell suggests (Chapter 20, page 301):

> [It] is necessary to identify the critical leverage points for the Global Compact to take action and avoid being overwhelmed by the scale of its challenge . . . The depth of the work suggests that it is critical for the Global Compact to develop some profound, deep-change, initiatives that will be long-term and require an interpersonal and inter-organisational intimacy that goes beyond the intellectual and into the emotional–spiritual dimension where stakeholders can 're-vision' their future.'

Most companies adopt a position that is, on the face of it, irrational because of an emphasis on short-term profits and bounded rationality. Jim Post and Tanja Carroll (Chapter 21, page 309) remind us that: 'Learning is a process, not an event. The organisational capacity to learn is the characteristic that most clearly separates successful from unsuccessful organisations.' The idea of seeing the world as a complex place and as adaptive and dynamic links Waddell's Global Action Networks, Ruggie and Kell's inter-organisational learning networks and Post and Carroll's extended enterprises. 'Within this rich picture our institutions can be seen as social systems that should work within an inclusionist view of "life in space" and on Earth' (McIntosh, Chapter 22, page 326).

Our corporations have become complex adaptive systems (but with unfortunately narrow purposes) and are now extended enterprises, intertwined with all aspects of life on the planet. Post and Carroll (Chapter 21, page 302) characterise this as a world of 'extended enterprises, with long supply chains, complex market channels and extensive networks of voluntary and involuntary stakeholders. There is interdependence, and risk, at every point in these networks.'

Global linkages, regional networks and multi-stakeholder dialogue characterise the Global Compact—and represent yet another new form of relationships among social actors, another form of extended enterprise. According to Post and Carroll (Chapter 21, page 305) these extended enterprises represent nodal points for a set of relationships. This notion suggests a shift in understanding what kinds of 'capital' are needed to run modern companies with their extended supply chains—and that is relational capital.

Klaus Leisinger (Chapter 5) acknowledges that society is a complex system of intertwined and yet (relatively) independent subsystems, including an economic subsystem, where interaction between these subsystems—described as 'organised complexity'—gives a whole (system) that is more than the sum of the parts (subsystems).

As we have seen, it is not possible for a company to truly embrace the principles of the Global Compact as envisaged by Annan without fundamentally changing the company orientation away from profitability for its own sake, and towards stakeholders and societies and towards nature. This shift occurs precisely because companies in the Global Compact must see themselves as extended enterprises and as complex adaptive systems if they are to negotiate successfully the relationships that networks imply.

Because of the ways it creates linkages among participating entities, whether they are businesses, NGOs, labour/trade unions, states or UN agencies, the Global Compact is structured as a new organisational form, what Steve Waddell (Chapter 20) calls a global action network (GAN). According to Waddell, GANs arise in situations of great complexity around issues that cannot be resolved through normal organising mechanisms. GANs, suggests Waddell, may represent a new form of inter-organisational and global governance—and the Global Compact is one of the more visible of these emerging entities. Waddell goes on to say (page 290) that

> GANs address issues that cross national boundaries and are recognised as being global in nature. This includes issues such as: corruption, which has produced the GAN of Transparency International; the environment, which has produced numerous GANs such as the Forest Stewardship Council; peace and security, which led to the Ban the Landmines initiative; and healthcare, which is the focus of the Anti-Malaria Campaign.

The problem for the Global Compact is that if the boundaries are too expansive, there will be lack of focus and inability to cohere. A major challenge for the Global Compact is thus to balance an expansive global vision with a highly strategic systems intervention based on a clear awareness of 'the system'.

For one of the companies discussed in this book, Pfizer, it was exactly this open systems view that encouraged the company to enter the Global Compact. Nancy Nielsen says (Chapter 16) that it was easy for Pfizer to join the open-network approach of the Global Compact as a place to engage and learn. So it may be that the strength of the Global Compact has to be in seeing it as an open system rather than as an 'old' hierarchical form.

The Global Compact, alongside other corporate responsibility initiatives such as the GRI, has the elements of a GAN. They are all synergistic with one another and with many of the in-house company systems (such as BT's—see Chapter 12). So perhaps Deborah Leipziger (Chapter 24, page 342) is correct when she says that 'The Global Compact can gain both depth and momentum by promoting convergence with other initiatives in the field of corporate responsibility that extend beyond principles.' But it must also be remembered that if the Global Compact seeks too much convergence it will, as Baker said in Chapter 10, become irrelevant. It must remain aloof and apart from the more mechanistic management technologies of some other systems thereby retaining its ability to raise the level of conversation to the humanisation of globalisation by utilising the moral authority of the UN.

In complex adaptive systems, such as the Global Compact, paradox, ambiguity and surprise are inherent characteristics. One of the greatest surprises has been the birth of the Global Compact Cities initiative led by the cities of Melbourne, Bath, Porto Alegre, San Francisco and Nuremberg. David Teller (Chapter 23) writes of using the Global Compact as a convening platform to bring together disparate actors from across the community in ways that have not been attempted previously.

Part 6: taking off

In concluding this brief introduction to a multi-dimensional collection of thoughts on the development of corporate citizenship via the Compact it is good to remember two points that Ruggie made back in 2000: that business created the single global economic space; business can and must help and that the Global Compact has explicitly adopted a learning approach to inducing corporate change, as opposed to a regulatory approach; and it comprises a network form of organisation, as opposed to the traditional hierarchic/bureaucratic form (see Chapter 2). These distinctive (and, for the UN, unusual) features lead the Compact's critics seriously to underestimate its potential, while its supporters may hold excessive expectations of what it can deliver (Chapter 2, page 33).

Georg Kell, in Chapter 25, provides some personal insights from inside the Compact Office; Gill Coleman, in Chapter 26, talks of learning and action.

The crucial questions from all the contributions to this book are: Can we learn to listen, to talk, and to walk the talk?

Part 1
The origins and development of
the UN Global Compact

1
An appeal to world business
31 January 1999*

Kofi Annan
Secretary-General, United Nations

I am delighted to join you again at the World Economic Forum. This is my third visit in just over two years as Secretary-General of the United Nations.

On my previous visits, I told you of my hopes for a creative partnership between the United Nations and the private sector. I made the point that the everyday work of the United Nations—whether in peacekeeping, setting technical standards, protecting intellectual property or providing much-needed assistance to developing countries—helps to expand opportunities for business around the world. And I stated quite frankly that, without your know-how and your resources, many of the objectives of the United Nations would remain elusive.

Today, I am pleased to acknowledge that, in the past two years, our relationship has taken great strides. We have shown through co-operative ventures—both at the policy level and on the ground—that the goals of the United Nations and those of business can, indeed, be mutually supportive.

This year, I want to challenge you to join me in taking our relationship to a still higher level. I propose that you, the business leaders gathered in Davos, and we, the United Nations, initiate a global compact of shared values and principles, which will give a human face to the global market.

Globalisation is a fact of life. But I believe we have underestimated its fragility. The problem is this. The spread of markets outpaces the ability of societies and

*   This chapter is the address of Secretary-General Kofi Annan to the World Economic Forum in Davos, Switzerland, on 31 January 1999. It was also issued as press release SG/SM/6881/rev.1 (revised to reflect text as delivered), titled 'The Secretary-General Proposes Global Compact on Human Rights, Labour, Environment, in Address to World Economic Forum in Davos'.

their political systems to adjust to them, let alone to guide the course they take. History teaches us that such an imbalance between the economic, social and political realms can never be sustained for very long.

The industrialised countries learned that lesson in their bitter and costly encounter with the Great Depression. In order to restore social harmony and political stability, they adopted social safety nets and other measures, designed to limit economic volatility and compensate the victims of market failures. That consensus made possible successive moves towards liberalisation, which brought about the long postwar period of expansion.

Our challenge today is to devise a similar compact on the global scale, to underpin the new global economy. If we succeed in that, we would lay the foundation for an age of global prosperity, comparable to that enjoyed by the industrialised countries in the decades after the Second World War. Specifically, I call on you— individually through your firms, and collectively through your business associations—to embrace, support and enact a set of core values in the areas of human rights, labour standards and environmental practices.

Why those three? In the first place, because they are the areas where you, as business men and women, can make a real difference. Secondly, they are the areas in which universal values have already been defined by international agreements, including the Universal Declaration, the International Labour Organisation's Declaration on Fundamental Principles and Rights at Work, and the Rio Declaration of the United Nations Conference on Environment and Development in 1992. Finally, I chose these three areas because they are ones where I fear that, if we do not act, there may be a threat to the open global market, and especially to the multilateral trade regime.

There is enormous pressure from various interest groups to load the trade regime and investment agreements with restrictions aimed at reaching adequate standards in the three areas I have just mentioned. These are legitimate concerns. But restrictions on trade and impediments to investment flows are not the means to use when tackling them. Instead, we should find a way to achieve our proclaimed standards by other means. And that is precisely what the compact I am proposing to you is meant to do.

Essentially there are two ways we can do this. One is through the international policy arena. You can encourage States to give us, the multilateral institutions of which they are all members, the resources and the authority we need to do our job. The United Nations as a whole promotes peace and development, which are prerequisites for successfully meeting social and environmental goals alike. And the International Labour Organisation, the United Nations High Commissioner for Human Rights and the United Nations Environmental Programme strive to improve labour conditions, human rights and environmental quality. We hope, in the future, to count you as our allies in these endeavours.

The second way you can promote these values is by tackling them directly, by taking action in your own corporate sphere. Many of you are big investors, employers and producers in dozens of different countries across the world. That power brings with it great opportunities—and great responsibilities. You can uphold human rights and decent labour and environmental standards directly, by your own conduct of your own business.

Indeed, you can use these universal values as the cement binding together your global corporations, since they are values people all over the world will recognise as their own. You can make sure that in your own corporate practices you uphold and respect human rights; and that you are not yourselves complicit in human rights abuses.

Don't wait for every country to introduce laws protecting freedom of association and the right to collective bargaining. You can at least make sure your own employees, and those of your subcontractors, enjoy those rights. You can at least make sure that you yourselves are not employing under-age children or forced labour, either directly or indirectly. And you can make sure that, in your own hiring and firing policies, you do not discriminate on grounds of race, creed, gender or ethnic origin.

You can also support a precautionary approach to environmental challenges. You can undertake initiatives to promote greater environmental responsibility. And you can encourage the development and diffusion of environmentally friendly technologies.

That, ladies and gentlemen, is what I am asking of you. But what, you may be asking yourselves, am I offering in exchange? Indeed, I believe the United Nations system does have something to offer.

The United Nations agencies—the United Nations High Commissioner for Human Rights, the International Labour Organisation (ILO), the United Nations Environment Programme (UNEP)—all stand ready to assist you, if you need help, in incorporating these agreed values and principles into your mission statements and corporate practices. And we are ready to facilitate a dialogue between you and other social groups, to help find viable solutions to the genuine concerns that they have raised. In doing so, you may find it useful to interact with us through our newly created website, www.un.org/partners, which offers 'one-stop shopping' for corporations interested in the United Nations. More important, perhaps, is what we can do in the political arena, to help make the case for and maintain an environment which favours trade and open markets.

I believe what I am proposing to you is a genuine compact, because neither side of it can succeed without the other. Without your active commitment and support, there is a danger that universal values will remain little more than fine words—documents whose anniversaries we can celebrate and make speeches about, but with limited impact on the lives of ordinary people. And unless those values are really seen to be taking hold, I fear we may find it increasingly difficult to make a persuasive case for the open global market.

National markets are held together by shared values. In the face of economic transition and insecurity, people know that, if the worst comes to the worst, they can rely on the expectation that certain minimum standards will prevail. But, in the global market, people do not yet have that confidence. Until they do have it, the global economy will be fragile and vulnerable—vulnerable to backlash from all the 'isms' of our post-Cold War world: protectionism, populism, nationalism, ethnic chauvinism, fanaticism and terrorism.

What all those 'isms' have in common is that they exploit the insecurity and misery of people who feel threatened or victimised by the global market. The more wretched and insecure people there are, the more those 'isms' will continue to gain ground. What we have to do is find a way of embedding the global market in a network of shared values. I hope I have suggested some practical ways for us to set about doing just that.

Let us remember that the global markets and multilateral trading system we have today did not come about by accident. They are the result of enlightened policy choices made by governments since 1945. If we want to maintain them in the new century, all of us—governments, corporations, non-governmental organisations, international organisations—have to make the right choices now.

We have to choose between a global market driven only by calculations of short-term profit, and one which has a human face; between a world which condemns a quarter of the human race to starvation and squalor, and one which offers everyone at least a chance of prosperity, in a healthy environment; between a selfish free-for-all in which we ignore the fate of the losers, and a future in which the strong and successful accept their responsibilities, showing global vision and leadership.

I am sure you will make the right choice.

2
The theory and practice of learning networks
Corporate social responsibility and the Global Compact*

John Gerard Ruggie
Harvard University, USA

Under the leadership of Secretary-General Kofi Annan, the United Nations has played an active role in promoting corporate social responsibility as one means to respond to the challenges of globalisation. 'You do not need to wait for governments to pass new laws,' Mr Annan has said to business groups. 'You can and should act now, in your own self-interest. The sustainability of globalisation is at stake.'

The Global Compact has been Annan's major initiative in this domain. It has attracted considerable acclaim in the world's press. In the United States, it was praised editorially by the venerable *Washington Post* while the *Christian Science Monitor* lauded it as Annan's 'most creative reinvention' yet of the United Nations. At the same time, the Global Compact has generated suspicion and in some instances sharp criticism in parts of the NGO (non-governmental organisation) community and from various anti-globalisation activists. Part of the difference is explained by differing attitudes towards globalisation. Thus, what the mainstream press views as an innovative practical response to some of its challenges, critics decry as 'bluewash': providing an opportunity for the private sector to drape itself in the UN flag without really mending its ways.[1]

* This chapter first appeared in *The Journal of Corporate Citizenship* 5 (Spring 2002): 27-36.
1 The standard critique, which unfortunately includes often-repeated factual inaccuracies, can be found in Bruno and Karliner 2000.

But even more fundamental issues are at stake. The Global Compact has explicitly adopted a learning approach to inducing corporate change, as opposed to a regulatory approach; and it comprises a network form of organisation, as opposed to the traditional hierarchic/bureaucratic form. These distinctive (and, for the UN, unusual) features lead the Compact's critics to seriously underestimate its potential, while its supporters may hold excessive expectations of what it can deliver.

Because organisational issues of this sort will continue to confront the search for viable global governance mechanisms for many years ahead, it is worth examining the Global Compact more closely as a case of things to come, spelling out both its advantages and its inherent limitations.

Below, I describe the Compact's organisational forms and the rationale behind them. But, first, I briefly place the current debates in their broader historical context.

2.1 Tina redux?

The globalisation mantra in corporate circles, at least until very recently, was the so-called 'Tina' hypothesis: 'There Is No Alternative'. But there is: Tina may prevail in the long run, but the road from here to there can be unacceptably rough.

History doesn't repeat itself; only historians do. But there is still great merit in the dictum that those who refuse to learn from the past may be condemned to repeat its errors. That is certainly true of globalisation and its consequences. Let us begin with some basic facts.

The speed and costs of global communications are plummeting to a fraction of what they were a decade earlier. The Internet? No, the laying of the transatlantic cables in 1866, which reduced the time it took to communicate between London and New York by 99.9%, from a week to a matter of minutes.

The ease of global transport is increasing by orders of magnitude. The latest Boeing or Airbus? No, the opening of the first Alpine tunnels, the Suez Canal and the Panama Canal in the late 19th/early 20th centuries.

Foreign trade accounts for a third or more of national product. Japan in the 1980s? No, Britain a century earlier. Emerging economies booming and global markets integrating, thanks to massive flows of foreign investment? Been there, done that, too, as European capital built railroads in the US, Canada, Australia and Argentina more than a century ago, and as raw materials, beef and agricultural products were shipped back to feed the industrial machines, and the stomachs, of Europe.

The era from 1850 to 1910 was the first 'golden age' of globalisation. Travellers required no passports or visas and capital flowed freely. Even more impressive, 60 million people left Europe between 1850 and 1914 to seek new economic opportunities and political freedoms elsewhere, something that is much harder to do today. And then it collapsed, horribly, into war and anarchy—followed, though not precisely in this order—by extreme left-wing revolution in Russia, extreme right-wing revolutions in Italy and Germany, militarism in Japan, the Great Depression, unprecedented international financial volatility and the shrivelling-up of world trade. Nor is that all. The social strains produced by those upheavals were so great that the world imploded into a second worldwide war in the span of a single generation. And in some respects globalisation was behind it all. How so?

Victorian globalisation was a system without popular roots and without social legitimacy. It reflected neither the needs nor the aspirations of the vast majority of ordinary people who, indeed, bore the brunt of the adjustment costs that open markets invariably produce. The demand for social protection proved irresistible, and it led, predictably, to economic protectionism—an entire generation of it.

What is the lesson? That societies will protect themselves from unrestrained market forces by whatever means they can muster.[2] The industrialised countries were slow to learn the lesson that markets must be embedded in broader frameworks of social values and shared objectives if they are to survive and thrive. When they finally did—after two world wars and a depression—they called this new understanding by different names: the New Deal, the social market economy and social democracy. But the underlying idea was the same: a grand social bargain whereby all sectors of society agreed to open markets, which in many places had become almost administered if not autarchic, but also to share the social adjustment costs that open markets inevitably produce.[3]

Governments played a key role: moderating the volatility of transaction flows across borders and providing social investments, safety nets and adjustment assistance; but all the while pushing liberalisation. In the industrialised world, this grand bargain formed the basis of the longest period of sustained and equitable economic expansion in human history, from the 1950s to the present.

2.2 Tina in trouble?

So what is the problem today? That grand bargain presupposed an *international* world; we have come to live in a *global* world. It presupposed the existence of *national* economies, engaged in *external* transactions, which governments could mediate at the *border* by tariffs and exchange rates, among other tools. But markets have gone global, leaving behind merely national social bargains. The backlash against globalisation has grown in direct proportion to the divergence between global markets and national communities.

In particular, the backlash against globalisation is driven by three of its attributes. First, its benefits are distributed highly unequally, both within and among countries. Large parts of the developing world are left behind entirely; these are the countries where 1.2 billion people somehow strive to survive on US$1 a day, or nearly 3 billion on US$2 a day; where half of humanity has never made or received

---

2 No subsequent account of these wrenching struggles yet surpasses Karl Polanyi's 1944 classic treatment in *The Great Transformation*.

3 In academic circles, this grand bargain is known as 'the embedded liberalism compromise'. See Ruggie 1982.

a telephone call; where one-fifth of the world's people lack access to safe drinking water.

Second, the backlash is triggered by an imbalance in global rule-making. Those rules that favour global market expansion have become more robust and enforceable in the last decade or two. Rules intended to promote equally valid social objectives, such as poverty reduction, labour standards, human rights or environmental quality, lag behind and in some instances have actually become weaker. So we find ourselves in the situation where considerations of intellectual property rights dominate fundamental human rights and even human life, at least until that clash became unbearable for the world's conscience over the AIDS treatment issue in Africa.

Third, there is emerging what might be called a global identity crisis. 'Who is *us*?' is being asked with growing shrillness all over the world. 'Who is in control of the unpredictable forces that can bring on economic instability and social dislocation, sometimes at lightning speed?' The answer, 'no one', serves only to feed the fear and paranoia in which ugly 'isms' thrive, apart from the fact that it is not, strictly speaking, accurate.

I am not suggesting that globalisation today will end as its 19th-century predecessor did; many of the fundamentals are very different. But I would venture two predictions. One is that the present state of affairs is not sustainable. The gap between market and community *will* be closed; the only issue is how and in which direction. The world needs open markets: for business to maximise its opportunities, for the industrialised countries to sustain prosperity and for the developing countries because an open world economy provides the only hope of pulling billions of poor people out of abject poverty.

But my second prediction is that rollback, a shift away from globalisation, is the more likely outcome unless we manage to strengthen the fabric of the global community.

2.3 Corporate social responsibility

That is where corporate social responsibility comes in. By itself, it cannot carry the burden of globalisation's many challenges. But the corporate sector can advance its own—and our collective—cause by embracing universal values and concerns in its own corporate sphere, and weaving them into global market relations.

Increasingly, society expects nothing less from the corporate sector. The signs of changing social expectations are not limited to the streets of Seattle or Genoa, Prague, Gothenburg or Washington, DC. Here are a few examples that hit closer to the boardroom:

- A 20 nation poll conducted by Environics International, a Canadian consultancy, finds that consumers' perceptions of companies are now determined as much by a company's social and environmental practices as by its product brands.

- The US public relations firm, Richard Edelman, in a cross-national study of thought leaders, finds that NGO 'brands', such as Amnesty or Greenpeace, enjoy greater public trust than corporate brands.

- CalPERS, one of the world's largest institutional investment funds, has targeted some US$1 billion directly for socially responsible investment, and is promoting the corporate social responsibility agenda more broadly at shareholder meetings and through other means.

- And the FTSE is but the latest index provider catering to the growing number of investors who want to do good while doing well.

The message here is crystal clear. Social expectations about what corporations are and how they should behave have moved well beyond the traditional realm of philanthropy or business ethics. The name of the game today is to align the corporation behind broader social and environmental goals, or at least to make sure that actions by firms do not undermine them.

The Secretary-General's Global Compact is an initiative intended to advance global corporate social responsibility. It engages the private sector directly to work with the UN, in partnership with international labour and NGOs, to identify and promote good corporate practices based on universal principles.[4]

The Global Compact encompasses nine such principles, drawn from the Universal Declaration of Human Rights, the International Labour Organisation's Fundamental Principles on Rights at Work and the Rio Principles on Environment and Development (see pages 11-12).

Companies are challenged to act on these nine principles in their own corporate domains, moving towards 'good practices' as understood by the broader international community, rather than relying on their often superior bargaining position *vis-à-vis* national authorities, especially in small and poor states, to get away with less.

Specifically, companies are asked to undertake three commitments:

- To advocate the Compact and its principles in mission statements, annual reports and similar public venues, on the premise that, by doing so, they will raise the level of attention paid to, and the responsibility for, these concerns within firms

- To post on the Global Compact website at least once a year concrete steps they have taken to act on any or all of the nine principles, discussing both

---

4   The Global Compact participants include the UN (the Secretary-General's Office, Office of the High Commissioner for Human Rights, International Labour Organisation, UN Environment Programme and the UN Development Programme); the International Confederation of Free Trade Unions (ICFTU); more than a dozen transnational NGOs in the three areas covered by the Global Compact, such as Amnesty International and the WWF; as well as individual companies and international business associations.

positive and negative lessons learned and triggering, thereby, a structured dialogue among the various participants about what deserves to be labelled as a good practice

● To join with the UN in partnership projects of benefit to developing countries, particularly the least developed, which the forces of globalisation have largely marginalised

In order to initiate participation in the Compact, the chief executive officer of the company sends a letter to the Secretary-General expressing the company's commitment, a step that typically requires board approval. Since an opening event in July 2000, some 400 companies worldwide—based in Europe, the United States, Japan, Hong Kong, India, Brazil and elsewhere—have engaged in the Global Compact. The target is 1,000 firms within three years.

2.4 Learning Forum

The major criticism of the Global Compact by the anti-globalisation front has been for what it is *not*: a regulatory arrangement, specifically a legally binding code of conduct with explicit performance criteria and independent monitoring of company compliance.

So how does the Global Compact propose to induce corporate change? Its core is a Learning Forum. Companies submit case studies of what they have done to translate their commitment to the Global Compact principles into concrete corporate practices. This occasions a dialogue among Global Compact participants from all sectors: the UN, business, labour and civil-society organisations. The aim of this dialogue is to reach broader, consensus-based definitions of what constitutes good practices than any of the parties could achieve alone. Those definitions, together with illustrative case studies, are then publicised in an online information bank, which will become a standard reference source on corporate social responsibility. The hope and expectation is that good practices will help to drive out bad ones through the power of dialogue, transparency, advocacy and competition.

Why did the Secretary-General choose this approach rather than propose a regulatory code, complete with monitoring and compliance mechanisms? First, the probability of the General Assembly adopting a meaningful code approximates zero. The only countries eager to launch such an effort at this time are equally unfriendly to the private sector, human rights, labour standards and the environment.

Second, the logistical and financial requirements for the UN to monitor global companies and their supply chains, let alone small and medium-sized enterprises at national levels, far exceed its capacity. For example, Nike, whose past labour practices have made it a frequent target of protesters, has more than 750 suppliers in 52 countries, and it is at the lower end among comparable firms in the number of factories as a fraction of its revenue base.[5] When it comes to effective regulation, there is simply no substitute for stronger national action.

Third, any UN attempt to impose a code of conduct would not only be opposed by the business community but also would drive progressive business leaders into a more uniform anti-code coalition.

But these strictly pragmatic reasons imply that a learning-based approach is merely a second-best solution. In fact, a far stronger intellectual case can be made for it. Many of the Global Compact's principles cannot be defined at this time with the precision required for a viable code of conduct. No consensus exists on what 'the precautionary principle' is—that in the face of environmental uncertainty the bias should favour avoiding risk—even though it was enshrined at the 1992 Rio Conference. Similarly, no consensus exists, even among advocates, on where to draw the boundaries around corporate 'non-complicity' in human rights abuses. Accumulated experience—through trial, error and social vetting—will gradually fill in the blanks. The Global Compact Learning Forum provides that experience.

Moreover, the extraordinary pace of change in corporate strategies, structures and production processes makes it exceedingly difficult to specify *ex ante* the full range of performance criteria and desired practices that a code should include. In contrast, the Global Compact Learning Forum helps companies to internalise the relevant principles so that they can shape and reshape corporate practices as external conditions change. Employees are turning out to be vital allies in this process.[6]

Finally, the accumulation of experience itself is likely to lead gradually to a desire for greater codification, benchmarking and moving from 'good' to 'best' practices, including by industry leaders who want to protect themselves against any possible competitive disadvantage. Laggards will have a harder time opposing actual achievements by their peers than *a priori* standards.

Thus, there are both pragmatic and principled reasons why the Global Compact adopted a learning model rather than regulation to induce corporate change. Nevertheless, there are certain things that such an approach cannot achieve. The fact that the Global Compact recognises and promotes a company's 'good practice' provides no guarantee that the same company does not engage in 'bad practice' elsewhere. Indeed, it may even invite a measure of strategic behaviour. Nestlé's recent interest in the Global Compact, for instance, undoubtedly reflects a desire

5 The following thought experiment illustrates the full magnitude of the task. A Hong Kong-based firm currently performs social audits ('Social Accountability 8000') for a number of US speciality and retail chains that source their products in China. It employs approximately 250 field technicians to monitor the production of US$1 billion in products. If we were to multiply that ratio for all US consumer product imports, the field staff requirement would amount to 55,000 technicians. That already is larger than the worldwide staff of the entire United Nations and all of its specialised agencies combined. But we would still need to add to it coverage for consumer product imports into all other countries, plus global imports from the extractive industries. The scale is mind-boggling. The escalating costs of monitoring Central American suppliers experienced by Gap, a large clothing chain, is reported in Kaufman and Gonzalez 2001.

6 A number of participating companies have set up internal websites or other discussion forums enabling employees to comment on company practices in relation to the Global Compact. A corporate-led Scandinavian workshop on diversity in the workplace resulted from one of these. On 'internal branding' of this sort, see Stamler 2001.

to balance criticism of the breast milk substitute, including that of the UN (UNICEF). Moreover, a learning model has no direct leverage over determined laggards. They require other means, ranging from legislation to direct social action.

In sum, the Global Compact's strengths and weaknesses both stem from its adoption of a model that promotes learning by recognising and reinforcing leadership. It helps to create and build momentum towards its universal principles, but it is unlikely to get there by itself.

2.5 Inter-organisational networks

Organisationally, the Global Compact is an expanding set of nested networks. The five participating UN entities constitute one network. The Global Compact Office in New York is by far the smallest component; its main functions are to provide strategic direction, policy coherence and quality control. The core network comprises the UN and the other participants: companies; international labour; transnational NGOs; and university-based research centres. Most of the heavy lifting gets done here.

The Global Compact has triggered several complementary regional, national and sectoral initiatives. Typically, they take a subset of interested Global Compact participants beyond its minimum commitments. For example, Norway's Statoil and the International Federation of Chemical, Energy, Mine and General Workers' Unions recently reached an agreement within the Global Compact framework whereby Statoil will extend the same labour rights that it applies in Norway, as well as health and safety standards, to all overseas operations, including Vietnam, Venezuela, Angola and Azerbaijan.

Finally, a number of initiatives intended for other purposes have associated themselves with the Global Compact. Such business associations as the International Chamber of Commerce, Prince of Wales International Business Leaders Forum, International Organisation of Employers and World Business Council for Sustainable Development support the Global Compact in various ways. The most unusual of these partnerships is with the multi-stakeholder Committee for Melbourne, which is incorporating the Global Compact into the strategic plan it is developing for that Australian city (see Chapter 23).

Accordingly, the Global Compact exhibits many of the defining attributes of inter-organisational networks (IONs), which should be better understood by critics and advocates alike.[7]

● IONs are formed by autonomous organisations combining their efforts voluntarily to achieve goals they cannot reach as effectively or at all on their own. They rest on a bargain, not coercion. The Global Compact's underlying 'bargain' is that the UN provides a degree of legitimacy and helps to solve co-ordination problems, while the companies and other social actors provide the capacity to produce the desired changes.

7   See Chisholm 1998. For a discussion of network-based organisations in the context of global public policy, see Reinicke and Deng 2000.

- IONs typically come into being to help their participants understand and deal with complex and ambiguous challenges. They are inherently experimental, not routine or standardised. Few challenges are more complex and ambiguous than internalising the Global Compact's principles into corporate management practices.

- IONs 'operate' as shared conceptual systems within which the participating entities perceive, understand and frame aspects of their behaviour. But the existing actors do all the doing that needs to be done. The Global Compact creates no new entities, but is a framework for normatively co-ordinated behaviour to produce a new collective outcome.

- IONs must be guided by a shared vision and common purpose. The Secretary-General is responsible for sustaining that vision and ensuring that network values and activities are compatible with it.

- IONs are loosely coupled organisational forms, resting on non-directive horizontal organising principles. Its participants meet in formats and frequencies required to conduct their work.

The major advantage of the Global Compact's network approach is its capacity to respond to the complex and rapidly changing environments that the UN seeks to affect. The UN otherwise lacks that capacity, as do governments, firms and civil-society organisations acting alone or in a different format.[8]

Again, the chief weakness is the same as its main strength. It *is* a network of autonomous actors, each with different interests and needs that intersect only partially. Criticism of the Global Compact for partnering with business fails to appreciate the advantages of inter-organisational networks. But, by the same token, anyone who sees in the Global Compact the cure for globalisation's many ills does not sufficiently grasp the fragile basis of all such networks.

2.6 The business of business

At this point, a business leader might well ask, why me? Isn't the business of business—well—business? Shouldn't governments take care of governance gaps? Indeed, sceptics of voluntary initiatives might well ask the same questions.

Of course, governments should govern. Voluntary initiatives in corporate social responsibility are no substitute for effective action by governments, alone or in concert. Indeed, governance failures—the unwillingness or inability of governments to live up to their own commitments—are among the main reasons that the consequences of globalisation are so painful.

---

8 For example, the Global Sullivan Principles for corporate social responsibility, a partnership of American firms and some NGOs, lacks the social legitimacy of the UN. As a result, the effort has picked up little support beyond the United States.

But society finds itself in a bit of race against the clock. Globalisation is operating on Internet time, while governments do not and probably cannot. Moreover, by definition, no government has full and legitimate global reach, which means they have to engage in intergovernmental negotiations, the outcomes of which are often determined by the lowest and slowest common denominator.

So society increasingly looks to the business community to couple its new global rights with new global responsibilities. But, beyond that, it is actually good business to step up. The most basic rationale is the protection and promotion of a company's brand in the face of new social expectations. Increasingly, as noted, it pays for companies to do 'good' things—and to be seen to be doing them.

Some companies have done 'bad' things in the past; they have paid a price in public embarrassment and perhaps even diminished sales or stock values, and they now want to pursue a different path. Think of Nike, or Shell. Others want to make sure they do not repeat the errors their peers have committed; BP Amoco is working hard in Angola to avoid repeating Shell's errant ways in Nigeria.

Some companies have come to view global corporate social responsibility as a natural extension of CSR in their home countries, as one of the rules of the game in the new global marketplace. It is probably no coincidence that the earliest of the first movers to support the Global Compact were companies based in Scandinavia. Still others—particularly companies in cutting-edge industries, where attracting absolutely the best personnel worldwide is the key to success—have found that they cannot sufficiently motivate the very best people with monetary rewards alone. In these cases, more elevated social purposes are becoming part of corporate culture.

In the environmental area, companies have discovered entirely new profit centres and developed entirely new businesses in response to the quest for greater 'eco-efficiency': squeezing more use out of raw materials in the production process, as well as out of its waste by-products. The somewhat broader concept of life-cycle management—expanding the search for these efficiencies further upstream and downstream—is also beginning to take root.

Finally, business has collective interests that are furthered by adopting an active global CSR posture. Quite simply, the more effective the CSR, the less the pressure will be to accomplish the same ends by other—and potentially far less friendly—means. The alternatives include having the whole bundle of social and environmental issues thrown into the World Trade Organisation, regional trade pacts or national trade legislation, where they would become part and parcel of the tit-for-tat of a new protectionism.

In short, *business* created the single global economic space; business can and must help to sustain it. And corporate social responsibility—through the Global Compact or some other vehicle—offers one viable and vital approach.

2.7 Conclusion

The Global Compact seeks to weave universal principles into global corporate behaviour. And it brings together all the relevant social actors in doing so: governments, who defined the principles on which the initiative is based; companies, whose behaviour the Global Compact seeks to shape; labour, in whose hands the concrete process of global production takes place; NGOs, representing the wider community of stakeholders; and the United Nations, the world's only truly global political entity.

It is a voluntary initiative intended to induce corporate change by identifying and promoting good practices. And it does so through a network form of organisation.

The Compact is not the only way to achieve those aims. But it does constitute a prototype of one way, the strengths and weaknesses of which need to be better understood by analysts and activists alike because it will become a more prevalent response to the challenge of closing global governance gaps in the years ahead.

3
The Global Compact Network
An historic experiment in learning and action*

Georg Kell
UN Global Compact

David Levin
University of Pennsylvania, USA

In his address to the World Economic Forum on 31 January 1999, UN Secretary-General Kofi Annan called on global business leaders to embrace nine shared values and principles in the areas of human rights, labour standards and environmental practices.[1] His well-received proposal catalysed the rapid, dynamic formation of a global network of unprecedented potential. The UN Global Compact network—consisting of several hundred companies, dozens of non-governmental organisations (NGOs), major international labour federations and several UN agencies—seeks to collaboratively contribute to a more stable, equitable and inclusive global market by making its principles an integral part of business activities everywhere (a full listing of the principles is given on page 12).[2]

* This chapter first appeared in *Business and Society Review* 108.2 (Summer 2003): 151-81. The authors would like to thank the Zicklin Centre for Business Ethics Research for financial support. They would also like to thank Ethan Kapstein, John Ruggie, Bill Laufer and the Global Compact Team for their excellent insights.

1 This address is reproduced in Chapter 1 of this book.
2 The nine principles were selected according to their relevance to international rule-making, their importance in advancing social and environmental issues and the degree to which they had intergovernmental support. Specifically, they were derived from the Universal Declaration of Human Rights (www.un.org/Overview/rights.html), the International Labour Organisation Declaration on Fundamental Principles and Rights at Work (www.ilo.org/public/english/standards/decl/declaration/text) and the Rio Declaration on Environment and Development (www.un.org/documents/ga/conf151/

The instability of the global market in its present form derives in part from the absence of strong social and environmental pillars to balance the developed system of economic exchange. The current global governance structure provides extensive rules for economic priorities such as intellectual property rights but lacks commensurate measures to protect the environment and human rights. The longevity of globalisation will remain threatened until this imbalance is rectified. The international economic order must also become more inclusive by giving the billions of marginalised poor open access to global markets in a manner that guarantees them equitable opportunities for advancement. This primarily requires a commitment by those who currently dominate the global market to assist the disadvantaged in building their economic capacity through long-term, sustainable development. It also necessitates the elimination of market asymmetries inimical to developing countries, such as trade barriers and subsidies in areas where the developing world has a comparative advantage.

The Global Compact cannot resolve all of the deficiencies of global capitalism, but it can make a significant contribution by laying a foundation of shared values and harnessing the skills and resources of the private sector. The ultimate measure of success for the initiative is the degree to which it promotes concrete and sustained action by its varied participants, especially the private sector, in alignment with broad UN objectives, the Global Compact principles, and the international Millennium Development Goals (see Appendix A). It does not substitute for effective action by governments, nor does it present a regulatory framework or code of conduct for companies. Rather, the Global Compact is conceived as a value-based platform designed to promote institutional learning with few formalities and no rigid bureaucratic structures. At its core, the Global Compact is simply a strategy to make the UN relevant by leveraging its authority and convening powers in ways that will actually produce the positive social change it aspires to create. This strategy is like any other, as defined by Prussian General Carl von Clausewitz in the 19th century: 'It is not a lengthy action plan; it is the evolution of a central idea through continually changing circumstances' (*Economist* 2002a: 16). Although in the broader sense the Global Compact is an idea, or strategy, the current circumstances have shaped the initiative into a global network.

We contend that this network constitutes a viable mechanism for partially filling the governance void of the global economy by engendering consensus around critical social and environmental crises and providing the means to ameliorate them through co-operative action. Furthermore, we argue that by facilitating transparency, dialogue and the dissemination of best practices, the Global Compact effectively encourages the implementation of good corporate citizenship. We refrain from making more ambitious claims about the initiative, as we recognise the inherent difficulties that challenge the strength and dynamism of the network.

aconf15126-1annex1.htm). The selection was reviewed and influenced heavily by non-governmental organisations and business associations such as Amnesty International and the World Business Council for Sustainable Development.

3.1 Current structure and governance

The conceptualisation and formation of the Global Compact network remains a work in progress. Figure 3.1 illustrates the current structure of the network and the actors involved. The Global Compact Office and UN agencies form the nucleus of the network, with academia, business, labour and civil-society organisations surrounding them on the periphery. Governments play an auxiliary role through outreach support, advocacy and funding but do not participate directly in the network. The Global Compact Office maintains primary responsibility for the facilitation of the network, but depends heavily on the collaboration of the four UN agencies and defers to the authoritative guidance of the UN Secretary-General and his Global Compact Advisory Council (for a list of Advisory Council members, see Appendix B). The specific responsibilities of this council formally consist of: (1) strategic planning; (2) reviewing standards and expectations for participation; (3) championing the initiative as it continues to expand in new countries and regions and (4) ensuring the integrity of the Global Compact as it encompasses larger numbers of participating companies and engages a more diverse range of activities.

The following four areas constitute the essence of the Global Compact's network activities, each of which officially began in 2001:

● The Learning Forum concept was developed as an ongoing analysis of cases studies and examples of good practice that companies report in order to demonstrate acceptance and integration of the principles into their core activities. Annual conferences and active management of the Global Compact web portal foster accountability and transparency regarding corporate activities.

● Global policy dialogues consist of thematic conferences on the contemporary challenges of globalisation. Participation in the dialogues is voluntary and open to all Global Compact participants, including business, labour, civil-society organisations and leading commentators from the academic and public policy communities.

● Multi-stakeholder collaborative development projects are fostered through participation in the network with the aim of furthering the Millennium Development Goals.

● Support for the spawning of national networks has led to the formation of local resource centres, Learning Forums and policy dialogues. Global Compact participants such as the International Organisation of Employers (IOE; www.ioe-emp.org) and international labour have facilitated this process by organising regional meetings around the Global Compact and building momentum at the national level. Furthermore, the addition of the United Nations Development Programme (UNDP) to the Global Compact network significantly strengthened national outreach efforts.

In the following sections we describe each of these four components in greater detail as we further discuss the network's structure and mechanisms for learning.

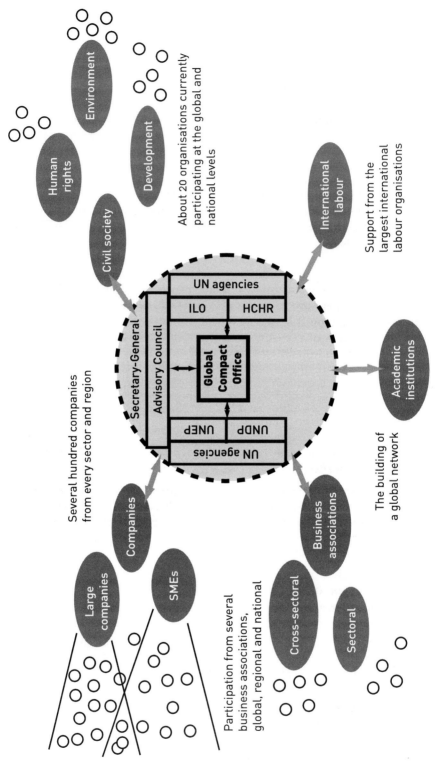

Figure 3.1 The Global Compact network today

HCHR = High Commission for Human Rights   ILO = International Labour Organisation
SME = small or medium-sized enterprise   UNDP = United Nations Development Programme
UNEP = United Nations Environment Programme

3.2 Network taxonomy and the Global Compact

The size, complexity and relevance of the Global Compact initiative qualify it as a premier example for analysis and classification according to established network theory. As mentioned in the introductory text to this chapter, the Global Compact is most appropriately described as an evolving strategic idea. However, the current status of the initiative allows us to describe it as an inter-organisational network embedded within a shared framework of values. More specifically, it is a global amalgamation of strategic and wide public policy learning networks that cultivates integrative learning at the organisational and network levels through inter-organisational interaction.

3.2.1 Classifying the structure of the Global Compact network

We elaborate on our classification of the Global Compact network by reviewing the terminology developed in academic literature and applying it to the components and activities of the Global Compact. In the most general terms, the Global Compact qualifies as an inter-organisational network (ION). Ruggie (see Chapter 2) used the attributes of IONs as defined by Chisholm (1998) to classify the Global Compact as such. We cite and slightly extend Ruggie's analysis:

- IONs are formed by autonomous organisations combining their efforts voluntarily to achieve goals they cannot reach as effectively or at all on their own. Together the members of the Global Compact network gather information and tackle difficult social and environmental problems that they could not effectively address independently.

- IONs typically come into being to help their participants understand and deal with shared complex and ambiguous challenges. They are inherently experimental, not routine or standardised. Experimentation and innovation are central to the *modus operandi* of the Global Compact, and few challenges are more complex and ambiguous than the goals of the initiative.

- IONs 'operate' as shared conceptual systems within which the participating entities perceive, understand and frame aspects of their behaviour. But the existing actors 'do all the doing that needs to be done'. The Global Compact Office maintains a non-bureaucratic support structure for the network. Working from a systems perspective (Senge 1990), it facilitates communication and partnership projects among members rather than organising or controlling projects through a separate institution.

- IONs are loosely coupled organisational forms, resting on non-directive horizontal organising principles. Relationships within the Global Compact are lateral, rather than hierarchical, and its participants meet in formats and frequencies required to conduct their work.

The Global Compact is thus a loosely formed aggregation of autonomous organisations that share a common vision and attempt to overcome difficult, ambiguous challenges. Its goals, members and methodologies characterise it as a specific type of inter-organisational network, as shown in Figure 3.2, which illustrates the organisation of the individual players within the Global Compact system, presenting this system as a series of networks. We explain how each of these categories applies.

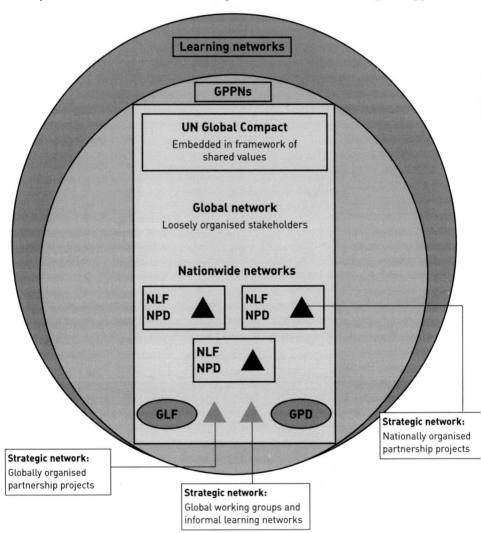

GLF = Global Learning Forum   GPD = Global Policy Dialogue   GPPN = global public policy network
NLF = National Learning Forum   NPD = National Policy Dialogue

Figure 3.2 Venn diagram of network structure

Knight (2002: 435) defines learning networks as 'groups of organisations that interact with the express purpose of learning together, from one another and through their interaction'. The Global Compact complies with this definition, for it has been designed as a multi-stakeholder learning platform that facilitates new understanding in the hope of achieving clear learning objectives (for a discussion of the modalities of learning fostered in the Global Compact, see Section 3.2.2).

We also characterise the initiative as an aspiring global public policy network (GPPN),[3] which falls within the broader category of learning networks. Certainly, not all learning networks concern themselves with public policy issues and neither do they necessarily take an orientation towards action and impact. However, all GPPNs seek to generate collective understanding that produces societal learning and change through global policy or independent, action-based solutions. We thus place GPPNs within the broader, better-known category of learning networks. Classification of the Global Compact as a GPPN has particular appeal, as learning, in itself, serves little purpose unless it functions as the means to accelerate positive social change.

Finally, the Global Compact consists of several nested wide and strategic networks. Wide networks are loosely connected groups of organisations that do not jointly share resources. In contrast, strategic networks are comprised of more closely bonded, autonomous organisations that engage in collective action (Knight 2002). We envision the entire Global Compact initiative as an extensive, wide network of loosely organised stakeholders. Labour unions, businesses and NGOs come together for annual Learning Forums and semi-annual policy dialogues, but they generally act independently and do not necessarily take concerted action. However, when these actors do unite in the global arena to undertake partnership development projects, they form smaller, more interactive, strategic networks. This type of network has also been created in the form of ad hoc working groups and informal learning networks that tackle specific problematic issues addressed in the broader policy dialogues and Learning Forums. Members of these communicate more regularly to devise action plans and facilitate implementation.

The microcosmic models that have arisen recently on the national and regional levels generally mirror the structure of the overall network but are often supported by local structures of varying forms and thematic orientations. These informal networks currently convene Global Compact companies that wish to learn from one another's experiences. The local structures have yet to include civil society and labour representation sufficiently, but they eventually will integrate these groups and host their own Learning Forums and policy dialogues. Moreover, the local-level wide networks will spawn a number of strategic networks to produce innovative solutions to local problems. This organic growth process of nested and related networks, in which collaboration continuously begets further collaboration (Powell *et al.* 1996), has already manifested itself within the Global Compact.

---

3   Two points of clarification are in order. First, the Global Compact is an aspiring GPPN in the sense that it relies heavily on the guidance of the UN and is still in the process of divesting ownership to stakeholders. Second, we define public policy loosely as any policy adopted by government, business or civil society that supports public interests.

The importance of the evolution of these local networks cannot be overstated. It represents a shift towards the decentralisation of the network and the distribution of ownership, both critical to the longevity of the initiative. Besides devolving responsibility to local networks, the Global Compact Office has increasingly empowered 'enablers', such as the World Business Council for Sustainable Development (WBCSD) and Business for Social Responsibility (BSR), to expand the network and to manage issues related to individual companies. Such decentralisation will enhance the potential of the Global Compact to embed markets around the world within a broader consensus of societal needs and concerns.

As the local structures grow, a new dynamic will emerge between the global wide network and its nested components that will leverage the capacity and efficacy of the initiative. The Global Compact Office hopes to nurture the creation of sustainable structures for national forums by establishing content and information protocols for how the global and national levels can collaborate. Besides offering financial and political support, the Office believes it can enhance the impact of locally designed solutions, proposals or practices in four ways:

- By offering a global communications platform to disseminate information about the local 'products'

- By facilitating broad acceptance of the local products by challenging other Global Compact participants to utilise them

- By developing the products further by adding variety and additional experience

- By continuing to grant legitimacy to these efforts through the affiliation of the UN and the leadership of the UN Secretary-General

This approach—encouraging the most advanced participants to develop knowledge around particular issues and facilitating the acceptance of innovative solutions by the broader movement—has great promise for maximising the potential of the network's leaders and pressuring the followers to catch up. The local structures thus have important implications both for the administration of the network and for the learning it generates, as discussed in further detail in Section 3.2.2.

3.2.2 Classifying the learning generated in the Global Compact network

The complex structure, diversity of actors and variety of activities within the network produce a unique context of multiple dialectics in which several types of learning occur. For instance, the Global Compact engenders both network learning and organisational learning. Organisational learning occurs when an organisation institutionalises new structures, routines or strategies that effect changes in action (Huysman 1999, cited in Knight 2002). Network learning refers to learning accomplished by organisations as a group, rather than as individuals. At both the network and organisational level, learning may be cognitive, behavioural or both (Crossan *et al.* 1995). When cognitive and behavioural changes combine and generate repeated, successful implementation, the network learning may be classified as integrative (Knight 2002). Each of these types of learning is manifested in the Global Compact network, as illustrated in Box 3.1 and in the following discussion on the network's learning mechanisms.

One method for generating learning in the Global Compact network is through the global and local Learning Forums. The Learning Forum, like the broader enterprise of the Global Compact, is neither an instrument for monitoring companies

---

Organisational learning

The United Nations learns:

- How to integrate the activities of four core agencies
- How to develop and operate a network form of organisation, rather than the traditional bureaucratic, institutional form
- How to operate according to its core competences by leveraging its authority and convening powers, but outsourcing implementation to others

Companies learn:

- How to institutionalise socially and environmentally responsible policies and practices

All stakeholders learn

- How to recognise one another's needs and concerns through engagement, transparency and dialogue

Network learning

The answers to the following questions are requested by all members of the network:

- Why should businesses be good corporate citizens and why should they contribute to development? What is the business case for corporate citizenship?
- How can good corporate citizenship be developed and implemented through responsibility management systems?
- How can long-term convergence of understanding of how sector, region, culture and scale affect the practice of corporate citizenship be reached?
- How can successful partnership models for strategic networks be developed?
- How can key issues such as business in zones of conflict be addressed?
- How is the network itself to be conceived and organised?

In relation to the last item, the Global Compact participants have collectively:

- Learned that the network would have to recruit CEOs, not just business associations, in order to secure commitment and implementation capability
- Learned that the initiative could not operate as a regulatory mechanism or business ethics ranking mechanism
- Learned that transparent and fair criteria must be established for entry, participation and exit to protect the integrity of the initiative

---

Box 3.1 Examples of learning in the Global Compact Network

nor a regulatory regime to legislate corporate behaviour. Rather, it is a mechanism to stimulate action, to enhance transparency and to encourage information-sharing. The Learning Forum should ultimately serve as an information bank of disparate experiences—some successful and some not—of company efforts to implement the Global Compact's founding principles. From this reservoir of organisational learning experiences, the network as a whole will, it is hoped, learn the general business case for corporate citizenship as well as how location, scale and industrial contexts influence the equation. The Learning Forum is also the mechanism by which the Global Compact seeks to fill knowledge gaps around all its activities and to disseminate cutting-edge research to participants.

The thematic multi-stakeholder policy dialogues are another key learning tool. The dialogues seek to address dilemmas and to develop innovative solutions, based on a multi-stakeholder model of shared but diverse interests. The aegis of the Global Compact lends legitimacy to this inquiry and access to a vast network of actors. The dialogues are designed to promote candid but constructive exchange and to culminate in concrete proposals for action. The conception of how to solve the problems presented in the policy dialogues entails network learning, for the participants collectively produce new knowledge and understanding. However, the process eventually also requires organisational learning when the solutions are implemented through organisations, working independently or in concert.

Although the global and local Learning Forums and the policy dialogues are primarily designed to stimulate cognitive learning, the partnership development projects fostered by the Global Compact focus on behavioural learning. The emphasis in these projects rests on the collective action taken rather than on the formation of common understanding. However, all of the learning that takes place within the Global Compact network should be both cognitive and behavioural, or integrative. Ideally, all cognitive learning should be followed by policy-setting and then action in a dynamic, continuous circle. All learning and policy-setting around best practices and methods to address critical social problems must be followed by effective and sustained action. The Global Compact is not an idea to produce other ideas, but an idea to produce action.

3.2.3 Dynamic change process

We offer the following model to illustrate how we conceptualise the dynamic process of change that links the goals of the network with the accomplishments that it produces.

As Figure 3.3a illustrates, the process of change initiated by the Global Compact begins with the ultimate objective of contributing to a more stable, equitable and inclusive process of globalisation. The specific goals of the initiative also include the UN Secretary-General's resolve to revitalise the UN and to make it relevant again by positioning it as part of the solution to the problems of globalisation. However, the three listed goals are more fundamental and more directly related to improving globalisation.

The dynamic change process itself consists of three products that continuously reinforce one another: learning, policy-setting and action. We derive this process from Waddell's (2002a) description of consensual knowledge development and

(a)

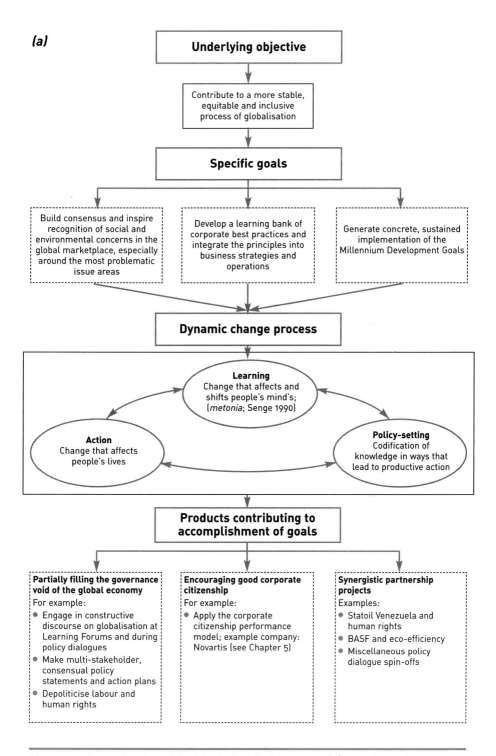

Figure 3.3 Operational model of the UN Global Compact: (a) flowchart of processes and products and (b) flowchart of determinants of effectiveness
(continued over)

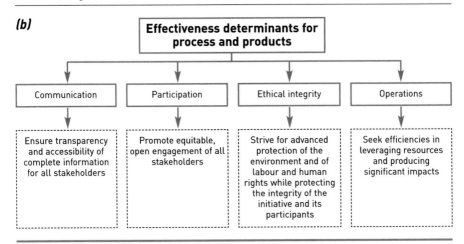

Figure 3.3 (continued)

implementation of large-scale systemic change within GPPNs. Within the context of the Global Compact, learning refers to the change produced in people's minds as a result of the leadership of the UN Secretary-General and the exchange of ideas among multiple stakeholders. Much of the impact of the Global Compact comes from the UN Secretary-General's role in changing perceptions about the division between public and private responsibility and the potential of co-operation. The Learning Forums and the policy dialogues facilitate social dialogue and foster the codification of collective knowledge into policies and plans for effective action.

We carefully distinguish between policy solutions that lead to action, and plans that lead to further dialogue, learning and policy-setting. For example, the Policy Dialogue Conference on Business and Sustainable Development in June 2002 produced two types of policy solutions. The first was generated by a working group on building sustainable business in the least-developed countries (LDCs). The group, comprising representatives of business, labour and civil society, collectively learned how Global Compact companies could best stimulate development in the world's poorest countries through sustainable investment. They then translated this consensual knowledge into a concrete plan for businesses and other stakeholders to consult, as they attempt to grow business in and build the capacity of LDCs. The second type of policy solution does not directly lead to improving lives or protecting the environment, but rather lays the groundwork for further learning and policy-setting. For instance, at the Conference on Sustainable Development, a working group created a method for promoting the financing of sustainable entrepreneurship and drafted a plan to hold further dialogue. These examples clarify the distinction between policy-oriented and action-oriented solutions and show how each supports the Global Compact's goals.

We strictly define action as change that improves people's lives in accordance with the Global Compact principles and the Millennium Development Goals. This enables us to judge the ultimate effectiveness of the initiative by focusing on specific measures companies take to implement the principles and to contribute to partnership projects. In other words, action can be conceived as either being internally or externally directed. Internally directed action refers to changes in corporate strategy, management and operations that benefit people within the organisation. For instance, a company could devise strategies to avoid discrimination and to ensure it pays its workers a living wage. Externally directed action consists of changes in corporate interaction with its surroundings that enhance greater societal welfare. Such action could take the form of a partnership project to eradicate poverty in the local community. In reality, of course, a company's internal action in support of the Global Compact's principles and action on broader corporate citizenship issues are closely intertwined.

We offer this classification scheme not to suggest that a true dichotomy exists between internal and external action but rather to demonstrate how the engagement mechanisms of the Global Compact relate to our 'comprehensive' notion of good corporate citizenship. We consider a commitment to the Global Compact principles as the necessary first step. Once a company has embraced the Global Compact and its principles, it may then wish to contribute to broader development goals and corporate citizenship issues through projects and initiatives. Undertaking projects without a prior commitment to making the principles an integral part of core business activities is not sufficient, since such projects may be isolated and detached from the core business of the company.

Box 3.2 describes the status quo, but the Global Compact Office is still experimenting with these engagement mechanisms. It constantly refines and solidifies them as the network holistically learns how best to conceive of and organise its activities.

Learning Forums

Business activities are as follows:

- Provision of example submissions (mandatory)
- Examination of business case studies
- The conduction of supportive research and analytical work
- Participation in informal, issue-specific networks
- Attendance of annual conferences

Policy dialogue

Working groups for the annual topic of the role of business in zones of conflict are as follows:

- Transparency
- Conflict Impact Assessment and Risk Management
- Multi-stakeholder Partnerships
- Revenue-Sharing Regimes

Working groups for the annual topic of business and sustainable development are as follows:

Box 3.2 Summary of UN Global Compact activities, by engagement mechanism
(continued over)

- Sustainable Investment
- Sustainable Entrepreneurship
- Corporate Management and Sustainability
- Investors and Sustainability

Partnership projects

It is suggested partnership projects should:

- Be inspired by the UN Global Compact
- Contribute to the Millennium Development Goals
- Be carried out with other actors such as UN agencies, labour, non-governmental organisations and public-sector entities
- Allow network participants to offer a substantial example of how they enact the principles (thus providing added incentives for them to do so)

It is also suggested that projects involving several companies be particularly encouraged.

Outreach and network-building

Replication of global structure should be found in:

- National Learning Forums
- National policy dialogues
- National partnership projects

Global Compact governance

Global Compact governance activities include:

- Building strategic alliances
- Searching for innovative operational concepts
- Seeking interagency co-ordination
- UN officials play an advocacy role and promote policy coherence
- The Global Compact Advisory Council:
  - Protects the integrity of the Global Compact
  - Provides leadership on key issues

Box 3.2 (continued)

3.3 Accomplishments and challenges

As an unprecedented, evolving experiment, the Global Compact has made substantial progress in advancing its goals since its inception nearly four years ago. However, the initiative has not accomplished all its objectives and perhaps it never will. We acknowledge that success is far from assured, but we argue that the Global Compact network represents a viable model for producing policy change and effective action. The greatest advantage of the network model is the flexibility that has enabled the initiative to transform itself and to overcome critical shortcomings. It will continue to do so, especially in the next couple of years, in order to resolve the deficiencies and challenges it currently faces. We return to our model of dynamic change to outline the accomplishments of the initiative thus far before analysing the major strengths and weaknesses of the Global Compact along several dimensions.

A few achievements of the Global Compact demonstrate its potential to partially fill the global governance gap between the economic, social and environmental spheres. Primarily, the Global Compact has held several successful policy dialogues that generated constructive discourse on globalisation. Besides the policy solutions mentioned above, the dialogues have also produced a set of policies for NGOs, companies and multilateral institutions to follow in order to enhance transparency and development in zones of conflict. Additionally, the diffusion of the principles of the Global Compact in many countries has shown that business pragmatism can help to depoliticise the debate over human rights and labour rights. The Global Compact has strengthened the efforts to promote UN conventions by directly influencing the protection of these rights through engagement with businesses. The Global Compact's hitherto success in raising awareness of human rights concerns in the private sector is particularly important, as up until six years ago very few companies considered these concerns to be relevant to business operations. Although the Global Compact, by itself, will never completely balance international governance structures and embed the global economic architecture in a framework of shared social values, the model it offers has the potential to substantially further these goals, especially as local networks develop around the world.

The Global Compact has also made progress in encouraging businesses to integrate the principles into their core strategies and operations. In fact, the network is currently creating a comprehensive performance model that could be applied universally by companies of all sizes and sectors. Several firms, such as the Swiss pharmaceutical company Novartis, have also pioneered the implementation of the principles through good corporate citizenship practices. Unfortunately, no company is a perfect corporate citizen, and even Novartis has come under fire for promoting genetically engineered agriculture. Despite this criticism, the firm has demonstrated serious efforts to comply with the principles. It created a Global Compact Steering Committee and Global Compact Clearing House to encourage corporate-wide commitment and to establish a knowledge infrastructure of internal and external information necessary for implementing the principles. The company then decided to provide its anti-malarial drug to the World Health Organisation (WHO) at cost, to support *pro bono* research on diseases of poverty, to donate significant amounts of tuberculosis (TB) treatments to African countries and to provide prevention and treatment services to its employees and their immediate family members for HIV/AIDS, TB and malaria. In addition, Novartis actively consults local NGOs to ensure it is paying living wages to their employees.

We acknowledge that few other Global Compact companies have shown such serious commitment to integrating the principles into their operations and to improving the quality of life in developing countries. But participation in the Global Compact network has pushed many firms down the long path towards good corporate citizenship. Several academics from around the world are currently writing case studies that will highlight the progress these companies have made and the obstacles they have yet to overcome. We emphasise that the permeation of UN principles into corporate boardrooms and the transformation of business practices will, as with most changes in human and organisational behaviour, remain a slow, gradual process. But as momentum builds, the Global Compact will give fresh impetus to core UN missions. We would estimate that, if these early efforts are successful, the critical mass of truly committed leaders necessary to fully implement and maintain the goals of the Global Compact will be reached within two years.

The Global Compact network has also succeeded in creating several action-oriented partnership projects in support of UN goals. For example, BASF contributes its expertise in eco-efficiency analysis to a training programme it founded with the United Nations Environment Programme (UNEP) and the United Nations Industrial Development Organisation (UNIDO) at the National Cleaner Production Centre in Morocco. In addition, Statoil Venezuela is working in partnership with the United Nations Development Programme (UNDP), Amnesty International and the Venezuelan judiciary to strengthen national awareness of human rights. The project utilises interactive training sessions conducted by Amnesty International to enhance understanding of human rights protection. Furthermore, several initiatives born out of the policy dialogues are currently being formed. These include programmes to provide electricity and water access to impoverished rural areas, to assist the UN in post-conflict reconstruction efforts, to support de-mining operations in Cambodia and to grow sustainable business in the 50 LDCs.

Finally, in a broader sense, the Global Compact has contributed to improving the effectiveness of the UN system by stimulating organisational learning and change within and between UN agencies. The Global Compact serves as a conduit for information exchange through which the involved agencies have developed synergies in learning the most reliable and productive solutions for their respective projects. For instance, through co-operation in the Global Compact, UNEP transferred knowledge to the Office of the High Commissioner for Human Rights (OHCHR) regarding the engagement of the private sector to advance UN goals. This shortened the learning curve significantly for the OHCHR, as it took them only one year to accomplish what UNEP struggled to achieve in ten. The participating UN agencies have also learned how to collaboratively improve their training and outreach efforts in developing countries. The Global Compact has served as a platform for them to integrate their tools, methodologies and training materials into a comprehensive package. Pooling resources and tools has enhanced the quality and attractiveness of UN operations in their workshops around the world.

3.3.1 Determinants of effectiveness

Despite giving several examples of the achievements of the Global Compact, we recognise that the efficacy of the network in its current state and structure remains subject to question. We attempt to clarify understanding about the effectiveness of the initiative through systematic analysis along four dimensions identified in the GPPN literature (see Reinicke 1998; Reinicke and Deng 2000; Waddell 2002a; see also Figure 3.3b). Admittedly, these lines of thought cross in various places; we categorise them only to provide some analytical structure and organisation.

3.3.1.1 Communication

The first dimension, or determinant of effectiveness, relates to the transparency and accessibility of information communicated within the network. The Global Compact's state-of-the-art web portal designed by German software company SAP AG provides complete information on the origins, goals, activities and major developments of the initiative. The site contains a database of participating companies, those that have submitted a letter of commitment from their CEO explaining their intent to implement the principles. At the end of 2002, the Global Compact discontinued the formal requirement that companies submit examples of how they have enacted the principles. The initiative now encourages companies to publish their progress in annual financial reports or in separate sustainability reports. The web portal will contain links to these documents in order to promote transparency and public accountability. However, the Global Compact Office still hopes to receive greater numbers of business examples and to disseminate knowledge of best practice. Despite these efforts, transparency remains a significant issue for the Global Compact, as it also confronts challenges in co-ordinating information flow throughout the network and improving the transparency of its governance procedures.

3.3.1.2 Participation

The second measure of effectiveness is the degree to which rules of participation offer all stakeholders open and equitable avenues of engagement. Since its inception, the Global Compact has faced the difficulty of joining traditionally antagonistic groups into one co-operative network. Yet the Global Compact remains committed to keeping the network inclusive and encourages participation from all stakeholder groups. The Global Compact also fosters the development of synergies and the convergence of efforts by welcoming major business ethics associations and proponents of other codes of conduct. Indeed, as previously mentioned (Section 3.2.1), the initiative is increasingly relying on these actors to strengthen and expand the network.

The flexibility and openness of the network structure enhance participation but do not guarantee co-operation and leave the initiative susceptible to tensions and conflicts of interest. For instance, many NGOs have expressed concern that partnerships with companies threaten the autonomy of the UN and that business wields too much influence over the design and goals of the Global Compact. They begin with the premise that business objectives necessarily conflict with their own priorities and those of the UN. However, the world's disadvantaged peoples significantly benefit from the business contribution to job creation, training and education, each of which cultivates economic development, peace and security. The Global Compact was constructed to advance only those goals of the private sector that coincide with broader societal objectives. It is neither intended to supplant regulation or other mechanisms of accountability nor to support any proponents of globalisation who disregard social and environmental concerns. On the contrary, Kofi Annan originally conceived of the Global Compact with the recognition that the world's poor will benefit from expanding market access, rather than social and environmental trade clauses that would subjugate them with de facto protectionism. The Global Compact strongly supports the strengthening of existing international social and environmental institutions and the creation of a global marketplace embedded in a framework of shared values. By no means does it promote the status quo or a particular ideology such as neoliberalism.

Enhancing our engagement with NGOs to avoid such misunderstandings is the principle challenge for the Global Compact to resolve in order to close current participation gaps. The network has maintained a policy of openness and inclusiveness, but several factors have complicated the involvement of NGOs. These include: the absence of hierarchical or representative structures, the multifaceted nature of their operations, their methods of work and their ideological orientations. Although a large number of NGOs have participated in country-level activities and projects, a clearly defined platform for their contribution at the global level is lacking. The Global Compact Office recognises this deficiency and has drafted a policy note on the issue, to be followed with major improvements in the upcoming months.

Regardless of any attempts to encourage the participation of NGOs, some will remain ideologically opposed to the initiative. A small but very vocal alliance of NGOs has rallied against the Global Compact, with various motives. Some use the Global Compact to gain profile for their own activities, some regard the opening-up of the UN to business as a zero-sum game with respect to their own standing and some take issue with specific features of the initiative. Nevertheless, their confrontational stance and vituperative reports have produced critical insight into how to identify and avert problems. For example, the self-imposed rule not to accept corporate funding for Global Compact activities and the elaboration of strict guidelines regarding the UN logo were activities greatly inspired by critical NGOs.

Another crucial participation gap results from the difficulty of motivating some firms that have committed to the Global Compact but fail to openly share complete information about their activities. They may not do so for several reasons. First, they may be hesitant to share proprietary information that could compromise some aspect of their competitive advantage *vis-à-vis* other firms. Second, 'free-riders' may wish to gain recognition and prestige by participating without really contributing to or abiding by the principles (Dyer and Nobeoka 2000). These 'competitive players' may opportunistically undermine the network by taking as much as they can and giving as little as possible, thus restricting transparency (Larsson *et al.* 1998). Third, companies may feel vulnerable to potential liabilities by exposing their practices to a global, critical audience. Last, firms may be fully motivated to participate but may lack the operational capacity to effectively communicate. We address some efforts to mitigate the free-rider problem below, but generally, these challenges will remain difficult to resolve. Any attempt to do so will have to confront the additional challenge of maintaining a positive internal dynamic between leading and lagging companies. The network will have to increasingly utilise informal networks to encourage the leaders to innovate and construct solutions that can be mainstreamed for those that lag behind. The stewardship role of the UN implies that, to mitigate potential friction between companies, it will have to continue to emphasise facilitating factors of participation, such as previous interaction experience, trust and long-term orientation, and to impede detracting factors such as opportunism and suspicion (Larsson *et al.* 1998).

A final challenge to the network relating to participation concerns the generation of negative marginal returns, as the addition of new participants beyond a certain point diminishes the effectiveness of the initiative. There exists an optimal level of collaboration beyond which the adaptive capacity of participants decreases because of a growing inward focus and a lack of interest in learning from and interacting with organisations outside of the network (Uzzi 1996). The Global Compact thus does not conceive of itself as an exclusive network, and it actively encourages co-operation with non-participating organisations. Diminishing marginal returns of participation also result from the difficulty of efficiently transferring knowledge among large numbers of participants (Dyer and Nobeoka 2000). Therefore, the Global Compact is developing a strategy to create small, independent working groups, distinct from those created through the policy dialogues, which will meet to discuss issues of shared interest and produce reports for the rest of the network.

3.3.1.3 Ethical integrity

The third determinant of effectiveness is the ability of the network to further its goals while protecting the ethical integrity of the initiative and its participants. As mentioned in Section 3.3.1.2, the Global Compact guards itself against conflicts of interest by refusing to take funds from companies or business associations. All funding comes from member-states and not-for-profit organisations, consistent with established UN policies and procedures. Furthermore, strict rules govern the use of the Global Compact logo, and companies are prohibited from publishing anything misleading or untruthful about their participation in the initiative. Appropriate measures will be taken if individual participants use their association with the Global Compact for purposes other than its stated goals or if their individual behaviour threatens the initiative's integrity.

Notwithstanding the implementation of these policies, the need to maintain lax entry rules presents a challenge for overcoming the free-rider problem. The network must maintain its inclusive policy for corporations because of the Global Compact's base in the UN. Political dilemmas would arise if the Global Compact attempted to exclude legal, tax-paying companies from sovereign member-states that indicated their desire to support and implement the principles. The Global Compact can effectively serve only as a learning platform that facilitates gradual, incremental change. It will attempt, no matter how difficult the task may be, to judge the intent of companies to improve their practices and abide by the principles. Although companies are strongly encouraged to report on their implementation of the nine principles, and are held accountable by public scrutiny for doing so, little else prevents them from free-riding.

The Global Compact is therefore constructing measures to enhance the participation of companies in the network. Future development of a multi-stakeholder business example review board and an analytical method of evaluating business submissions and reports will provide incentives for companies to improve their performance and the quality of their examples. In addition, the public is encouraged to comment on business examples published on the Global Compact website and to broach broader concerns about corporate behaviour at the annual Learning Forum conferences. The ability of all stakeholders to freely exchange ideas and concerns about one another's behaviour at the Learning Forums is crucial for guaranteeing the legitimacy of the Global Compact. The network also supports and contributes to the development of reporting standards and accountability mechanisms. Finally, nearly a dozen business case studies have been commissioned from independent academic authors to analyse companies' implementation of the principles. These measures help address the moral hazard problem, which arises from the incentive for corporations to act carelessly, or even fraudulently, without the threat of monitoring and enforcement. Good corporate citizens and those truly wishing to improve their conduct welcome the transparent feedback and the support of other accountability structures, for they would not benefit from participation in an initiative that might otherwise be rendered socially illegitimate.

One final issue that potentially threatens the integrity of the Global Compact relates to the implicit messages promulgated through public advocacy. We emphasise here that the UN does not endorse any individual company participating in the Global Compact. We consider companies to be participants engaged in a multi-stakeholder network, not members of a club that have met some performance standard to gain entry. Participating firms have sufficiently indicated their willingness to publicly support the principles and have demonstrated their aspirations to abide by them. In their public advocacy of the Global Compact, companies should officially label themselves as 'participants' that believe in and aspire to abide by the principles. They should not, explicitly or implicitly, untruthfully advertise full compliance with the Global Compact. Indeed, this measure not only protects the integrity of the initiative but also protects the firms themselves from regulation against false advertising and misleading commercial speech (see *Kasky v. Nike* 2002). We acknowledge that companies enhance their reputation and social legitimacy by participating in the Global Compact insofar as the public considers it admirable that these companies aspire to comply with the principles, but we cannot accept misleading statements that besmirch the reputation of the initiative and the UN as a whole. Of course, the Global Compact will never be capable of preventing companies from issuing misleading statements via unpublished, unofficial media. We encourage the public to consult official Global Compact literature and to perform its own due diligence when possible.

Our efforts to defend the network's integrity respond to scathing attacks on the legitimacy of the Global Compact. Some NGOs have labelled the Global Compact 'a smuggling of a business agenda into the United Nations' (CorpWatch 2002) that 'has undermined UN social and ecological responsibility' (IFG 2002). They have accused the Global Compact of 'bluewashing' companies, or allowing them to drape themselves in the UN's blue flag without forcing them to change their ways. As we discussed above, the Global Compact has developed several methods of protecting itself from abuse and encouraging gradual reform. It could never dispel all allegations of bluewashing, however, unless it were to become a regulatory force, which it has neither the mandate nor the capacity to do.

3.3.1.4 Operational effectiveness

The fourth determinant of effectiveness refers to the network's efficiency and impact. The Global Compact is generally very efficient and cost-effective out of necessity. The Global Compact Office has few staff members and little funding, making it imperative to leverage the donated time and energy of consultants and participants. Even without a large budget, the network is capable of producing substantial change due to its emphasis on utilising the core competences and comparative advantages of its participants. The exact amount of positive change generated is difficult to measure without established metrics of value, but it is clear that the potential impact is very significant. Of course, by itself, the Global Compact will never be enough to alter the course of globalisation, but, given sufficient time to engender incremental changes in attitudes and behaviour, the initiative could bring the world closer to the Millennium Development Goals.

3.3.2 Open questions

The fate of the Global Compact only partially depends on the structures and protocols it employs to achieve its objectives. Those stewarding the direction and shape of the initiative can influence, but not control, several exogenous factors. The following are critical issues still open to question:

- Are the companies participating in the Global Compact network serious and committed to working with the principles, or are they disingenuous and simply using the initiative as a public relations tool?

- Will confrontational NGOs be satisfied with changes to the Global Compact and eventually participate in the network, or will they continue their attempts to derail the initiative?

- Will the UN have the courage and flexibility to interact with the real world and continue this historic experiment, or will the immense bureaucracy and those committed to the traditional division between public and private responsibility stifle the growth and innovation of the Global Compact?

- Will the climate of globalisation shift towards bilateralism and protectionism and radically change the parameters for shaping a better global economic order?

The model presented here and the vision it represents will succeed if the stake-holders involved *want* it to succeed. The network has the flexibility and capacity to collectively determine its future. Volition, commitment and understanding are the truly fundamental determinants of success.

We have offered an extensive analysis of the Global Compact by using established theory surrounding networks and dynamic change, but we have barely scratched the surface. The Global Compact is an extremely complex, unique network that requires further study from the perspective of many academic disciplines. For instance, research could focus on the debate over voluntary initiatives compared with command-and-control regulation (see Streeck and Schmitter 1985; Ayres and Braithwaite 1992; ICHRP 2002; Robinson 2002), metrics of value for assessing the business case for corporate citizenship and the impact of the Global Compact[4] and normative frameworks for the Global Compact such as integrative social contract theory (Donaldson and Dunfee 1999). Researchers may also wish to extend the implementation model for corporate citizenship recently developed within the Global Compact network or apply empirical evidence to theories of total responsibility management (TRM) systems (see Waddock *et al.* 2002). Alternatively, academics might analyse the game-theoretic implications of global multi-stakeholder engagement within the Global Compact and explore the weaknesses that the network confronts.

3.4 Conclusions

Since Kofi Annan's call to action at the 1999 World Economic Forum, the notion of the Global Compact has evolved into one of the most expansive and ambitious networks in the world. We have described the UN Secretary-General's initiative as an experiment with the aim of making 'globalisation work for all the world's peoples'. This entails stabilising the global governance system by strengthening its social and environmental pillars and making the global market more inclusive by providing equitable opportunities for advancement to the billions of marginalised poor.

The Global Compact's inter-organisational, public policy learning network has the power to further these goals by generating a process of incremental, but comprehensive, change. Over time, this dynamic process will progressively alter attitudes and behaviour, insofar as it engenders consensus around critical social and environmental issues and facilitates co-operative action. The reach of the initiative is global not only because of the UN's leadership but, more importantly,

---

4 One way researchers have attempted to measure the economic returns and losses from responsible behaviour has been through the study of socially responsible investment (SRI). For a meta-analysis of 95 empirical studies on SRI, see Margolis and Walsh 2001. For an example of analysis by finance academics, see Geczy *et al.* 2004, which brings the latest asset management benchmark factor models to bear on the question of the performance of socially screened funds.

because of the emphasis on creating local networks, each embedded within the same shared framework of values.

Again, we argue for the viability of the model presented; yet we acknowledge that success is far from assured. The Global Compact has produced constructive social dialogue at the global level, has promoted the adoption of the principles, has stimulated action-oriented projects in support of UN goals and has played a role in enhancing the effectiveness of the UN system. Going forward, the initiative must confront several challenges in order to sustain these efforts. It must work to manage tensions and conflicts of interest, to improve the participation of NGOs and laggard firms and to institute a fair system of checks and balances. These efforts will require the collaboration of all participating stakeholders.

The Global Compact can only partially resolve the problems associated with globalisation. It is clearly not the beginning of the solution, nor is it the end, but it can play a significant role in improving people's lives around the world. It will succeed in doing so as long as it secures the necessary volition, commitment and understanding from key stakeholders. These stakeholders have the capacity to shape the initiative, to enhance its strengths and to overcome its weaknesses. The Global Compact is not a fixed entity, but a strategy, or idea, continuously evolving through changing circumstances. It is, in short, an historic experiment in learning and action.

Part 2
The Global Compact
and human rights

4

De-compacting the Global Compact*

Thomas Donaldson
Wharton School, Philadelphia, USA

By announcing the Global Compact, Secretary-General Kofi Annan has set the world a tall, tall task. Indeed, the remarkable ambitiousness of the Compact project is matched only by the remarkable stakes it holds for all of us. I want here to explore the sorts of value-oriented justifications necessary to make this tall task at least a theoretical success. What justificatory account is required to support the Compact adequately? I propose that any such account must ascend eventually three distinct rungs of a 'ladder of justification'. The three justificatory rungs are: first, 'egoism'; second, 'co-operative egoism'; and, third, 'citizenship'. To justify the full Global Compact, companies must somehow be capable of reaching the third, and most difficult, rung.

Rung 1 is simply 'corporate egoism'. That is, some principles of the Global Compact can be justified by showing that following them will make a company more money, assuming at least that doing so doesn't cause significant auxiliary harm or violate other key ethical principles. Consider the claim embedded in Principle 8 that companies should 'undertake initiatives to promote greater environmental responsibility'. In the explanatory notes to Principle 8, it is claimed that 'Investing in production methods that are not sustainable, that deplete resources and that degrade the environment has a lower long-term return than investing in sustainable operations.' Here we have a justificatory 'no-brainer', or at least a 'small-brainer'. The battle at this rung of justification is entirely empirical, and theoretically winnable.

* This paper was first presented at All-Academy Symposium, 'The Global Compact: Building Corporate Citizenship in a World of Networks', at the 2002 Academy of Management conference in Denver, CO, 12 August 2002.

However, we are wise to pause and reflect on the difficulty of getting the studies we want, not only because the facts may not turn out as we like, but because of the logical problems surrounding certain elements of the Compact and that form of justification. To take only one example, consider the issue of human rights. A key aspect of a right, as the political philosopher Ronald Dworkin notes, is that it constitutes a trump over interests or goals (Dworkin 1979). If free speech is a right, one cannot justify violating it by showing that by violating it a person or people will be better off. Because they are trumps, rights cannot be hostage to consequences, collective or individual. Put simply, one should honour a right because it is the right thing to do—*period*. This deontic, unconditional nature of a right means that, if a company's honouring a particular right—say, the right of workers to bargain collectively—does *not* advance the long-term self-interest of a particular corporation, the right must *still* be honoured. Hence, rights in general, by their nature, cannot be justified by this first rung of the justificatory ladder.

Consider a similar, but non-rights, example from the Compact: namely, Principle 2's requirement that corporations do not engage in acts of bribery or intimidation that undermine the host country's political or judicial system. Unfortunately, it is logically possible that an individual act of bribery or intimidation by company XYZ *might be* in the long-run self-interest of XYZ's corporate shareholders.

It follows that to justify rights and other important precepts of the Global Compact principles, we must move to the second rung of justification.

That rung is 'co-operative egoism'. Adam Smith (Smith 1976) never anticipated the modern corporation or its grand role in a global market. Yet most of his arguments for the superiority of the market still stand—so long as the very backdrop of ethical co-operation and government's selective involvement that he endorsed occurs at a global level. Consider the importance of ethical co-operation to markets. What I've called the 'efficiency hypernorm' elsewhere (Donaldson and Dunfee 1999) requires corporations to co-operatively adhere to those principles necessary for systemic market efficiency. In 2002, as I write this essay, the United States is reeling from such failures today. Blocking transparency and providing systematically misleading information to investors makes transactions less efficient, as in the instance of the dot.com bubble or the many Enron/WorldCom/Qwest scandals. Other principles falling under the 'efficiency hypernorm' include:

1. Respect for intellectual property

2. Engaging in fair competition and avoiding monopolies

3. Avoiding nepotism and 'crony capitalism'

4. Not abusing government relationships

5. Avoiding bribery

6. Respecting environmental integrity

All companies have a stake in the efficiency of the economic system in which they participate, and, if companies co-operatively follow certain principles, most will be better off. Prisoners' dilemmas, and the failure of Amartya Sen's 'paradox of the Paretean liberal' are thus avoided. At least four of the principles just mentioned are key components of the Global Compact, and thus find potential justification in 'co-operative egoism'. Examples would include Principle 2's honouring the right of governments to have legitimate political and judicial systems by not undermining them through intimidation or bribery. Under co-operative egoism, companies co-operate around norms such as those in the Global Compact to secure their collective advantage.

But the task of the Global Compact is taller than even these two rungs can reach. Justification of the full Compact means reaching rung 3 or 'corporate citizenship'. This is the toughest and requires what Lee Preston and others have called 'a redefinition of the corporation' (e.g. Post *et al.* 2002a).

Consider the inadequacy of rungs 1 and 2, i.e. egoism and co-operative egoism, when it comes to many requirements of the Compact. For much of the Compact seems to require not only enlightened self-interest, but heart. Principle 1 asks corporations to honour rights to basic health, education and housing, at least when operations are located in areas where these are not provided. This means corporations should sometimes reach out to boost the welfare of workers to some threshold human standard. The rights here, i.e. to minimal housing and food, are known by theorists as 'positive' rights rather than 'negative' ones. Negative rights, such as the right to free speech, require only that others abstain from violating them, but positive rights require more than abstention: they require that people and corporations actually *do* things, perhaps sometimes even build houses, and provide education for workers.

And the Global Compact does contain a number of norms that ask companies at least sometimes to *do* things. For example, in Principle 9 the Compact asks that companies 'encourage the development and diffusion of environmentally friendly technologies, and communicate with stakeholders about the environment'. And in Principle 3 the Compact asks that companies provide facilities to help worker representatives carry out their functions.

Moreover, the trumping nature of rights, noted earlier, means that the Compact holds companies responsible for honouring a given right *even if* it cannot be shown that doing so serves the egoistic or co-operative egoistic advantage of most companies. The Compact is asking companies to do many things simply because *they are the right thing to do.* Here we must appeal directly to value theory, for it is values that are at stake. Jim Post put it well when he said: 'Global business is about *value*; global corporate citizenship is about *values*' (Post 2002a).

It is clear that from the standpoint of the Global Compact the conception of the corporation must be a stakeholder one, not merely a stockholder one. The interests of constituencies other than shareholders, such as labour and customers, must be taken as having intrinsic worth, as being valuable in themselves, and the goals and mission of the corporation must reflect that plurality of interests.

How do we justify this new conception of the corporation as a global citizen? The answer is too long to sketch here but it will surely follow avenues of research and analysis already in evidence. Social contract theory, along lines first charted by John Rawls (1971) and in evidence in much current business writing, is promising in explaining the evolving social contract between global corporations and the global citizenry that the Global Compact recognises. The very name 'Global Compact' suggests a hypothetical, implicit, social contract.

And then there is the traditional justification for rights, justification that can be easily be adapted to the Global Compact. Henry Shue's (1980) method is well respected, for example, and involves beginning with a handful of basic rights that everyone accepts, and then systematically determining which additional rights are necessary for the maintenance of the basic rights. Thus the less fundamental rights become legitimised through their connection to the more basic rights.

I do not mean here exhaustively to canvas the kinds of normative justifications that might be used to support the third rung of 'corporate citizenship'. I mean only to show that some such justification is finally necessary for the social compact, and that some obvious candidates for justificatory mechanisms are standing in the wings.

I have sketched the ladder that we must climb. For those who, as I do, think the Global Compact has merit, the next task is to climb it.

5
Business and human rights[*]

Klaus M. Leisinger
Novartis Foundation for Sustainable Development
and University of Basel, Switzerland

> Companies cannot and should not be the moral arbiters of the
> world. They cannot usurp the role of governments, nor solve all the
> social problems they confront. But their influence on the global
> economy is growing and their presence increasingly affects the
> societies in which they operate. With this reality comes the need to
> recognise that their ability to continue to provide goods and services
> and create financial wealth—in which the private sector has proved
> uniquely successful—will depend on their acceptability to an
> international society which increasingly regards protection of
> human rights as a condition of the corporate licence to operate.
>
> *Sir Geoffrey Chandler*[1]

5.1 Human rights: a business duty?

Largely unnoticed by the management of most companies, an intense debate has
developed in recent years on the issue of business and human rights. But, actually,
the issue is not new, because specialist human rights groups even back in the 1980s
linked multinational companies in the extractive sector (oil, diamonds, gold,
precious metals) with human rights abuses at their local mining sites (for examples
of current problems, see Amnesty International 2003; AI DRC 2003; see also

[*] This chapter represents the author's personal opinion and does not reflect the opinion
of the Novartis corporation or its directors, officers or staff.
[1] Chandler 2000: 5.

Chandler 1998; Gberie 2003). The *Human Development Report 2000* (UNDP 2000: 79 ff.) pointed out that 'global corporations' have an 'enormous impact on human rights—in their employment practices, in their environmental impact, in their support for corrupt regimes or their advocacy for policy changes' and called for corporate human rights standards, implementation measures and independent audits'. The OECD Guidelines for Multinational Enterprises, revised in 2000, had already included a reference to human rights (OECD 2000a: 19). What is new, however, is the dynamic increase over the past three years or so in the breadth and depth of the general business-related human rights debate.[2]

This may be unexpected, but it does not pose a problem for companies competing with integrity (see de George 1993). Today, all actors in civil society must perceive a responsibility for human development and thus respect the equal and inalienable rights of all members of the human family as enshrined in the Universal Declaration of Human Rights (UDHR) adopted by the General Assembly of the United Nations on 10 December 1948. 'Good' corporations and those responsible for their corporate conduct will therefore perceive a duty to support and respect human rights and do their utmost to ensure that the spirit of the Universal Declaration is upheld in their sphere of activity and influence. At a minimum, they will refrain from actions that obstruct the realisation of those rights. Where, then, are the problems?

The present debate suffers from the fact that, at one end of the political opinion spectrum, human rights activists create the impression that the whole misery of people in developing countries is largely the consequence of cynical orgies of human rights abuses by multinational companies (see CETIM/AAJ 2002: 10). At the other end of the spectrum, institutions with close ties to business go on record saying that there are no business-specific human rights problems, as all demands of the Universal Declaration of Human Rights are directed exclusively at the state and its regulatory authorities (ICC/IOE 2003). Human rights demands being made of other actors in society (e.g. of business enterprises), they say, detract from the actual perpetrators—widely known despots and their entourage abusing basic human rights within their sphere of power.

The tenor of the human rights debate has become increasingly critical of transnational corporations because of a deep-seated disquiet about globalisation. Opinion polls show that nine out of ten respondents who are interested in development policy and work in non-governmental organisations (NGOs) or who have close ties to that work see too much globalisation emphasis on trade and investment and far too little attention being paid to human rights or other non-economic issues.[3]

Against this background, the UN Global Compact initiative of UN Secretary-General Kofi Annan continues to be of major importance. It takes up this disquiet and aims to counteract it by encouraging companies to commit themselves

---

2 Anyone who enters the two terms in an Internet search engine such as Google will find over 5 million contributions to the debate.

3 See www.globescan.com for the Corporate Social Responsibility Monitor 2003 and 2003 (33 Bloom Street East, Toronto, Canada M4W 3HI).

publicly to compliance with certain minimum standards of a political, social and ecological nature. Convinced that weaving universal values into the fabric of global markets and corporate practices will help advance broad societal goals while securing open markets, Kofi Annan challenged world business leaders to 'embrace and enact' the Global Compact, both in their individual corporate practices and by supporting appropriate public policies and promoting fair business practices. Such fairness is expressed by good labour standards and enlightened protection of the environment—and also by corporate efforts to 'support and respect the protection of the international human rights within their sphere of influence' (Principle 1) as well as to 'ensure that their own corporations are not complicit in human rights abuses' (Principle 2).

The principles relating to social and ecological issues were not a problem for companies working responsibly because they correspond to state-of-the-art practices of good corporate citizenship or corporate social responsibility (CSR). The two human rights principles, however, led the managers of most companies into territory that was new and unfamiliar to them.

At about the same time, a sub-commission of the UN Commission for Human Rights (UNCHR) started its work to develop a set of UN Norms on the Responsibilities of Transnational Corporations and other Businesses on Human Rights (UNCHR 2003a, 2003b). One of the central aims of this sub-commission was to strengthen and put into operation the two human rights principles of the Global Compact. The Norms were unanimously approved in Geneva on 13 August 2003 and will be submitted to the full UNCHR for acceptance. Although it is true to say that the UN Norms represent a welcome strengthening of Principles 1 and 2 of the Global Compact in terms of content, they are unclear—at least in their present form—on a number of important procedural issues.[4]

Whatever the tune of the debate, the fact remains that business enterprises have a moral obligation to respect human rights. If they do not comply with these most essential elements of their social responsibility, they surely risk their societal (if not legal) licence to operate. Hence, at the very least the management of enlightened companies see themselves confronted with the question of how to respond to the increasing importance of human rights demands on business enterprises.

4 Whereas the Global Compact is a voluntary framework for promoting good corporate citizenship, the Norms are seen as becoming a part of international law and are perceived to suggest that companies should be subject to the kind of enforcement by the UNCHR that has previously applied only to nation-states. Another point to be discussed in more detail in the negotiation process ahead is the 'periodic monitoring and verification by the United Nations and other international and national mechanisms already in existence or yet to be created' (see Amnesty International's contribution to this debate: AI 2004).

5.2 What constitutes a fair societal distribution of labour?

Modern societies are highly complex systems of human co-existence. They contain a multitude of actors (individuals, groups, organisations) whose interests, objectives and differing modes of behaviour and regulations are entwined in a circularly interdependent relationship.[5] To meet the superordinate aims of a modern society (such as respect for and fulfilment of human rights) the various actors must contribute according to their resources and abilities in the context of a social contract (see e.g. Donaldson and Dunfee 1999).

With many demands made on business enterprises by interest groups, it is not the question of their fundamental justification that is at issue. For example, demands to fulfil the rights and grant the freedoms set forth in the Universal Declaration of Human Rights are doubtless justified from the perspective of people-centred human development. The issue that is contentious is the question of who is the appropriate bearer of duty. To demand rights without determining at least the direction for collateral duties creates the risk of raising expectations that cannot be fulfilled. No societal actor has all the obligations to bear and no one enjoys all the rights. This is especially true in the context of human rights.

Paul Streeten (2003) helps to sort out the different duties by distinguishing four different areas of human rights:

- In the narrowest sense they are rights of personal integrity: the right not to be tortured or murdered, not to be imprisoned without due process of law. Freedom of conscience and expression, freedom from arbitrary deprivation of liberty, the right to assembly and freedom of association belong in this group. These rights apply under all governments, irrespective of their political colour—and take little more resources than the political will.

- A second group consists of civil rights, or what in Anglo-Saxon countries is described as the 'rule of law' and in German as the *Rechtsstaat*. This group comprises the rights of citizens against their government. The rulers themselves are subject to the law.

- In the third group are political rights. These enable citizens to participate in government by voting for their representatives, 'throwing them out' and restricting those elected regarding what they can do while they are in power. Representation can take many forms, of which one adult person/ one vote or a multi-party system is only one example.

- The fourth group is that of economic, social and cultural rights, embodied in the Universal Declaration of Human Rights of 1948 and the International Covenant on Economic, Social and Cultural Rights of 1966 (OHCHR 1966). Economic, social and cultural rights are positive rights to

5 This sentence conceals an even greater complexity, which has best been explained in Luhmann 1997.

scarce resources and therefore distinct from the negative rights not to have certain things done to one. In the case of cultural rights, conflicts can arise between the rights of communities and the rights of individuals. The rights to universal primary education, to adequate health standards, to employment and to minimum wages and collective bargaining are quite different from negative rights. It has taken enlightened societies three centuries to achieve these civil, political and social dimensions of human development.

The 18th century established civil rights—from freedom of thought, speech and religion to the rule of law. In the course of the 19th century, political freedom and participation in the exercise of political power made major strides, as the right to vote was extended to more people. In the 20th century, the welfare state extended human rights to the social and economic sphere, by recognising that minimum standards of education, health, nutrition, well-being and security are basic to what may be termed 'civilised life' as well as to the exercise of the civil and political attributes of citizenship.

The interpretation of economic and social rights therefore cannot be made irrespective of the stage of development of a country, its available capabilities and resources, and competing claims on these resources. Social services (such as support for unemployed citizens through 'dole' [social security] systems) that have been financed by a 'mature' European nation such as Germany in the past 20 years seem no longer sustainable there—and they are well out of reach for the financial capability of any Sub-Saharan African nation. It is therefore recommended to distinguish in this context, as Streeten (2003, emphasis added) has done, between

> *aspirations*, which are ideals we hope to attain eventually, and *rights*, about which there is something absolute . . . by calling some human aspirations a *right*, the objective in question has been given a moral absolute and categorical supremacy, irrespective of the nature of the right, its appropriateness to the circumstances in which it is proclaimed or to the possibilities or costs achieving it.

There is no doubt that all actors in every civilised society should aspire to opportunities for comprehensive human development, including such rights as expressed by Article 24 (such as the right to rest and leisure), Article 25 (the right to a standard of living adequate for health and well-being of the individual and the family, including food, clothing, housing, medical care and necessary social services, and the right to security in the event of unemployment, sickness, disability, widowhood, old age or other lack of livelihood in circumstances beyond a person's control) and Article 26 (right to education) of the Universal Declaration of Human Rights. It would be unrealistic, however, to expect poor nations to guarantee full and immediate implementation.

Accepting this poses highly political questions: if those carrying the primary responsibility to deliver on these rights are not able to do so, who is next in line of responsibility? One thing is certain: a flourishing economy that benefits all social groups—carried by flourishing enterprises—is the most important prerequisite for the satisfaction of basic needs and the fulfilment of economic, social and cultural rights. In terms of responsibility for pursuing pro-poor economic development, for restructuring budgets to provide adequate expenditure on primary human concerns, for ensuring participation and social reforms, for protecting environmental resources and the social capital of poor communities and for securing human rights in law, there is clearly one duty-bearer: the nation-state.

5.2.1 Characteristics of modern society

According to Niklas Luhmann (1989), a characteristic feature of modern society is its differentiation into a variety of functionally specialised subsystems, such as the economy, law, politics, religion, science, education and so on. None of these subsystems of society is able to substitute for another, let alone all others: 'function systems cannot step in for, replace or even simply relieve one another' (Luhmann 1989: 48). The quality of co-operation of the different subsystems determines the degree of possible synergies and allows for the whole (society) to be more than the sum of its parts (subsystems).

The case of the economy illustrates the limitations of a subsystem. Money is the medium of communication in the modern economy. For Luhmann the economy is the totality of those operations that are executed by payments. Business enterprises and individuals engaged in business form the economic subsystem. Its prime function is to ensure that the needs of all citizens are satisfied as cost-effectively as possible. The self-interest of individuals and competition are the organising forces in this process (von Nell-Breuning 1990: 64). Decisions are made according to the economic efficiency principle (benefit–cost ratio) and other criteria of business rationality. This results in rules of conduct that differ fundamentally from those of other societal subsystems. As a functional subsystem of modern society the economy can treat problems only insofar as they are communicated as matters of economic costs and benefits, otherwise it will regard them as 'noise' and refrain from such action (Luhmann 1995: 462). To apply rules and values of other subsystems is not suitable for the functional capacity and effectiveness of the economic subsystem. Redistribution policies or social transfers of wealth in the name of charity, for example, belong to the functions of other societal subsystems. The economic subsystem acts on and through markets; a compassionate anti-economy could not be sustained owing to constraints inherent in the system. Under 'normal' circumstances (i.e. given a functioning society and good governance) other subsystems assume responsibility for the issues that cannot be dealt with by the economic subsystem.

It is a subject of debate in modern societies as to what a self-evident duty is for a company and what constitutes an unreasonable demand. Different stakeholders define the responsibilities of business enterprises differently as a result of their differing values and interests. Not every demand of every stakeholder becomes the moral duty of the company. In defining the corporate social responsibility of companies—the human rights dimension is just one of several—a distinction should be drawn between three dimensions of responsibility involving differing degrees of obligation, namely:

● The 'must' dimension: this includes non-negotiable essentials incumbent on the respective industry that, by general social consensus, 'go without saying'

- The 'ought to' dimension: this includes good corporate citizenship standards through the application of internal guidelines for sensitive business areas, particularly in countries where the quality of the law is insufficient or where law is not enforced

- The 'can' dimension: this involves the assumption of further responsibility, not covered in the first two dimensions

5.2.1.1 The 'must' dimension of societal responsibility

The dimension of responsibility that is absolutely essential for good companies is not much different today from that in the past. A company has to produce good-quality goods and services for which there is a demand from potential buyers with purchasing power and to sell them at profitable prices. In the process, the business enterprise—like all other societal actors—has to comply with all the laws and regulatory requirements as well as to respect relevant customs. To conduct its business activities, the enterprise creates and maintains healthy and safe jobs, pays employees competitive wages and treats them fairly. The 'must' dimension of corporate activity also includes securing a fair interest on the capital invested by the owners of the company: the shareholders.

Other essential responsibilities include the protection of the environment, contributions to pension funds and insurance systems and the payment of taxes. With the taxes paid, the state should finance its operations and fulfil its tasks. Since most companies also provide training and education, further value-added accrues to society. Added value also arises from the productive use of products and services. In the case of a pharmaceutical company, considerable benefit to society arises from the use of medicines because mortality is reduced and sickness and disability are cured or relieved.

By accepting this essential dimension of corporate social responsibility as a matter of course, a company contributes to the fulfilment of economic, social and cultural human rights of citizens just by doing business under 'normal' circumstances. By 'normal' circumstances I mean that the countries in which corporations operate are characterised by good governance (e.g. legitimised exercise of political power; correct financial, economic, social and other policy decisions; the rule of law and the rational allocation of resources). Unfortunately, circumstances in many countries are not 'normal'. The most difficult human rights problems occur in countries in which the state and its organs are either unable or unwilling to meet their responsibilities. Under such circumstances, a company is well advised to go beyond the 'must' dimension of human rights and other societal responsibilities.

5.2.1.2 The 'ought to' dimension of societal responsibility

The European Green Paper 'Promoting a European Framework for Corporate Social Responsibility' defines the 'ought to' dimension as the actual social responsibility of companies and as a 'concept whereby companies integrate social and environmental concerns in their business operations and in their interaction with their stakeholders on a voluntary basis' (CEC 2002: 366). If we understand the 'must' dimension as compliance with legal and conventional modes of behaviour, then the 'ought to' dimension can be seen as the constructive and generous filling of unregulated space as proposed, for example, in the Global Compact.

Enlightened labour and environmental standards are applied even if local law and regulations would allow for lower standards. The reason for adherence to the enlightened spirit of the rule and not just the letter of actual national law is based on values: 'It is the right thing to do'. By adopting corporate citizenship guidelines, enlightened companies create a framework of self-commitment that guarantees legitimate business behaviour even if local legal preconditions are lacking. Since these activities are voluntary and therefore to a certain degree dependent on the financial muscle of a company, the 'ought to' dimension of social corporate responsibility is fulfilled in different ways by different companies and over time. This is even more so in the case of the 'can' dimension.

5.2.1.3 The 'can' dimension of societal responsibility

The 'can' dimension of social responsibility describes special activities that are neither set out by law nor customary in the industry yet can be of substantial benefit to people. A company, for example, may offer free or subsidised meals to its employees, free or subsidised transport, free or subsidised kindergarten facilities for children of working parents, free further training opportunities by using the company's infrastructure or scholarship programmes for the children of employees in lower-income groups. Special activities for diagnosis, therapy and psychosocial care, such as for employees with HIV/AIDS also fall into this category.

The establishment and funding of foundations with a philanthropic mission also come into the 'can' category. In addition to financial resources, some companies have knowledge and experience that they can deploy in projects and programmes relating to development co-operation and humanitarian aid. Given such support, these projects and programmes will greatly benefit in terms of effectiveness, efficiency and significance (see e.g. NFSD 2003). Creative fantasy in the context of the 'can' dimension knows no boundaries.

5.2.2 The human rights dimension of corporate social responsibility

Several companies can be lauded for their efforts to integrate an ethical approach to multinational operations. Although none has been specific in stating that it has used the Universal Declaration of Human Rights developed by the United Nations, it is not difficult to see that its incorporation is possible, because they accept a number of duties related to human rights.

5.2.2.1 Obligations in the context of civil and political human rights

Although the civil and political rights of the Universal Declaration of Human Rights are, above all, incumbent on states and their institutions, the preamble of the Declaration stipulates that 'every individual and every organ of society' is called on to respect and promote these rights. Business enterprises are 'organs of society' and enlightened corporations therefore accept—to different degrees—responsibilities to human rights. The prime responsibility is to ensure that a company's activities do not contribute directly or indirectly to abuses of civil and political human rights and that the company under no circumstances should knowingly benefit from such abuses. This implies that a corporation should inform itself of the human rights impact of its principal activities and major strategic decisions so that it can avoid complicity in human rights abuses.

5.2.2.2 Obligations in the context of economic, social and cultural human rights

The respect and promotion of economic, social and cultural rights is also primarily a duty of the state and its regulatory authorities. Whereas civil and political rights are defensive rights that aim to prevent state interference in individual freedoms, economic, social and cultural rights are positive rights and are more difficult to enforce, as their implementation requires the material support of duty-bearers.

Today, for a large number of poor people, far from all rights encased in the Universal Declaration of Human Rights and set out in the International Covenant on Economic, Social and Cultural Rights are respected or fulfilled. The lives of more than 1.2 billion people living in absolute poverty are characterised by the sad fact that their right to adequate food, clothing and housing as well as their right to the highest attainable standard of physical and mental health remain unfulfilled (enshrined in Article 25 of the Universal Declaration of Human Rights and in Articles 11 and 12 of the International Covenant on Economic, Social and Cultural Rights). The sheer dimension of today's global poverty problems makes it obvious that private companies can only contribute toward the support and respect of the economic, social and cultural rights in the context of their normal business activities (see also ICHRP 2003: 23ff.). Economic and social rights such as the right to work (Article 23 of the Universal Declaration), the right to a standard of living adequate for the health and well-being of a human being and his or her family, including a right to medical care (Article 25) and the right to education (Article 26) cannot be progressively implemented without good governance, effective public services and the appropriate allocation of resources. Corporate contributions toward the fulfilment of such rights come through the provision of employment, the payment of fair wages and the provision of social benefits as well as through the creation of economic value-added through normal business activity and by obeying all laws and regulations. Through specific corporate citizenship guidelines relating to human rights and their incorporation into normal business activities, companies contribute to the fulfilment of various economic, social and cultural rights.

Right to equal opportunity and non-discriminatory treatment

Enlightened corporations have non-discriminatory business policies, including, but not limited to, those relating to recruitment, hiring, discharge, pay, promotion and training.[6] All employees are treated with equality, respect and dignity. Dis-

---

6　Discrimination means any distinction, exclusion or preference made that has the effect of nullifying or impairing equality of opportunity or treatment in employment or occupation.

crimination based on race, colour, gender, religion, political opinion, nationality, social origin, social status, indigenous status, disability, age (except for children, who may be given greater protection) or other status of the individual unrelated to the individual's ability to perform a job are not tolerated within the sphere of the corporation's influence. Nor is intimidation or degrading treatment tolerated. No employee is disciplined without fair procedures.

Right to security of persons
Responsible corporations will not engage in or benefit from war crimes, crimes against humanity, genocide, torture, forced disappearance, hostage-taking, other violations of humanitarian law and other international crimes against the human person as defined by international law, such as the UN Basic Principles on the Use of Force and Firearms (United Nations 1990). Their security arrangements observe international human rights norms as well as the laws and professional standards of the country in which they operate and are used only for preventative or defensive services. Security personnel are instructed to use force only when strictly necessary and only to an extent proportional to the threat.

Rights of workers
Responsible corporations do not use forced or compulsory labour and respect the rights of children.[7] Workers are recruited, paid and provided with working conditions that meet or exceed the package necessary to cover basic living needs (providing 'living wages'). All workers and employees have the right to choose whether to join a trade union or employee association. Responsible corporations also make special efforts to respect the rights of children to be protected from economic exploitation[8]—they do not employ any person under the age of 18 years in any type of work that by its nature or circumstances is hazardous, interferes with the child's education or is carried out in a way that is liable to jeopardise the health, safety or morals of the young person.

For all employees and workers, a safe and healthy working environment is provided, at the very least in accordance with the national requirements of the countries in which they are located and with international standards.[9]

Respect for national sovereignty and local communities
It goes without saying that corporations competing with integrity will recognise and respect all norms of relevant international and national laws and regulations

---

7   As encoded, for example, in the Conventions 29 and 105 of the International Labour Organisation (www.ilo.org).
8   Economic exploitation of children includes employment or work in any occupation before a child completes compulsory schooling and, in any case, before the child reaches 15 years of age. Economic exploitation also includes the employment of children in a manner that is harmful to their health or development or that will prevent the children from attending school or performing school-related responsibilities. Economic exploitation does not include work done by children in schools for general, vocational or technical education or in other training institutions.
9   For example, in accordance with the standards found in the International Covenant on Economic, Social and Cultural Rights and in the respective Conventions of the International Labour Organisation.

as well as the authority of the countries in which its group companies operate. Within the limits of its resources and capabilities, such companies strive to encourage social progress and development by expanding economic opportunities. Enlightened corporations respect the rights of local communities affected by their activities and the rights of indigenous peoples and communities consistent with international human rights standards.

5.2.2.3 Obligations with regard to environmental protection

In many respects, socioeconomic development facilitates the enhancement of human capabilities, which in turn helps to secure basic freedoms and realise human rights. The use of nature may, on the one hand, be the price for economic development and may, on the other hand, make economic growth unsustainable (for examples of conflicts between resource use and subsistence rights, see Sachs 2003).

As the environmental impact of business activities differs substantially between sectors (e.g. the impact of crude oil production differs from that of insurance enterprises) every sector has specific environmental problems to solve and obligations to bear. It is, however, inconceivable that responsible corporations would not carry out their activities at least in accordance with national laws, regulations, administrative practices and policies relating to the preservation of the environment of the countries in which they operate. As with social standards, enlightened corporations voluntarily set higher standards if the standards required by local law and regulations do not meet the corporation's understanding of environmental stewardship.

5.2.2.4 Other obligations

In accordance with state-of-the-art business ethics, enlightened corporations do not offer, promise, give, accept, condone, knowingly benefit from or demand a bribe or other improper advantage. Long-term self-interest demands corporate actions in accordance with fair business, marketing and advertising practice and takes all necessary steps to ensure the safety and quality of the goods and services provided. Such corporations therefore adhere to the relevant international standards of business practice regarding competition and anti-trust and ensure that all marketing claims are independently verifiable, satisfy reasonable and relevant legal levels of truthfulness and are not misleading.

5.3 Entrepreneurial options

Companies respond in different ways to political challenges, depending on corporate culture, historical experiences or the philosophy of top management. In the context of the human rights debate, the management of a company has in principle three options for action:

- Defend the perceived status quo or even actively resist

- Duck, wait and hope for the best

- See the human rights debate as an opportunity for corporate citizenship leadership

5.3.1 Defending the perceived status quo: 'human rights are not the business of business'

There are a number of understandable reasons why managers of companies would not feel that demands of a human rights nature on their company have anything to do with them. First, they usually associate 'human rights' with civil and political human rights only (Articles 1–21) and not with economic, social and cultural human rights (Articles 22–29) of the Universal Declaration of Human Rights. Second, they see the state and its institutions, and not private companies, as the primary bearers of duty. Third, even managers who are empathetic to human rights concerns are surprised that, at a time when the most horrific abuses of the most fundamental human rights—the right to life and to freedom from bodily harm— are documented almost daily from notorious countries (see AI various years), it is the business community that is the focus of interest with regard to human rights policy. Last, but not least, a considerable portion of the debate on human rights and business consists of completely non-discriminating and generalising charges against businesses, and this makes many concerned people from the private sector hesitant to engage in a debate that could turn out to be too politicised to yield constructive results (see e.g. Swithern 2003: 50; Kinley *et al.* 2003: 92).

Indeed, it is primarily the implementation of national and international law through responsible government that is called for as a way out of existing human rights deficits. Without the acceptance of essential national obligations no sustainable and essential progress can be achieved for those people whose shattering destiny we are familiar with from the annual reports of Amnesty International (AI various years). But one thing does not preclude the other: the commitment of the state and its bodies does not exclude the assumption of responsibility by 'other organs of society'.[10] On the contrary, this becomes a duty precisely when the holders of state power are not able or willing to protect the citizens of a country from violation of their rights. Looking at the annual reports of Amnesty International, it is precisely in places where the state fails to meet its primary responsibilities that the potential vulnerability for companies is particularly high, because in these cases companies have to operate in an extremely difficult socio-political environment (Davis and Nelson 2003: 3):

- Legal frameworks and governance structures are inadequate to ensure fair and equitable administration of justice and regulations.

10 The text of the preamble to the Universal Declaration of Human Rights says 'that every individual and every organ of society, keeping this Declaration constantly in mind, shall strive by teaching and education to promote respect for these rights and freedoms and by progressive measures, national and international, to secure their universal and effective recognition and observance'.

- Public-sector institutions are weak, authoritarian or failing and corruption thrives.

- There are high levels of poverty and inequality in the distribution of resources and livelihood opportunities.

- There is a lack of access to basic services such as education, healthcare, energy, water and sanitation, and telecommunications.

- Strict press controls are in force.

- There is existing or potential civil conflict, with politically or ethnically motivated human rights violations.

Lack of good governance gives rise to a vacuum that has to be responsibly filled by other actors in society, including companies: only in this way can companies minimise the risk of not becoming part of the problem themselves, but more on this later . . .

5.3.2 Ducking, waiting and hoping for the best

Most multinational corporations have so far not responded to the human rights debate, at least not visibly or audibly.[11] It seems as if they are waiting until the 'discussion caravan' has moved on and the globalisation debate has turned its attention to other issues. If, unexpectedly, the debate is ultimately to have consequences for national legislation, then a company just has to do what cannot be avoided (any longer) because of the new laws. Other arguments brought forward in favour of 'ducking and waiting' relate to a fear similar to that of the 'ratchet effect' described by James Duesenberry (1967): corporate performance within the framework of a corporate citizenship policy (i.e. beyond what is stipulated by law) could, by virtue of the normative force of what has become fact, establish a performance level below which it is no longer acceptable to fall and that becomes the baseline for additional (including legal) demands.

In my perception, companies that opt for the duck-and-wait strategy unfortunately have a good chance of success. In many cases, the attention of the critical public is focused not so much on those companies that use local deficits of the law and refuse to engage in debate but on those that behave responsibly, face up to the company-related human rights debate and take an active part in it with arguments of their own. The more prominent a company, so it seems, the greater the size of the sounding board for critics, apparently almost regardless of the severity of the issue that is being criticised. This situation supports the rationale that the crucial element for management deciding to deliver corporate performance standards beyond the legal minima must be its conviction that it is 'the right thing to do'.

The situation is different for companies that have signed up to the Global Compact—in doing so, they have already committed to two human rights principles. Since these are relatively open in their wording, such companies only have the

---

11 The Global Compact, too, so far enjoys the support of fewer than 1,200 of the 70,000 or more companies with international operations.

choice of defining for themselves what commitments they believe they have entered into—or of leaving this interpretation to other actors of civil society and then finding themselves confronted with demands that they either have to or want to reject. As this would be a strategically poor choice, the right thing to do is to take an active part in the human rights and business debate and to perceive this as an opportunity for leadership in corporate citizenship practices.

5.3.3 Seeing the human rights debate as an opportunity for corporate citizenship leadership

Successful business enterprises are organised for constant change and innovation—and the current focus on human rights is just one of those changes. As Peter Drucker observed many years ago (Drucker 1993: 57f., 80, 97-101), successful companies are those that focus on responsibility rather than on power, on long-term success and societal reputation rather than on piling short-term results on top of short-term results (for support for this notion, see Avery 2000). Getting the human rights dimension correct—correct in the sense of achieving a creative balance between the common good and enlightened corporate self-interest—is no longer only a question of moral choice but also, increasingly, an important asset on the reputation market created by a growing part of global civil society. Good managers realise that it will be very difficult to be a world-class company with a second-class human rights record—and they act upon this (Avery 2000: 46).

Companies that have signed up to the principles of the Global Compact will set in motion an internal process of definition and implementation with regard to all commitments entered into, the human rights obligations being one such commitment (Leisinger 2003). A process of this kind has different phases:

● Reflection and consultation

● Discussion and decision-making

● Implementation

5.3.3.1 Reflection and consultation

Rory Sullivan (2003: 14) describes the intersection between human rights and business as 'chaotic and contested':

> On the one hand there are those who see companies as 'the source of all evil'. On the other are those who have a touching faith in the abilities of companies, economic growth and 'the market' to resolve all of these human rights problems. Yet the truth, if there is such a thing, is far more complex and indeterminate than either of these extreme perspectives allows. Despite the increasing use of human rights language in public policy discourses, the expectations of companies remain unclear.

Indeed, few companies had any clear idea before signing up to the Global Compact what it meant for them 'to support and respect the protection of international human rights within their sphere of influence' (Principle 1) as well as 'to ensure that their own corporations are not complicit in human rights abuses' (Principle 2). In normal cases (i.e. in the case of companies operating within the law and committed to basic ethical values) there seems to be an intuitive assumption by companies there are no human rights violations through their own activities and therefore no problems were to be expected. This assumption largely corresponds to my experience. Much of the action that is demanded today in the human rights debate already forms part of the social and ecological management processes of enlightened companies.

It is nevertheless inadvisable to carry on as if nothing had happened without any further reflection; a deeper consideration of the problems is called for. On the one hand, the issues surrounding the human rights and business debate are defined by many stakeholders in a way that is substantially broader than most managers assume. On the other hand, as far as actual human rights performance is concerned, it is not wise to operate with assumptions when empirical knowledge can be gained. The more facts that can be ascertained on sensitive issues and the more insight there is on the existing pluralism of values with regard to the facts the better the decision-making basis for informed policy choices. What need to be answered first and foremost are questions such as:

- What could be the potentially sensitive aspects of our business activity?

- Where do stakeholders outside the company see potential or actual issues of relevance to human rights in the context of our business activity?

- Are there vulnerabilities that arise through co-operation with others, and, if so, how do we cope with this?

A conscious human rights assessment, if not a human rights audit, of current corporate practices might be recommended if a rough assessment does reveal unexpected negative surprises.

The intense search for answers to these complex questions triggers important sensitising effects within the company, especially for managers whose area of responsibility is confined in the day-to-day routine of work to purely business or financial functions or, depending on the field of work, to biological, chemical or other matters. The very fact that human rights issues are discussed internally on the company's own initiative—not out of a defensive compulsion—and that critical questions are posed increases the corporate social sensibility and hence competence.

In internal and external consultation processes, the broadest possible spectrum of opinion needs to be obtained. Managers whose workplace is located in countries with a poor human rights performance can make hugely important contributions to the discussion that are of relevance to day-to-day practice. Procurement managers have a view of things that differs from that of communications officers, and the legal department in such a process has still different functions to perform. As Ernst Schrage (2003: 16) states, 'General counsels are paid to worry about possible threats of litigation, however remote.' The legal view of things is becoming increasingly important if only by virtue of the way in which US courts currently interpret the Alien Tort Statute of 1789.[12] A serious analysis of potential vulnerabilities and corresponding guidelines for corporate activities in sensitive areas are a credible first 'good faith effort'. Best practices are always anticipatory—a proactive approach, however, presupposes appropriate reflection on different fact and value scenarios.

Internal consultation processes are also necessary to broaden ownership for what are at least initially 'non-mainstream' positions: anyone who wants to change paradigms of corporate policy must create majorities for the envisaged changes within the company through persuasion. Experience shows that when something is perceived as being imposed 'from above' it will have little effect in daily practice. If a policy change is perceived as a threat (to investment plans, marketing policy, customer relations and so on), it may—despite the decision being accepted at the level of corporate policy—lead to passive resistance, cover-up practices and refurbishment for some Potemkin façades. All this makes it more difficult to retain a dispassionate grasp of the essentials—and thus to make a rational analysis of the status quo.

Since intra-institutional analyses always involve the risk of being self-referential and therefore of leaving out important aspects from the analysis, external consultations contribute to a better basis for decision-making. This is especially true in the case of complex political judgements such as on company-specific human rights issues. Not only is it wise to use the knowledge and experience of specialised NGOs for a company's own decision-making processes, society's pluralism of interests also gives rise to opportunities. Potentially fatal deficits of perception arise where people or institutions confuse their view of things with the things themselves. Sustainable solutions to complex problems usually transcend the initial preferences of corporate management, taking into account the differing life experiences, value premises and constellations of interest to improve the quality of the eventual decision. Specialised interest groups are best able to present the relevant portfolio of values, to articulate special interests and to show ways to preserve those values and interests.

5.3.3.2 Discussion and decision-making

After a good decision-making basis has been developed through broad consultation and deep reflection, an intensive internal discussion process must follow. Weighing the pros and cons of different options and wrestling with them in order to come up with what will be the corporate position to be implemented contributes to a further sensitisation within the company. This in turn increases the ability to understand corporate responsibilities and their limits. The fact that differing views are presented not only between outside stakeholders and the management but also within management itself should be seen as an opportunity

---

12   A so far little-known, one-sentence law enacted in 1789—the Alien Tort Statute (ATS)— stipulated: 'The district courts shall have original jurisdiction of any civil action by an alien for a tort only, committed in violation of the law of nations or a treaty of the United States.' Recent court interpretations of this law allow a plaintiff to claim actual or punitive damages in the United States for inadequate labour or environmental standards in developing countries. See Hufbauer and Mitrokostas 2003.

to improve mutual understanding and as a chance to discover better solutions. Precisely in the case of politically prestructured questions, it would be dangerous for a company to reach a concluding judgement too early based on the personal preferences of individuals. Here, too, the principle applies that consultation with people with different personal inclinations or professional or cultural backgrounds, different value judgements and experiences of life or other characteristics that influence their judgement enriches the debate and thus enhances the quality of the decision-making.

The consultation process must also be used to clarify ambiguous terms (such as 'sphere of influence', 'complicity' and 'precautionary principle'). 'Sphere of influence' in the context of the Global Compact is relatively clearly understood as the core operations, the business partners and the host communities (see www.unglobalcompact.org; see also AI/PWBLF 2000: 28ff.). Mary Robinson refined this concept with the remark: 'Clearly, the closer the company's connection to the victims of rights violations, the greater is its duty to protect. Employees, consumers and the communities in which the company operates would be within a first line of responsibility' (personal communication; quoted in United Nations 2003c).

Analysing the wide variety of possibilities for the definition of 'complicity', it seems much more difficult to come to an accepted corporate understanding of the concept (Clapham and Jerby 2001). And yet differentiations are possible: With a small number of known corporate commonsense measures it should be possible to rule out 'direct complicity' in the sense of consciously assisting a third party in violating human rights. A well-informed and sensitive management should also be able to avoid 'beneficial corporate complicity'—defined as benefiting directly from human rights violations of a third party.

Staying clear of 'silent complicity' is a bigger challenge, as this notion reflects the expectation that companies raise a certain quality of human rights violations with the appropriate authorities. To speak out about human rights, whether in corporate management development courses, contract negotiations with third parties or on other occasions, helps create a business environment that supports the protection of human rights. Individuals working in corporations may raise human rights issues at private meetings with higher-ranking officials, politicians or ministers—even there, diplomatic suggestions may achieve better results than overt criticism. Many companies, however, do not encourage their managers to adopt a highly political role while on corporate duty. They see no corporate mandate to act as a vehicle for global diplomacy. As public perceptions of corporate behaviour might differ significantly from corporate perception regarding 'silent complicity', the creation of a position paper is advisable on this topic.

The 'precautionary principle' is another term that is used widely but differently by stakeholders. The concept was developed in the context of the UN Conference on Environment and Development in 1992 and dealt exclusively with environmental issues surrounding global warming. Today there are a number of vague definitions and demands, such as 'the burden of proof of harmlessness of a new technology, process, activity or chemical lies with the proponents, not with the general public'. But what does 'harmlessness' mean for a research-based company working with pharmaceutical compounds active, for instance, against cancer but not at all 'harmless' as far as side-effects are concerned? Even if different stakeholders (mis)use the precautionary principle in widely different contexts (such as against the use of genetic engineering for third-world agriculture), a corporate definition of this principle in the original environmental context seems appropriate.

The use of the 'precautionary principle' implies a certain way of thinking that ought to be made transparent if the use of this principle is to be suggested. There are two points of view when we face risk and uncertainties. One is based on the precautionary principle. The precautionary principle says when there is any risk of a major disaster, no action should be permitted that increases the risk. If, as so often happens, an action promises to bring substantial benefits together with some risk of a major disaster, no balancing of benefits against risks is to be allowed. Any action carrying a risk of a major disaster must be prohibited, regardless of the costs of prohibition.

The opposing point of view (which is mine) holds that risks are unavoidable, that no possible course of action or inaction will eliminate risks and that a prudent course of action must be based on a balancing of risks against benefits and costs. The precautionary principle asserts that faced with a possibility, however remote, of some catastrophic development, prudent policy demands that whatever action is required to prevent it should be taken. This implies that the required action has to be taken however high the costs. When we buy a padlock to prevent our bicycle being stolen, we compare the value of the bicycle with the chances of theft and the costs of the padlock. If the bicycle is worthless and the cost of the padlock is very high, we do not buy the padlock.

To apply the precautionary principle means that, irrespective of the chances of future loss, the scale of the loss and the costs of preventing it one must incur these costs. We have the choice between (1) accepting some remote and unquantifiable possibility of severe effects and (2) accepting the occurrence of some catastrophes provided policies are adopted to avoid them. The economic costs of avoiding all conceivable possibilities of a major disaster could be astronomic.[13]

As a result of the discussion processes, the company has a better understanding of all aspects of its activities in relation to human rights and is able to decide on the best course of action in the matter. Different issues will have a different weight and importance for different sectors (such as the oil, textiles, banking, data-processing or pharmaceutical industries). Even within a specific sector (the pharmaceutical industry, for example, and there again between research-based and 'generics'[14] companies), different problems will lead to different decisions regarding corporate human rights policy. For companies competing with integrity in all sectors, however, it should be possible to develop a relatively broad basic corridor for their human rights performance.

---

13   I am grateful to Paul Streeten for his comments on the precautionary principle. All errors remain my responsibility.

14   Those who produce only drugs the patents of which have expired.

5.3.3.3 Implementation

Once a company has self-regulated the details of its corporate human rights endeavours, a 'normal' management process has to be implemented—that is, compliance with the human rights guidelines must become 'part and parcel' of normal business activities. The usual process parameters for this are as follows (see AI/PWBLF 2000: 30ff.):

- Appoint a senior manager to be in charge of the human rights responsibility, including mainstreaming and supervising the human rights strategy throughout the corporate world.

- Initiate an interactive communication strategy for all employees (not only for management) and develop an attractive roll-out campaign in different languages to enhance interest in the issues.

- Provide internal training for key personnel worldwide, including a toolbox (including the use of dilemma sharing) and details of case studies of relevance to corporate business (e.g. Fussler *et al.* 2004). Involve relevant NGOs to provide an 'out-of-the-box view' to add to the quality of such endeavours.

- Develop 'measurables' in the sense of qualitative and quantitative benchmarks that are relevant to the human rights debate of the sector to which the company belongs.

- Set performance targets for sensitive areas of responsibility (such as security and human resources) and link achievement to the income of the managers responsible.

- Ensure compliance monitoring throughout the corporation, with special emphasis on the potential vulnerabilities of corporations in the given sector.

- Develop and implement external verification mechanisms.

- Report on the success as well as the failure of performance as well as on other activities, according to sector of activity.

As such a complex implementation process will take some time, the management should set milestones to keep track of progress. If this is done, the promise 'to support and respect the protection of international human rights within their sphere of influence' (Global Compact Principle 1) as well as 'to ensure that their own corporations are not complicit in human rights abuses' (Principle 2) becomes a self-evident part of normal business activity.

The concrete effects of all corporate efforts made in good faith, however, depend not only on the company itself but also on what other actors of civil society do. The challenges involved in ensuring respect for and support, if not fulfilment, of human rights are so huge and complex that individual societal actors can usually make only a contribution to solutions—on their own, they would be overtaxed.

5.4 Open issues for discussion in a learning forum

The human rights and business debate has progressed a lot in recent years. There are, however, still a number of open issues that need further debate, in good faith, among the different stakeholders. Four will be touched on here:

- How far does the corporate arm reach?

- What constitutes an appropriate verification process for corporate human rights performance?

- What are useful indicators?

- How can we develop a human-rights-related 'Richter scale'?

5.4.1 How far does the corporate arm reach?

No reasonable person would dispute that corporate activities must be carried out in a manner that upholds the rights of employees and workers as well as of the local communities in which the companies operate. The issue at stake is to define reasonable boundaries to the human rights responsibilities of business enterprises. It is relatively easy to determine where such responsibilities begin: a company should adopt explicit corporate guidelines on human rights and establish procedures to ensure that all business activities are examined for the human rights content. Wherever a company has direct control (i.e. predominantly in its own operations) it can be held accountable for its human rights record. This includes the moral duty to protect the rights of employees against illegitimate interference from local authorities (e.g. by providing them with legal assistance in cases where they suffer violations of their civil and political rights).

It gets a bit more difficult to exert indirect control—to influence suppliers, subcontractors and business partners to adhere to the spirit of one's corporate responsibility standards, including those relating to human rights. But there are ways (processes) and means (carrots and sticks) to correct deficits and to initiate policy changes that will prevent such deficits in future.

But where are the limits? What is the permissible nature and extent of corporate contributions toward the creation of an enabling environment for the realisation of human rights in states in which human rights performance gives rise to justified criticism and in which local standards conflict with international norms. In contrast to the long-standing disapproval of transnational corporations interfering in domestic political affairs,[15] recent thinking from advocacy groups and well-

---

15 After the 1973 coup d'état of the Chilean military against President Salvador Allende, the suspected support of the US-American ITT Corporation led to widespread protests and to a UN General Assembly Resolution (on 1 May 1974) calling for an international code of conduct preventing interference with the 'internal affairs' of the countries within which companies operate (ECOSOC-CTC 1976: Section 59). This view was confirmed in the UN Charter of Economic Rights and Duties (United Nations 1974) and taken up by the 1976 version of the OECD Guidelines for Multinational Corporations (OECD 1976). See UNCTAD-DTCI 1996: 54 ff.

intentioned NGOs seems to call for corporate involvement in political activities relating to human rights when the company operates in 'difficult' countries.

It is relatively easy to determine that, at the very minimum, corporations have a moral obligation to ensure that they do not undermine elected governments or the democratic process, but it is much more difficult to draw the line about where direct interference in the political process—such as against repression of religious, ethnic or political opposition groups—is acceptable and where it is inappropriate. Should a multinational corporation working in a country that does not allow, or that severely restricts, unions contravene local laws? Should General Motors contribute to the fulfilment of Article 18 of the Universal Declaration of Human rights (the right to freedom of thought, conscience and religion) by permitting Falun Gong meetings at its Shanghai plant (see Litvin 2003: 68-72)? Is a 'good' company expected to close down its plants in a country after an undesirable change of government from a legitimate regime to a regime abusive of human rights? How would one balance the value of such an affirmative human rights 'gesture' against the personal losses of employment and income? Would one have to ask the workers who are direct victims of a boycott decision—mostly poor people, who anyway suffer most from such regimes—whether they accept a deterioration of their personal life conditions as the price of an external pressure that could lead in the long run to an improvement of the human rights record of their nation?

It is obvious that tolerance of other cultural and political systems must stop short of the violation of absolute moral norms—as a consequence, a violation of human rights (such as apartheid) should not be tolerated with the pretext of cultural or ethical relativism. As a private individual, I share Sir Geoffrey Chandler's belief that the days when companies could remain silent about human rights issues are over: 'Silence or inaction will be seen to provide comfort to oppression and may be adjudged complicity . . . Silence is not neutrality. To do nothing is not an option' (Chandler 1997: 3; quoted in Avery 2000: 22). I am also aware of the dilemma that, on the one hand, industry associations or chambers of commerce are stronger because they are collective voices for corporate human rights lobbying but that, on the other hand, associations 'too often adopt a lowest-common-denominator approach to human rights issues, doing as much in the human rights sphere as their least courageous members (i.e. often nothing at all)' (Avery 2000: 24).

It would be an encouraging first step if managers were to send the right signals to human rights violators at non-official events by refusing to rationalise what cannot be rationalised, by refusing to level down what should not be levelled down and by not trivialising what is not at all trivial to the victims of the human rights violations. Martin Luther King Jr left us with the legacy that 'we shall have to repent in this generation, not so much for the evil deeds of the wicked people, but for the appalling silence of the good people'.

5.4.2 What constitutes an appropriate verification process for corporate human rights performance?

Christopher Avery reminds us that 20 years ago most people probably would have given business the benefit of the doubt in a human rights controversy but that this is no longer the case:

> In the past two decades they [people] have been disappointed too many times by disclosures about the human rights record of particular companies. While they welcome news that a company has adopted a human rights policy, they now withhold judgment to see whether the company follows through with action and whether the results have been verified by an organisation truly independent of the company and without any motive to sugar-coat the findings (Avery 2000: 23).

For this reason, companies propose verification processes by external auditors along the same lines as with the auditing of company books. Following the scandals of Enron and others, representatives of NGOs are sceptical of such solutions. They see a risk that auditors that are profitably associated with the company in other business areas are not 'credible third parties'. For human rights verifications, for instance, they are probably not prepared to jeopardise their main business (auditing of the books) through a critical reporting on possible deviations from the path of virtue.

The 'general overall principles of independent monitoring' for claims of good employer practice, as developed by Elaine Bernard, director of the Harvard Trade Union Programme, offer a good point of reference for external verification of a corporate human rights performance (Bernard 1997, quoted in Avery 2000: 51). Credible human rights verifications must be:

- **Independent** of the business enterprise being monitored. This independence, however, should not be defined so restrictively that the corporation monitored is not allowed to pay for monitoring services—this is not sustainable for any monitoring institution.

- **Ongoing**: that is, according to a plan being announced on a relatively short-term base and not simply a superficial 'celebrity' visit. All parties affected by a business activity in terms of human rights violations must be able to talk with monitors in complete confidentiality and without reprisal.

- **Institutional**, in the sense that the monitoring agency must have independent authority and sufficient resources.

- **Indigenous**: where local indigenous people are affected, the monitoring process must include people who speak the language and live in the country where the human rights performance is being monitored.

- **Trusted**: that is, with a track record within the area of competence.

- **Knowledgeable** about the business activities under review and with an appreciation of what is common practice and what is not.

● **Transparent:** that is, as open as possible and—after giving the monitored corporation an opportunity to comment on and, if necessary, initiate necessary to correct deficits—with the right to communicate information without corporate pre-screening or control.

The monitoring system developed and implemented in the context of the Mattel toy company by S. Prakash Sethi's Monitoring Council, in which the claims that a company has made voluntarily and publicly are the focus of monitoring, holds much promise for serious companies that 'walk as they talk' (see Sethi 2003).

So who would be suitable candidates as monitors? Theoretically, it would be ideal if specialised institutions that enjoy high levels of authority and credibility, such as Amnesty International or Human Rights Watch, were to take on such verification on behalf of companies. To do this with any sustainable success, however, it would, on the one hand, have to be possible for companies to pay for these services, just as is the case with financial auditing companies. On the other hand, it would have to be ensured that the verification process meets the requirements of both company and verifier.

A company that systematically puts publicly proclaimed values into practice in the form of corporate citizenship guidelines and lives up to these in the form of consistent business practices has little to fear from external verification. However, it is in the nature of human beings that they tend to commit individual lapses, make stupid mistakes or get priorities wrong. Every company with more than 1,000 employees must expect a normal distribution of individual virtues, social competence and other elements of the collective profile of strengths and weaknesses—and thus also individual misconduct. Where corresponding management processes are implemented and such misconduct can be uncovered and corrected as a result, it can at least be shown that individual problem cases by no means represent 'company policy'. In this respect, too, the presumption of innocence should apply—or at least there should be a certain 'power sharing'. In the case of external verification it would not be acceptable for the functions of 'police', 'prosecutor' and 'judge' to rest in the same hands.

Even best-practice companies will seek alternative processes where a deviation from the rule is the exception and not the norm but where external verification reports fail to make this transparent. Activist groups that engage in naming and shaming, and holding generalised preconceptions, are understandably not at the top of the wish list of companies seeking verification services—but the dislike is probably reciprocal. With institutions on record for activism, there is at least a risk that there is a self-imposed compulsion to detect some form of misconduct in order to retain credibility with their own constituency—and then perhaps to turn a 'molehill' of individual laxness into a 'mountain' of a business policy that violates human rights.

5.4.3 What are useful indicators?

An important step toward the acceptance of verification processes is a broad-based agreement on practicable human rights indicators—for example, in collaboration with the Global Reporting Initiative (GRI; www.globalreporting.org). Indicators help a company to translate its commitment to human rights into tangible and concrete human rights 'deliverables'. At the same time, indicators communicate to the outside world and to human rights NGOs what responsibilities the company is willing to fulfil and in what way. There are no harmonised expectations and thus there will not be consensus among human rights stakeholders on all indicators, and so the debate will continue—but at a higher and better-informed level.

The general human rights indicators proposed by the GRI (see Table 5.1) encompass all essential problems of relevance to business and therefore offer a good approach to gaining a *general* picture of a company's human rights performance.

To prevent unnecessary and high administrative costs, duplication of effort must be avoided. Unlike in the current business and human rights debate, no new indicators should be created for labour standards and the environment, but those already in place should be drawn on (the GRI, for example). After reaching agreement on a selection of these indicators (HR 5, 6 and 7 might be taken care of by labour standards, whereas HR 11 and 14 might not be relevant to all sectors), a deeper sector-specific work-up is needed, because factors of importance for different industries differ.

Owing to the dimension of human rights deficits and the characteristics of the different generations of rights ('freedom from torture' is a first-generation right, for instance, whereas 'right to medical care' is a second-generation right), it is further advisable to differentiate the indicators along the dimensions of 'respecting', 'protecting' and 'fulfilling' rights (as in UNDP 2000: 93ff.). Companies must respect human rights in the sense of refraining from interfering with people's pursuit of their rights, and they must, to the best of their abilities, protect in the sense of preventing violations by other actors. But they can only to a limited degree ensure, for example, economic, social and cultural rights are respected when and where the primary bearer of duty, the state, is not able or willing to do so. Philanthropic efforts, as laudable as they may be in ensuring respect for economic, social or cultural rights, will not compensate for non-compliance with human rights essentials in normal business activities (such as by benefiting from child labour).

For pharmaceutical companies, it has to be expected that, in the context of economic, social and cultural rights, particular importance is attached to Article 25 of the Universal Declaration of Human Rights and, specifically, to the 'right to medical care'. To measure individual corporate human rights performance, the following indicators may be useful:

- 'Generics' as a proportion of total production or business volume
- The use of intellectual property rights in least-developed countries
- Willingness to offer differential pricing for life-saving medicines for special patient groups
- *Pro bono* research activities for tropical, neglected or poverty-related diseases
- Specific policies in place for the regulation of clinical trials in countries with no local laws (or at least no enforced laws) to ensure protection from abuse

Indicators	Description
Core indicators:	
HR 1	Description of policies, guidelines, corporate structure and procedures to deal with all aspects of human rights relevant to operations, including monitoring mechanisms and results
HR 2	Evidence of consideration of human rights impacts as part of investment and procurement decisions, including selection of suppliers and contractors
HR 3	Description of policies and procedures to evaluate and address human rights performance within the supply chain and contractors, including monitoring systems and results of monitoring
HR 4	Description of global policy and procedure and programmes preventing all forms of discrimination in operations, including monitoring systems and results of monitoring
HR 5	Description of freedom of association policy and extent to which this policy is universally applied independent of local laws, as well as a description of procedures and programmes to address this issue
HR 6	Description of policy excluding child labour as defined by ILO Convention 138 and the extent to which this policy is visibly stated and applied, as well as a description of procedures and programmes to address this issue, including monitoring systems and results of monitoring
HR 7	Description of policy to prevent forced and compulsory labour and the extent to which this policy is visibly stated and applied, as well as a description of procedures and programs to address this issue, including monitoring systems and results of monitoring
Additional indicators:	
HR 8	Employee training on policies and practices concerning all aspects of human rights relevant to operations
HR 9	Description of appeal practices, including but not limited to human rights issues
HR 10	Description of non-retaliation policy and effective, confidential employee grievance system (including but not limited to its impact on human rights)
HR 11	Human rights training for security personnel
HR 12	Description of policies, guidelines and procedures to address the needs of indigenous people
HR 13	Description of jointly managed community grievance mechanisms or authority
HR 14	Share of operating revenues from the area of operations that is distributed to local communities

ILO = International Labour Organisation (www.ilo.org)

Table 5.1 The Global Reporting Initiative: indicators for general human rights performance

Source: GRI 2002: 53-54

- Donations of medicines for needy patients in poor, developing, countries and in emergencies brought on by war or natural disaster

- Further activities in the healthcare sector of poor countries (such as through corporate philanthropy)

5.4.4 How can we develop a human-rights-related 'Richter scale'?

If the media report on the human rights abuses of a company, it is highly likely that concerned people will associate these with very severe human rights abuses. People are likely to think of 'complicit[y] in the abuses by foreign governments related to genocide, war crimes, slavery, torture, executions, crimes against humanity or unlawful detention' (Robinson 2003: 10). In reality, however, it may be that the facts in question are an abuse of human rights only from the point of view of specific, individual preferences. Human rights violations can be in the eye of the beholder, and the public debate reflects different views, all of them with merit. But, if the critical view is situated well away from the mainstream of the debate, it will not represent a relevant benchmark for a company—still, the damage to reputation is done.

The current spectrum of the discussion on human rights and business is extremely broad, covering questions of free trade and investment (ECOSOC 2003) as well as bioethical issues concerning the human genome (UNESCO 2003) and research priorities of the pharmaceutical industry (Swithern 2003). If we assume that violations of the right to life, slave labour or child labour represent a different 'quality' of human rights abuses compared, for example, with the profit focus rather than the poverty focus of the research priorities of a pharmaceutical company, then it becomes necessary to differentiate between varying degrees of human rights violations.

A good simile for what is sought here is the 'Richter scale'. Earthquakes are measured on the Richter scale, by which even people untrained in seismology can approximately estimate the severity of an earthquake. But what about human rights abuses? Are we talking here about research with embryonic stem cells to which people, on the basis of their religious beliefs or value systems, attribute the whole potentiality of a human being and thus also attribute rights and a dignity that are capable of being abused? Or are we talking about contempt for humanity as manifest, for example, in child labour in gold and diamond mines of poor countries? Does the severity of the violation in the various cases not differ enormously, and should this not be taken into account with an appropriate weighting? Even given acceptance of the 'universality, indivisibility, interdependence and interrelatedness of all human rights', it is clear that at the level of socioeconomic development different rights carry different degrees of weight. For example, there can be no legitimacy for 'torture' or 'political murder' at any level of development (a '10' on my human rights measurement scale), but the 'right to rest and leisure, including reasonable limitations of working hours and periodic holidays with pay' (Universal Declaration of Human Rights, Article 24), however, although while important, comes under a less essential category (a '2' on my scale).

Through general indicators such as those of the GRI in conjunction with sector-specific indicators it should be possible to take the political heat out of human rights reporting and to depoliticise the verification process. Through the grouping and weighting of different indicators it becomes possible to draw distinctions, such as:

- Code Green. This would refer to lesser 'sins of omission' that can be easily remedied. Example violations of rights in this category would be to require women working in production to undergo pregnancy tests (Article 12, on 'interference with privacy') or to expect members of management to work overtime on a regular basis (Article 24, on the 'right to leisure').

- Code Orange. This would include 'sins of omission' such as unknowingly violating human rights but not making an effort to find out.

- Code Red. This would indicate the systematic violation of human rights within corporate activities or direct benefit from violations by subcontractors or subsidiaries.

In his first lecture series in Germany following the end of Nazi power, in the winter term of 1945–46, the German philosopher Karl Jaspers reflected on 'The Question of German Guilt' (Jaspers 1949, 2000). He identified four types of guilt, which are also of relevance to the present discussion; the following is quoted from the English version (Jaspers 2000: 25-26):

- **Criminal guilt**: crimes are acts capable of objective proof and violate unequivocal laws. Jurisdiction rests with the court, which in formal proceedings can be relied on to find the facts and apply the law.

- **Political guilt**: this, involving the deeds of statesmen [and stateswomen] and of the citizenry of a state, results in my having to bear the consequences of the deeds of the state whose power governs me and under whose order I live. Everybody is co-responsible for the way he [or she] is governed. Jurisdiction rests with the power and the will of the victor, in both domestic and foreign politics. Success decides. Political prudence, which takes the more distant consequences into account, and the acknowledgement of norms, which are applied as natural and international law, [serve] to mitigate arbitrary power.

- **Moral guilt**: I, who cannot act otherwise than as an individual, am morally responsible for all my deeds, including the execution of political and military orders. It is never simply true that 'orders are orders'. Rather—as crimes even though ordered (although, depending on the degree of danger, blackmail and terrorism, there may be mitigating circumstances)—so every deed remains subject to moral judgement. Jurisdiction rests with my conscience and in communication with my friends and intimates who are lovingly concerned about my soul.

- **Metaphysical guilt:** there exists a solidarity among men [and women] as human beings that makes each co-responsible for every wrong and every injustice in the world, especially for crimes committed in his [or her] presence or with his [or her] knowledge. If I fail to do whatever I can to prevent them, I too am guilty. If I was present at the murder of others without risking my life to prevent it, I feel guilty in a way not adequately conceivable either legally, politically or morally . . . jurisdiction rests with God alone.

With these distinctions between different types of guilt, Jaspers sought to 'preserve us from the superficiality of talk about guilt that flattens everything out on a single plane, there to assess it with all the crudeness and lack of discrimination of a bad judge' (Jaspers 2000: 27). Enlightened corporations, under all circumstances, will shy away from criminal guilt; they will create a corporate governance structure to avoid the political guilt of not making unmistakably clear what are the corporate 'do's' and the 'don'ts' and, last but not least, strive for a management that feels also morally accountable for actions and omissions. As long as the annual reports of Amnesty International have more than 20 pages, we all will have to live with metaphysical guilt.

5.5 Preliminary conclusions

The Universal Declaration of Human Rights represents the most important value catalogue for human beings in all cultures and at all times. This declaration affirms that there are certain non-negotiable rights that should be enjoyed by all people in all places at all times based simply on the fact that they are human beings. It is precisely in the context of globalisation, where different cultures, social constitutions and socioeconomic conditions meet that this common denominator is also of utmost importance to companies. Business enterprises need to do their respective 'homework' and act consistently in order to adjust the corporate social responsibility concept to the changed sociopolitical framework of a globalising world (Leisinger and Schmitt 2003).

Beyond the day-to-day responsibilities of business, one of the most important questions for managers of global companies is: 'What kind of a world do we wish for ourselves and our children?' Whatever the individual value-based preferences may be regarding a right to life in dignity, justice, equality of opportunity and fairness, it cannot be a world in which human rights are not respected. And what duties are we prepared to assume to ensure that our vision of an 'ideal' world as we see it can be achieved? This is something that has to be decided by all individuals in their families, in their jobs and in their role as citizens. In elections, anyone can say

if [I do] not vote, it will not change the election result, but [I] will vote anyway because [I know] that all individuals together make up the result. So the moral force of the seemingly vanishing individual is the only substance and the true factor for what becomes of humanness (Jaspers 1949: 734).

Change—even corporate change—is always initiated by minorities, by intellectual elites who take the risk on themselves of being pioneers in uncharted territory; 'the big values always remain closely tied to the small number' (Guardini 1986: 56). All those who are making their contribution to the world they would like to see for their children should be confident, for, as Margaret Mead once reminded us, 'Never doubt that a small group of thoughtful, committed citizens can change the world; indeed it's the only thing that ever has.'[16]

16   I owe this quote to a poster shown at the 2003 Business and Human Rights seminar of the Business Leaders Initiative on Human Rights (Honorary Chair: Mary Robinson), London, 9 December 2003.

6
Operationalising the Global Compact with a focus on the human rights principles
Learning to walk the talk

Errol P. Mendes
University of Ottawa, Canada

The goal of this chapter is to demonstrate that the Global Compact represents one of the most important stages in the evolution of attempts to enhance the global private sector's actions in the critical task of sustainable human development globally while respecting and promoting international human rights. However, as will be discussed, perhaps the greatest challenge in this evolutionary stage will be to operationalise the anti-complicity principle established in the human rights principles of the Global Compact.

6.1 The explosion of codes

The first major attempt by the United Nations to develop a code of practice for what were termed transnational corporations (TNCs) began in 1977, and a draft code was completed in 1990. Within two years it was dead, killed by the TNCs and Western governments that fiercely opposed it (see O'Reilly and Tickell 1999). In the vacuum left by the inability of the institutions of global governance to act, a plethora of international and national organisations, non-governmental organisations (NGOs) and business groups have attempted to develop codes of conduct, benchmarks and verification systems applicable to the multinational enterprises (MNEs) globally. One study, sponsored by the Organisation for Economic Co-operation and Development (OECD) in 2001, identified at least 233 codes, and an International Labour Organisation (ILO) report in 2002 (Urminsky 2002) claimed that the number has risen to several hundred more (for a comprehensive review of many of the leading codes, see BSR 2000).

These codes are said by those who study the area (including the authors of the two reports described above, from the OECD and the ILO) to share common weaknesses. They have been formulated by a limited number of participants, whether business or NGOs, without a rigorous examination of the context and history of the sector, company or issues involved. They are also critiqued for being too vague or for being too detailed or too rigorous for the MNEs to adopt and implement. Most of the existing codes are voluntary in nature and do not have formal verification systems by independent third parties. As several recent OECD and ILO reports indicate, there is tremendous variation in the sponsors of the codes, the content of such codes and the public endorsement of such codes (see Gordon 2001).

Some codes have tried to address the deficiencies critiqued in other codes, especially in the areas of addressing multi-stakeholder concerns, reporting and independent third-party monitoring and verification. However, even attempts to fill in deficiencies in other codes are subsequently met with critiques that the codes are too narrow in scope and focus only on process as opposed to substance. A very brief sample of such codes include:

- Social Accountability 8000 (SA8000)
- The Global Reporting Initiative (GRI)
- The Caux Round Table Principles
- The Global Sullivan Principles

6.1.1 Social Accountability 8000

Social Accountability 8000 (SA8000) is a detailed code that includes third-party certification and auditing. This code was developed by Social Accountability International (SAI), an organisation formerly known as the Council on Economic Priorities Accreditation Agency (CEPAA).[1] SA8000 includes global standards on labour and human rights, including the call for a living wage. These standards, formulated by a broad range of unions, companies, NGOs and auditing and certification firms, are asserted to be based on ILO Conventions,[2] the Universal Declaration of Human Rights[3] and the UN Convention on the Rights of the Child.[4]

---

1 For details of SA8000 go to www.cepaa.org.
2 For more details of the ILO Conventions, go to www.ilo.org/ilolex/english/index.htm (accessed 2 April 2004).
3 For more details of the Universal Declaration of Human Rights, go to www.un.org/ Overview/rights.html (accessed 19 May 2004).
4 For more details of the Convention on the Rights of the Child, go to www.unicef.org/ crc/crc.htm (accessed 22 April 2004).

Regarded by many private-sector organisations and companies as laying down stringent standards, companies who sign up to the standard agree to be monitored by an independent auditor, and the standard also allows for NGOs and labour unions to challenge a company's SA8000 certification or the accreditation of an audit entity.

It is difficult to obtain information as to how many companies have subscribed to what is called the Corporate Involvement Programme (CIP) of SA8000. One study asserts that, as of mid-2000, 66 companies, including 50 from developing countries, have been certified for SA8000 (see Gordon 2001: 6). The website of the initiative states:

> The CIP was launched in late 1999 and has attracted entities representing more than $100 billion in annual revenue, including Amana SA, Avon, Cutter & Buck, Dole, Eileen Fisher, Otto Versand, Tex Line, Toys 'R' Us, UNOPS and Vögele Mode.[5]

6.1.2 The Global Reporting Initiative

The GRI, established in 1997 by the Coalition for Environmentally Responsible Economies (CERES), is not so much a code as an attempt to develop universal guidelines for corporate reporting on economic, social and environmental performance. The Guidelines, which are periodically revised, are an attempt to reduce the mass of variable and inconsistent reporting in the above-mentioned areas.[6] The GRI has succeeded in getting co-operation from key stakeholders such as companies, accounting firms, trade unions, environmentalists and other NGOs to produce a framework for reporting based on agreed-on environmental, social and economic and integrated indicators.

The GRI's list of social indicators is integrated to a certain extent into the information that corporations subscribing to the SA8000 code are providing. Some have criticised the GRI for demanding too much information from companies and not really measuring performance (see e.g. Baker 2004).

With regard to how much buy-in there has been for the GRI, again accurate information is difficult to obtain, but one report asserts that, in 2000, 21 major MNEs with headquarters in North America, Europe and Japan participated in one of the pilot tests of the GRI standards (see BSR 2000).

6.1.3 The Caux Round Table Principles

The Caux Round Table Principles were developed in 1995 by a coalition of US, European and Japanese business leaders, with assistance from the Minnesota Center for Corporate Responsibility, to establish general principles of ethical

---

5   See www.cepaa.org/SA8000/SA8000.htm (accessed 8 January 2004).
6   For details of the Guidelines, go to www.globalreporting.org/guidelines/2002.asp.

behaviour and corporate social responsibility (CSR).[7] The principles are designed to be very general, avoiding complexity, and to reflect two ethical ideals: *kyosei* and human dignity. The Japanese concept of *kyosei* means acting for the common good by co-operation and mutual prosperity, which co-exists with fair competition. The Western concept of human dignity refers to the sacred principle of treating persons as ends in themselves.

Although the Caux Principles could be regarded as being too general and as lacking appropriate complexity, the main goal of the Principles is to act as a catalyst for action and dialogue among business leaders from different cultural perspectives (see Gordon 2001: 3).

Again, there is no generally available information as to the number of MNEs adopting the Caux Principles. The Caux Round Table is officially affiliated to the UN Global Compact.

6.1.4 The Global Sullivan Principles

On 2 November 1999 the late Reverend Sullivan launched the Global Sullivan Principles (GSP), which promote a worldwide set of corporate ethics and social responsibility standards.[8] The principles, like the Caux Principles, are general in nature and were formulated by Sullivan with input from several major companies.

The GSP cover eight areas, dealing with the environmental, labour and business ethics conduct of MNEs and their partners. Companies that have endorsed the GSP are required to commit to integrate the principles into their operations, to make an annual renewal of corporate commitment and to reveal progress on the implementation of the principles. The GSP were endorsed both by the Clinton Administration and by Kofi Annan, the UN Secretary-General. By the end of 2000, the GSP had attracted more than 50 corporate sponsors (see Gordon 2001: 6).

6.1.5 Overview

Although some critics have argued that the growing list of codes, benchmarks and verification systems by NGOs and business groups have the potential to create a system overload, one could also present a more positive result of all this activity. The growing global consensus on corporate integrity has been furthered by those who have developed and been consulted on this plethora of codes and by those companies that have agreed to comply with these codes. One can see them as ripples coalescing in the pond of ethical consciousness of the global human family.[9] We shall also see how some of these leading codes, reporting systems and

---

7 For more details, see the website of the Caux Principles and follow-up dialogues, at www.cauxroundtable.org/index.html (accessed 8 January 2004).

8 The Global Sullivan Principles can be found at www.globalsullivanprinciples.org (accessed 2 April 2004).

9 For a more extensive analysis by leading experts of the codes described in this chapter and of other important codes, such as the CERES Principles, see Williams 2000; Leipziger 2003.

principles can or cannot be regarded as duplicating, opposing or supporting the Global Compact.

6.2 Initiatives by multilateral organisations

In the wake of the failure of the United Nations to promote a universal code, other multilateral organisations have attempted to develop their own. I shall examine two of the leading results of such attempts, one by the ILO and the other by the OECD, to demonstrate how one was incorporated into the framework of the Global Compact whereas the other led to an alternative method of promoting fundamental values necessary for the promotion of sustainable development and human rights among multinational companies.

Beginning with the ILO's efforts, there has been relatively recent effective and positive developments at the ILO in terms of the focus on core labour standards, which has led to the tripartite consensus on the 1998 Declaration on Fundamental Principles and Rights at Work. The Declaration clearly states that all member-states, even if they have not ratified the previous ILO Conventions that had established these core labour standards, have an obligation, arising from their membership in the ILO to respect, promote and realise in good faith the principles contained in the 1998 Declaration.[10] The core labour standards set out in the 1998 Declaration were substantially incorporated into the labour principles of the Global Compact. This Declaration was preceded by the 1977 ILO Tripartite Declaration of Principles Concerning Multinational Enterprises and Social Policy, aimed at encouraging the positive contribution of MNEs to economic and social progress and to minimise and resolve the difficulties to which their various operations may give rise.[11] By incorporating the core labour standards of the 1998 Declaration into the Global Compact, the drafters of the Global Compact have incorporated the legitimacy of the consensus-building at the ILO that involved not only member-states but also the representatives of labour unions and employers that are participants in the unique tripartite structure at this multilateral organisation. The drafters of the Global Compact attempted to achieve the same type of 'legitimacy by reference' for the human rights principles in the Global Compact by incorporating the spirit behind the 1948 Universal Declaration of Human Rights. Likewise the environmental principles of the Global Compact incorporated the legitimacy of the 1992 Rio Declaration of the United Nations Conference on the Environment and Development (UNCED).[12]

In contrast, the OECD Guidelines for Multinational Enterprises, first adopted in 1976, are recommendations by governments to MNEs operating in or from the 33

10 International Labour Conference, 86th Session, Geneva, June 1998. The Declaration can be located at the website of the ILO at www.ilo.org.
11 For further discussion of this Declaration, see Avery 2000: 27; for the text of the Declaration, see www.ilo.org/public/english/standards/norm/sources/mne.htm.
12 For further discussion of this approach, see Mendes and Mehmet 2003; for the text of the Rio Declaration, see www.un.org/documents/ga/conf151/aconf15126-1annex1.htm.

member countries that subscribe to the Guidelines. The Guidelines are asserted to be the only comprehensive, multilaterally endorsed code of conduct (although the number of countries subscribing to the Guidelines is relatively small) that set ethical, social, economic and, most recently, human rights standards for MNEs (see Gordon 2001: 1). The 29 members of the OECD, together with Argentina, Brazil, Chile and Slovakia, adopted a revised version of the Guidelines in June 2000.[13] The standards include those relating to worker rights and industrial relations, environmental protection, bribery, consumer protection, competition, taxation, disclosure of information and, for the first time, a provision relating to respect for the human rights of those affected by corporate activities.

The Guidelines are accompanied by detailed, but rather weak, implementation procedures that are binding on OECD member-states (for further discussion see Karl 1999: 89). Although the Guidelines are voluntary in nature, subscribing governments are required to set up national contact points (NPCs) that are responsible for encouraging observance of the Guidelines in each member country, gathering information as to implementation and to allow business, unions and NGOs to request consultation with the NPCs over issues relating to the Guidelines and corporate compliance with the Guidelines. There is no attempt to impose sanctions on those who violate the Guidelines, despite the establishment of relevant infrastructure surrounding the NPCs and the Guidelines in general. This weak implementation structure seems at odds with the character of the Guidelines, being undoubtedly one of the most comprehensive multilaterally endorsed codes. I suggest that this contradiction undermines the value of the Guidelines and was a model to be avoided in the evolution of the Global Compact.

6.3 The UN Global Compact

UN Secretary-General Kofi Annan, in a dramatic address to the global private sector at the World Economic Forum in Davos in January 1999,[14] proposed that the world's most powerful MNEs enter into a global compact with the United Nations to promote universal values in the area of human rights, labour standards and the environment if they wished to see the benefits of globalisation being sustained. The UN Secretary-General chose these areas for reasons that are fundamental to the evolving nature of global governance: first, because he and others believe that in these three areas the global private sector can make a real difference; second, these are three areas in which, according to the UN Secretary-General, universal values have already been defined by international agreements, as described above.

The message at the beginning of most of the official Global Compact literature may be a great surprise to many. It states clearly that it is not intended to be a code of conduct or aimed at providing an independent monitoring or verification

13 The OECD adopted a revised version of the Guidelines on 27 June 2000 that for the first time included a reference to human rights. For the full text of the revised Guidelines see the web page at www.oecd.org/dataoecd/46/36/2075173.pdf (accessed 2 April 2004).
14 This address is reproduced in Chapter 1 of this book.

system for those MNEs that have endorsed the principles. For this reason, it cannot and should not be regarded as an equivalent to the SA8000 certification system (described in Section 6.1.1) or the GRI reporting system (described in Section 6.1.2). There would be enormous obstacles and potentially insurmountable challenges to the United Nations attempting to duplicate the efforts of the broad range of actors that led to the establishment of the SA8000 and GRI initiatives. However, as will be discussed below, the GRI has great potential to enhance the commitment made by the MNEs to the principles of the Global Compact.

The Global Compact professes to be above all a 'values-based platform' to promote institutional learning and implementation of best practice based on the universal principles listed at the front of this book (page 12). In this regard, the Global Compact shares some essential features with the Caux Round Table Principles (described in Section 6.1.3) and the GSP (described in Section 6.1.4). Like the Global Compact, the Caux Round Table Principles and the GSP use their values platform to bring together ethical coalitions of the willing to promote dialogue and real and substantial progress in defined areas. A cursory examination of the websites of all three initiatives will quickly demonstrate the reality of the similarity between them. It is not, therefore, surprising that the Caux Round Table and the GSP are affiliated with the Global Compact and support each other's activities.

More recently, we have also been seeing potential for leverage between the Global Compact and the GRI. The Global Compact has announced co-operation with the GRI under which the companies endorsing the Global Compact can report on progress by using the GRI framework to fulfil their 'walking the talk' requirements. In 2002, the chairperson of the GRI, Robert Massie, in asserting that the alliance was a 'natural fit', was quoted as saying: 'The UN is not empowered to set disclosure standards and we are not here to do the UN's work, so this way everyone wins' (quoted in Ribanns 2002: 45).

By 2002, the Global Compact hoped to have 100 major multinational and 1,000 other corporations committed to internalising the principles in their corporate management practices. By all accounts, the Global Compact is well on its way to achieving the expected number of corporate commitments that were expected at the start of the initiative. With the growing number of MNEs getting involved, there are increasing examples of concrete results and benefits attributable to the values-based platform of the Global Compact. The Office of the Secretary-General has initiated dialogues between the global private sector, multilateral organisations and civil-society groups in areas critical to the principles. The first such dialogue focuses on the role of the global private sector in zones of conflict (as in the address at Davos; see Chapter 1). I assisted in the development of this first dialogue of the Global Compact and co-chaired a working group that produced the cutting-edge *Business Guide to Conflict Impact Risk Assessment* (this Guide, available to the global private sector for adoption or adaptation, can be located on the website of the Global Compact, www.unglobalcompact.org). Following the first production of the Business Guide, the Global Compact Office has organised regional workshops to field-test this practical tool of the Global Compact dialogue with business, civil society and other partners. Such practical outcomes are illustrations of what the Global Compact can achieve. These are results which the SA8000 or the GRI cannot accomplish, given their specific mandates.

Likewise, the Global Compact has established a learning bank of best practice in the areas covered by the principles and continues to promote partnership projects between the global private sector and other partners that reflect and advance the principles (see Chapter 1).

These results are practical outcomes of a values-based platform that most of the several hundred other codes in existence cannot reproduce. In order to achieve these levels of voluntary outcomes, it is suggested that a values-based platform such as the Global Compact must balance two key characteristics. First, the platform must appeal to universal principles that are general in nature, thereby avoiding the fear of where the devil may be hiding in the details. The Global Compact achieves this by comprising a few short principles based on international agreements that have been universally recognised as legitimate. Second, the values-based platform must highlight the importance of implementation of the principles in real-world business settings, given the great complexity involved in bringing the principles into practice. This is best illustrated by the complexity involved in 'walking the talk' on the human rights principles in general and the anti-complicity principle in particular, as I will demonstrate in the following section.

6.4 Learning to walk the talk on the human rights principles in the UN Global Compact

The human rights principles of the Global Compact could appear to present the greatest challenges to the global private sector. These principles were based on the International Code of Ethics for Canadian Business established by a group of private-sector companies in Canada, led by Nexen Inc., one of Canada's largest independent energy companies.[15] I was also one of the principal drafters of the Code and assisted the Office of the Secretary-General in the formulation of the human rights principles in the Global Compact. The intellectual foundations of the human rights principles in the Global Compact are based on the following premises.

First, there are few who would expect MNEs to duplicate the role of Amnesty International or Human Rights Watch. What is expected of business is that, within its sphere of influence, it can promote the universally recognised human rights norms and lead by example. The UN Secretary-General at Davos in 1999 gave some sound case studies (Chapter 1, page 30):

> Don't wait for every country to introduce laws protecting freedom of association and the right to collective bargaining. You can at least make sure your own employees, and those of your subcontractors, enjoy those rights. You can at least make sure that you yourselves are not employing under-age children or forced labour, either directly or

15 The code can be found at: www.cdp-hrc.uottawa.ca/globalization/busethics/codeint.html.

indirectly. And you can make sure that, in your own hiring and firing policies, you do not discriminate on grounds of race, creed, gender or ethnic origin.

More difficult is the second human rights principle of the Global Compact, which advocates non-complicity in human rights abuses. Here, there is a need for the global private sector to begin a dialogue and develop practical frameworks on what constitutes both worst and best practice. The international legal dimensions of complicity must also be taken into account. The following is a brief account of some of the important international legal dimensions of complicity in human rights abuses.

Under Article 25 of the Rome Statute of the International Criminal Court, corporations as entities cannot be prosecuted for a crime under the Statute (for a detailed analysis of the provisions of this Statute, see Schabas 2001). However, when an employee or officer of a corporation knowingly 'aids, abets or otherwise assists in its commission or its attempted commission, including providing the means for its commission' or 'in any other way, contributes to the commission or attempted commission of such a crime' those individuals can be subject to prosecution. For example, there were allegations that some coffee companies in Rwanda aided in the genocide by storing arms and equipment used in the massacre, and that a local radio station, Radio-Television Libre des Milles Collines, helped create the environment that precipitated the genocide by broadcasting hate propaganda.[16] The Ad Hoc International Tribunal for Rwanda has recently confirmed this thesis by convicting individuals involved with the media in Rwanda at the time of the genocide with the most serious of international crimes. On 3 December 2003 the UN International Criminal Tribunal for Rwanda (ICTR) convicted three Rwandan media officials of genocide and sentenced two of them to life imprisonment and one to 35 years in prison. The ICTR sentenced Ferdinand Nahimana, a founder and chief hate propagandist of the radio station, and Hassan Ngeze, editor-in-chief of the *Kangura* newspaper, to life in prison for their role in advocating the 1994 genocide that saw the killing of over 800,000 Rwandans. The third defendant, Jean-Bosco Barayagwiza, a board member of the radio station, was sentenced to 35 years in prison. The convicted media officials were found guilty of genocide, incitement to genocide, conspiracy and crimes against humanity (for more details, see GPF 2003).

There is also the possibility that such acts of complicity on the part of officials of corporations or other corporate bodies or political parties, if proved, may give rise to criminal prosecutions of individuals in jurisdictions that have incorporated the principles of universal jurisdiction. This emerging jurisdiction can be asserted over individuals who commit acts amounting to crimes against humanity that have become part of the most fundamental norms of international law *(ius cogens)* and impose a duty *erga omnes* on all states to ensure that prohibitions against such crimes be enforced. Many countries around the world, but especially in Europe and

16 According to Metzl (1997), the radio station was created in mid-1993 by 'leading Hutu extremists' in the Rwandese government. However, despite being ostensibly controlled by Hutu extremists from various walks, including the government, the radio station was established as a private jointly funded stock company (see Metzl 1997: 630).

the Americas, have enacted legislation that expressly gives their courts universal jurisdiction over crimes against humanity, war crimes and other international crimes such as torture, as the former ruler of Chile, General Pinochet, discovered (for a detailed discussion of the concept of universal jurisdiction and a description of countries that have implemented prosecutions under the principles of universal jurisdiction, see ICHRP 1999; see also Princeton University 2002; on the case of Pinochet, see Brody and Ratner 2000).

These international legal norms should be taken very seriously by MNEs in their decisions on where and how to invest in conflict zones around the world. The greatest possibility of violating the non-complicity human rights principle can arise from situations in which private investors are lured into being a direct link in the gross abuse of human rights. Let us look at a hypothetical example:

> An oil and gas MNE invests in a conflict zone. As part of its operations it builds an airstrip, which is then used, with the knowledge and consent of the corporation, as a military staging post for aircraft to bomb civilians as part of the genocidal strategy of those in power.

There could be international criminal liability attaching to the officers of such a company, which would destroy the reputation of the corporation in its worldwide activities. This highlights the need for corporations involved in international operations in conflict zones to engage in an appropriate risk assessment before investing in these zones.

In a company such as the one in this example it is often too late for a corporation to prevent a rights-abusing government from using company facilities if, for example, it has already commenced its operations and built the airstrip. (Corporations operating in war zones such as the Sudan should be very careful about this type of scenario; see Harker 2000; see also AI 2000.) There is also the reality that, once large amounts of resources have been sunk into the investment in the conflict zone, which raises the possibility of direct complicity, corporate officials may find it economically imperative to defend the indefensible. The possibility of such complicity in international crimes should be a key factor in the decision of MNEs to invest in conflict zones around the world. The *Business Guide to Conflict Impact Risk Assessment* produced by the Global Compact working group is designed to help companies avoid this risk of direct complicity.

Other forms of direct complicity that profoundly violate the non-complicity human rights principles of the Global Compact and that could also involve the international criminal liability of corporations include the following:

- The exertion of pressure on governments to crack down on certain parts of society that may be opposed to some of the corporation's activities, leading to executions, torture, and other forms of human-rights abuses. There have been many allegations of such corporate complicity across the world, prime examples of such allegations being those that have been documented in the rich oil-producing areas of Nigeria (see AI 1996).

- The bribery and corruption of local officials to abuse the land-tenure and other rights of local citizens, leading to ethnic group displacement and other serious human rights abuses. Again, there is a plethora of allegations against corporations around the world concerning such bribery and corruption, with cases in Cambodia providing some of the worst examples (see HRW 2002).[17]

- Contracting or agreeing with governments and local officials to utilise army or police personnel to use 'strong-arm' tactics that violate human rights for site and personnel security, or to encourage forced labour on projects. Again, there are many allegations of such corporate complicity around the world, especially in Myanmar (see Earthrights International 2003).[18]

- The encouragement of rebel groups to use child soldiers or to inflict civilian casualties in order to gain access to mineral wealth. There are allegations that such complicity may be rife in the war-torn parts of Africa where there also happens to be abundant mineral wealth (see Oxfam America 2003).

The most difficult analysis will concern the framework for assessing when the human rights principles of the Global Compact have been violated where there is indirect complicity in human rights abuses by governments or others in the country where the investment is located. Many human rights activists and advocacy groups would argue that the non-complicity principle would be broken if the revenues from business operations were used by the governments of the host countries to wage war or to purchase armaments that are used to kill and maim. Some also argue that complicity is established where revenues are being used to promote the abuse of human rights by dominant racial, ethnic or linguistic groups in the country or by paramilitary groups ostensibly operating without government backing. The problem with taking the non-complicity principle so far is that it would encompass virtually all business operations in virtually all countries, including European and North American countries. The problem is where to draw the line. It is suggested that a framework for assessing when indirect complicity—especially in terms of the use of revenues or the manufacture of armaments—may result in an undermining of the human rights principles in the Global Compact could include consideration of the following regarding the impugned situation:

- Do the foreign private investors have foreknowledge that the business operations in which they are either partners or sole proprietors were designed substantially to raise revenue or manufacture armaments to assist in conducting a conflict in which gross human rights abuses are taking place? A proper conflict impact risk assessment before the investment takes place should alert all, but the most reckless, that it may be

17 From a discussion, on 7 October 2003, with Professor Peter Leuprecht, Representative of the UN Secretary-General to Cambodia, it appears that this is a growing problem not only in Cambodia but also in Indonesia and elsewhere in Asia.
18 The ongoing litigation involving Unocal and other oil and mining company operations in Myanmar under the US Alien Tort Claim Act centres on such allegations. For details of the Doe v. Unocal litigation see the Earthrights website at www.earthrights.org/unocal/index.shtml.

unwise to proceed to invest and, if the decision to invest is made, the onus would be on the companies to rebut a presumption that they are violating the non-complicity principle.

● Can the foreign private investors, within their sphere of influence, stop or prevent the abuse of human rights of their employees or other key stakeholders by the host government or other entities? If they choose not to do so (e.g. to stay in favour with the government), if they have the ability to stop or prevent the human rights abuses, this form of indirect complicity would also be a violation of the human rights principles of the Global Compact.

● Do the foreign investors engage in corrupt practices with government officials and other entitles and promote the abuse of power in the host jurisdiction? Such complicity, in the view of many, is the cause of a cancer in societies that leads to the abuse of human rights of all citizens in the country.

The above list is only a starting point regarding how to start learning to 'walk the talk' on the human rights principles of the new Global Compact between the UN and the international business community. The same needs to be done with regard to the other principles of the Global Compact. In all areas of the Global Compact, there is a need for more examples of best practice to be followed and worst practice to be avoided—proffered by the international business community itself—if the Global Compact is to become an effective guide for international business learning on how to 'walk the talk' of the principles.

6.5 Conclusions

The clear message that the Global Compact is not intended to be a regulatory instrument, a code of conduct or any verification or compliance system promoted by the leader of the main institution of global governance reveals a significant turning point in enhancing the role of the global private sector in sustainable development while respecting and promoting international human rights. The major interest of the global private sector in participating in the Global Compact should be its interest in making the global free-market system sustainable. The fundamental monitoring and verification systems of the Global Compact and indeed all the other variations of codes described in this chapter should come from the realisation that with power comes responsibility. If this does not happen, ultimately the backlash against the lack of responsibility, even among the MNEs that have endorsed the Global Compact, will undermine the very sources of corporate power.[19] Before that happens, we will also see an increasing attempt to

---

19   We see this backlash even against the Global Compact by some activist NGOs that assert that the United Nations is being co-opted by the MNEs; see the harsh criticism at the website of one activist group, Corporate Watch, located at www.corpwatch.org/un. This

impose increasing legal duties on the global private sector by domestic and international law, which may not be to the liking of many MNEs. 'Walking the talk' on the anti-complicity principle will provide the greatest challenges for MNEs operating in conflict zones around the world.

No code, however comprehensive, can encompass all the possible parameters of how to 'walk the talk' on avoiding complicity in human rights abuses by governments or other entities. The real impact of the Global Compact in this area will come when the accumulated consensus of the member-states of the United Nations together with the knowledge of experts and the real-world challenges of operating in extremely sensitive environments are combined to arrive at frameworks and best practice that may never be perfect but will genuinely attempt at continuous improvement on the Global Compact principles. It must always be remembered that 'perfection is the enemy of the good'.

organisation is also keeping a watch on corporations that have endorsed the Global Compact but, in the view of the organisation, is violating its principles. Insofar as these assertions are accurate, this 'watch' on the Global Compact will be of great benefit to prevent this initiative of the UN Secretary-General from degenerating into a public relations exercise for some MNEs.

7
Institutionalising global standards of responsible corporate citizenship
Assessing the role of the UN Global Compact

Mara I. Hernandez
Massachussets Institute of Technology, USA

During the past decade, multinational corporations (MNCs) such as Shell, Nike, Reebok, GAP and Nestlé (Spar 1998; Ruggie 2003) have been the target of several different boycott campaigns organised by non-governmental organisations (NGOs) in response to alleged violations of basic human rights, environmental and/or labour standards. As a result of these pressures, many MNCs have adopted codes of conduct that include a commitment to respect human rights, labour and environmental standards.

Meanwhile, the rhetoric of the UN and other international institutions such as the World Bank and the Organisation for Economic Co-operation and Development (OECD) has seen a considerable transformation in an attempt to address similar concerns. The traditional focus on nation-states has been gradually shifting towards other actors that operate through transnational networks, such as NGOs and MNCs. In 1999, Kofi Annan announced the creation of the UN Global Compact 'to advance responsible corporate citizenship so that business can be part of the solution to the challenges of globalisation'. Since then, this initiative has engaged a growing number of participants from different stakeholder groups, but has also been subject to severe criticism from several NGOs.

The Global Compact aims to be a 'multi-stakeholder network bringing business together with UN, governments, labour, NGOs and others to advance responsible corporate citizenship'.[1] Its mission statement describes it as a learning forum that seeks to open channels of communication and collaboration between business and society to promote 'a more sustainable and inclusive global economy'. Companies that sign up are expected to act on principles (listed on page 12) drawn from the Universal Declaration of Human Rights,[2] the Declaration of Fundamental Principles and Rights at Work of the International Labour Organisation (ILO)[3] and the Rio Declaration on Environment and Development.[4] The Global Compact does not monitor or sanction the behaviour of corporations but 'relies on public accountability, transparency and the enlightened self-interest of companies, labour and civil society to initiate and share substantive action in pursuing the principles on which the Global Compact is based'.

In short, the Global Compact seeks to enhance the institutionalisation (Scott 2001) of responsible corporate citizenship (RCC) at a global level by creating shared understandings and a normative framework to guide the behaviour of corporations. In this chapter I explore the forces underlying this process of institutionalisation at the cognitive, normative and regulatory level and discuss the role of the Global Compact in this process.

7.1 The current institutional environment: responsible corporate citizenship in the context of 'embedded liberalism'

The resilience of institutions can be explained, at least partly, by their mutually reinforcing nature. Beliefs, values, norms and law often influence organisational behaviour in the same direction and are interwoven in a complex, over-determined system. As D'Andrade (1984: 98) argues, 'social sanctions plus pressure for conformity, plus intrinsic direct reward, plus values, are all likely to act together to give a particular meaning system its directive force'.

Hence, we can think of the three pillars of institutions (Scott 2001)—regulatory, normative and cognitive—as sets of distinct social mechanisms (Hedstrom and Swedberg 1998) that may be interdependent but nonetheless discernable and functioning independently. In fact, they may sometimes operate in conflicting directions at certain periods of history, creating disequilibria and hence pressure for institutional change.

In the aftermath of the Second World War a set of institutions emerged whereby the dominant nation-states engaged in multilateral co-operation and trade but

1 See www.unglobalcompact.org.
2 For details of the Universal Declaration of Human Rights, go to www.un.org/Overview/rights.html.
3 For details of the ILO Fundamental Principles, go to www.ilo.org/public/english/standards/index.htm.
4 For details of the Rio Declaration, go to www.un.org/documents/ga/conf151/aconf15126-1annex1.htm.

retained the capacity to regulate the private sector and were able offer a welfare system (and even developing countries were able to use state intervention to complement and enhance markets) within their territorial domains. Ruggie (1998) refers to this set of institutions as an 'implicit contract' that he calls 'embedded liberalism'.

On the regulatory front, a rich body of international law emerged, whereby the nation-state (and to some extent individuals) were the only entities subjected to obligations and rights. In particular, states reserved the right to regulate corporations at the national level as long as they did not violate basic human rights. At the cognitive level, this arrangement made sense, because relatively low levels of trade and capital flows led to the belief that: (1) the law and regulation set in one country would not greatly affect actors in other countries and (2) such regulations would be binding on most actors in each nation-state, since most of them lacked mobility and hence the state could impose a cost to violating these rules. At the normative level, this period was characterised by a fair degree of consensus around Milton Friedman's definition of RCC, where, beyond the fulfilment of legal requirements, 'the social responsibility of business is to increase its profits' (Friedman 1984).

Hence, the beliefs, norms and rules that emerged in this period reinforced each other and supported a rather coherent institutional environment for international relations. However, in the past couple of decades, these institutions have increasingly been questioned, as economic integration has weakened the capacity of states to regulate corporations and set standards unilaterally (see Ruggie 1998). Hence the implicit contract of 'embedded liberalism' no longer seems suitable in an increasingly interdependent world.

In response to the perceived weakening of the nation-state there is a growing consensus among different stakeholders regarding the need to redefine the social responsibility of corporations, at a global scale. In the past decade several UN summits have produced emphatic declarations in favour of establishing internationally acceptable minimum environmental and social standards (Nadvi and Wältring 2001). Furthermore, in spite of the heated debate over how RCC should be defined and implemented, businesses, governments, non-governmental organisations (NGOs) and the like increasingly understand that the concept of RCC transcends the notion that the sole responsibility of the private sector is to maximise shareholder value, subject to the constraints imposed by the legal framework (UNCTAD 1999).

7.2 Redefining responsible corporate citizenship

According to structuration theory (Giddens 1984), actors tend to reproduce existing scripts and structure, but they are also knowledgeable and reflexive agents. When confronted with additional resources or information they are capable of improvisation that may lead to structural change. Today, a growing number of actors is choosing to participate in some form of collective effort to address RCC at an international level. These initiatives might be interpreted as part of an ongoing structuration process through which corporations and other stakeholders are improvising with new scripts and roles in response to changing assumptions regarding the social responsibility of corporations. This process of structuration could eventually lead to the institutionalisation of global standards of RCC.

An exact definition of RCC is still the subject of ongoing debates, which reflects the fact that standards of RCC are still in the process of being institutionalised. Nonetheless, for the purposes of this chapter, it seems appropriate to define RCC as the 'implicit social contract' (Ruggie 1998) between corporations and their host society, encompassing the set of beliefs, norms, shared values and regulations that shape the institutional environment in which corporations operate. This contract may take different shapes depending on the values, norms and so on of each society.

The term 'institutionalisation of global standards of RCC' refers to the process by which these different 'implicit social contracts' will converge (at least partly) towards internationally agreed principles and guidelines. Such a process of institutionalisation would require a set of shared norms, rules and beliefs at the global level.

There is also an ongoing debate as to whether RCC is the most adequate concept to address these issues. Other widely used concepts include corporate social responsibility (CSR), strategic philanthropy and corporate engagement. The literature that uses strategic philanthropy and corporate engagement is directed primarily at managers and, in the eyes of many observers, is intended primarily to highlight the strategic advantage (from the corporations' viewpoint) of engaging stakeholders and/or implementing certain types of philanthropic practices (Porter 2002; Weiser and Zadek 2001). In contrast, both RCC and CSR refer to a set of 'rights and obligations' that corporations should be subjected to in any country in which they operate. The United Nations Environment Programme (UNEP) is currently conducting a survey on its website, asking people to vote on which of these two concepts is better and why.[5] This suggests that these have almost identical meanings and might be, in fact, two competing names for the same underlying idea. The Global Compact uses these constructs as well as other similar constructs (such as 'global citizenship' or 'responsible citizenship') interchangeably. But, most of the time, the Global Compact uses the construct 'responsible corporate citizenship', which seems to be a combination of 'corporate social responsibility' and 'corporate citizenship'.

The Global Compact requires commitment to principles based on UN declarations and conventions but does not restrict its definition of 'responsible corporate citizenship' to these principles. Rather, MNCs that sign up to the Global Compact are expected to experiment with innovative policies to reduce their negative impact of and engage stakeholders affected by their operations in order to seek mutual gains.

Hence, we can think of RCC as a dynamic concept that might 'mean different things in different places' and that will evolve as different stakeholders engage

5 See www.uneptie.org/outreach/about/csr.asp.

through the Global Compact or other similar forums, even if these different meanings converge to some degree towards basic principles and criteria.

The Global Compact is one of many efforts to define RCC at a global level and institutionalise basic principles to regulate the behaviour of corporations. Underlying these efforts are changes in beliefs, norms, rules and power structures that need to be understood if we are to assess the role of the Global Compact in what could be an ongoing process of institutionalisation of global standards of RCC.

7.3 Cognitive level: interdependence mismanaged

Any process of institutional change is generally affected by various forms of theorising and sense-making (Strang and Meyer 1993) through which prevailing assumptions and beliefs are examined and often replaced by new assumptions. In the case of a global standard of RCC, there are a number of competing theories and a heated debate that suggest an underlying process of sense-making. This process involves different types of actors that are reacting in different ways in response to these new theories (as structuration theory suggests).

An increasing number of NGOs, consumers, investors and scholars believe that economic integration without any kind of environmental and labour standards is leading to a 'race to the bottom', where inequality and environmental degradation are increasing as countries seek to attract foreign investment from MNCs by offering lower environmental and labour standards (Nadvi and Wältring 2001; Sengenberger 2002). In response to this belief, different stakeholders have been improvising with new ways to increase the accountability of MNCs and set clearer standards of RCC.

This stands in stark contrast to the set of beliefs that have been dominant in major international institutions such as the World Trade Organisation (WTO), the International Monetary Fund (IMF) and the World Bank. Much of the debate in these organisations, along with the set of policy prescriptions that have come to be known as the Washington Consensus,[6] have been based on assumptions of neoclassical economic analysis and the belief that sustained economic development requires institutions that protect property rights, promote competitive markets and enhance a free flow of capital and goods. Under these assumptions, the attempts of rich countries with high wages and costly environmental regulations to impose labour and environmental standards on developing countries has been viewed as an inefficient form of protectionism that hurts the competitive advantage of the poorest countries (Bhagwati 1995; Sachs 1996).

However, scepticism regarding the Washington Consensus has been growing fast even among mainstream economists. Nobel prize-winner Joseph Stiglitz (2000) has been critical of the World Bank's orthodoxy with regard to recom-

---

6   These policies include low inflation rates, balanced fiscal budgets, the lowering of trade barriers, and market-oriented reforms, among other neoliberal prescriptions. For an in-depth description of these policies see Williamson 1994.

mending more labour-market flexibility without taking into account the downsides of increased flexibility. Stiglitz (2000) also argues that increased economic integration, particularly after the Asian Crisis (1997–98), has eroded the capacity to attain a 'high road' of development (with high levels of trust and mutual cooperation between labour and management) in emerging economies as they face the need to cut labour costs and increase 'efficiency', at the cost of implicit contracts and social cohesion.

Several other authors have explored the connection between social standards (labour and environmental) and economic integration. Bagwell and Staiger (1999) conclude that under the current rules in the General Agreement on Tariffs and Trade (GATT, now the WTO) countries might be trapped at a suboptimal equilibrium where they cannot improve their labour and environmental standards without losing competitiveness. Chau and Kanbur (2000) have argued that the benefits of free trade for developing countries might be eroding as national governments compete against each other by lowering environmental and labour standards in their efforts to attract foreign direct investment (FDI).

These concerns regarding the connection between standards and competitiveness have been pointed out as central to the impasse that the WTO reached in 1999, as developed countries refused to further eliminate barriers to trade without including environmental and labour standards as part of the trade negotiations (Ruggie and Kell 1999). Therefore, it would be naïve to think that Kofi Annan's decision to launch the Global Compact in that same year was merely a coincidence.

Additionally, leading strategy gurus such as Michael Porter and Simon Zadek are now advocating different forms of corporate engagement with stakeholders. Porter (2002) has written persuasively about 'the competitive advantage of corporate philanthropy', and Weiser and Zadek (2000) have engaged in an ongoing 'conversation with disbelievers' in an effort to make the business case for RCC (or what they call 'corporate engagement').

Boston College has established a Center for Corporate Citizenship 'because it's good for business'. This Centre has existed since the mid-1980s as the Centre for Corporate Community Relations but about three years ago changed its name to the Center for Corporate Citizenship to reflect the broader agenda of corporate citizenship now emerging globally. Among other things, it claims that good corporate citizenship:[7]

- Builds brand loyalty
- Attracts and retains high-calibre employees
- Helps judge and then strengthen mission-critical partnerships
- Enhances a company's official and unofficial 'licence to operate'
- Smooths the path for entering new markets and completing real estate plans

7   See www.bc.edu/centers/ccc/Pages/a_bus.html.

- Reduces safety liability for employees and customers

- Appeals to the growing number of socially responsible investors

- Polishes the corporation's public image and enhances its reputation

Underlying these prescriptions are two main assumptions. First, there seems to be a shared belief among leading business strategists that the implementation of principles of RCC can lead to opportunities for mutual gains between corporations and stakeholders. The argument used by Porter (2002) is that it is in the interests of corporations to invest in human capital and to implement policies that increase among stakeholders a commitment to the goals of the corporation. Porter's view of RCC has been criticised for being too narrow and almost akin to philanthropy. Nonetheless, it reflects an increasing concern among business strategists with respect to the relationship between some form of RCC and the bottom line.

Second, these opinion leaders recognise a shift in the power structures, where non-state actors (NGOs, unions, grass-roots activists, consumers and corporations), working across national boundaries, have been increasingly successful in using 'soft power' to influence the decision-making process in government, international organisations and transnational corporations (TNCs). These actors have created a powerful alliance with consumers in developed countries and are now perceived as a significant counterbalance to the power of MNCs (Florini 2000).

It has become clear to these gurus that globalisation strategies (such as global production chains and outsourcing) have created opportunities for MNCs, but also vulnerabilities (Wild 1998). Many of the largest MNCs have been able to establish world-renowned brand names that have become an important asset of corporations, accounting for up to 40% of their market value (Ruggie and Kell 1999). In turn, the value of these brand names is now perceived as a source of power for activists seeking to call the attention of consumers in developed countries to RCC.

Under the emerging set of beliefs, activists, corporations, the UN and nation-states have an incentive to seek a common understanding of what RCC means, how it should be implemented and how it should be enforced.

At the core of the mission of the Global Compact is the goal of providing a 'learning forum' and a network of social actors from different stakeholder groups to 'advance responsible corporate citizenship'. If this initiative is successful, we should be able to observe increasing 'consensus among organisational decision-makers concerning the value of a structure [in this case, standards for RCC], and the increasing adoption by organisations on the basis of that consensus' (Tolbert and Zucker 1996: 182). We should observe, for example, convergence in the language used to address the issues of RCC. We should also observe the emergence of a common understanding with respect to the role of the Global Compact and other actors in creating or enforcing the standards. These changes should permeate through to the local level, since one of the strategies of the Global Compact is to replicate itself at the national and local levels.

However, the Global Compact is just one of many initiatives attempting to institutionalise global standards of RCC at the cognitive level through multi-stakeholder engagement. Initiatives such as the Strategic Advisory Group on Corporate Social Responsibility (from the International Organisation for Standardisation

[ISO]),[8] AccountAbility,[9] the Global Reporting Initiative (GRI)[10] and the Global Corporate Citizenship Initiative (from the World Economic Forum),[11] among others, are examples of similar efforts.

The first of these initiatives, the Strategic Advisory Group on Corporate Social Responsibility, differs from the Global Compact in that its main objective is to define mechanisms for the enforcement of global standards of RCC by establishing a certification process. The second two, AccountAbility and the Global Corporate Citizenship Initiative, are also somewhat different in that they aim to set standardised criteria for the process of reporting and measuring the performance of the standards of RCC. In this sense, these three initiatives might be complementary to the Global Compact. Nonetheless, the language they use varies (the ISO initiative talks about 'responsible corporate citizenship' whereas the Global Compact uses the term 'responsible citizenship') and the issues are framed in different ways (AccountAbility is concerned primarily with information disclosure whereas the Global Compact provides very loose guidelines in terms of reporting business practices). Finally, the Global Corporate Citizenship Initiative 'hopes to increase businesses' engagement in and support for responsible corporate citizenship as a business strategy with long-term benefits both for the companies themselves as well as society in general'.[12] Hence, its mission is almost identical to that of the Global Compact but seems to be more in line with the interests of MNCs and less concerned with the inclusion of other stakeholders.

Overall, in spite of the increasing number of participants (up to May 2003, over 800 had signed up), there is still no evidence suggesting that the Global Compact has been central to the process of generating consensus at the cognitive level. However, it seems to be contributing to the institutionalisation of RCC by increasing the level of awareness among key stakeholders and by proving that there is a constituency of MNCs interested in addressing these issues.

7.4 Normative level: redefining norms, responsibilities and roles

Normative systems are composed of values and norms that introduce a prescriptive and obligatory dimension into social life. Values are conceptions of the preferred or the desirable whereas norms define legitimate means by which agents can pursue their interests (Scott 2001).

---

8 For details of the Strategic Advisory Group on Corporate Social Responsibility, go to www.iisd.org/standards/csr.asp.
9 For details of AccountAbility, go to www.accountability.org.uk/resources/default.asp.
10 For details of the GRI, go to www.globalreporting.org.
11 For details of the Global Corporate Citizenship Initiative, go to www.weforum.org/corporatecitizenship.
12 www.unglobalcompact.org

Shifts in beliefs and power structures often lead to changes in values and social norms as different actors adjust their behaviour and their expectations regarding the behaviour of other actors. As structuration theorists have argued (Giddens 1984), what may begin as isolated improvisations in the behaviour of individual actors can eventually lead to structural changes in the social norms underlying the roles and scripts assigned to entire categories of actors.

In the past couple of decades, the community of nation-states has managed to reach consensus on a number of principles, based on broadly shared values, regarding environmental and labour standards. Such principles are reflected in a number of UN conventions, have been ratified by most countries and are notably reflected in the Global Compact's principles.

However, the gap between these principles and their level of enforcement is an example of decoupling (Meyer and Rowan 1977) to which NGOs, consumers, investors and other non-state actors have reacted forcefully (as structuration theory would predict). But, instead of pressuring governments, these actors have focused on other players that actually have the power to enforce these internationally agreed principles. The counter-hegemonic globalisation, as Evans (2000) calls this network of non-state actors, has been successful in placing the spotlight on large corporations and in generating wide public support among consumers with respect to the idea that corporations should be held accountable in terms of their efforts to enforce these 'universal principles'.

At the early stages of the movement against corporations, activists were focusing on the practices of MNCs within their vertically integrated structures. In response to this constraint, many MNCs opted in favour of outsourcing part of the production process and established arm's-length relations with their suppliers in developing countries. Today, there is broad support, even among leading MNCs, regarding the idea that corporations should work to enforce labour standards throughout the entire production chain of which they are part, even if that means monitoring their subcontractors (Spar 1998; see also HBS 2000). Spar (1998: 7):

> US corporations are finding it difficult to sustain their old hands-off policy. Under pressure [from activists], they are beginning to accept responsibility for the labour practices and human rights abuses of their foreign subcontractors.

The boycott against Nike during the early 1990s because of the labour practices of its suppliers in developing countries and the protests against the environmental damage caused by oil companies in Africa are well-documented examples of how the 'counter-hegemonic globalisation' is operating (HBS 2000).

In response to these changes in expectations and values in their environment, corporations have engaged in different initiatives. The proliferation of voluntary codes of conduct, eco-labelling (OECD 2001a) and other private initiatives to certify 'environmentally friendly products' (such as ISO 14001 for environmental management standards)[13] exemplify the efforts of businesses to establish norms and standards.

---

13   For details of ISO 14001, go to www.iso.ch/iso/en/prods-services/otherpubs/iso14000/index.html.

Scott's (2001) argument that 'the state's role in eliciting change is obscured by managers' interest in collectively crafting normative justification that creates a market rationale for their conformity' can be applied to the process of institutionalisation of global standards of RCC. The role of nation-states in enforcing the UN declarations has indeed been obscured by the collective effort of MNCs seeking legitimacy in the eyes of key stakeholders through a number of different initiatives.

In fact, these initiatives are so numerous and so different in their normative content that it is in the interests of corporations to work together through a forum such as the Global Compact to engage in the collective effort of defining clear norms that do create a 'market rationale' for company conformity to standards of RCC instead of duplicating efforts and overwhelming consumers with different standards and labels.

One of the strengths of the multi-stakeholder approach of the Global Compact in terms of its ability to contribute to the institutionalisation of RCC is that, at least in principle, the normative outcome of this initiative should enjoy legitimacy among a wide constituency, because the concerns and values of different stakeholders will presumably be addressed. However, of late this strength has been severely questioned, as Human Rights Watch (HRW) and other NGOs have grown increasingly critical of the United Nations Global Compact because, among other things, the 'progress report issued in July failed to address key NGO concerns' (HRW 2003).

Some corporations participating the Global Compact seem more optimistic about the future of this initiative. In a recent interview, a spokesperson representing DaimlerChrysler stated that, in spite of its pitfalls, the Global Compact was having a positive effect in advancing RCC, because of 'validation that goes in both directions', with the United Nations validating responsible corporate behaviour and the companies endorsing the UN initiative, which in turn has encouraged other corporations to follow (Fiorill 2002). Interestingly, this statement ignores the role of NGOs in this process and thus might be a signal of obliviousness both of the United Nations and of corporations towards the concerns of other stakeholders. The risk of losing the support of key NGOs is that even corporations might lose interest in participating because they may no longer perceive a gain in terms of legitimacy. And if the expected benefit of participating in the Global Compact is merely to create learning and common understanding within the corporate sector then it might be more profitable for corporations to participate in the Global Corporate Citizenship Initiative of the World Economic Forum, because this Forum relies on an extensive network of the world's most influential business leaders and is explicitly committed to the interests of corporations.

However, even if NGOs remain critical of the normative content of the UN Global Compact, their continued engagement in the Global Compact could have an effect at the cognitive level if it helps members of the different stakeholder groups to understand their different interests and beliefs. This effect could permeate through to the local level, as one of the main strategies of the Global Compact is to create networks cross-cutting stakeholder boundaries at the national and local level in order to disseminate the principles of the Global Compact. However, if key stakeholders remain sceptical of the Global Compact at the global level, they will also tend to be sceptical of it at the local level. If this is the case, the effect of the Global Compact at the normative level might be limited.

7.5 Regulatory level: the need for a coherent regulatory system

According to Scott (2001: 52), 'Regulatory processes involve the capacity to establish rules, inspect others' conformity to them, and, as necessary, manipulate sanctions—rewards or punishments—in an attempt to influence future behaviour.' In this sense, nation-states are still the main sources of regulatory power of MNCs, within their territorial domains.

As discussed in Section 7.4, several UN declarations and resolutions have endorsed general principles and guidelines that are relevant to RCC. These statements reflect changes at the cognitive and normative levels. However, because they impose no binding legal obligations on states or MNCs, they have often failed to produce changes at the regulatory level. Nonetheless, these cognitive and normative changes are generating pressures to reform the regulatory system, as key stakeholders understand that adequate monitoring and sanctioning systems are needed in order to effectively influence the behaviour of corporations in the direction of higher standards of RCC.

The proliferation of labelling systems and codes of conduct to which MNCs have voluntarily subscribed as well as the pressure of activists have partially filled the gap in the regulatory system. NGOs working with other non-state actors have been successful at creating an informal sanctioning system by shaming corporations that violate their own codes of conduct or basic principles contained in UN declarations. Similarly, business associations have encouraged the institutionalisation of certification processes (e.g. the ISO 9000 series)[14] for environmental standards, backed by independent monitoring systems whereby corporations are induced to comply with certain standards in order to gain a desired certification.

However, it is mostly the largest MNCs with considerable brand recognition that are vulnerable to the strategies of activists, and even these corporations are not usually monitored on a regular basis, so it is not always possible to shed light on their practices. And, even when monitoring does take place, the legitimacy of the monitors has often been questioned. As illustrated by O'Rourke's (2000) critique of Price Waterhouse's monitoring practices, many monitoring firms have business relations and/or strong ties to the corporate sector, which may create a conflict of interests.

Additionally, as labelling systems proliferate, consumers are losing the power to truly evaluate their options, and hence the value of these labels could be declining, as suggested by the decline in demand for eco-labelled products (OECD 2001a). Furthermore, as Freeman (1994) argues, it is not clear how much consumers are willing to pay in order to buy 'socially responsible' products and services. Finally,

14   For details of the ISO 9000 series, go to www.iso.org.

the weakness of the regulatory system has also been attributed to a lack of transparency regarding the practices and standards of corporations, along with the need for a common set of indicators to report and evaluate the performance of MNCs (Fung *et al*. 2001).

Hence, activists have been vocal in demanding the definition of clear standards of RCC, along with a coherent regulatory system that guarantees legitimate monitoring and effective enforcement. Even MNCs have sought to move forward in the regulatory front, as suggested by their participation in the Global Reporting Initiative and the ISO's Advisory Board on RCC.

For corporations that are trying to implement higher standards of RCC, the lack of coherence at the regulatory level is generating: (a) relatively higher transactions costs, because of the economies of scale associated with any regulatory system, (b) confusion among key stakeholders, such as socially responsible investors and consumers, resulting from the proliferation of standards and (c) declining value added in terms of legitimacy as a consequence of the lack of consensus regarding 'the right' regulatory system.

Despite all these pressures, the Global Compact has explicitly avoided the task of creating any kind of monitoring or sanctioning system to enforce its principles, stating that it 'does not "police", enforce or measure the behaviour or actions of companies'.[15] Corporations participating in the Global Compact are expected to implement 'changes to business operations so that the Global Compact and its principles become part of strategy, culture and day-to-day operations' and are required to submit a yearly report describing efforts to implement the principles of the Global Compact. However, no sanctions are considered for those participating corporations that fail to present a case study or for those that present a cutting-edge case of their operations in one country but are then accused of violating the principles in other countries.

In several meetings of the Global Compact, participants have raised their concerns regarding the lack of 'teeth' in this initiative and the risk of it losing legitimacy if its participants are not made accountable.

Human Rights Watch (HRW 2003) and other NGOs have criticised the Global Compact over several issues, including the lack of

> specific guidelines to clarify the broad standards contained in the compact; a mechanism for standardised, consistent and public reporting of corporate practice under the compact; a formal structure for stakeholder—particularly civil society—involvement; strong criteria for expelling from the compact companies that fail to meet minimum standards; and a link between the compact and the UN's own procurement and contracting activities.

Bayer AG, among several other participating companies, has been accused of 'using its "membership" in the Compact to deflect criticism by watchdog groups, without addressing the substance of the criticism' (Mimkes 2002: 1).

The critical stance of NGOs regarding the Global Compact was accentuated further when, according to Human Rights Watch (HRW 2003),

15 www.unglobalcompact.org

a UN panel investigating the illicit exploitation of economic resources in the context of the conflict in the DRC [Democratic Republic of the Congo] named at least three transnational companies that were formally members of the Global Compact who were in violation of Organisation for Economic Co-operation and Development (OECD) guidelines.

NGOs are not the only group of stakeholders represented in the Global Compact that have expressed concern regarding the need to make progress at the regulatory level. A recent report (Waddock 2002b: 4) on the progress of the Global Compact emphasised that 'through multiple discussions and workshops, it became clear that most participants supported the notion of a transparency principle' (which was originally not included in the nine principles). According to Waddock, the concept of transparency, as discussed within the Global Compact Learning Forum, goes well beyond that of anti-bribery and anti-corruption measures and 'implies responsibility and accountability, which creates the need for credible (internal and external) auditing, monitoring and assurance systems' (2002b: 4).

In short, although the Global Compact is not explicitly committed to advancing RCC at the regulatory level, through its work at the cognitive level (in the context of its Learning Forum), this initiative might eventually create a common understanding with regard to the need to create a coherent regulatory system and might even contribute to the generation of consensus regarding the content of such a system.

7.6 Conclusions

A number of facts discussed throughout this chapter suggest that there are several sources of pressure favouring the institutionalisation of global standards of RCC, at the cognitive, normative and regulatory levels.

The Global Compact is just one of many initiatives that aims to contribute to this process of institutional change. Up to this point, the main contribution of the Global Compact seems to have been at the cognitive and normative levels. Through an ongoing conversation between MNCs and different stakeholders (NGOs, labour unions, the UN and national governments, among others), this initiative seems to be contributing to the process of sense-making with regard to what RCC means and why and how it should be implement. It has also provided a learning forum with respect to best practice in the implementation of socially responsible business practice. Yet competing initiatives with similar goals are using different language, and some seem to have a different agenda. Therefore, there is still no conclusive evidence suggesting the convergence in meaning and understanding that is needed to institutionalise RCC.

The Global Compact might also be contributing to the institutionalisation of a normative system by shaping societal expectations with respect to the behaviour of MNCs and by increasing the commitment of MNCs to a few basic principles. However, to date, this initiative has been criticised by key stakeholders for the lack of monitoring, accountability and enforcement mechanisms. Growing scepticism with regard to this initiative among leading NGOs could be eroding the legitimacy of the Global Compact and hence its ability to institutionalise norms regarding the behaviour of corporations. One of the main incentives of corporations participating in the Global Compact is the search for legitimacy in the eyes of consumers in rich countries, NGOs, employees and other key stakeholders, so if influential NGOs withdraw their support to the Global Compact then participation in this initiative might not have the desired pay-off in terms of the image of corporations.

In short, without complementary efforts to create a coherent and legitimate regulatory system to enforce standards of RCC, the efforts of the Global Compact at the cognitive and normative level might have a limited effect. In the end, efforts to institutionalise global standards of RCC run the risk of having similar results as the attempts to diffuse total quality management (TQM) in the USA:

> Although expert gurus offered insights, consulting companies proffered advice, professional associations . . . offered normative justification, and award programmes . . . offered prestige and financial incentives, little consensus developed regarding the core ingredients of TQM. The movement was not sufficiently theorised, nor was it supported by adequate normative and regulatory structures, to diffuse widely or to have deep effects in this country [USA]. Some practices, such as quality circles, were widely discussed but they tended to receive *more lip service than use*. Companies felt the need to change, but the directions and recipes they were offered did not provide clear guidelines. Perhaps the most important change associated with TQM was the *cognitive framing of quality*, shifting attention from the concerns of internal engineers to external customers and from a 'detect-and-repair' to a *'prevent-and-improve'* mentality . . . All attempts at institutional diffusion do not succeed (Scott 2001: 121; emphasis added).

Without clear guidelines and an adequate regulatory structure, the principles of the Global Compact might receive 'more lip service than use'. If the mission of the Global Compact is to advance RCC by using the 'globally-agreed values of the United Nations as a framework for responsible business' (Waddock 2002b: 1) all participants should probably think twice before dismissing the critics of Human Rights Watch and other NGOs.

Nonetheless, even if global standards of RCC fail to be institutionalised, the Global Compact might contribute to a new shift in the 'cognitive framing of quality', from customer satisfaction to stakeholder engagement, building on the 'prevent-and-improve' mentality of TQM.

In a more optimistic scenario, the Learning Forum of the Global Global Compact could play a key role in building consensus among key stakeholders with regard to the need to move forward at the regulatory level and on how to do so. Considering the huge divergence in interests, world-views and values represented at the Global Compact, this would be a major contribution to the process of institutionalising global standards of RCC.

All in all, it is too early to assess the impact of the Global Compact in advancing corporate citizenship and to predict whether or not RCC will become institutionalised. It is also problematic to evaluate the Global Compact, as there is no way of isolating the effect of such an initiative in the context of so many efforts to advance RCC.

Part 3
The evolution of the UN
and the UN Global Compact:
critical perspectives

8

Growing big,
learning that small is beautiful[*]

Cornis van der Lugt

United Nations Environment Programme, France

Three decades ago, when governments showed interest in exploring the regulation of the conduct of transnational corporations, they responded to growing evidence of environmental pollution in the 1960s and 1970s. This phenomenon questioned the assumed overlap between profitability to the company and profitability to the community. It questioned the old belief, reflected in a remark by the US Secretary of Defense at the time, saying 'What is good for the country is good for General Motors, and what is good for General Motors is good for the country' (Dell 1990: 55). When Americans celebrated their first Earth Day in 1970, the focus was on the local backyard. Yet over the years citizens had to learn that environment knows no borders. Similarly, companies had to learn that an absolute separation of what happens inside and outside the factory gate is impossible. The ensuing debate about command-and-control enforcement and voluntarism was related to the degree of involvement of business in society. Today, the question is: 'Does the elastic concept of corporate social responsibility (CSR) know no borders?' Tackling the issue from a UN platform, the Global Compact has been on a steep leaning curve over the past four years.

---

[*] The views expressed are those of the author and not necessarily those of the United Nations Environment Programme.

8.1 Let's talk business: the UN entering new fields

It was in July 1997 that UN Secretary-General Kofi Annan unveiled his UN reform proposal, developed by a team headed by Maurice Strong. It included provision for working more closely with civil-society organisations, including the private sector. The Secretary-General embarked on a policy of rapprochement with the private sector, based, among other things, on the view of globalisation as a business-led process (Tesner and Kell 2000: 145). The new approach represented what one analyst called 'the UN third way' of working with corporations (Suter 2000).[1] Its arrival overlapped with what some interpret as the emergence of co-regulation, following the emphasis on command-and-control regulation in the 1960s and 1970s and self-regulation in the 1980s and 1990s. Speaking to world leaders at the Millennium Summit in September 2000, Annan reminded them that 'the world around us is changing . . . we have to adapt to the realities outside' (*IHT* 2000).

The world around business has been changing as well. Two years later at the World Summit on Sustainable Development (WSSD) in Johannesburg, non-governmental organisations (NGOs) demanded a framework convention on corporate accountability. The Johannesburg Declaration (United Nations 2002a) and Plan of Implementation (United Nations 2002b) encouraged business to display greater environmental and social responsibility and accountability. The WSSD showed a willingness from various stakeholders to work together in partnership, underlining that business needs to be part of the solution. Still, a number of NGOs criticised business for promoting a development model 'in which corporate rights are carved in stone while corporate responsibilities remain voluntary' (*IHT* 2002). During a high-level Global Compact dialogue with CEOs and heads of stakeholder organisations at the Johannesburg Summit, a number of heads of state spoke on private-sector responsibilities.

References to rights and responsibilities turn the spotlight on the use of the term 'corporate citizenship' under the Global Compact. The term 'citizenship' generally refers to membership of a political community and the practices that define a person as a member of that community. The practices involved are determined by the relationship between the public and the private sphere. Looking at the relationship between the individual and the collective, the realisation that the citizen has not only rights but also duties is important. Accordingly, the concept of corporate citizenship underlines that companies—like citizens—have duties as well as rights. Companies benefit from the expansion in rights that for example trade liberalisation brings, but at the same time the UN Secretary-General is reminding them of the duties they have wherever in the world they operate.

---

1 The two earlier 'ways' occurred in the early days of the debate when corporations were ignored in discussions about a 'new international economic order' and in a subsequent era in which there was an attempt to use the UN to regulate corporations and create an international code of conduct for transnational corporations. Some non-governmental organisations have asked for a return to the second approach, asking for a citizens' compact between the UN and civil society and the regulation of transnational corporations. The Alliance for a Corporate-Free UN advocates these concerns.

Will they rise to the challenge? Before ministers in the Organisation for Economic Co-operation and Development (OECD) approved the revised OECD Guidelines for Multinational Enterprises in mid-2000, OECD Secretary-General Donald Johnston wrote that the unveiling of the Guidelines signalled to the world 'that multinational enterprises are important agents of change for the better throughout the developing as well as the developed world' (Johnston 2000). Visiting Washington, DC, at the time, the CEO of AB Volvo spoke of a definite move within industry to become 'greener', with companies recognising the benefits of staying ahead of new regulations aimed at reducing pollution (*Reuters* 2000). This came ten years after the pre-1992 wave of international environmental awareness, when *Newsweek* (1990) announced in a front-page article that companies in the OECD world are eager 'to clean up their act'. In the United Kingdom it was reported that 'environmental friendliness has replaced "new" and "free" as the main consumer inducement' (Simpson 1990: 34). This was a wake-up call for many companies. Markets can be more coercive than governments. There are times when private surveillance or the watchful eye of the consumer can be more penetrating than the eye of the regulator.

8.2 The organisational challenge in the UN: sectoral and other approaches

A service performed by the UN on behalf of business, often overlooked in the past, is the provision of global governance and regulation as a public good. A good example dating back to the 1970s has been that of the United Nations Environment Programme (UNEP) working with industry in an effort to protect the ozone layer. After the UNEP Governing Council asked its Executive Director in 1977 to convene a Co-ordinating Committee for the Ozone Layer, industry representatives were invited to attend its meetings and join the ongoing co-ordination of research and assessments. Business involvement and representation in the form of individual companies and associations increased at meetings over the following ten years. After the Montreal Protocol took effect in 1989, one author remarked: 'The agreement marks one of the first times that the community of nations, working together with the private sector, has anticipated and taken positive steps to manage a world problem before it could lead to an irreversible crisis' (Dell 1990: 134).

A unique feature of UNEP's work with the private sector has been its sectoral approach. A core part of this is a network of sectoral industry associations with which it meets annually in Paris. Opening the 20th Annual Consultative Meeting with Industry Associations in Paris on 9 October 2003, Klaus Töpfer quoted French Prime Minister Laurent Fabius who said in his concluding remarks at the first such meeting held at the Palais des Congrès in Versailles in 1984:

> Could such a conference have been held 20 years ago, or even 10? In
> effect our work here suggests a dawning awareness by industrialists

that they too must participate in the managing of the ecological problems engendered by their activities.[2]

The 1984 audience included Gro Harlem Brundtland, whose commission was to come up with the internationally renowned definition of 'sustainable development'.

Over the years, UNEP's work with the private sector has recognised the value of voluntarism in complementing regulatory approaches. It has recognised 'the contribution of voluntary agreements and initiatives in terms of cost-effectiveness, flexibility, lower administrative costs as well as collective learning, generation and diffusion of information' (Töpfer 2000: 40). Since the early 1990s UNEP has been involved in the creation of a number of international voluntary initiatives in different industry sectors. These include the finance sector, tourism, telecommunications, automotive, advertising and communication, mining, building and construction (see Nelson 2002: 89-93).[3] Each of these provides an avenue for companies to explore the meaning of the Global Compact principles at the sectoral level. Their work programmes include research and sharing knowledge on sector-specific ways of advancing sustainable production and consumption through life-cycle approaches. Companies have also used these initiatives to develop sector-specific supplements to the Global Reporting Initiative (GRI) Sustainability Reporting Guidelines.[4]

Different UN agencies, of course, follow different approaches in their co-operation with the private sector and other stakeholders (see Cohen 2001; Nelson 2002). In interviews conducted in 2001 for a UN Secretary-General report on co-operation between the UN and the private sector, one of the barriers to more effective co-operation with the UN identified by business representatives was a lack of consistency between UN agencies on guidelines for working with business (Nelson 2002: 160). Different approaches between agencies have been evident in meetings of the UN agency private-sector focal points in New York. This follows from the different mandates of UN agencies. They can be categorised in terms of entry points, based on philanthropy, development and market considerations. These are set out in Table 8.1, in which the focus of each is given. The transition from one to another is, of course, fluid, and many agencies will argue that their approach covers more than one of these three categories. Also, some issues can be treated through more than one approach. As an example, HIV/AIDS is being approached as both a humanitarian and a business case challenge. The examples in Table 8.1 are only suggestive of core focus areas. Looking at these, one can also expect activities under the philanthropy approach to be more short-term and project-based, with

---

2   See www.uneptie.org/outreach/business/2003-presentations.htm.
3   The Finance Initiative involves over 200 banks and insurance companies, the Tour Operators Initiative 20 tour operators, the Global e-Sustainability Initiative 14 telecommunications companies, the Mobility Forum 12 automotive manufacturers and related companies, and the Advertising and Communication Forum 12 advertising agencies, associations and companies (see www.uneptie.org/outreach/vi_home.htm). In a similar approach, the World Business Council for Sustainable Development (WBCSD) has launched sectoral initiatives with, for example, the paper, mining and minerals, cement and mobility industries.
4   For details of the GRI Guidelines, see www.globalreporting.org/guidelines/2002.asp.

Entry point	Focus	Example
Philanthropy, humanism	Ethical case, social cause (e.g. refugees)	UN High Commission for Human Rights
Material, developmental	Development case	UN Development Programme
Material, market-based	Business case	UN Environment Programme

Table 8.1 **Different approaches of UN agencies in working with the private sector**

longer-term initiatives with business and industry being easier to establish under the business case approach. Important to note is that the business case approach is not per se a private-sector approach; rather, it involves seeking win–win solutions in delivering public and private goods.

8.3 The organisational challenge in companies: learning to change course

Advising corporations on managing green issues, Curtin and Jones (2000: 5) made it clear at the outset that corporate reputation 'should be built up from the micro-level'. Behind their pragmatic approach the key consideration is 'always be prepared for incidents'. The focus on micro-level details and building from the bottom up highlights the organisational challenge large corporations face in making the link between what happens at corporate headquarters and what happens at the site level. Downsizing and decentralisation within the corporation only adds to the complication. It presents a perfect scenario for dialogue and learning.

Discussions with possible participants in the Global Compact in early 2000 highlighted issues such as the legal implications of different ways of 'committing' to the Global Compact and the fine line between being prescriptive and sharing good or best practice. Who defines 'best' practice? When does 'best' practice become 'standard' practice? Today, participants seek answers to these questions at the Global Compact Learning Forums. This is where experience in the implementation of the principles are shared, including its environmental principles, which are more aspirational in nature. For example, at the 2003 Annual Learning Forum in Belo Horizonte a group of companies from Brazil, France, Spain and South Africa presented case studies on the precautionary approach. Company representatives joined their case-study authors from business schools in presenting examples of how they apply precaution in their daily operations. In a workshop environment, this provides the opportunity for participants to share learning experiences of what constitutes best practice across different sectors.

Often feeding ideas into the Learning Forums have been the Global Compact policy dialogues, the platform where corporate policies are debated. In 2002 UNEP co-hosted the Global Compact Policy Dialogue on Business and Sustainable Development. Led by Claude Fussler of the World Business Council for Sustainable Development (WBCSD), a working group of this Dialogue developed the Global Compact performance model. Based on total quality management, the model presents company operations in its different components and phases, ranging from company vision to products and communicating results.[5] If we start at the level of vision, policy and strategy, the role of visionary and committed leadership is key in the Global Compact. This is why the Compact requires that company participation starts with a letter signed by top management. That is where awareness of the organisation joining the initiative needs to register at the start. Some like to refer to CEOs as the 'change agents'. This does not imply an elitist model in which the role of management and employees is secondary. The knowledge, capabilities and skills of the company's human capital represents its greatest asset. But the captain of the ship needs personal conviction. A recent survey by Cambridge Business School of the CEOs of *Fortune* 500 companies showed that they perceived leadership and vision as the element likely to have the most crucial future impact on the preservation of a positive corporate reputation (JIM 2002).[6]

Moving from the individual CEO to the institution it is clear that corporate governance has a decisive role to play in mainstreaming sustainability into core business activities. What role do senior and middle management play once a high-level commitment to sustainability has been made? Does management practice reflect the commitment to CSR? Some argue it is at the level of middle management that the real work is done. Others argue that middle management represents 'the wall of China', that this is where transformation is blocked. Does middle management for example operate in silos, or do managers show an appreciation for integration and the relevance of broader societal issues to core operations?[7]

The advancement of implementation internally is more complicated than simply issuing standard operating procedures for all sites. Plans discussed under the International Organisation for Standardisation (ISO) to develop management standards on CSR will tend to result in drawn-out negotiations to produce process rather than performance standards. The introduction of management systems needs to be accompanied by re-evaluation of the values and attitudes that underpin performance. A survey of senior managers in OECD-based companies

5   Its core involves 'enablers' such as leadership and innovation, and 'results' in the form of impacts on people and environment. It ends with reporting, which feeds into stakeholder dialogue and again takes us back to corporate vision, policy and strategy to complete the full cycle of continuous improvement (see Fussler *et al.* 2004).
6   Leadership and vision was followed by quality, knowledge and skills, all ranking above financial, social and environmental credibility. Noteworthy is that, most probably as a result of corporate scandals, controversies around managerial awards and lay-offs of employees at the time, CEOs listed both financial credibility and social credibility higher than environmental credibility.
7   For many companies it takes an outsider to catalyse internal change agents. Discussion in the 2002 Berlin Learning Forum meeting highlighted the role consultants and business school academics can play in helping those at company headquarters to enable the principled commitment to permeate or trickle down within the company.

during the 1990s suggested that wealth creation is, in essence, a moral act, driven by values—values that flow from national and corporate cultures (Elkington 1997: 140). Yet the shift in human and societal values, one of seven impending sustainability revolutions identified by John Elkington (1997), does not imply simply replacing an old ideology or organisational culture with a new one. It has been argued that the complexities of the environmental debate require exploration of difference and of conflicting views rather than conformity to common values. This position reflects scepticism about the ability of a uniform 'corporate culture' to bridge the gap between organisational morality and social morality. More important than attempting to discover 'ideal types' of culture that ensure better environmental or CSR performance, concluded Crane (1997: 142) is for managers to examine more closely how organisational life is culturally and ecologically framed. This approach represents a call for diversity and open dialogue to help the company to be flexible and be prepared for the unexpected. As Zadek *et al.* (1999: 31) noted, for companies to know what is happening and what to expect requires effective systems of reporting and two-way communication with stakeholders internally and externally.

Attempts to create a unitary organisational culture may inhibit the expression of those personal thoughts and reflections that may be necessary in finding new sustainability solutions. The Global Compact both challenges companies to advance universal values and to discover that employees actually have a desire to take value or moral positions. Describing new approaches for multinational companies to enter developing-country markets in partnership with local entrepreneurs, Prahalad and Hart (2002: 4) noted some orthodoxies that must be re-examined. These include the belief that managers are not excited by business challenges that have a humanitarian dimension, as well as the belief that it is hard to find talented managers who want to work in poor markets because the intellectual excitement is in developed markets.

Are we underestimating the potential of individual employees? In discussion of the performance model participants considered an image of the company that starts at the policy or board level and ends with checklists at the level of the shop floor. One comment was that this pyramid needs to be turned upside down. It highlights the role of individual employees. Workers can play a key role in the implementation of, for example, an effective environmental management system in the company. This was underlined by Jim Baker of the International Confederation of Free Trade Unions (ICFTU) in a Global Compact panel discussion during UNEP's consultative meeting with industry associations in 2001.[8] It requires all workers to be trained and involved, with tasks not left only to some environmental manager. It is an approach of general engagement reflected in an environmental case study presented by the Brazilian company Samarco at the 2002 Learning Forum in Berlin.[9]

8 See the report of the meeting, at www.uneptie.org/outreach/business/ind_meeting. htm.
9 See the case studies at www.unglobalcompact.org.

8.4 What price voluntarism?

In an article titled 'The Dangers of Corporate Social Responsibility', *The Economist* (2002b) argued that 'even allowing for some recent corporate scandals and the odd crooked chief executive, most law-abiding companies do good simply as a by-product of their pursuit of profits'. So, business as usual is good enough? Should we be doing more? How much more is good enough? It is often said that being socially responsible is a process and not an outcome. CSR tends to be an elastic concept: the more the company does the more it is expected to do. It appears we should not assume a positive correlation between expenditure and recognition. Will voluntary action through a collective effort find the winning recipe?

At a conference on Global Governance and Sustainability held in Berlin on 30 September to 1 October 2002, and hosted by the Friedrich Ebert Stiftung and Institute for Ecological Economy Research, the representative of the NGO group World Economy, Ecology and Development (WEED), Jens Martens, expressed scepticism over the role of voluntary initiatives, arguing that they tend to be based on statements of business ethics that lack implementation goals (cf. Williamson 2003). This is a popular criticism. Naomi Klein branded company statements of principles and voluntary codes as 'pieces of paper' that tend to be 'drafted by public relations departments . . . in the immediate aftermath of an embarrassing media investigation' (Klein 2000: 430).

People such as US architect William McDonough argue that 'regulations are signals of design failure' (Williams 2002: 61). Regulation can at best prevent bad practice; it can hardly promote best practice. Yet others such as Friends of the Earth International warn of 'a potential cocktail' of greater corporate power and weaker regulation that contributes to growing levels of environmental damage (*Financial Times* 2002). Writing on UN–business partnerships, Utting (2000) of the UN Research Institute for Social Development argued that the partnership approach seems to be straining rather than strengthening relations between the UN and actors in the global corporate accountability movement. CorpWatch warned of companies 'wrapping themselves in the UN flag' and argued that the Global Compact 'undermines the UN potential for demanding corporate accountability' (Karliner and Bruno 2000). UN advisor John Ruggie responded that they make it sound 'as if we are supposed to work only with companies that have trouble-free pasts', adding, 'what would be the point?' (Ruggie 2000b).

The impact of the voluntary initiative can, to start with, be measured in terms of its uptake by the target organisations. In addition to this, the quality of its impact is closely related to the level of detail of its participation requirements, which implies that the soft entry rules for the Global Compact pose us with potentially predetermined difficulties. There has been a growing literature on the effectiveness of voluntary initiatives and agreements (see e.g. ten Brink 2002). In a report from its Environment Policy Committee's series of studies on voluntary environmental agreements in OECD countries, the OECD (2003) came out with a critical conclusion. The report concluded that although the environmental targets of most of the case-study voluntary approaches have been met there are only a few where such approaches have been found to contribute to environmental improvements significantly different from what would have happened anyway. The OECD's Business and Advisory Committee described the conclusion as 'disappointing'. The report did note, however, that voluntary approaches can offer higher economic efficiency than command-and-control policies by providing increased flexibility in how environmental improvements are to be accomplished (OECD 2003: 14-15).

A critical factor appears to be the right combination of voluntary approaches in policy mixes with other instruments such as economic instruments, the involvement of key stakeholders in the setting of appropriate targets as well as credible monitoring (including reporting) and regulatory threats (see OECD 1999; see also Gunningham and Grabosky 1998). Finding the right and more representative policy mix involves finding a combination between 'the electoral accountability of governments' and 'the accountability of the market to consumers' (Grabosky 1995: 221).

The range of voluntary initiatives can be characterised as follows (Jenkins 2002: 36-37; Moffet and Bregha 1999: 15-18; OECD 1999; UNGA 2001a: Annex II):

- Public voluntary programmes, where authorities invite individual companies to participate

- Negotiated agreements, where a bargain is struck between authorities and industry

- Unilateral commitments, set by industry acting independently of public authorities

- Private agreements, involving direct bargaining between stakeholders

- International or UN voluntary initiatives

Voluntary initiatives may relate to policies (including principles and norms), strategies and management systems, guidelines or codes of conduct and certifiable processes or performance standards with associated targets. In addition to being categorised in terms of the participants, voluntary initiatives can therefore also be classified in terms of content. Some have a macro managerial focus, looking at the level of policy and management systems, whereas others have a micro operational focus on technical aspects, the improvement of performance and on the meeting of targets at the site level. The Global Compact and the voluntary initiatives of UNEP and its partners fall in the former, macro managerial, category. It is more likely for a voluntary initiative at the global level—in particular multi-sectoral initiatives—to focus on policies and management systems steered from corporate headquarters.[10] Much of the impact of these global voluntary initiatives lie in 'soft' informational effects, taking the form of sharing knowledge, building capacity and publishing best-practice guides. These impacts dare not be underestimated, as can be seen in the development of very specific tools in the form of sector-specific supplements and guidelines on reporting developed under the GRI.

10 At the global level, specific targets tend rather to be the domain of intergovernmental agreements.

8.5 So why bother?
Building on the emerging business case

Companies are confronted with three considerations:

- Why should I incorporate corporate citizenship and sustainability into my operations?

- Why should I join other companies and stakeholders in collective action to advance corporate citizenship and sustainability?[11]

- If I join collective action, why should I join a particular initiative of the United Nations?[12] Specifically:
  - What value impact does my involvement in this initiative have?
  - Does it enhance my reputation?
  - Does it improve my ability to obtain social licence to operate?
  - Do I find new ideas and solutions through its learning network?
  - Does it help me enter into a dialogue with international stakeholder organisations with which I am unlikely to share the table at other platforms?

To start with, a growing body of research is building the business case to answer the first consideration listed above. An overview study by the Division of Technology, Industry and Economics (DTIE) of UNEP and SustainAbility Ltd (SustainAbility and UNEP 2001) concluded that a strategic focus on triple-bottom-line performance aligns well with mainstream business purpose. The business case is based on various drivers that catalyse the early mover. These include macro-level drivers or forces such as globalisation and deregulation (Andriof and McIntosh 2001: 17; Kemp 2001: 11-17). The micro-level drivers are more evident in daily operations of individual companies. During the 4th Warwick Annual Corporate Citizenship Conference in mid-2001, organised by the Corporate Citizenship Unit of Warwick Business School, Brad Googins of the Boston College Center for Corporate Citizenship mentioned the following drivers in support of the business case:

- Value drivers (e.g. charity, philanthropy)

- Compliance drivers

---

11 Let us take the example of certification systems in the forestry industry. Timber companies have started introducing 'umbrella' certification programmes through their industry associations rather than developing firm-specific certification programmes. The reason for this is that these companies face a 'shared reputation problem': consumers tend not to distinguish between wood harvested by company A and company B, which means that individual company action does little to solidify a green reputation (Gereffi *et al.* 2001: 61).

12 From early discussions in London regarding the Global Compact, business participants noted that the UN offers them global reach, local presence, experience in specific areas and the lowering of transaction costs.

- Intangible drivers (e.g. social issues, reputation)

- Market drivers (e.g. location, suppliers, labour)

A year later, during the Global Governance and Sustainability Conference in Berlin mentioned in Section 8.4, Mark Wade of Shell stated that attention to sustainable business:

- Attracts and motivates talent

- Turns the waste-stream into a value-stream

- Reduces costs through eco-efficiency

- Promotes and serves innovation

- Attracts loyal customers

- Enhances corporate reputation

All of these point to instances where the social responsibility of business becomes a 'near rational' economic choice, as noted in a 2001 UN report on business and development (UNGA 2001b: 11). Corporate citizenship thus becomes more than traditional corporate philanthropy (cf. UNCTAD 1999: 3).

In preparation for the 2003 Summit of the Group of Eight in Evian, where corporate responsibility was set to be a key item on the agenda, the French government convened a multi-stakeholder forum to discuss corporate environmental responsibility. During the discussion business representatives argued that corporations should consider environmental responsibility as a source of long-term value creation (Novethic 2003: 2). Financial markets have slowly started to take note. A working group of the 2002 Policy Dialogue on Business and Sustainable Development started an examination of the receptiveness of financial markets to sustainability performance.[13] Earlier, a study by the Conference Board of Canada reviewed 18 research studies and reports on sustainable development and value creation. It concluded that the practice of sustainable development is most certainly a value driver, a revenue generator that relates positively to share price performance (Feltmate *et al.* 2001: 17).

Monitoring corporate ethical, social and environmental performance has became a growth industry in many OECD countries. Non-financial rating agencies are taking the rating market by force. Shareholders have been making their voices heard as well, filing resolutions on social and environmental issues at annual meetings. Compared with the social dimension, the inherent link between the environment and economy is an easier one to quantify. (Looking at the business case from a human resources point of view, examples of the link between employee values, levels of satisfaction and business performance can be found in case studies summarised by Kemp 2001: 25.) It is therefore easier to argue the environmental case from a purely instrumental point of view, as opposed to a normative point of view. Yet, looking at the 22 industry sector reports prepared for the WSSD in a process facilitated by UNEP, one commentator from the field of environmental and

---

13 See uneptie.org/outreach/compact/unep-role.htm

social accounting commented that that it lacked recognition that there are conflicts between good business practice and sustainability issues. He argued that the new agenda could not be driven entirely by what makes good business sense (Bendell 2002: 8). This reminded me of a labour union leader who said 'there is not always a business case; if there was one everybody would have been doing it by now'.[14]

If the business case is that obvious, why isn't everybody taking action? Most companies adopt a position that is, on the face of it, irrational because of an emphasis on short-term profits and bounded rationality. Gunningham and Grabosky (1998: 415, footnote 89) listed the following reasons for companies failing to exploit the economic advantages of being more proactive on environmental issues: insufficient technical expertise, lack of information, middle-management inertia, ignorance of marginal cost curves, insufficient resources to focus beyond core business functions, a reluctance to borrow capital and uncertainty about future returns. The main blind spot here is for the business leader regarding the belief that corporate citizenship and sustainability is some 'new form of religion . . . rather than a new form of value which society will demand and which successful businesses will deliver through transformed markets' (Elkington 1997: 5).

8.6 Communicating progress: transparency and accountability

The general critique against voluntary initiatives—one with which the Global Compact has been confronted with as well—can be summarised in the words *transparency* and *accountability*. Sceptics argue that voluntary initiatives involve (Muldoon and Nadarajah 1999: 57-60; cf. Utting 2002: 88-92):

● The resurgence of the backroom approach to decision-making, being negotiated behind closed doors

● The pre-emption of more stringent regulatory initiatives and public policy debates

● A lack of verification and accountability

In addition, on the occasion of the WSSD, CorpWatch published *Greenwash + 10* in which it argued that there is a fundamental conflict between the two approaches—between corporate responsibility and corporate accountability. Acknowledging that the two 'may be mutually supportive in some circumstances', in critical moments 'the purpose of voluntary corporate responsibility is not to

14 More unions are seeing the material case for integrating environmental and social concerns. This realisation is driven by findings such as that of a study by the United Farm Workers in California which examined cancer incidences during 1987-97. It showed a positive correlation between pesticide use and the health of farm workers (*GEL* 2002).

improve the behaviour of corporations on behalf of sustainability, but rather to avoid accountability mechanisms that would be more difficult for corporations to control' (CorpWatch 2002: 3). In the same report CorpWatch highlighted what it regarded as examples of violations of the Global Compact principles by some participating companies.

Today, the Global Compact is displaying transparency by publicly listing on its website all participants, indicating next to each company name whether the company has submitted examples, case studies or projects since it joined the initiative. An ongoing question is how to deal with free-riders or sleepers, as well as the possible difficult case of grave ongoing violation of the principles. The Global Compact Advisory Council discusses these issues. After the first meeting of this multi-stakeholder body in January 2002, International Federation of Chemical, Energy, Mine and General Workers' Unions (ICEM) union representative Fred Higgs underlined that 'the advisory process is extremely important to ensure that the Global Compact continues to be relevant and credible' (Higgs 2002: 12).

During the first three years of the Global Compact, the participation requirement that companies annually submit case studies or examples of how they are implementing the principles resulted in the immense task of trying to analyse these centrally. The new approach of developing and analysing case studies through a decentralised network of business schools has proven much more effective. In addition, since January 2003 learning and accountability has been advanced through the requirement of annual communications on progress. Any company wishing to participate has to 'publish in its annual report or similar corporate report (e.g. sustainability report) a description of the ways in which it is supporting the Global Compact and its nine principles'.[15] For many companies the annual communication will take the form of highlighting actions in support of the principles in their annual financial or sustainability reports. In making an annual communication on progress companies are encouraged to use indicators included in the Sustainability Reporting Guidelines of the GRI.[16]

UNEP has always argued the case for sustainability reporting with independent verification to accompany voluntary initiatives, helping to ensure transparency and accountability (see UNEP-DTIE 1998). The value of the GRI, with its Secretariat being a UNEP Collaborating Centre based in Amsterdam since 2002, has been recognised by the UN Secretary-General. In his statement to the 2nd International GRI Symposium he stated, 'I see great potential for the GRI and the Global Compact to profit from each other' (Annan 2000b). Since then, a co-operative agreement has been signed between the Global Compact and the GRI. Addressing business representatives at the Business Day on 1 September 2002 during the Johannesburg Summit, Annan confirmed that the GRI is 'a crucial complement to the Global Compact' (Annan 2002).

As Sir Mark Moody-Stuart noted, the fact that over 200 multinational companies 'now routinely report non-financial performance using the Global Reporting

15   See www.unglobalcompact.org → 'View Examples'.
16   A table on the Global Compact website lists some GRI indicators next to the relevant Global Compact principles, giving companies a practical indication of what can be reported on (see www.unglobalcompact.org → 'How to Participate').

Initiative's sustainability reporting guidelines, and are winning public recognition of their efforts, is confirmation that Cinderella has finally arrived at the ball' (Moody-Stuart 2003). In the WSSD Johannesburg Plan of Implementation, the GRI received explicit recognition for providing an instrument that can be used by companies in their pursuit of corporate environmental and social responsibility. The multi-stakeholder GRI process provides a natural complement to the Global Compact in helping to facilitate the communication of information that is so essential in the learning approach followed under the Global Compact. This underlines the fact that there is also a business case for reporting within management systems, and that sustainability reporting is not a mere backward-looking monitoring exercise. Looking at materiality or relevance, one of the key challenges for companies is not to overwhelm different user groups with a 'carpet bombing' of information (SustainAbility and UNEP 2002).

8.7 The future: growing big, learning that small is beautiful

The future of the Global Compact will revolve around 'outreach' in the quality sense of the word. This will require support in the building of the capacity of companies in all regions to implement and integrate the principles in their daily operations. The initiative has been introduced in all regions, and word of the challenge is spreading. In February 2003 in Cairo, during a meeting organised for Arab-speaking countries by the International Labour Organisation (ILO) and the International Organisation of Employers (IOE), IOE representative Brent Wilton encouraged employers to become proactive, warning that, 'if business does not respond to the challenge, others will'.[17]

In future, the role of reporting in communicating progress and sharing learning experiences will become more important. The debate concerning the Global Compact and the GRI has been particularly topical in France, the first country where legislation, in effect from 2002, made reporting on sustainability performance mandatory. The same holds for South Africa, where the Johannesburg stock exchange agreed that all listed companies must produce GRI-type sustainability reports. This is of historical importance in a country where the apartheid debate in the 1970s and 1980s triggered the Global Sullivan Principles and laid early foundations for the launch of the GRI process by the Coalition for Environmentally Responsible Economies (CERES) in partnership with UNEP (see also Sections 6.1.2 and 6.1.4, on the GRI and on the Global Sullivan Principles, respectively).

The introduction of a decentralised approach in building the Global Compact network is critical to facilitating the involvement of the small role-players. This is

---

17   A Global Compact workshop on networks and outreach hosted by the Swiss government in Bern in June 2003 highlighted different approaches taken in different regions, with national offices of UN agencies and associations having to give more support in developing countries.

necessary to avoid one of four limitations of voluntary initiatives, raised by Muldoon and Nadarajah (1999: 60): namely, the introduction of new inequities, which often takes the form of the favouring of large companies with greater resources, expertise and political access. A report prepared for the United Nations Industrial Development Organisation (UNIDO) referred to the 'CSR paradox', arguing that it is easier for large companies to respond and make commercial gain from their actions than it is for small companies to do so (Raynard and Forstater 2002: 50). It has been warned that the Global Compact may harm the small players, overwhelmed by big business and big NGOs from the industrialised world (Kapstein 2001). This implies the need for special attention to small and medium-sized enterprises (SMEs), which, UNIDO reports, represent around a fifth of company participants (see UNIDO 2004). Discussion on SMEs in the roundtables of the EU Multistakeholder Forum on CSR has noted that SME-friendly management systems are being developed in a number of European countries.

The argument for special attention to be given to small companies is part of an argument for working more closely with all types of entrepreneurs working on a small scale, including social entrepreneurs in the form of NGOs. Our global initiatives tend to start with the big, including big companies and big NGOs. A key part of outreach is to involve more NGOs at the local level, where the United Nations Development Programme (UNDP) has been gaining much experience. In 2002 it was estimated that up to 80% of NGOs accredited to the UN act on behalf of the three value areas (human rights, labour rights and the environment) targeted by the Global Compact (Tesner and Kell 2000: 126).

The decentralised network also includes the growing involvement of management institutes from all regions. They are challenged to rethink old approaches. Many business schools barely have corporate citizenship or CSR on their curricula. Some address the issues but do not brand them as CSR, and it is clear that there are many old-style course outlines that require redesign (see Galea 2004). We also need to look beyond business schools. At UNEP's 20th Consultative Meeting with Industry Associations, David Vidal of the Conference Board spoke of the role of company lawyers and underlined that we need to focus not only on the management schools but on the law schools to advance new thinking. A call for convergence between two mind-sets has also been made by a number of analysts, against the following background:

> Where the CSR agenda focuses on responsibility, legal risk management focuses on liability. Whereas the CSR agenda focuses on transparency, legal risk management focuses on confidentiality, and where the CSR agenda focuses on bridge-building and partnerships, the legal risk management approach is typically one of cautious defensiveness (Ward 2003: 27).

The Global Compact remains an innovative experiment in testing the ability of the UN to work effectively with a diversity of stakeholder organisations worldwide. When Annan spoke at the launch of a Global Compact network in Spain in April 2002, he described the Global Compact 'as a chance for the UN to renew itself from within, and to gain greater relevance in the 21st century by showing it can work with non-state actors, as well as States, to achieve the broad goals in which its member-states have agreed' (UN Secretary General 2002b). This ability to transcend old divisions was echoed in the conclusion by Hawken *et al.* (1999: 317) in their book, *Natural Capitalism: Creating the Next Industrial Revolution.* They underlined that businesses will be able to grasp the opportunities offered by the resource productivity revolution only if they move 'across industrial sectors and solicit co-operation from competitors, critics and perceived adversaries alike'. The Global Compact is offering a global platform for doing exactly this.

If, ten years from now, we were to look back to the present day, we would in all probability conclude that the greatest impact of the Global Compact has consisted in raising the profile of human rights, labour and environmental issues in core business operations. Here lies the strength of voluntarism: namely, the prospect of finding voluntary mechanisms that 'build, rather than hinder, the development of a custodial ethic, and . . . make environmental protection [labour standards and human rights] part of the "community norm" ' (Gunningham *et al.* 1998: 59).

9
Flags of inconvenience?
The Global Compact and the future of the United Nations

Jem Bendell
Nottingham University Business School, UK

> We all have to recognize—no matter how great our strength—that we must deny ourselves the license to do always as we please.
>
> *Harold Truman, 1945*

9.1 Compact context

In 2004 the United Nations moved into its 60th year of existence. The organisation faces a different set of political and economic forces than those at its founding, which has led some to suggest it is slipping toward early retirement. How can an organisation established to mediate between (and influence) nation-states in order to promote peace and progress pursue this mandate in a world where global business and civil society have become major powers and while one nation-state and one economic system have become dominant in international affairs?

A variety of UN staff and commentators have suggested that increasing collaboration between the UN system and non-state actors in the business and voluntary sectors is one means of adapting to this new context. The Global Compact is often discussed in this context. Increasing collaboration with non-state actors is, however, a complicated challenge if the UN is to uphold the fundamental principles set out in its founding charter.

The UN was established to foster the two goals of peace, understood as the absence of civil and international war, and progress, understood as the realisation of human rights. These goals were sometimes complementary, and sometimes not, depending on the political systems and our perceptions of progress. I argue the UN pursued these goals on the basis of two main philosophies. The first approach was to bring together the most powerful groups that might have the most destructive confrontations and give them supreme and undemocratic power in international affairs. The second approach was to engage other powerful groups, identified as the governments of other nation-states, in a more democratic process of dialogue and resolution. The first invention was called the Security Council, the second was called the General Assembly. Therefore the UN embodied both a Hobbesian view of how to achieve peace, by helping to promote a monopoly of the justified use of force through the Security Council, and the more Locke-ite idea of justifying systems of governance through mechanisms of accountability, through the General Assembly.

In the 21st century the context seems somewhat different; growing terrorism reminds us that nation-states do not have a monopoly on violence within their political communities. Globalisation means nation-states neither have a monopoly on political power in the international sphere nor continue to represent competing politico-economic ideologies, as most now administer variants of capitalism. It appears that mediation between states alone, either in democratic or in undemocratic ways, will not achieve either the original goal of peace or progress.

One basic premise of the UN, explained by Harold Truman at the founding conference of the organisation in 1945, is as pertinent today as it was then: 'We all have to recognize—no matter how great our strength—that we must deny ourselves the license to do always as we please'. This came from the president of a nation whose global dominance was even greater then than it is today. After the Second World War, all other great powers lay in ruins, whereas the USA's mainland itself was unscathed by bombing or invasion. US factories were working at full tilt, its armed forces were by far the most powerful in the world and it was only months away from unveiling the atomic bomb, which no other country possessed. Some estimates put US economic output at half of the world's total (Schlesinger 2003). The UN came about in part because the most powerful organisation in the world— the USA—recognised that it must establish constraints on its own power, that it must help establish systems that would require itself and others to be accountable to a new international community.

It is this premise that needs to be remembered and upheld within the UN system as it engages with other players in the international sphere—including business. As some companies and finance have become transnational they are able to both influence and escape the actions of states. There is a lack of global regulation to match the global operation of private enterprise. Worse, those mechanisms that do exist to regulate trade, investment and business operations have been developed with questionable accountability to people affected by them and by the global economy.

The UN has not been able to deal with this governance gap directly, as its mandate has been to engage states to make pronouncements on, influence and work with other states—not non-state actors such as business. In addition, its mandate has been to *promote* peace and progress, rather than *enforce* this. Enforcement can only come when the Security Council resolves to do so—a situation that has limited the ability of the UN to achieve its aims because of the constituents in that Council.

Therefore, within the context of globalisation and the aim of promoting peace and progress, the UN has begun working more closely with non-state actors. Civil society has become increasingly involved in UN processes (Gordenker 1996). During the 1990s relations with another non-state actor—business—also increased. Business had been involved in some aspects of the UN system, such as the International Labour Organisation (ILO) since its inception, but large companies were now becoming sponsors of projects run by various UN agencies such as UNICEF (the United Nations Children's Fund) and the World Health Organisation (WHO). The range of relations with companies, often called 'partnerships', was chronicled in a book prepared for the Global Compact (Nelson 2002). Some relations involve financial support from companies, others do not. The launch of the Global Compact in 1999 was a significant example of this trend, as well as facilitating it, through encouragement of more relations between the UN and business. As various UN agencies are using corporate participation in the Global Compact as a sign of good faith on behalf of the company, it is becoming a factor in such agencies' own decisions about relations with the corporate sector. Growing interest in these relations and in the Global Compact in particular is illustrated by a number of publications, such as a special issue of *The Journal of Corporate Citizenship* (McIntosh *et al.* 2003a), and this book.

The contributors to this book are all generally supportive of the Global Compact. Many echo the arguments of its founders and supporters—that it is an innovative response from UN Secretary-General Kofi Annan to the challenges of globalisation. The Global Compact is indeed an innovative approach, as it escapes the bureaucratic restrictions placed on the work of most UN agencies and seeks to promote action on the basis of values rather than to control action on the basis of rules. Some have applauded it as a 'network model' of organisation, with activity dispersed through the network and new initiatives arising from the network, not from the centre. Although this does create potential for innovation, it also causes a range of problems, which will be discussed in this chapter.

These problems are leading to increasing criticism of the Global Compact, its role, its effects and its accountability. In this chapter I argue that these criticism are not marginal and will become more central as the Global Compact grows. In response, I suggest that we need to understand that the UN is a complex set of institutions, with a unique political mandate. Consequently, we must remember the politics involved when we consider the role of the Global Compact in promoting corporate citizenship and reducing corporate irresponsibility. I suggest that a more open dialogue is required on the UN's relations with the private sector, as these relations will help determine how the UN serves the goals of peace and progress in future decades. I make some specific suggestions on how the Global Compact should move forward in addressing this. I conclude that the Global Compact must reconsider its relationship with UN member-states. These states have helped give the UN its unique role in the world and thus the power of its 'brand' to mobilise action. Although narrow governmental interests have stultified the process of international co-operation, we must not ignore these states as 'flags of inconvenience'. Instead, the UN secretariat should aim for its relations with corporations to help states serve 'we the peoples'. In sum, this chapter is a call for a major overhaul of the UN's relations with business.

In Section 9.2 I highlight the concerns of some of those persons and groups that have criticised the Global Compact and wider UN relations with the private sector. I suggest that these are important enough for their concerns to be looked at and responded to progressively. In Section 9.3 I detail some of the specific problems that are being raised and briefly discuss some possible ways of addressing them. In Section 9.4 I suggest what is ultimately required from institutions of global governance in relation to the private sector and thus call for the development of a work programme for the Global Compact that will help, not hinder, that goal. Finally, in Section 9.5, I explain why corporations should support the Global Compact in this process, both in terms of the personal ethics of managers and the economic case for their companies.

9.2 Dangerous liaisons?

'The Global Compact and its cousin partnerships at other UN agencies threaten the mission and integrity of the United Nations', argued the US group CorpWatch (Bruno and Karliner 2000: 1). The group acts as Secretariat for an 'Alliance for a Corporate-Free United Nations'. Alliance members have written to the UN Secretary-General and heads of other UN agencies to express their concern. Other groups, including the International Baby Food Action Network (IBFAN), the Third World Centre Europe (CETIM) and the Berne Declaration have published critiques of the Global Compact (Richter 2003) that call for a coalition to be formed to disband the Global Compact. The response of the Global Compact's officers has generally suggested that these groups misunderstand the Global Compact and that they represent a marginal viewpoint.

However, groups that participate on the Global Compact's Advisory Council have also begun raising concerns. Oxfam International, Amnesty International, the Lawyers' Committee for Human Rights, and Human Rights Watch wrote a joint letter to the Deputy Secretary-General publicly expressing their concerns about the Global Compact and that although these had been expressed internally they had not been acted on. They indicated that their continued participation was becoming problematic (Hobbs *et al.* 2003).

There has also been criticism from within the UN system. The UN's specialist research institute on development issues—the UN Research Institute for Social Development (UNRISD)—has questioned the role of the Global Compact. The Deputy Director of UNRISD published a critique in the *UN Chronicle*:

> [the UN's] growing proximity to big business is generating tensions with certain sectors of civil society that are critical of this relationship. Such criticism cannot be dismissed as the lone voice of radical single-issue advocacy NGOs. As was evident from the large gatherings

of NGOs and grass-roots organisations at the World Social Forum and the Johannesburg Summit; it is these voices that are at the forefront of much of the thinking and advocacy on 'alternative globalisation' that is gathering momentum worldwide' (Utting 2003: 1).

UNRISD also co-published a major study that critiques the Global Compact (Zammit 2003). Concerns about the Global Compact have been expressed directly to me by members of three other UN agencies.

It does not appear that there has been much constructive dialogue between these critics and the Secretariat of the Global Compact. I relayed a variety of the specific concerns I had heard directly to the consultant drafting the UN Secretary-General's report to the General Assembly on the development of partnerships between the UN and the private sector (United Nations 2003b). However, this report, the writing of which was co-ordinated by members of the Global Compact Office, did not address those concerns. Avoiding criticism and critics is not a sustainable strategy, especially as some of these exist within the UN itself. A more substantive process of dialogue on the issue of the organisations' corporate relations is still required. This process must look closely at the various concerns raised, and it is to these that I now turn.

9.3 Specific challenges for the Global Compact

There are five key criticisms of the Global Compact, which I review in this section, along with some brief suggestions for how these could be addressed. First, some argue that it is wrong for business with questionable practices to participate in the Global Compact, that there is little monitoring of their commitments and that participation can thus diffuse criticism of individual companies. Second, some suggest that the Global Compact could compound the power of large companies in the global economy, with negative implications for development. Third, it is said that key issues necessary to improving the practice of all corporate actors are being sidelined or undermined, such as those relating to macroeconomic questions and concerns about mandatory corporate accountability. Fourth, it is felt by some that the Global Compact is allowing its own agenda, as well as other parts of the UN, to be shaped by business and is allowing the organisation's name to be used by some companies to promote their own perspectives and interests. Fifth, it is argued that these problems cannot be addressed while the Global Compact is not itself more accountable to the UN system of agencies and member-states.

9.3.1 Who participates, how they are monitored and how they benefit

The following points have been made:

- It is wrong for businesses with questionable practices to participate in the Global Compact.

- There is little monitoring of the commitment of companies to the Global Compact.

- As a result of the lack of monitoring, participation can diffuse criticism of specific companies.

For example, IBFAN has complained about the participation of the Swiss-based transnational corporation (TNC) Nestlé (IBFAN 2002). The organisation accuses the company of a long-standing record of poor compliance with the 1981 International Code of Marketing of Breastmilk Substitutes, which was developed by the WHO, a UN body, in response to the marketing malpractices of baby food companies which led to death and poor health in infants and young children around the world. The company has challenged whether the provisions of the code apply to all breastmilk substitutes and all countries, something that UNICEF (2000) criticised as illustrative as an 'attempt to limit the application of the code'.

In response the Global Compact Office stresses that it focuses on helping companies to learn about how to improve their practices. Exclusion is currently limited to a few sectors involved in specific activities, such as landmine production. The idea that no matter how bad you are you can improve is an interesting starting point, although it is questionable given the guidelines on UN relations with business, which I discuss below. In any case, this starting point creates an obligation to demonstrate that participants are committed to learning and are, over time, learning in ways that correlate with the espoused aims of the Global Compact.

However, there is concern that systems for monitoring company performance and learning have weakened. Some members of the Global Compact's Advisory Council have also raised concerns that such mechanisms have weakened since the start of the initiative, with companies no longer obliged to report on their performance in relation to all the principles and with the information not being made public and not the basis for commentary by, and dialogue with, civil society. They also argue that criteria need to be adopted to deal with cases where companies are alleged to breach the Global Compact principles (Hobbs *et al.* 2003).

A related concern here is that by participating in the Global Compact companies with poor practices may be able to diffuse criticism. The Global Compact Office has been careful to communicate that it is not an endorsement of participating companies, yet association with the UN is one of the key motivations for participation. In addition, other UN agencies are using a company's participation in the Global Compact as an indicator of a company being suitable as a potential partner. Therefore, systems for screening and monitoring companies would still be important, even if no official endorsement is involved.

How might these concerns be addressed? Clearly, there is a need to look at the issue of initial screening, and then monitoring of practices or hearing complaints. Although continuous improvement may be the philosophy of the Global Compact this does not mean there need not be an initial threshold of performance. It is important to note at the outset that UN staff, including those of the Global Compact Office, have been requested by the UN Secretary-General to check corporate practices in ways that go beyond the Global Compact principles. The *Guidelines on Co-operation between the United Nations and the Business Community* (United Nations 2000a) explain that 'co-operation with business can take many forms, such as advocacy, fund-raising, policy dialogue, humanitarian assistance and development co-operation', which means they apply to the Global Compact staff. This raises two issues. The first issue relates to whether the Global Compact Office should check member companies against the exclusion criteria of these guidelines, which state that

> business entities that are complicit in human rights abuses, tolerate forced or compulsory labour or the use of child labour, are involved in the sale or manufacture of anti-personnel mines or their compo- nents, or that otherwise do not meet relevant obligations or respon- sibilities by the United Nations, are not eligible for partnership.

The second issue relates to whether they should assess member companies against the provision in the guidelines that 'business partners should demonstrate responsible citizenship by supporting UN causes and core values as reflected in the Charter and other relevant conventions and treaties'.

With a small secretariat such monitoring appears to be an impossible task. However, four activities could be considered as a basic response:

- Awareness and understanding of the guidelines across the UN system needs to be promoted, as well as that of current and potential corporate partners.

- Documenting of what these guidelines actually mean in practice is necessary (i.e. to look at what the conventions mean for companies)

- Public and transparent systems to hear complaints about companies who either do or do not co-operate with the UN system need to be established.

- Internal processes to hear complaints about UN staff who might not abide by the guidelines need to be established.

The Sub-Commission for the Promotion and Protection of Human Rights may have helped in the process of documenting what the conventions imply for corporations. A working group of this Sub-Commission developed the UN Norms on the Responsibilities of Transnational Corporations and Other Business Enter- prises with Regard to Human Rights (UNCHR 2003a). The Norms make clear a range of legal obligations for companies, based on existing international human rights and labour and environmental standards. Their use by the Office of the High Commissioner for Human Rights (OHCHR) is yet to be seen and depends on decisions made at the Commission for Human Rights. Proposals include the establishment of a working group that would hear complaints about companies breaching the Norms. This may go some way to addressing the unacceptable situation that arose when the UN Security Council issued a report on the civil war in the Democratic Republic of Congo. The report noted that commercial interest in the country's natural resources helped fuel the four-year civil war in which more than two million people died. It listed 85 companies considered to be in breach of the Guidelines for Multinational Enterprises developed by the Organisation for Economic Co-operation and Development (OECD 2000a). The OECD questioned whether the UN could determine this and also said that unless complaints were formally filed with their national contact points they would not be able to act in the matter.

This situation raises two questions. The first question relates to why the highest council of the world's premiere intergovernmental body needs to refer to a code developed by a different organisation, the OECD, that represents only some states. Some of the companies criticised were not from OECD countries, and the Congo is not an OECD country and does not have a say in the OECD Guidelines. The UN is tasked with the promotion of human rights and peace and has its own conventions and codes that relate to various aspects of business practice. The Norms developed by the Sub-Commission are therefore essential for the UN to carry out its mandate.

The second question relates to why the UN does not have its own system of complaints and adjudications, which could conduct investigations to a standard that would have legal standing and that would be linked to an internal process to ensure UN agencies did not have commercial dealings with companies judged to be in contravention of UN standards, either by the UN or by courts of law. Proposals from the Sub-Commission for a working group to be established to hear complaints about the Norms is a step towards this, as are the recommendations from the Advisory Council to the Global Compact that the UN system move to put its own operations in alignment with the principles it espouses. This will mean assessing the companies with which is has commercial relations, including suppliers, subcontractors and those invested in through the UN Joint Staff Pension Fund and other savings. It would also mean looking at the environmental management and labour practices of UN agencies. The Global Compact should promote this agenda of work, although it should not necessarily conduct this itself, as it would require an interagency task force. This issue is returned to in Section 9.3.5.

The Global Compact has set its own, additional, requirements on companies, related to institutional learning, which it must itself seek to monitor. Once companies have joined, there need to be criteria for demonstrating progress in one's application to and achievement of learning. Monitoring and evaluation of both personal and institutional learning is an area of existing expertise, so movement on this should be forthcoming. Who will then be able to assess learning performance is a key issue to consider. There may need to be procedures for when the Global Compact Office considers that the commitment and learning is not enough, or when others inside or outside the Global Compact believe this. Thus, a transparent process for hearing complaints on learning performance, for expulsion from the Global Compact and for appeals could be developed.

There is much to be done. The trend has been for the Global Compact to move toward taking a less robust approach. For example, some UN staff explained to me that companies are qualifying their commitment to the principles, with one mining company arguably reneging on its full commitment to the principle of freedom of association in a letter to the Global Compact Office, which was accepted. Given the variety of other issues that have been raised, which I now examine, it is urgent that officers and participants in the Global Compact do not seek to weaken its procedures.

9.3.2 Compounding corporate power?

Some commentators on the Global Compact have suggested that its efforts could compound the power of large companies in the global economy, with negative implications for development. This argument is made most strongly by the UN's own research institute for development issues—the UNRISD—and relates to four issues:

- Enhancing the image and thus financial performance of TNCs based in the northern hemisphere

- Facilitating large corporations' policy advocacy to governmental and intergovernmental bodies

- Promoting an uncritical attitude towards foreign direct investment (FDI)

- Promoting notions of corporate responsibility that have been developed in the West

9.3.2.1 Enhancing image and financial performance

TNCs are the usual partner for most UN partnership projects (Nelson 2002). This is because many, if not most, partnerships between the UN and business involve financial contributions from the corporate partner. Not only do TNCs have such funds but also they have an interest in associating with the global 'brand' of the UN and its agencies. I was once asked by someone assessing potential corporate 'partners' for one UN agency which banana-producing TNC would be the most ethical to work with. Given the existence of fair-trade and organic banana producers and traders, who have preferable social and environmental credentials to TNCs and who compete with banana-producing TNCs, my suggestion was that they look beyond the major TNCs. This was, however, unworkable advice for that UN staff member, as such companies would not be particularly interested in the reputational benefits of sponsoring the UN. However, if the widely touted reputational benefits for a sponsoring TNC are real, then these relationships are helping certain TNCs to improve their performance and thus profits. Given that most of the corporate beneficiaries of such partnerships are large corporations, most often with headquarters in the richest countries, these new relationships could be challenged as a contravention of the role of the UN. This is because the UN Charter is clear that the organisation should not work to benefit the particular interests of any one nation-state, its enterprises or citizens to the detriment of others. As the guidelines on relations with business say, there should be 'no unfair advantage: every member of the business community should have the opportunity to propose co-operative arrangements' (United Nations 2000a). We should remember here that business involves competition—if one company increases market share, another can lose market share.

This is the somewhat awkward context within which the Global Compact sits. It has been argued by its founders and participants that the Global Compact is not about raising funds—it is about encouraging better corporate practices. However, the existence of the Global Compact does indeed facilitate corporate sponsors of other UN activities and agencies, so this issue needs to be considered.

9.3.2.2 Facilitating policy advocacy

By 2004, TNCs and Northern-based companies had been more heavily represented in the Global Compact's activities, such as the policy dialogues, than had smaller companies. Some member-states of the UN may begin to question the political implications of any influence on the agendas and programmes of intergovernmental bodies. The Global Compact has focused on increasing membership from companies from the southern hemisphere, particularly with the establishment of national compacts. However, Zammit (2003) argues that corporate participation in national compacts provides opportunities to influence national development policy to suit corporate interests in a way that may be contrary to the interests of other companies and stakeholders. This relates to the question of promoting policy environments favourable to FDI.

9.3.2.3 Promoting foreign direct investment

A further aspect to the concern that the Global Compact may compound corporate power arises from the perceived uncritical promotion of FDI by the Global Compact Office and its partners. Zammit (2003) argues that they seem to imply that, in view of the lack of capital in southern-hemisphere countries, foreign investment in them by Northern-based businesses is a clear manifestation of corporate responsibility. There is, however, a significant literature from across the ideological spectrum on FDI and TNC presence in Southern countries that points to potentially significant costs and risks for host countries as well as benefits (UNRISD 1995). Balance-of-payment problems, the 'crowding-out' of competitors and anti-competitive abuses of market power, transfer pricing and tax evasion, de-skilling, price rises, currency instability, labour rights problems and environmental damage are among the negative impacts that can be associated with FDI. With privatisation and takeovers, FDI does not necessarily entail the introduction of new technology or productive assets. Moreover, in developing countries with little limited local capabilities any benefits attached to inward FDI may be transient (TADB 2002: 3). Therefore, any assumption that FDI is itself an expression of corporate responsibility is entirely unfounded, and any belief that removing restrictions on FDI is compatible with corporate responsibility and the aims of the UN is misguided. Zammit (2003) therefore argues that in providing additional encouragement to and opportunities for FDI in southern countries the Global Compact not only overlooks potential costs and risks for those countries but also runs the risk of being perceived as overlooking these because it is captive to TNC interests.

9.3.2.4 Promoting Western notions of corporate responsibility

The fourth area of concern relates to whether the Global Compact is promoting not only the power of Western corporations but also a Western view of corporate responsibility, promoted also by Northern-based NGOs, which may not be congruent with the values and practices of Southern nations. For example, there is growing evidence that small and medium-sized enterprises (SMEs), as well as larger enterprises, in the global South manifest corporate responsibility in ways that, although not always registering points on the Global Compact principles scorecard do qualify as ethically and socially responsible behaviour (UNIDO 2002). My own research has shown that models of monitoring, verifying and certifying codes of conduct on workplace issues reflect the interests of Western-based auditing companies and undermine Southern local initiatives with more transformative approaches (Bendell 2001; Prieto and Bendell 2002). Even the definition of 'ethical trade' by Western groups such as the Ethical Trading Initiative (ETI, www. ethicaltrade.org) locate the problem in Southern suppliers rather than the practices of Northern buyers, to the detriment of Southern stakeholders and their own proposals and practices (Bendell 2004). Given growing concerns about the protectionist effects of social and environmental standards in trade, the Global Compact must be careful not to enhance a Western agenda as it supports the interpretation and implementation of its global principles.

9.3.2.4 Suggested responses

There are a variety of responses to these problems that could be considered. On the question of corporate sponsorship, there is a need to assess the 'end-game' of this funding mechanism—for example, what would be the political implications if 50% of the UN's funding came from the private sector? Would this be acceptable? The UN should consider the implications of not seeking corporate sponsorship at all (which is already the policy of many UN agencies). There are, after all, various non-governmental organisations (NGOs), universities and companies that could accept this funding from private corporations to undertake development and peace-related work. Alternatively, geographical balance in corporate sponsors could be sought, as there are large corporations in the South that may be interested, or new rules could be developed that require any corporate partnership to involve domestic entrepreneurs and be the result of a proactive agenda from the UN and not the response to approaches by corporate donors. The Global Compact could usefully serve the UN system by facilitating a dialogue within the UN on this.

On the issue of unbalanced corporate participation in dialogues, the Global Compact could embrace the concept of 'stakeholder democracy' as a way of operationalising the values in the UN Charter. This would mean that the dialogue-oriented activities of the Global Compact focus on providing a meaningful opportunity for involving those who are affected by an issue or decision to have a voice. Therefore, the Global Compact could renew its efforts to pluralise participation in its events, particularly encouraging the participation of civil society and enterprise from Southern countries, both in its national events and in its global events. Some steps have been made in involving Southern businesses and in establishing national compacts. However, to address the challenge properly will require funds to pay for the costs of participation.

For such participation to happen, the current agenda and possible assumptions of the Global Compact must be open to debate. Therefore the pursuit of a comfortable consensus could be avoided. One of the assumptions that may be challenged when pluralising participation is that FDI from TNCs in Southern countries is always a good thing. Instead, the focus should shift to how governments and corporations can be supported to ensure that FDI enhances the capacity of Southern countries to provide social investment, products and services and to enhance the capacity of their firms to compete nationally and internationally. The Global Compact should seek to ensure its work with TNCs does not create dependency either on particular foreign companies or foreign capital more generally but helps to build local competence.

9.3.3 Systemic issues are sidelined, initiatives undermined

As the Global Compact has grown and become more well known, so people have developed very different opinions as to what it proves or what it implies. Some participants in and commentators on partnerships suggest that partnerships demonstrate how we can achieve social progress through voluntary measures and that regulation of corporate activities is not required. Therefore, when criticising voluntary partnerships, many people describe not what the partnership does but what it prevents from being done. The same is true of the Global Compact, as various participants and commentators suggest that it means that we do not need regulatory innovations or systemic changes to global capitalism and the international trading regime. Therefore a number of critics, including Peter Utting (2003) of UNRISD, have questioned whether the key issues necessary to improving the practice of all corporate actors, such as macroeconomic policies and mechanisms for mandatory corporate accountability, are being sidelined or undermined by the existence of the Global Compact.

The first issue to consider here is macroeconomics and trading relations, which have a major effect on the development realities and potential of Southern countries and which have been shaped by corporate lobbying over previous decades. Two examples will suffice here. Increasing corporate consolidation of access to markets and lobbying against co-operation between Southern governments to control their production levels have led to falling prices in the past three decades. For example, prices of agricultural commodities have been on an almost continuous decline since 1980, and as Southern countries are heavily reliant on agricultural exports falling commodity prices have contributed greatly to the difficulties of those countries. Annual losses in purchasing power as a result of deteriorating terms of trade are estimated to cost developing countries US$2.5 billion a year and mean that countries have to run faster merely to stand still (ILO 2000).

Taxation provides a second example. Transfer pricing is the practice where one company reports that it sells products to another company in the same group at a higher or lower price to ensure the profits can be recorded in the company that faces lower tax rates. It is about moving money from one country to another to avoid tax and has been estimated to cost over US$50 billion a year to countries in the global South (Bendell and Young 2003). This practice is not without social consequences, given the poor state of national budgets in many Southern countries and because governments have little option but to shift the tax burden onto labour, raising the costs of employment and reducing the take-home wages.

These are just two macroeconomic problems that companies have influenced and are influenced by and are among a range of systemic issues that must be tackled if the global economy is to be more supportive of social development. In the past the business world generally has promoted frameworks that facilitate greater freedom for enterprises both at the national level and at the international level while at the same time narrowing the room for policy manoeuvre for Southern governments. If the Global Compact continues to sidestep the negative influences of corporate political lobbying on these macroeconomic issues, while its existence is used by some to support that lobbying, then the benefits of the Global Compact that are described in this book will come at a high price.

The second issue to consider is how the Global Compact relates to calls for improved legal mechanisms for holding corporations to account. It should be noted that available research suggests that the economic case for companies voluntarily acting on social and environmental issues is not certain and depends on the industry and the context. Although some companies may begin to act voluntarily, and should be encouraged to do so, this does little to protect society from those who do not. Even though only hundreds of the 65,000 TNCs are involved in the Global Compact, some participants, such as the International Chamber of Commerce (ICC), have suggested that the Global Compact illustrates that voluntary approaches are the way forward. Global Compact officers themselves have stressed that they do not have an opinion on this and that they hope the Global Compact's efforts can be complementary to any regulatory innovations. However, the experience of the relationship of the Global Compact to the UN Norms, mentioned in Section 9.3.1, has raised concern that the Global Compact could be, whether its staff want it or not, undermining the progress of work on corporate accountability elsewhere in the UN system. Echoing the arguments of the ICC a year earlier, the President of the US Council for International Business criticised the Norms, basing his argument on the growth of voluntary initiatives such as the UN Global Compact (BBC 2003). Therefore some members of the Advisory Council to the Global Compact have criticised the Global Compact officers for not calling on its members to show leadership in supporting the Norms (Hobbs *et al.* 2003).

Their concern is supported by the guidelines on the UN's co-operation with business, detailed in Section 9.3.1. These are clear that corporations co-operating with the UN should support the UN's role and activities. This includes support for the UN's implementation of conventions and treaties and the implementation of mandates given to its agencies by member-states. As the Sub-Commission was acting on a mandate from governments, in lobbying against this process while using the Global Compact as evidence, the ICC could be contravening the provisions in the guidelines and thus by not disciplining the ICC the Global Compact officers may leave themselves open to criticism for failing to uphold the guidelines.

The Global Compact Office could respond to this possible sidelining or undermining of macroeconomic issues and progress toward mandatory corporate accountability by beginning a dialogue on ways of creating change across all business actors, not just its partners. First, it could seek to expand the debate about corporate citizenship to include how companies use their political power and economic freedoms in ways that create an unhelpful macroeconomic environment, and how this could be changed. Thus the Global Compact should apply its learning approach to political economy questions rather than just to projects. As Peter Utting (2003) suggests, 'Social learning should focus not only on the technicalities of specific interventions, dialogue and stakeholder relationships but also on the macro issues'. Participants need to be 'learning to talk' about economics and politics. This could relate to the arguments of the UN Conference on Trade and Development (UNCTAD), that we look at the economic dimensions of corporate citizenship (Bendell and Concannon 2003).

The expanded dialogue would also need to include a new look at the role of regulation. The partnership agenda must be separated from a voluntarist perspective and neoliberal economics paradigm, neither of which the UN has been mandated to promote. Therefore, partnerships should not undermine efforts at the UN to encourage intergovernmental agreement on regulatory innovations to stimulate peace, security and sustainable development. Partnerships could even seek to support such efforts. Therefore the Global Compact should *actively* seek to complement the work of the UN system that has been formally mandated by member governments rather than allowing its name to be used against this. Specifically, the Global Compact could promote the UN Norms as a means of further understanding its two principles on human rights, perhaps through policy dialogues, improve the understanding of its own staff and co-operators of the implications of the guidelines and the broader role and work of the UN system and discipline those participants who knowingly work against this.

9.3.4 Hitching a ride with business?

A fourth concern that has been raised is that that the Global Compact is allowing its own agenda to be shaped by business, and perhaps other parts of the UN, as well as allowing the UN's name to be used by some companies to promote their own perspectives and interests. One co-publication by the Global Compact Office illustrates this. In 2003 the British consulting firm SustainAbility produced a report on NGO accountability, funded by a range of corporate sponsors (SustainAbility 2003). The report was problematic for a number of reasons, detailed elsewhere (Bendell and Visser 2003). However, the Global Compact and the UN Environment Programme (UNEP) lent their names to this report, although not directly involved in its preparation, and thus the report was advertised and reported as coming from the UN. 'Adding the UN's name to this work might anger those who think the Compact is about diffusing criticism of companies by NGOs', said Jules Peck, of WWF-UK, and Judith Richter argued that 'the UN's support, via the Global Compact, for the simplistic analyses presented in this study may damage efforts to hold corporations accountable to the world's citizens' (quoted in Bendell and Visser 2003: 15-16).

The question of NGO accountability is one that has been with us for decades. Within development studies, various commentators have stressed the need for NGOs to be more accountable to those they aim to support, and various groups such as ActionAid have sought to empower their beneficiaries by putting representatives on their board (Hulme and Edwards 1996; Hudock 1999). If the Global Compact Office is interested in the issue then it could approach centres of methodologically sound research expertise, institutions with a trust and mandate from civil society, or agencies within the UN system, such as the Non-Governmental Liaison Service (NGLS) that have experience and expertise in this area. However, the Global Compact Office responded to a for-profit consultancy with corporate funding that had identified a co-branding opportunity with the UN.

Therefore some suggest that the Global Compact Office has been responding to those corporations and consultants that knock loudest and soonest on their doors and that are able to fund the projects they propose. This reveals the downside of the network model of organisation: if action and energy are dispersed through the network, then it is those actors in the network that have most access to funds that shape the agenda and work programme of the network.

To deal with this problem the Global Compact needs a strategic change of direction. As the premiere international organisation in the world, the UN should be in the driving seat in its relations with business, not hitching a ride. UN agencies need to define their agenda on partnerships, in keeping with their mandates, and be proactive not reactive. Otherwise, partnerships with the UN will serve the agendas of those with privileged access to the UN system. The Global Compact could consider the following developments in order to avoid this. First, it could work with UN agencies to establish a joint strategy and a proactive work programme. Second, it could assess how proposals arising from its network relate to this central strategy. Third, it could seek to use its corporate convening power to serve the existing UN agencies in executing their mandates. Fourth, it could initially look within the UN system when addressing policy issues and, if the expertise is not available, then approach independent centres of research excellence and not rely on the consultancy industry involved in corporate responsibility issues. Ultimately, it should seek a core budget to help it execute this strategy.

9.3.5 Questionable accountability to the UN system

In summarising their various concerns with the Global Compact, some have argued that their concerns derive from the fact that this is an initiative of some staff of the UN Secretary-General's personal office, and that it has remained outside formal procedures of accountable governance. It is true that the various issues outlined above will probably be addressed only if the personalities involved in the Global Compact decide to act. Should international civil servants have such unaccountable power?

The answer has to be no. The civil servants involved should be commended for innovating something that has grown as quickly as the Global Compact. Their actions stand in contrast to the typically slow bureaucracy of the UN system. They have been able to achieve this, in part, because there is no intergovernmental board directly controlling what they do. The reasons why intergovernmental disagreements seem to paralyse the UN system is something I discuss further in Section 9.4. However, the UN is an intergovernmental body, and so systems of accountability to governments are essential, even if government delegations are kept at arm's length from specific operational decisions. The absence of this has led to criticisms that the Global Compact is being driven more by the ideologies of its administrators and partners than by the UN (Zammit 2003).

The Global Compact is not alone in having its accountability challenged. By the end of 2003 there were fairly weak, sometimes non-existent, accountability mechanisms for most UN partnerships. The World Summit on Sustainable Development (WSSD) provided UN backing for specific partnerships. This necessitates future monitoring, evaluation, sense-making and reporting on the conduct of these partnerships to the UN.

If the Global Compact and corporate partnerships really are to be a significant part of the UN's future, then governance issues need to be addressed now. The following steps could be taken. First, the Global Compact Office, the UN Secretary-General's Office, the UN agencies that are involved in the Global Compact and other interested groups within the UN system should all examine whether a new mechanism for governing the Global Compact could be devised. One option to consider would be to give the UN agencies a direct role in its governance: it could become an interagency project. Moreover, all the agencies that participate in the Global Compact could seek, with the help of the UN Secretary-General's Office, a mandate from their governing bodies to be active participants in the Global Compact and thus have the necessary capacity and resources to work on it proactively. By the beginning of 2004, the OHCHR did not have a mandate from the Commission for Human Rights to fully participate in the work of the Global Compact, even though it is a founding participant. Alternatively, an agency such as UNCTAD could be mandated to work on Global Compact issues, so the Global Compact Office could have the option of becoming a programme of that agency.

This issue of accountability, as well as the four areas of concern discussed above in Sections 9.3.1–9.3.4 need to be addressed directly. Unfortunately, some of the NGOs and UN staff that are raising such issues say that they feel ignored or sidelined, and that the problems are becoming more acute. Although procedures for how the UN relates to businesses are young, and teething problems are understandable, these are too important to the future of the UN for policies and practices not to be more co-ordinated and to result from wider dialogue both within and outside the UN system.

9.4 Learning to talk more broadly: a new agenda for the Global Compact

In Section 9.3 I mapped out a range of areas that the Global Compact could explore, and procedures it could adopt, in order play a constructive role in the future of the UN. A key theme in this analysis is that the participants in the Global Compact need to begin to learn to talk more broadly about politics and economics and to face the fundamental questions about why globalising capitalism is not currently delivering for all the world's people. In doing this, we should remember that the Global Compact would not be necessary were the UN's government delegations truly to represent the long-term interests of their peoples and were able to work together on issues of common concern. Like many people, I believe that with the relevant information on the situation of our planet, people would not choose to be represented in ways that undermine the global sustainable development of humankind. However, for a variety of reasons, governments do not seem to represent their people's longer-term interests.

The UN must respond to this fact: Governments may be masters of the institution, but they are not masters of the situation. Current patterns of corporate power and global finance have impaired the ability of states to represent and serve 'we the peoples'. Consequently, in its relations with business, the UN secretariat should seek to free governments from these undemocratic pressures so that they can effectively represent and serve the peoples of the world. The Global Compact could therefore seek to engage corporations in a dialogue on how to free the democratic spirit of member-states. The full implications of this philosophy will have to be developed, and here I present nine initial ideas.

The Global Compact could engage the corporate sector in dialogue and action to help liberate is member-states from:

- The undemocratic power of global financial flows

- The undemocratic power of historic debts and the resultant economic and political prescriptions from international financial institutions and foreign governments

- Corruption, which undermines democratic governance

- Rebel movements and civil war

- Declining revenues

- The monopolising practices of some companies

- Opaque corporate lobbying, as well as that directed at intergovernmental bodies

- The undemocratic power of the corporate financing of election campaigns

- The institutionalised bias of corporate-owned mass media

9.4.1 Freedom from the power of global financial flows

The Global Compact could engage the corporate sector in dialogue and action to help liberate its member-states from the undemocratic power of global financial flows.

The equivalent of over a trillion dollars are traded every day in currency markets. This creates currency volatility that is responsible for increasing poverty in various regions, an example being Indonesia, where poverty doubled as a result of the East Asian currency crisis (Weller and Hersh 2002). Moreover, the currency markets exert an undemocratic pressure at all times, as any negative perspectives from finance companies on the politics of a sitting or prospective government can lead to a devaluation of its currency. Thus there was a run on the *real* as Inacio Lula Da Silva moved toward the presidency of Brazil (Beck 2002). Consequently, governments such as that of Brazil are restricted in their political freedom by international banks. This situation needs to be addressed multilaterally, via currency transaction taxes or capital control agreements, and could be supported by some companies that also suffer from currency volatility, as well many banks, as only the top 20 banks account for about 80% of currency trading.

9.4.2 Freedom from debts and associated policy interference

> The Global Compact could engage the corporate sector in dialogue and action to help liberate its Southern members from the undemocratic power of historic debts and the resultant economic and political prescriptions from international financial institutions and foreign governments.

As monies lent to Southern governments were lent unaccountably and have been paid back many times over, so-called 'third-world debt' is a travesty, killing 19,000 children every day as governments have to service the debts by cutting health, education and various social services and by adopting ill-thought-out trade policies (UNDP 1997: 93). Debt relief could be supported by some companies, in the North and the South, as it would help economies to grow.

9.4.3 Freedom from corruption

> The Global Compact could engage the corporate sector in dialogue and action to help liberate its member-states from corruption, which undermines democratic governance.

The blessing of natural resources has turned into a curse for many states in the South as foreign companies have sought to exploit them. Billions of dollars have been paid by foreign companies to African politicians to gain access to oils and minerals (Global Witness 1999). This rewarding of corruption has led to ruthless and unaccountable governance. Voluntary responses have not worked. Laws on corrupt practices by companies operating overseas need to be developed further and better enforced and companies should be obliged to publish what they pay to governments. Companies could support campaigns on this, as they gain nothing from corruption in the longer term. The Global Compact has begun work in this area, which should be extended.

9.4.4 Freedom from rebel movements and civil war

> The Global Compact could engage the corporate sector in dialogue and action to help liberate its member-states from rebel movements and civil war.

Democracy requires peace. As discussed in Section 9.3.1, one of the worst wars in human history, in the Democratic Republic of Congo, killing over 2 million people, was carried out by armed groups that obtained much of their funds from foreign companies that were exploiting the country's mineral resources (Kassem 2002). To prevent this from happening again, and to provide redress, will require a variety of measures, including the establishment of mechanisms for prosecuting international corporate criminals. Companies could support this, because abiding by their voluntary codes could lead them to being out-competed by unscrupulous competitors. The Global Compact's work on this should therefore move beyond promoting codes of practice and towards engaging corporations in dialogue and taking action on the question of mandatory rules for corporate accountability.

9.4.5 Freedom from declining revenues

> The Global Compact could engage the corporate sector in dialogue and action to help liberate its member-states from declining revenues.

As discussed in Section 9.3.3, transfer pricing and tax evasion is becoming increasingly problematic for governments. The response must be a regional or global regulatory innovation that requires transparency of the internal pricing and tax activities of TNCs. Many large corporations that are not able to conduct transfer pricing could support such a move, as these practices put them on a less competitive footing.

9.4.6 Freedom from monopolies

> The Global Compact could engage the corporate sector in dialogue and action to help liberate its member-states from the monopolising practices of some companies.

Free-trade rhetoric has masked a reality of market monopolisation, where two-thirds of world trade now occurs between the subsidiaries of the same groups of companies (ILO 2000). Basic economic theory describes the societal problems that arise from monopolies, yet today half the member-states of the World Trade Organisation (WTO) do not have competition law. The time is right for a global competition framework. True entrepreneurs would support this, and thus many companies could support this, although probably not the TNCs that control or seek monopolies.

9.4.7 Freedom from corporate lobbying

> The Global Compact could engage the corporate sector in dialogue and action to help liberate its member-states and intergovernmental bodies from opaque corporate lobbying.

Trade negotiations and agreements have been subjected to corporate lobbying, with either damaging or highly questionable effects. The General Agreement on Trade in Services (GATS) and the Agreement on Trade-Related Aspects of Intellectual Property Rights (TRIPs) would not exist without corporate lobbying. Pharmaceutical companies have been criticised for lobbying government delegations to the WTO to prevent agreements that would facilitate access to medicines. Some companies could support moves to require transparency in corporate lobbying, given the unequal access and influence of some of their competitors.

9.4.8 Freedom from corporate financing of elections

The Global Compact could engage the corporate sector in dialogue and action to help liberate its member-states from the undemocratic power of the corporate financing of election campaigns.

Around the world, there are increasing calls from commentators on political processes to curb the influence of special-interest money on politicians (Palast 2002). In many countries you cannot become a viable candidate in elections unless you successfully appeal to corporate donors, a situation that is a travesty of democracy. Even in the USA there is a movement towards 'clean elections', with a number of States having such elections. Again, some companies could support moves to remove corporate funding of parties and election campaigns, as otherwise their competitors have unequal access and influence and can win policy concessions that undermine their own interests.

9.4.9 Freedom from a biased mass media

The Global Compact could engage the corporate sector in dialogue and action to help liberate its member-states from the institutionalised bias of corporate-owned mass media.

Diverse forms of media are crucial to the functioning of a democracy. Recent decades have seen the consolidation of mass media by large corporations, so that 40% of the world's media industry is now controlled by just five corporations (Simms *et al.* 2000). The political agenda is sometimes explicit, as illustrated by the corporate media's factual inaccuracies during the attempted coup in Venezuela (Adams and Gunsun 2002). However, most often it works in a more insidious manner, as profit-seeking translates into a range of filters on the news and programming agenda (Chomsky and Hernan 1994). Renewing democratic discourse will require pluralising forms of mass media, including the promotion of different forms of ownership—by the state, and by community, not-for-profit and domestic companies, rather than just by TNCs. Some smaller media corporations could support work on this agenda.

9.4.10 Summary

These nine areas concern problems that have arisen as a result of an over-concentration of unaccountable corporate power. They must all be addressed if the UN is to help its member delegations become masters not servants of the global economy. If the Global Compact were to seek to address these problems of corporate power it would not be surprising if there were little leadership on this from its corporate participants. The UN and civil society must therefore take an initial lead.

The current funding model of the Global Compact, and its network approach, will not help: leadership on this agenda will require resources.

When embarking on this new agenda the Global Compact and its participants may need to adopt a new approach to dialogue and learning. Those Global Compact events I have attended have been hierarchical in approach, with a traditional conference format of speakers who are senior within their organisations. However, participants will need to acknowledge that those at the top of their profession in the corporate sector may not be the best people to understand the complexities of global political economy. Corporate executives have much to learn and unlearn. I am not alone in my frustration at sitting through speeches from people who have scaled their respective hierarchies and talk of their conversion to making the world a better place after a short poverty holiday. Instead, there are people with years of work and research on development, politics, economics, sociology, anthropology and law who should be engaged more centrally in the future of the Global Compact as it engages in a more systemic analysis of corporate relations with society. The academic network of the Global Compact may have a greater role in this regard, especially involving those who are trained in disciplines additional to management studies.

9.5 Conclusions: citizenship revisited

The areas of work I have outlined in Section 9.4 are an enactment of a systems view of a corporation's relationship with society. Work on corporate responsibility has largely adopted a methodological individualism, believing that we can understand the problem and how to improve it by focusing on what one company does by itself. Take the issue of working standards. The methodological individualist focuses on what codes a company might adopt to improve the working conditions of its suppliers. Taking a systems view, we might ask why the problems have arisen in the first place, including why employees, communities, unions, local governments and so forth do not have their own power to rectify the situation. Such an approach would then consider a corporation's responsibility for influencing policies that undermine the power of these constituents.

Thus the concept of 'corporate social responsibility' can be reconceived. Given the need for all companies to change if we are to promote sustainable development, voluntary corporate responsibility need not, perhaps by definition should not, be 'voluntarist' and promote deregulation. Instead, the responsibility of one is to promote the accountability of all.

This brings us back to the concept of 'corporate citizenship'. There appear to be three definitions in use. The first definition relates to when corporate citizenship is used to describe a company that acts to improve its own internal behaviour and also becomes involved in the community (McIntosh *et al.* 1998). The second relates to when corporate citizenship is used to describe a social situation where companies take on the role of providing some of the basic needs and rights of citizens (Matten and Crane 2003). However, a third definition sees citizenship as implying membership of a political community, to which rights and freedoms are relinquished, in return for benefiting from the fact that others must do the same. It is a concept of mandatory rights and mandatory obligations. Therefore, in the absence of an international framework of mandatory obligations of corporations to society, so corporate citizenship should mean support for developing such a framework, in return for the right to international ownership and movement of capital assets (Bendell 2000).

Some companies, especially those that are already making a better impact on society than their competitors are, would have nothing to fear from societies and governments being freed from oppressive corporate power and thus more able to intervene in markets for sustainable outcomes. It is these companies that could adopt a deeper understanding of corporate citizenship, adopt a systems view of their responsibilities and engage the Global Compact on a more transformative agenda. Nevertheless, there will be many participants who will fight against such an approach. A comfortable consensus is therefore impossible if the Global Compact is to be a progressive force in the future of the UN.

The echoes of Harold Truman's statement at the founding of the United Nations, quoted at the head of this chapter, are loud and clear. If global financial institutions and TNCs are the most powerful force on the planet today, so they should acknowledge that they must deny themselves the licence to do always as they please. That principle of citizenship is at the very heart of the UN. Thus, it should be at the heart of the UN's relations with corporations.

If this does not happen then the Global Compact could play a key role in transforming the UN into a tool of vested interests in the global economy, which would be a travesty of the vision of its founders and staff and would undermine its ability to mediate between competing views, ideologies and power bases, as it is meant to do. The bombing of the UN headquarters in Baghdad, in 2003, illustrates the dreadful consequences that may arise when some people, mistakenly or not, regard the UN as an agent of dominant and self-serving forces.

The UN is about politics as well as values. It is an intergovernmental body, and its member-states are not 'flags of inconvenience' to be held at arm's length but are central to the UN's role and profile. A future for the Global Compact lies in engaging corporations to help and not undermine states in better serving 'we the peoples'.

10
Labour and the Global Compact
The early days

Jim Baker
International Confederation of Free Trade Unions

10.1 The context of the Global Compact

The Global Compact initiative is rooted in the traditions of the UN and its family of organisations and also in more recent, largely private, developments related to 'globalisation' and 'corporate social responsibility' (CSR). These traditions are, in theory, complementary, but may conflict in practice. The two approaches create a certain tension inside the Global Compact.

The original nine principles of the Global Compact, covering human rights (Principles 1 and 2), labour standards (Principles 3-6) and the environment (Principles 7-9), are universal principles already adopted by governments and, in the case of labour standards, by the International Labour Organisation's (ILO) tripartite constituents, representatives of governments, employers and workers.[1] In other words, all nine principles, although handled differently by the respective organisations responsible for their implementation, have established legitimacy and were not invented by or for the Global Compact.

In the case of the ILO, the principles, developed for governments in a series of conventions, were used in the ILO Tripartite Declaration of Principles Concerning Multinational Enterprises and Social Policy, adopted in 1977 to guide the behaviour of enterprises.[2] The Declaration has been updated subsequently from time to time. The meaning of those principles has been defined over decades by the super-

---

1 The principles are listed on page 12.
2 For details of the Tripartite Declaration, see www.ilo.org/public/english/standards/norm/sources/mne.htm.

visory machinery of the ILO, including in response to specific complaints against governments.

Some decisions by the supervisory machinery would not easily apply to companies. For example, companies presumably would not have the authority to imprison trade unionists. However, the jurisprudence of the ILO can provide guidance in very many areas.

The meanings of the six non-labour principles are not always quite as clear. However, they are, nevertheless, internationally accepted universal standards.

Most of the principles date from the postwar period and are fundamental to the protection of human freedom and the establishment and maintenance of democracy. They, including the principle on freedom of association and the right to collective bargaining (Principle 3), were central to the radical changes in Europe in the years following the war and to the early struggles for independence from colonial powers. A more recent and better-known example of the power for change of these principles is the struggle of Solidarnošc in Poland, where changes in an entire region and system were dramatically touched off by the strike of shipyard workers in Gdansk in 1980. Another is the crucial role of black trade unions in resisting and helping to bring down the apartheid regime and building a mass movement that provided the basis for a stable, non-racial democracy in South Africa. The strikes and mobilisation of black workers were critical to engaging business on a multiracial basis, engendering political change and, more broadly, changing society.

The realisation of these principles, in this 'traditional' approach, requires real actors. That means rights-based dialogue, involving more than one party, and representation of interests and institutions. It can take time, and organisation and can be messy, but it has the big advantage of working.

In contrast to the rights that, when used by trade unions and others, have changed history, CSR is often rooted in paternalism in a historic sense and, more recently, in public relations actions. It has evolved since the early days, but to understand it, one must understand its origins as these help to shape both the concept and its evolution.

CSR is not drawn from the long experience that many companies have in establishing and maintaining good relations with the representatives of their employees and negotiating in good faith. Responsible industrial relations, as critical as they are to real rights and responsibility, are not part of the CSR marketing process. Often, such responsible firms were not involved in CSR and were sometimes considered by the CSR industry as 'backwards'. It did not matter what they did in practice; rather, what mattered was what declarations they made, what management systems they used and how they reported.

CSR was, in large part, a response to the effects of massive shifts of production over a relatively short period of time, particularly in the textile and garment industry. In many cases, manufacturing was separated from markets and brand names. Sales in major markets were no longer related to production in those same markets. Production had been transferred to supply chains in other countries. The experience of Nike, held responsible by many for the violation of workers' rights by suppliers, is but one example of the reputation effects of this rapid shift of production.

This shift of production had been facilitated by a number of new possibilities related to the organisation and distribution of work. One important factor in this development was the drastic reduction in transport costs related to the introduction of technology, including the containerisation of cargo. It allowed companies to take advantage of lower production costs in far-flung parts of the world.

In labour-intensive industries, that cost advantage was largely in the form of low wages, and workers had no role in determining their own wages, hours and working conditions in those sourcing countries where trade union rights were not protected.

One can ultimately understand, even if it is very difficult for affected workers, that jobs leave one country for another in order to lower costs even if the markets remain largely the same, but it is another matter when companies and their production and supply chains shift jobs away from countries where there is respect for fundamental workers' rights to take advantage of the economic edge provided by tyranny. That is comparative advantage through comparative abuse. A further problem is that, in certain cases, companies can argue with some justification that 'the market made us do it'. That fact, in itself, begins to establish the limits of voluntary initiatives.

Cases of abuse of workers' rights in supply chains, including use of child labour, came to light, and those companies that took advantage of these cost advantages found that they had an image and reputation problem. Campaigns mounted by elements of civil society, including trade unions, and revelations in the press began to affect brand names. Public relations problems received public relations responses. The lack of respect for fundamental rights and the unacceptable conditions for workers were seen through a marketing lens.

Another crucial CSR difference compared with those approaches that are based on internationally accepted standards is that the marketing orientation means that one is addressing the concerns of consumers and not of the affected workers. Unlike in Poland or South Africa, there is no direct connection between the problem and the solution, and there is therefore no automatic role for the representatives of those workers. Far too often, they have no real opportunity to defend their own rights and interests.

In the course of controversies and campaigns, the responsibility of governments to protect the rights of their citizens was often forgotten as well. That is true even in the case of China—a country that systematically violates the rights of workers to organise. Workers are prevented by law from organising outside the office of ACFTU, a 'trade union' controlled by the ruling Communist Party. This fundamental issue and government responsibility tends to get drowned out in discussions about company behaviour as if there were no relationship between what companies are doing and what they are allowed to do.

In this context, the trade union movement and some non-governmental organisations (NGOs) sought real change 'on the ground'. In other words, they wanted to use the embarrassment of companies to try to create the space for workers to organise freely without being victims of violent attacks, reprisals and fear, at least in countries where that is possible. To the extent that image problems and associated CSR measures could help alter the environment so that it could help workers to become actors and participants in their own lives, they were seen as something that could help to achieve progress.

In other words, CSR could be good to the extent that it created space for workers to organise. Recently, however, there has been an increasing tendency to try to occupy that space with techniques and methods, including the creation of what is close to what used to be called 'company unions', that leave little room for free and independent trade unions established and controlled by the workers themselves. Even though the public relations approach has evolved it has too often not changed its fundamentally unilateral and outward-oriented approach. False interlocutors, including some social auditing firms and NGOs, end up occupying the space that should be filled by the workers themselves. Far too often the object of CSR seems to be the development of management systems where workers and their organisations are, in effect, excluded.

Essentially, the Global Compact, owing to the circumstances of its birth and the times in which it was born, is caught between two quite different orientations. One is a top-down CSR view in which pressure builds to go more and more deeply into management systems, performance models, verification or assurance and reporting as a complete package to fend off hostile public opinion, but that renders the affected workers irrelevant. It is a revival of 19th-century paternalism with the benefit of a new vocabulary. In this context, the Global Compact runs the risk of losing its uniqueness and, instead, competing with or accommodating itself to a multitude of other measures developed and being developed by the CSR industry. In seeking to be 'relevant' it runs the risk of becoming irrelevant.

However, the Global Compact can also be used to promote and deepen global dialogue based on its principles. And the Global Compact and dialogue should really be based on those principles. The behaviour of companies needs to conform to standards, rather than standards conforming to the behaviour of companies. The most obvious case is China concerning the issue of freedom of association where many companies have sought to redefine this standard rather than admit that they cannot respect it. Dialogue can lead to problem-solving, trust and agreement among legitimate actors. On those grounds, the Global Compact has little competition and bases itself on long and successful national experience.

The Global Compact must therefore build on its global dialogue function. That is its 'added value'. This is where it can be most effective. It should drive dialogue and be driven by it, and, dialogue, again, should not simply be defined as meetings that can be then mentioned in reports so that one can tick the right box on a list. It needs to be real dialogue, designed to achieve something.

Often, the best dialogue is never reported. Its results are evident in improvements in the lives of workers, communities and the environment and not by the number of attempts to measure something that may or may not be measurable nor by the number of kilos of company reports that are published. To the extent that measurement and reporting can be useful, they need to be a means to an end and not the end itself. After all, weighing a pig does not make it any heavier, even if you write the weight down and print it.

10.2 Trade union participation in the Global Compact

The trade union movement was not invited to participate in the Global Compact at the time of its launch. The subsequent evolution of the Global Compact in terms of certain key issues made it possible for trade unions to become involved and help to shape the Global Compact.

UN Secretary-General Kofi Annan launched the Global Compact at the World Economic Forum at Davos in January of 1999 (see Chapter 1). Although the Global Compact was important as a leadership initiative and was a challenge to business to respect its principles, it had a serious design flaw as it was set up. By being seen as a UN–business initiative, it implied that government and business were the only actors in globalisation, even though that was not intended.

The Global Compact, however, had the great advantage of being a personal initiative of the UN Secretary-General based on international instruments that were already accepted. In other words, the standards already existed and could not be changed, even if there was a great deal of flexibility as to how the Global Compact idea could be carried forward.

At that early time, UN officials had not decided to seek or accept the involvement of others. It seemed as if they still had a fairly undifferentiated notion of civil society and it was not clear how or whether there would really be a possibility of broadening the dialogue beyond business and the UN. There were, however, some early, informal, discussions with labour and with some NGOs.

Another misstep at the beginning was the notion that voluntary action in the social and rights area, including the Global Compact, somehow balanced out binding rules to protect property rights and commercial interests at the global level. This idea was reflected in a joint UN statement with the International Chamber of Commerce (ICC) that specifically opposed addressing non-trade issues at the World Trade Organisation (WTO). This was particularly sensitive because of the fact that the launch took place just a few months prior to the WTO ministerial meeting in Seattle.

Informal, but serious, discussions began between those responsible for the Global Compact at the UN and the International Confederation of Free Trade Unions (ICFTU) in late 1999. Although there were aspects of the Global Compact that had appeal for the ICFTU, it sought assurances in three areas:

- The Global Compact should be depoliticised. The ICFTU did not believe that the Global Compact should take positions on controversial international political issues such as the link between workers' rights and trade at the WTO but should, rather, stick to its purpose.

- The Global Compact should not be seen as a 'code of conduct'. This was particularly important because the trade union movement did not wish to see the Global Compact undercut the OECD Guidelines for Multi-national Enterprises,[3] which were being revised at that time.

---

3   For details of the OECD Guidelines, see www.oecd.org/department/0,2688,en_2649_34889_1_1_1_1_1,00.html.

● Trade unions need to be recognised as full dialogue partners grouped separately from business and from other civil-society organisations, even though the Global Compact challenge itself was directed at companies.

10.2.1 Depoliticisation of the Global Compact

On the first point, the ICFTU argued for the depoliticisation of the Global Compact. As a private initiative launched by the UN Secretary-General, the status of the Global Compact has benefited from the leadership of the UN Secretary-General while remaining informal enough to allow experimentation. The danger of placing this initiative, by its very nature not very official, in a major faultline of global political debate was clear.

The ICFTU has never shared the notion that it is necessary to put binding, enforceable rules into place at the global level to protect commerce, while at the same time considering it inappropriate to protect basic human rights, including workers' rights, with only moral force. In other words both property and people should be worthy of global rules. A division between the economic and social is an ideological choice that does not exist in people's daily lives. Respect for rights as fundamental as, for example, the right to organise and to bargain collectively does not depend on levels of development. That does not mean, of course, that in fact the results of such bargaining in terms of wage levels and other economic issues do not reflect the level of development or other factors.

Trade unions have never asked for support for their position on workers' rights and trade from the Global Compact. When a decision was made by the international trade union movement to participate in the Global Compact, however, it was agreed with the UN that 'global markets required global rules', the same language that was contained in the joint UN–ICC statement a year earlier.

10.2.2 Codes of conduct and the Global Compact

The second major issue concerned 'codes of conduct'. From the beginning, the international trade union movement saw the value of the Global Compact mainly as a catalyst and basis for global dialogue rather than as a code of conduct. The trade union movement had participated in the development of the OECD Guidelines for Multinational Enterprises, adopted in 1976, and in shaping the ILO Tripartite Declaration of Principles Concerning Multinational Enterprises and Social Policy in 1977. Those were considered codes of conduct at the time when the UN 'transnational' code exercise was carried out. This process took more than ten years and, ultimately, failed to be completed and adopted.

More recently, unilateral company initiatives, largely responding to the scandals related to abuses of workers in the supply chain resulted in the issuing of new 'codes of conduct'. These codes were not related to the OECD and ILO codes. Most of them, especially at the beginning, did not even contain core labour standards. There was, therefore, at the time of the launch of the Global Compact, some confusion over terms.

At the same time that the Global Compact was being developed and launched, the OECD was engaged in a review process of the OECD Guidelines. The context for the review was the failure to agree and adopt the Multilateral Agreement on Investment (MAI), a proposal designed to provide a multilateral instrument covering investment. Fixing terms for investment was already taking place in a fast-growing number of bilateral agreements. The MAI generated a great deal of controversy and revived concerns about the role of enterprises in the world. The OECD Guidelines were originally adopted in a climate of scepticism and concern about the role of multinational enterprises. In the intervening period, most governments tended to devote their efforts to obtaining investment from multinational enterprises (MNEs)—even, in some cases, using violations of workers' rights as investment incentives—rather than trying to influence their behaviour in a positive way. Except during the early years, the OECD Guidelines remained largely dormant. That was even truer for the ILO Tripartite Declaration; which still lacks an effective implementation mechanism.

There are consultative bodies that work with the OECD—the Business and Industry Advisory Committee (BIAC) to the OECD, and the Trade Union Advisory Committee (TUAC) to the OECD. BIAC and TUAC participated in the work that led to the adoption of the OECD Guidelines in 1976 and in subsequent reviews and revisions. A section on the environment as well as sections covering other issues were subsequently added, and recent revisions have also included consultations with a group of NGOs.

The Ministerial Council of the OECD adopted the revised Guidelines in June 2000. Although the Council made some changes in content—including making it clear that the Guidelines apply to companies from OECD countries wherever they operate in the world and not just in OECD countries, and extending them in a limited manner to supply chains—the most significant changes related to the implementation of the Guidelines.

OECD and other adhering governments (several non-OECD countries adhere to the Guidelines) must establish national contact points (NCPs) that are responsible for making the Guidelines work. The NCPs are also charged with promoting the Guidelines with external and internal investors. The requirement to establish NCPs is not new. However, they are now expected to make public the outcomes and conclusions of cases (unless there is agreement among the parties not to do so), to report on their activities to the OECD and, on an annual basis, to meet and discuss the effectiveness of their work. Although the effectiveness of the NCPs still varies enormously, the revision has brought hope that they can become more useful and has generated several dozen useful cases.

Although they are not legally binding, unlike the unilateral or 'new' codes of conduct the Guidelines are not voluntary. Companies are not free to pick and choose among their provisions. Cases are handled on alleged breaches of the Guidelines in the same manner, regardless of whether or not companies have endorsed the Guidelines. BIAC and TUAC support the Guidelines. The ILO Tripartite Declaration was adopted by the tripartite ILO Governing Body and, like the Guidelines, can credibly claim to have that extra legitimacy of support from the social partners.

That the Global Compact is not considered to be a code of conduct is important in this context. It cannot be seen as a stripped-down version of the Guidelines by companies and as an alternative to it. It is also important that it not be seen as a more credible imitation of the new codes of conduct, which depended neither on dialogue nor on well-defined, universal standards.

Although the OECD Guidelines are fairly simple and are not very detailed they do, nevertheless, incorporate general provisions that are not contained in the principles of the Global Compact, although they do not conflict with them. In addition to the areas covered by the Global Compact's original nine principles, they include the issues of bribery and corruption, information disclosure and con-sultation (including information relevant to corporate governance), employment and industrial relations, consumer protection, science and technology policy, competition and fiscal (tax) responsibilities.

10.2.3 The Global Compact and the role of the trade unions

The role of trade unions was the third major issue in the early discussions between the Global Compact and the ICFTU. Trade unions are, at the same time, part of industry and part of civil society. They do not comfortably fit into either. They are also representative, grouping large numbers of workers in organisations that these workers control and govern (the ICFTU alone has affiliates representing 158 million workers).

If the dialogue built into the Global Compact is to work, it is important for trade unions to be grouped apart from organisations from industry, business and busi-ness associations, as well as from other civil-society organisations (in the organisa-tion of the Global Compact, civil society is a narrow concept, being essentially a grouping of NGOs). This is vital in terms of organising dialogue in a sensible way. It is also fundamental in order to avoid the danger that, on workers' rights issues, some companies might consider that they have satisfied their dialogue responsi-bilities relating to their employees by meeting with non-union civil-society organi-sations rather than engaging in social dialogue with representative organisations in their sectors.

10.2.4 Conclusions

The ICFTU carried out informal consultations with the UN on these three issues, de-politicising the Global Compact, making sure that it was not billed as a code of conduct, and ensuring that trade unions have a place in the Global Compact that reflects their unique nature and role. After these informal consultations, it was necessary, however, to consult the rest of the international free trade union move-ment. The ICFTU does not directly represent workers in specific companies and sectors; in other words, it is not the counterpart of individual enterprises. The global union federations (GUFs), which group trade unions by sector and occu-pation, play that role. They represent private-sector and public-service workers.

There is close co-operation between the ICFTU, TUAC and the ten GUFs, but they are all autonomous from one another, with their own democratic governance structures and decision-making processes.

The elected general secretaries of those trade union bodies considered the informal assurances from the UN on the above three questions (discussed in Sections 10.2.1–10.2.3). After a debate, a delegation was designated to meet with UN Secretary-General Kofi Annan. That meeting, which took place in New York on 20 January 2000, confirmed the assurances that were given by the UN Secretariat. This discussion resulted in trade union support for the Global Compact and the issuing of a joint statement with the UN. Subsequently, the agreement of trade union leaders to engage in the Global Compact was put to the Executive Board of the ICFTU where, following discussion, it was approved. A number of Global Union Federations and TUAC have also discussed the Compact with one, the International Metalworkers' Federation, having decided not to support or participate in it.

10.3 Trade unions and Global Compact policy dialogues

Global Compact policy dialogues have helped to encourage and foster global dialogue. The participation of the trade union movement, although often limited, and the issues raised by unions in Global Compact policy dialogues illustrate the specificity of trade union concerns.

10.3.1 Zones of conflict

The first policy dialogue was on zones of conflict. Much of the focus of the discussion was on specific issues facing MNEs doing business in such zones, including, for example, security issues. The International Federation of Chemical, Energy, Mine and General Workers' Union (ICEM), one of the GUFs, participated in the negotiation of an agreement on security and human rights in oil, gas and mining industries, sponsored by the UK and US governments. The ICEM was involved in the discussions leading up to the agreement and supported it. However, the essence of the trade union contribution related to the role of institutions, particularly trade unions, in dealing with conflict.

At one of the zones-of-conflict meetings a case study was presented on the role played by the Irish Congress of Trade Unions (ICTU) in Northern Ireland. The ICTU includes Catholic and Protestant workers and engages in representation and bargaining. As such, it is by far the largest and most powerful social institution in Northern Ireland that brings together both groups. The case study also presented an organisation created by the ICTU for the purpose of helping enterprises combat sectarian violence at the workplace.

Trade unions, with few exceptions, bring together workers based on their employment rather than their ethnic, religious or other divisions. That does not, of course, eliminate all tensions and conflicts, but it provides an orderly and democratic way, through compromise, to find common ground on common interests and promotes an important self-interest or stake in solidarity. In spite of conflicts, workers also find ways, 'for the greater good', to govern their unions together. Engagement with trade unions by foreign investors can help to ensure that there is a democratic space to acknowledge and resolve conflict in a way that maintains production and furthers the economic interests of enterprises and workers. More importantly, trade unions are schools for democracy that can contribute to the resolution of conflict in the broader society.

Trade unions are finding ways to deal with groups in conflict in their unions: from Rwanda, where the major trade union organisation relaunched itself following the genocide, they organised with, from the beginning, both Hutus and Tutsis and elected people from both groups on its governing bodies; to Bosnia–Herzegovina, where efforts are being made to bring ethnically based unions into closer co-operation. This natural role of trade unions is key to their survival in difficult situations. In this continuing work, it may be worth looking at the potential for labour-management co-operation to contribute not only to economic development but also to the resolution of conflict.

10.3.2 Sustainable development

The second Global Compact policy dialogue was on sustainable development and took place in conjunction with the World Summit on Sustainable Development in Johannesburg from 26 August to 4 September 2002. Although trade unions had been involved in sustainable development for many years, the recognition of the separate roles of business, labour and other civil-society organisations in the Global Compact facilitated a better understanding of worker interests and concerns and improved the quality of the dialogue with NGOs and business.

Workers and their trade unions have an interest in all three pillars of sustainable development (economic, social and environmental). However, these interests are not automatically the same as those of companies or those of environmental NGOs. Even though workers have a concern about the environment in general, but also because they are often the first and most directly affected by dangerous substances and processes, they also have an economic interest in the survival of the enterprise. The workers' interest is therefore both economic and social and it is more focused on the employment aspects of economic and sustainability questions than on the purely financial aspects of the enterprise.

There is no reason to assume that, when restructuring is considered necessary for environmental reasons, either business or advocacy groups will necessarily speak for workers. The independent and representative voice of workers, through their unions, is the only proven way to ensure that economic transition entailing employment effects, if it must happen, takes into account the interests and needs of workers and that it will be 'just'.

Another interesting aspect of issues relating to corporate responsibility emerged from the discussions: that is, the different manner, in spite of the undeniable connection, in which social and environmental responsibilities need to be addressed by business, on the one hand, and by society in general on the other. The social responsibilities of business are large and, to some degree, we have become prisoners of terms that limit those responsibilities. But, whatever term is used, one important origin of CSR is experience with the environment. It is one of the reasons that legitimate scientific notions applied to environmental problems are frequently applied to non-scientific social situations where, often, they cannot work.

Unlike protecting the environment, the crucial factor in the protection of workers is the right to organise, not monitoring and corrective action by others. Although, in some cases, the environment is capable of cleansing itself of pollutants over many years, it cannot act or intervene to protect itself. Humans must take responsibility for the environment. There is no alternative. But, with human beings themselves, outside protection from 'on high' is neither fully effective nor democratic.

Only workers with unions that they control have effective power to protect themselves. Even outside monitoring, or one of the other systems of assurance or verification of trade union rights that may be intended to give workers the right to defend themselves, are problematic. How does one determine, in the absence of a trade union, that freedom of association is being respected? A sensitive device that can measure parts per million of a dangerous substance is much more likely to yield an accurate result than a series of questions about the right to organise addressed to a frightened young woman working in an export-processing zone surrounded by barbed wire.

10.3.3 HIV and AIDS

The Global Compact policy dialogue on HIV and AIDS provided an opportunity to gather together UN agencies and others working in this area. Business, labour and other civil-society organisations were given a chance to discuss the fight against the pandemic. Much of the discussion focused on the workplace. It was clear that workplace programmes to fight the problem were much more effective if companies and trade unions co-operated. Among other things, the fight against HIV and AIDS becomes more credible to workers if their trade unions are involved from the beginning.

In connection with the policy dialogue on this issue, the International Organisation of Employers (IOE) and the ICFTU issued an unprecedented joint statement calling for co-operation among employers and trade unions all over the globe. Although recognising existing co-operation, the statement becomes the basis for expansion of common work that can contribute to more effective mobilisation and use of resources. It is also expected to give a boost to the use of the ILO code of practice on HIV and AIDS. The two organisations have, subsequently, recognised and promoted labour management in eight pilot countries in Africa where such relations were already positive and will extend their joint work to other continents.

10.4 Rights, social dialogue and sustainable corporate social responsibility

The OECD Guidelines can help to produce global social dialogue, but they are an accidental by-product that is not built into the process. The ILO, through its tripartite structure, is, in fact, functioning through global dialogue, but largely in order to produce standards, results or activities for application at the national level. There is a deficit of global social dialogue in terms of producing truly international processes in the ILO, yet there may still be some possibilities at this level to develop more useful global dialogue in order to find some global, as opposed to purely local, solutions to the challenges of an increasingly integrated global economy. The Global Compact, in contrast, was specifically designed to be a place where global dialogue, including social dialogue, can take place.

There is a relative explosion, at the international level, of social dialogue, defined as dialogue between employers and trade unions. 'Relative' is an important word. Such dialogue is still atypical, although no longer truly exceptional. It is hard to determine the connection between this expanded dialogue and the Global Compact. Is there a relationship between the social dialogue that we see and the Global Compact or are they both just part of the same phenomenon? If there is not a connection, there should be one.

In spite of their initial exclusion, one of the reasons that the Global Compact held interest for the trade union movement, something that led unions to try to influence it rather than attack it, is that it combined standards with dialogue. Companies made a commitment to standards, not standards that they made up or defined themselves but standards originating in UN bodies. Companies also made a commitment to global dialogue.

This combination of standards and dialogue means, in theory at least, that a multinational company that supports the Global Compact should be willing to talk to its global trade union counterpart. And, given the Global Compact principles, it should be willing to discuss the question of employer interference in the workers' right to organise. This is a major switch for some companies that, historically, would refuse even to meet union representatives or that would meet simply to make the appropriate noises while explaining that they could not possibly override the prerogatives of local management. The opening of doors for serious, credible and representative interlocutors is an important part of the Global Compact and, to the limited extent that it has been tested, it has tended to work. A number of participating companies, particularly in extractive industries, have met with ICEM and resolved problems or reached agreements.

The Global Compact has no system to make judgements on company behaviour, but nothing prevents it from explaining the meaning of the principles if asked. The meaning is based on definitions by the appropriate agencies. Nothing prevents the Global Compact from using its good offices to open up dialogue, at least on an informal basis. The Global Compact Office has already been willing to do that and has helped produce useful social dialogue, leading in some cases to the resolution of problems.

The international trade union movement is realistic and pragmatic. It is not interested in enhancing or destroying company reputations. It is interested in protecting the rights of workers and enabling them to participate in their own lives. It seeks dialogue and agreement, not because it believes and wishes to prove that there are perfect companies but rather because it recognises that no such thing as a perfect company exists. At a national level, collective bargaining agreements are not negotiated and signed to prove that a company is good; rather they are approved on the assumption that there are going to be problems and that there need to be ways to resolve those problems that do the least possible damage to the workers, their companies and their industries.

This approach is the reverse of the CSR reasoning that derives from public relations traditions and motivates many CSR practitioners and their critics. The trade union and industrial relations approach does not seek to prove or certify virtue but rather to establish it. It does not seek to embarrass a company that has made a slip but rather to correct the slip as soon and as quietly as possible. It is dialogue based on rights, and is also dialogue designed to protect rights. It does not exist in order to establish and report on dialogue but rather it exists to further rights and solve problems.

It also assumes that only workers, organised in their own free trade unions, can really protect their rights. Workers are present in their workplace every day the enterprise is doing business and, if they have their own union, they change the balance of power at the workplace. They have power, not empowerment. That is the key to sustainable CSR, not the use of more and more elaborate and detailed management systems or methods or the employment of firms to check and cross-check data from outside. These firms cannot be at the workplace every minute of every day and even when they are at the worksite they are unlikely to see what is really going on. Freedom of association is also a central element of sustainable society, because it gives workers the tools to participate in their own societies and to build and enlarge democracy from below. In doing so, unions also make space for other elements of civil society.

One visible sign of a growing global social dialogue is the growing number of international framework agreements signed between GUFs and MNEs. It indicates a relationship and is the tip of the iceberg of global social dialogue. Just seven years ago, there were only two such agreements; now there are 25, and negotiations are under way to conclude even more. They vary considerably in content, reflecting industrial relations practices, cultures and sector-specific and company-specific factors, but none of them is a collective bargaining agreement. They are, rather, agreements on general principles that serve as the basis for looking into and resolving problems and conflicts.

There is, however, one exception. There is one global collective bargaining agreement. It covers all the usual issues of wages, hours and working conditions. It was signed in July 2000 between the International Transport Workers' Federation (ITF) and an association of shipowners and ship managers, created for that purpose—the International Maritime Employers' Council (IMEC). It is not, by itself, a solution to a generations-long problem of flags-of-convenience shipping. Regulation and law enforcement are also required, but this is a private, negotiated part of the solution to those abuses.

10.5 Perspective, problems and opportunities for the Global Compact

The Global Compact has been launched at the national level in many countries. Unfortunately, when it has done so it has far too often abandoned its commitment to involve a wide variety of actors, even in some counties with long traditions of tripartism and social dialogue. Often, national Global Compact activities have been carried out without any consultation with or involvement of trade unions. In some cases, the representative national employers' organisations have been ignored as well. This failing has repeatedly been brought to the attention of the Global Compact Office, but with little response. This has undermined support for the Global Compact at the national level with growing numbers of excluded trade unions considering the Compact to be an empty promise. In addition, international trade union support for the Global Compact is not as strong as it once was.

This failure risks seriously damaging the impact of the Global Compact. The vast majority of the world's workers do not work for multinational firms; nor do they work in the supply chains of those firms. If national activities had involved companies, including small and medium-sized enterprises (SMEs), trade unions and civil-society organisations in a way that was linked with the Global Compact at the international level it might have helped to bring the principles to life in some of the areas where they are needed the most. Even though this would not substitute for legal adoption and enforcement of standards, it would at least have set off the right kind of dialogue.

Another important issue is that an understanding of the meaning of the standards at the national level should not be assumed. Much should be done by the Global Compact to ensure that the meaning of the principles is understood if real support for them is to be expected.

Another weakness of the Global Compact is the lack of links to existing, legitimate, instruments that can play an important complementary role with the Global Compact. The ILO Tripartite Declaration of Principles Concerning Multinational Enterprises and Social Policy has not proven effective in handling specific cases, but its provisions, which contain the labour standard principles of the Global Compact, as well as many other labour standards, could be used to enrich Global Compact dialogues at the national, regional, sub-regional and sectoral levels. They would also be helpful to companies and trade unions wishing to go beyond the fundamental rights and develop better standards and practices. The OECD Guidelines for Multinational Enterprises should also be considered a complementary set of standards that could form part of a global dialogue and, because of the role of governments and the expectations of governments, help create a better climate for standards and rights.

The Global Compact has focused on individual enterprises but, until now, very little has been done at the sectoral level, in spite of the fact that sectors play a very important part in determining the nature and characteristics of dialogue. Stronger sectoral work could help companies work together and begin to develop employer dialogue with their partners from the international trade union structures, thus enhancing the reach and quality of global dialogue.

There needs to be realism and an understanding of the limits of voluntary action in the face of a combination of government and market realities. The policies of governments and their governance capacities are far from irrelevant to company behaviour. If we oversimplify a bit, we can say there are some countries where companies are forced to respect rights, others where they are not allowed to do so and a large third group where they are not forced to respect rights but are allowed to do so. In fact, it is in that third situation where enlightened management policies can have the greatest impact. Combined with the legal situation, there are market pressures that make it very difficult to avoid operating in some countries where full respect of rights is not possible.

It is better to recognise that reality than to try to redefine the standards to meet the lowest common denominator. There are many situations in the world that are not 'win–win'. There are places where ruthless exploitation and abuse are daily facts of life. Large numbers of companies in China declaring their support for the Global Compact will not constitute progress unless those companies are willing to live by the principles, even if it means being kicked out of the country.

With all of its weaknesses and imperfections, however, the Global Compact has already stimulated a much-needed global dialogue, and it has the potential to create more. It carries the seeds of success as well as failure. Its future is not assured, but it is has promise.

The Global Compact is not a 'magic bullet' that can cure the ills of the world. However, dialogue, including social dialogue, is a process that is indispensable if globalisation is to better serve the interests of the people. And it can and must be used by the global social actors to move the world forward.

The Global Compact does not offer binding rules but, even if those standards were in place, the world, like the nation-state, could not rely on regulation alone. The potential for the Global Compact is perhaps best understood in the context of national experience. The countries in which the protection of rights is most effective do not depend on regulation and state solutions alone. It is true that they establish binding frameworks of rights, but the actors in society do the rest. For example, the right of workers to organise and engage in collective bargaining is protected but, through free bargaining, it is the parties, not the government, that determine the outcome. In many countries, the regulations themselves are not put in place without careful consideration and, sometimes, at the initiative of the social partners.

Human rights and workers' rights have never been fully protected at the national level, nor has the environment been cleaned up without binding rules. There is no reason to believe that the market alone will produce at the global level what it has never produced at the national level. Global, binding frameworks to protect rights will emerge in the global economy. In the long-term, the Global Compact, in some form or another, must continue and progress. Global dialogue, including social dialogue, needs to become a serious means to develop global and binding frameworks. It is also needed to begin to build the necessary trust and wisdom to establish effective global dialogue traditions and habits to help create a globalisation that produces both wealth and justice.

11
The UN Global Compact
A triple-win partnership*

Michael Hougård Pedersen
Novozymes, Denmark

As 'the most creative reinvention of the UN to be seen yet' (*CSM* 2000: 10), the Global Compact more than anything else symbolises the end of 'decades of mutual hostility and suspicion' (Capella 1999: 25), 'sometimes antagonism' (ICC 2001a), between the UN and business—a change that Kofi Annan, the UN Secretary-General, initiated shortly after he took office in 1997 by declaring the importance of redefining the organisation's relationship with business (Cohen 2001: 188). Thus, acknowledging the fact that 'the goals of the United Nations and business can be mutually supportive' (ICC 2001a), 'the way the United Nations regards international business has changed fundamentally' (Cattaui 1998):

> The Organisation has undergone a complete overhaul that I have described as a 'quiet revolution'. We are becoming better equipped to face the challenges of a new global era. And we are in a stronger position to work with business and industry. If reform was the dominant theme of my first year in office, the role of the private sector in economic development was a strong sub-theme. A fundamental shift has occurred. The United Nations once dealt only with governments. By now we know that peace and prosperity cannot be achieved without partnerships involving governments, international organisations, the business community and civil society. In today's world, we depend on each other (Annan 1998).

---

* This chapter, the contents of which do not necessarily reflect the official positions of the entities mentioned, is based on the author's MSc dissertation in political science (Pedersen 2003).

In that respect the Global Compact clarifies the fact that business in general and multinational corporations (MNCs) in particular have become very important players in international relations, just as the initiative makes clear that the business community for the first time acknowledges the UN's 'role as a stabilising force in economic and social affairs' (Capella 1999: 25), takes on itself broader societal responsibility and engages in international relations. At the same time, the Global Compact also proves that a new relationship between governments and the UN is evolving, with the UN taking on itself an unprecedented autonomous role *vis-à-vis* the member-state governments.

The incentives of the UN, governments and business that are enabling these changes are subject to analysis throughout this chapter and indicate that the Global Compact constitutes a triple-win partnership and possibly 'the only way to achieve [the UN's] increasingly complex missions with scarce resources in the 21st century' (Reinicke *et al.* 2000: xxi). In fact, 'the future of the world body may well depend on the judgement it exercises in managing its relationship with business' (Cohen 2001).

11.1 UN incentives

By intentionally launching the Global Compact without formally asking the member-state governments in advance, the UN has proven that international relations can be in the nature of more than just the sum of bargains between governments. Accordingly, by taking on itself an unprecedented autonomous role *vis-à-vis* member-state governments, despite initial opposition from a substantial number of these, the UN is now for the first time in the history of the organisation co-operating closely and directly with business.

Overridingly, the UN holds four main incentives for launching a ground-breaking initiative as the Global Compact: advancing the objectives of the organisation, regaining respect and relevance, promoting a more balanced global governance regime and remedying the lack of funding.

With regard to advancing the objectives of the organisation the UN has come to acknowledge the fact that business is much in the ascendant *vis-à-vis* governments. Thus, private capital flows 'now represent close to 80% of the total resources that accrue to developing countries each year' (Bellamy 1999), whereas official development assistance is decreasing. As a result, engagement with business is seen as imperative for advancing the objectives of the organisation (Annan 2001a). Inasmuch as business can support advancement of the UN's peace and development objectives (ICC 2001b):

> Let there be no mistake: the United Nations needs the world's businessmen and businesswomen: as promoters of trade and investment; as employers and entrepreneurs; as experts on globalisation; in short, as full partners in our global mission of peace and development (Annan 1999a).

More specifically, the UN sees the Global Compact as a way of fostering multilateral development assistance through profiting from the financial, technological and managerial resources of participating MNCs (Annan 1997), either in the form of MNCs introducing a more socially responsible way of doing business globally and/or in the form of partnerships (Annan 2001b: 8, 10). As a beneficial ripple effect the Global Compact also advances the UN's 'mounting frustration with many governments' failure to impose humane labour and human rights standards at home' (*Washington Post* 2000: A06) in the sense that the initiative shows those member-state governments that are unresponsive to their people's needs a better way of governance (*CSM* 2000):

> You don't need to wait for governments to pass laws before you ensure that your operations do not pollute the lake or water that produces fish for the people. You don't need to wait for governments to pass laws before you pay a decent wage. You don't need to wait for governments to pass laws before you refuse to employ children (Annan, quoted in United Nations 2000b).

Furthermore, acknowledging that safeguarding open markets has a vital role to play in achieving the objectives of the UN, the organisation has come to the conclusion that thriving markets can help to create the conditions necessary for development and peace, and that 'open markets offer the only realistic hope of pulling billions of people in developing countries out of abject poverty' (Annan 2000c). In that respect, the Global Compact constitutes a means of ensuring that human rights, environmental and labour issues are not introduced within the framework of the World Trade Organisation (WTO), where they inevitably would end up as a pretext for protectionism (Ruggie, Source 7).[1] Such a backlash 'would hurt the developing countries more than anybody else' (Ruggie, Source 7).

As for the incentive of regaining respect and relevance, 'there was an enormous amount of internal politics within the UN to get [the Global Compact] off the ground' (Weintraub, Source 9) at a time characterised by the World Bank poaching on other intergovernmental organisations' preserves, the unique power of the WTO and the devaluing of member-state governments *vis-à-vis* MNCs (Buchan and Hoyos 2000):

> The world around us is changing, and we change with it or we will be left behind. We have to adapt to the realities outside (Annan, quoted in Crossette 2000: 1).

More specifically, the UN believes that there is a political 'window of opportunity' for regaining the organisation's relevance in the backlash to globalisation by 'position[ing] the United Nations as part of the solution to tensions; both at the global rule-making level and at the micro-level for social change' (Kell 2001a). Hence, responding to the fact that 'rules favouring the expansion of global markets have become fairly robust, while those intended to promote social objectives . . . continue to lag behind' (Kell 2001a), the Global Compact 'provides an opportunity

---

1 For more details of the sources, see the Sources section at the end of this chapter.

to experiment with new approaches to global governance and standard setting' (Annan 2001b: 10f.) in areas such as human rights, environment, labour and development:

> Probably most importantly, [launching the Global Compact] would offer a new point of departure for developing a broader case for balancing global governance in favour of developmental, social and environmental concerns. This could be achieved by strengthening the link between progress on economic regime making with progress on non-market institutions and mechanisms, thus using the diverging forces that are influencing the formation of the former for a positive approach on the latter (Kell 1998).

At the same time, projecting the UN's values and principles as defining a framework of universal standards, against which business behaviour can be judged, the Global Compact is seen a way of 'creating greater public awareness and reaching a wider audience by having companies speaking out in favour of the [organisation]' (Annan 2001b: 10f.). In that sense, the Global Compact is perceived as particularly boosting the three UN agencies charged with human rights, labour and the environment: the Office of the High Commissioner on Human Rights (OHCHR), the International Labour Organisation (ILO) and the United Nations Environment Programme (UNEP), respectively (Kell 2001a).

Last, the Global Compact also represents a response to the UN's funding crisis at the end of the 1990s, which originates from the 'pinch in donations from governments' (Hoyos 2000: 1) and billions of dollars in back dues remaining unpaid; largely from the USA (Knight 2000: 34). In that respect, launching the Global Compact represents a way of getting support from a very strong player in the form of MNCs advocating government funding for the UN and channelling direct financial contributions to the developing countries through partnership projects (Knight 2000: 34).

However, although the UN holds many and weighty incentives for launching the Global Compact, the organisation had actually no intention of 'embark[ing] on a major initiative' (Kell 2001a), as Kofi Annan went to the World Economic Forum in Davos, Switzerland, in January 1999 to present the Global Compact to business:

> Honesty requires us to say that this was an accidental project. It did not start out as a project. It started out as a speech. [The] Secretary-General was considering whether or not to attend the Davos meeting in January 1999, and he essentially said: 'I will only go if we can come up with a major challenge to the business community. Otherwise, I am staying home. I went last year' (Ruggie, Source 7).

Contrary to expectations, the response to Kofi Annan's speech was extraordinary, and in six months the UN realised that the organisation had to develop the idea further and build on an organisational framework (Kell 2001a).

In this process, the UN had to deal with numerous difficult dilemmas regarding the structure of the Global Compact, not least devising a framework that was both true enough to the organisation's conviction of meeting criticism and attractive enough to get business to sign up. Additionally, defining the areas to cover, the rules for entry and the players to involve were also seen as involving difficult dilemmas.

With regard to the areas to cover, it was decided to frame the Global Compact around global issues such as trade and globalisation, corporate citizenship, human rights, environmental protection and labour rights, as these issues are most important at the business level as to 'operational and strategic relevance' (Annan 2001b: 32-34). However, in order to avoid having to ask for authorisation from the member-state governments in the UN General Assembly, the rooting of these issues in intergovernmental agreements constituted a prerequisite too:

> We had to base the principles on something that states had already agreed to . . . and then we could turn around and say: 'well, you already agreed to this, we are just implementing—that is what secretariats do; governments decide and secretariats implement . . . What we are doing is, we are implementing it in the context of a universe of actors that you did not have in mind when you formulated those principles. You thought of only states, but we have learned that private actors and civil-society groups are important players in this, and so we are just extending what you, our masters, have decided . . . If you threw this into the General Assembly in 1999, the process would have been hijacked by countries that do not like the private sector, do not like human rights, do not like the environment and do not like labour standards. So it would not have been a pretty code . . . For every Denmark [the home country of this author] there are five or six countries that are on opposite sides of all of those issues, and it would have gotten all wrapped up in Group of 77 politics and would have produced something that was not going to advance the cause (Ruggie, Source 7).

For that reason, it was decided not to include principles on corruption, community involvement and development, although there was both preference and pressure for doing so (Kell, Source 5).

In line with that, the idea of a mandatory code of conduct was never really an option for the UN, predominantly because the organisation wanted to take advantage of the existence of progressive business leaders, but also because the member-state governments would necessarily have to negotiate such a code. From a logistical, financial and judicial point of view such a code would also be very difficult to enforce (Ruggie, Source 7).

Additionally, as one of the main objectives of launching the Global Compact was to establish a model of global governance, the UN realised at an early stage that the initiative 'needed to be broadly based and rooted in different social actors and communities' (Ruggie, Source 7). For that reason, it was decided to pursue a multi-stakeholder approach:

> The world cannot be run by an alliance between business and the United Nations. It is not credible; it is not legitimate; it does not have the expertise. And so, we wanted not only to enlist the business community to achieve certain substantive objectives; we also wanted the Global Compact as a test case . . . a model of global governance, and that had to be by definition multi-stakeholder in character (Ruggie, Source 7).

However, throughout the process business was seen as the critical and first partner, with other partners coming in afterwards. Thus, 'the key challenge was to motivate businesses to act out of self-enlightened interest' (Kell 2001a) and, for that reason, the UN decided to bring along both business associations and individual MNCs: business associations, as they are key to institutional follow-up and are the only actors to circumvent the collective problems faced by individual MNCs; individual MNCs, because they are seen as key opinion-makers within business associations and as doers and pace-setters at the practical level (Kell 1998).

As for the selection of non-governmental organisations (NGOs) to be included in the Global Compact framework, pleasing business again played a major role. Thus, the UN invited only those NGOs 'work[ing] at the global level that are responsible, knowledgeable, with high reputations and that want to work with business and labour to make a difference' (Doyle, Source 3).

Last, but not least, the UN decided to set up a particular Global Compact Trust Fund, which accepts donations only from UN member-state governments and not-for-profit entities (United Nations 2002c: 9). Financing the Global Compact through this trust fund and not directly via private capital was seen as a means to ensure the integrity of the initiative.

11.2 Governmental incentives

The position of member-state governments towards the Global Compact to a large extent reflects the attitude of major MNCs based in their respective countries. Thus, European member-state governments initially favoured the Global Compact along with a substantial number of European-based MNCs. The US government was 'sitting on the fence', as were the vast majority of US-based MNCs, because of a general suspicion of the UN (Ruggie, Source 7). In addition to that, a substantial number of member-state governments from developing countries and MNCs based in these countries originally raised objections against the Global Compact, predominantly because they were afraid that the initiative was just another protectionist set-up to be imposed on them by the developed countries (Kell 1998):

> The Swiss were delighted already at Davos [in 1999]. Most of the EU members, the Scandinavians in particular, were very excited. The British were very strong almost from the very beginning . . . objections came from a number of developing countries . . . those countries included . . . Egypt, . . . India, . . . Algeria, [and] Cuba (Ruggie, Source 7).

Despite this conflict of interests, however, more than 70 member-state governments from both North and South ended up endorsing the Global Compact at the conclusion of the UN General Assembly debate on partnerships, which took place at the end of 2001 (Doyle and Kell 2002). This consensus, which is 'unusual for the General Assembly' (Doyle and Kell 2002), indeed indicates a favourable bargaining position of MNCs *vis-à-vis* governments. Thus, participating companies, especially those based in developing countries, successfully lobbied the support of their respective governments. As a result of that, many sceptical member-state governments ended up endorsing the Global Compact as a useful means of capacity-building and of achieving recognition, and thereby market access, internationally:

> Last summer's debate on partnerships was a very important turning point. When the General Assembly went into that debate, the Group of 77 countries that were interested in it were interested in it because they thought it would be a way to pull back the Global Compact. [The General Assembly] ended up essentially endorsing the approach, and the reason it ended up endorsing the approach was because of countries like Brazil, like India and several other major developing countries, which had had some experience with the Global Compact in the meantime, and encouraged their colleagues in the Group of 77 to give it a chance and to see what it could produce, before . . . yanking the carpet out from under its feet (Ruggie, Source 7).

In addition, a substantial number of governments favour an enhanced regime for intergovernmental co-operation, acknowledging the fact that they have become subject to conflicting policy pressures on trade, social issues and the environment (Kell 1998). In that respect, many governments see the Global Compact as a means of pursuing national policy goals in a conflict-ridden policy environment without risking a tough national politicisation of sensitive issues such as strict rules of conduct for MNCs.

Along the same lines, governments have also come to realise that MNCs possess gargantuan capabilities in the form of financial resources, transfer of technology and management expertise (Kamyab 2001), which give them real potential in advancing developmental objectives. Thus, many governments believe that 'the Global Compact has the potential to make bigger changes for the poor around the world, than [their] traditional aid programmes, [which are even undergoing cuts,] have ever done' (Brittain 2000: 12).

Last, some governments support the Global Compact as a means of advancing national capacity-building (e.g. the Russian government):

> The involvement of Russian business circles in the co-operation with the [UN] in the framework of the Global Compact has major advantages both in terms of the development of the socially responsible national private sector and as a possible way to strengthen its international positions. We also see there certain opportunities for attracting foreign private capital and technologies to the Russian economy. Such partnership relations are equally important for the introduction to and promotion in Russian business practice of international standards in the field of management, accounting, audit and environmentally safe production (Ordzhonikidze 2001).

On the other hand, however, some governments still do not support the Global Compact, because they fear that the initiative could strengthen the autonomy of the UN at the expense of member-state governments (Pfaff 2000).

11.3 Business incentives

Although MNCs do not constitute a homogenous group as to attitudes towards corporate citizenship in general and towards the Global Compact in particular, the notion of corporate citizenship is increasingly becoming a competitive parameter. Thus, incentives of the MNCs participating in the Global Compact predominantly include reputation and risk management as well as access to expanding markets.

As regards reputation and risk management, companies participating in the Global Compact acknowledge that 'the successful companies [to come] will be those that are better and have more to offer than the competition' (Tandy 2001: 2). To these MNCs, participation in 'the Global Compact makes perfect business sense' (*IHT* 2001) inasmuch as the initiative constitutes a global reference point of universal principles with 'a critical element of social legitimacy that ad hoc arrangements lack' (Ruggie 2001). Hence, the Global Compact gives participating MNCs the opportunity of formulating a legitimate response to globalisation sceptics that is not subjected to varying single-issue pressure (Kell 1998). In that sense, the Global Compact provides better risk management, because the initiative can be used as a global management tool to create added value in the relationship with a broad circle of stakeholders (e.g. employees, customers and society at large), thereby proactively 'securing "license to operate" internationally' (Geir Westgaard, Vice President of Statoil, quoted in UN News Service 2001).

However, the reputation and risk management strategies of the MNCs participating in the Global Compact vary to a large extent. Accordingly, some MNCs, predominantly active either in the natural resource sector or in selling high-branded consumer products, 'have paid a high price for "shaming and blaming" in the media' (Kell 1998) because of their exposure in terms of operations 'on the ground' or in terms of their supply chain. These MNCs join the Global Compact to re-establish a good reputation (Ruggie, Source 7), not least with a view to attracting and retaining the best talent. Other MNCs, especially Scandinavian-based ones, have come to view global corporate citizenship as a natural extension of corporate citizenship in their home countries (Ruggie, Source 7). In addition, another group of MNCs join the Global Compact purely for reputational purposes, without the intention of actually changing the way in which they do business (Kell 1998). Last, but not least, MNCs from developing countries, although relatively small in number, have their own particular motive for joining the Global Compact; they believe that participation in the initiative is 'required to be taken seriously as a global player' (Ruggie, Source 7).

As to the incentive of gaining access to expanding markets, MNCs sign up to the Global Compact with a view to maximising business opportunities. Thus, having realised that their home markets are characterised by 'highly competitive low margins' (Clements-Hunt, Source 2), and that the market of the next 50 years therefore lies in the rest of the world (Clements-Hunt, Source 2), MNCs, particularly the ones active in the field of energy, participate in the Global Compact expecting to gain 'access to development expertise' (Annan 2001b: 10f.) and to gain from specific activities. In addition, consulting MNCs have a definite marked related interest in supporting and promoting the Global Compact, because the initiative 'creates a new market for auditing' (Kell 1998).

Along with acknowledging the importance of corporate citizenship, the companies participating in the Global Compact also attach importance to the fact that the Global Compact provides the hitherto best framework for sparring and mutual learning within the field of corporate citizenship—a business area still lacking clear international standards:

> It is beyond doubt that participating in the [Global] Compact enables you to be ahead in the discussions on corporate responsibility and globalisation; there is no better place to discuss these issues. It is also beyond doubt that at the closed discussions, where we discuss the problems surrounding these issues, you get marvellous sparring. The openness surrounding these numerous questions is very constructive, because it is obvious that discussing these issues is everything but simple; they are all-encompassing (Berthelsen, Source 1).

At the same time, the voluntary and non-binding Global Compact set-up receives a lot of sympathy from many MNCs (Weintraub, Source 9).

On the other hand, however, the majority of MNCs 'continue to reject the notion of corporate citizenship' (Kell 1998). The incentives of these MNCs (e.g. companies making heavy of energy), for not joining the Global Compact are twofold: suspicion towards the UN, as well as the risk of added exposure and losing out to competitive free-riders.

With regard to their suspicion of the UN, 'some companies perceive the UN to be a slow, cumbersome and difficult organisation to work with' (Moorcroft, Source 6). As for the risk of added exposure and losing out to free-riders, these notions are rooted in the fact that the business case for environmental, human and labour rights is not yet fully established. Thus, a participating MNC may expose itself to criticism to an unnecessary degree and leave competitors with a competitive advantage as free-riding non-participants:

> I am well aware that adhering to the [Global] Compact requires you to take some risks. After all, the business case for human and labour rights and the environment is not yet established fully, and those who help to make it—those who are at the forefront of change—are exposing themselves to heightened scrutiny. Labour and civil society will question your sincerity, while your competitors, who remain silent, get a free ride (Annan 2002).

MNCs not participating in the Global Compact also have structural reasons for hesitating to join the initiative. Hence, these MNCs fear a prescriptive evolution of the Global Compact into a more binding framework; either at the national and/or at the international level (Clements-Hunt, Source 2). Furthermore, particularly US-based MNCs have difficulties accepting the labour component (Ruggie, Source 7), just as they hesitate to participate in the Global Compact, because of the particular juridical system in the USA (Weintraub, Source 9).

In line with these observations, although there was a lot of tension within the International Chamber of Commerce in terms of how to play the Global Compact (Clements-Hunt, Source 2), the business community generally acknowledged that the objectives of the UN are essential in achieving the collective business goals of wealth creation and prosperity (Töpfer 2000: 39). In that respect, the Global Compact is seen as an attractive means of sustaining the multilateral trade regime and creating new markets.

Consequently, supporting and promoting the Global Compact offers the possibility of safeguarding the functioning of open markets by 'building bridges between trade and environment, between trade and labour and between trade and human rights' (Annan 1999b). Keeping these issues out of the WTO lowers the risk of damaging the effectiveness of the multilateral trade regime; a risk that the business community has taken seriously since the rise of massive globalisation protests, which were initiated at the 3rd Ministerial Meeting of the WTO in Seattle at the end of 1999:

> Labour unions, NGOs and others are keen to bring social issues back to the WTO. They keep under close scrutiny progress made at the ILO. The international business community regards the ILO Tripartite Declaration of Principles Concerning Multinational Enterprises and Social Policy as the second best choice. It is aware that unless real progress is made this issue will bounce back to the WTO. This has built up enormous pressure to show progress and provides the single most important motivation for the business community to collectively engage in a search for solutions (Kell 1998).

Finally, as to the Global Compact's prospects of creating new markets, the business community has come to recognise that 'much of the dramatic [economic] growth in the world today is led by [developing] countries' (Annan 1997). Therefore, 'a strong United Nations is good for business' (Annan 1998), just as a stronger UN constitutes a major source of bringing '60% of the world's population into the market' (Annan 1997) by creating an environment within which business can function and succeed (Annan 1998).

11.4 Conclusions

The analysis of incentives of the UN, governments and business for co-operating within the framework of the Global Compact indicates that the initiative constitutes a triple-win partnership.

Overridingly, the UN holds four main incentives for launching the Global Compact:

- To advance the objectives of the organisation
- To regain respect and relevance
- To promote a more balanced global governance regime

● To remedy the lack of funding

In addition, governments predominantly support the Global Compact for three reasons:

● To advance the realisation of the UN's objectives

● To handle conflicting national policy pressures

● To advance national capacity-building

Governmental incentives for opposing the Global Compact mainly include the creation of a more autonomous UN and suspicions that the initiative may represent hidden protectionism.

Last, but not least, the business incentives for participating in the Global Compact are primarily twofold:

● To enhance reputation and to manage risk

● To gain access to new markets

The reputation and risk management strategies vary to a large extent. Some MNCs join the Global Compact to re-establish a good reputation, whereas others join for purely reputational purposes without the intention of actually changing the way in which they do business. Additionally, some MNCs believe that participation in the initiative is required in order to be taken seriously as a global player.

The business incentives for not joining the Global Compact mainly include suspicion towards the UN and the risk of added exposure and of losing out to competitive free-riders.

Sources

Source 1 Interview with Jens Berthelsen, then Senior Consultant, Danish Federation of Industries, 16 January 2002, at Danish Federation of Industries Headquarters, Copenhagen, Denmark.

Source 2 Telephone interview with Paul Clements-Hunt, former Advisor on Environment and Energy, International Chamber of Commerce, then Head of Unit, UNEP Finance Initiatives, 12 February 2002.

Source 3 Interview with Michael Doyle, then Assistant UN Secretary-General and Special Advisor to the UN Secretary-General, 8 February 2002, at UN Headquarters, New York, USA.

Source 4 Interview with Pernille Fabricius, former Chief Financial Officer, ISS A/S, then Chief Financial Officer, GN Netcom, 16 January 2002, at GN Netcom Headquarters, Copenhagen, Denmark.

Source 5 Interview with Georg Kell, then Executive Head of the Global Compact Office, 7 February 2002, at United Nations Headquarters, New York, USA.

Source 6 Interview with Dave Moorcroft, then Sustainable Development Director, BP, 8 May 2002, BP Headquarters, London, UK.

Source 7   Interview with John Gerard Ruggie, former Assistant UN Secretary-General and former Chief Advisor for Strategic Planning to the UN Secretary-General; then Director of the Centre for Business and Government as well as Evron and Jeane Kirkpatric Professor of International Affairs at Kennedy School of Government, Harvard University, 5 February 2002, at Harvard University, Boston, MA, USA.

Source 8   Interview with Preben Sørensen, then Global Partner in Charge, Deloitte Touche Tohmatsu Environment and Sustainability, 16 January 2002, at Deloitte Touche Tohmatsu Denmark Headquarters, Copenhagen, Denmark.

Source 9   Telephone interview with Mark Weintraub, then Policy Advisor, Royal Dutch Shell, 7 April 2002.

Please note that quotes from interviews that were carried out in Danish have been translated by the author.

Part 4
Action and learning

12
Reflections on the Global Compact

Chris Tuppen
British Telecommunications, UK

As many of the old centralised economies give way to the ideology of free trade and open markets, governments everywhere are turning to public–private partnerships for practical solutions and financial investment. In this respect, many people recognise that the private sector has much of the expertise needed to address some of the greatest challenges facing the world.

Against this backdrop, Kofi Annan's original 'call to arms' had much logic to it. To create a compact between government, civil society and business seemed to be a way to new fruitful partnerships. Yet in the summer of 2003, whereas non-governmental organisations (NGOs) are complaining that not enough has happened, many businesses are being bombarded with a multitude of Global Compact initiatives and are trying to find links between these and their core business strategies at a time of economic downturn.

BT has been involved in the Global Compact from the very beginning. It participated in the early meetings in New York that formulated the nine principles and felt comfortable from the start that there was a coherence between these principles and the foundations of the company's own management approach to social and environmental issues. It was essentially this coherence of ideology that led the company to 'sign up'.

At this point it is worth remembering that the actual commitment was to:

● Support the principles

● Engage in partnership with the UN

● Post an annual review of progress on the Global Compact website

In this sense the Global Compact felt similar to many other 'charters' BT had committed itself to. In fact, it was already doing much to address the nine principles through its existing corporate social responsibility (CSR) programme and believed that the main result of signing up would be to demonstrate that point in a transparent way—in essence, the aim was to be held accountable for actions (or lack of action!) taken against the commitments the company was making.

At the same time, BT was working with the UN Environment Programme (UNEP) and the International Telecommunications Union (ITU), one of the oldest of all UN institutions, to create an industry-led voluntary initiative in the information and communications technology (ICT) sector. The Global *e*-Sustainability Initiative (G*e*SI) was launched on World Environment Day, 5 June 2001.[1]

12.1 Held to account

Of the three obligations expected of Global Compact signatories, the third (to provide an annual review of progress) was originally linked to the Global Compact Learning Forum, which was designed to encourage experiential learning among signatories and was structured around the submission of case studies.

At that time, BT had just published its first fully integrated, externally verified sustainability report. Within the report it created an index that linked content of the report to the Global Compact's nine principles. In a similar vein it also included an index in relation to the Global Reporting Initiative (GRI)—another initiative with strong UN backing and involvement.[2] It was BT's contention that this approach was the best way of demonstrating its progress against the commitments it had made. Figure 12.1 is taken from the BT 2003 Sustainability Report[3] and illustrates the company's approach in action.

Following the 2001 submission BT received anonymous critical feedback that was clearly more in favour of a highly detailed single case-study submission. Stating, for example, that 'Given the breadth of work showcased, it would be valuable for other Global Compact participants to have at least one worked example of (or a clear signpost to) a project that covered all the issues of development.'

In our experience, such public-domain case studies are often self-selected to demonstrate the company in the best of light and therefore do not give a general overview of the sustainability performance of the business. Also, being in a public space, they are often 'cosmetic' and do not disclose the really valuable learning points: barriers, dead ends and keys to success. One generally finds that such 'behind-the-scenes' comments come out under more intimate discussions conducted under Chatham House rules with no more than 20 people round the table.

In addition, BT had put a huge amount of effort into preparing its sustainability report and had ensured it had a significant external component. The company recommended that the Global Compact recognise this and not expect additional

1 For more details, see www.gesi.org; see also Section 12.5.
2 For details of the GRI, see www.globalreporting.org.
3 See www.bt.com/betterworld.

Global Compact Principles: BT's Communication on Progress

Global Compact principle	BT information
Principle 1: support and respect the protection of international human rights within their sphere of influence;	The Human rights section of the report summarises BT's approach to Principles 1 and 2. BT's potential impact - both positive and negative - on human rights is managed by a number of departments and units throughout the business.
Principle 2: make sure their own corporations are not complicit in human rights abuses.	See above.
Principle 3: freedom of association and the effective recognition of the right to collective bargaining;	The Employee relations section of the report sets out our relationship with trade unions. The Ethical trading section contains details of BT's efforts to ensure freedom of association in our supply chain.
Principle 4: the elimination of all forms of forced and compulsory labour;	The Ethical trading section presents information on BT's efforts to eliminate forced and child labour in our supply chain.
Principle 5: the effective abolition of child labour;	See above
Principle 6: the elimination of discrimination in respect of employment and occupation.	The Equality and diversity section sets out BT's policies and practices relating to the elimination of discrimination in our own employment practices. The Ethical trading section contains details of our efforts to eliminate discrimination in our supply chain.
Principle 7: support a precautionary approach to environmental challenges;	The Mobile phones and health section sets out BT's approach to this issue.
Principle 8: undertake initiatives to promote greater environmental responsibility;	The Environment section includes details of our accreditation to ISO14001 and our performance in each of the eight 'aspects' that we manage.
Principle 9: encourage the development and diffusion of environmentally friendly technologies.	The Benefits section presents the positive social and environmental impacts of communications technology. Our eBusiness and the environment 'Hot Topic' is an independent study into the benefits of BT's own use teleworking and conferencing.

Figure 12.1 **BT's Sustainability Report, July 2003: global compact navigation**   © BT

Source: www.bt.com/betterworld

reporting which the company felt was being driven more by the academic fraternity than by other participants in the Global Compact process.

It is reassuring that the Global Compact has now turned to a more accountability-focused reporting model and explicitly supports the application of the GRI.

12.2 Help please, you're a Global Compact signatory

What does the UN and NGO world expect of Global Compact companies? From inside a company it sometimes feels like the answer to this question is 'deep philanthropic pockets and a capability to address all the world's ills'. Over the past few years BT has been invited to participate in Global Compact initiatives designed to address, *inter alia*: global hunger, HIV and AIDS, operations in zones of conflict, market growth in least-developed countries (LDCs) and communicating sustainability to the financial community.

This often reminds me of the time when, as BT's Environmental Issues Manager, I was telephoned by a campaigning NGO for the company's position on whaling. I explained we didn't have a position on whaling. 'Why not?' the enquirer asked, 'After all, you have a good record on environmental issues'!

Some people have, in all good faith, found it quite difficult to understand that becoming a Global Compact signatory does not mean a company has the resources (in a financial sense or in terms of people) to participate in everything. In fact, some organisations have found it so difficult to take 'no' for an answer that they have escalated their requests to the highest levels in BT, with multiple avalanches of e-mails going to all the main executive directors.

Although this kind of activity certainly raises the profile of the Global Compact, it does so in a way that probably does more harm than good. It casts the Global Compact in a campaigning, almost aggressive light, and endangers an alienation of the Global Compact concept in the business community.

In a note to Georg Kell, the UK group of Global Compact businesses put it 'straight down the line' in a pretty robust fashion:

> Given the Global Compact's objective of raising the level of CSR performance in business, the current mix and involvement of academics, NGOs, government and business is felt to be out of balance. Academics, in particular, are felt to be hijacking the initiative, leaving business sometimes as bemused onlookers. If the object is to change *business*, we would be better served by having a business-led initiative and projects with strong participation from the other parties.
>
> Business should be invited to conceive and lead projects or, at the very least, be involved in their planning at inception rather than being invited to participate later, almost as an afterthought. The approach adopted in a recent ill-conceived initiative was typically unfortunate in that businesses were approached at the last minute

with no opportunity to frame the project to give it a more business-oriented focus. The timetable was set, the deliverables were fixed and business was only approached when funding was required. This modus operandi should be avoided in future (emphasis added).

This is not to say that many of the ideas that people come to the company with are not good ideas, but the approaches are often not thought through from the company's perspective. If they were then I think they would be far more selective. It may, at this point, be worth exploring how that selectivity might develop.

12.3 I'm a Global Compact partner, how can I help?

One of my roles in BT is to embed considerations of sustainable development or CSR into the main commercial programmes of the company. Although I have a strong personal sense of the underlying values behind sustainable development, if I attempt to use these as the basis for CSR integration then I often hit a brick wall. And this is not because the people I am talking to do not share some of those values as well, but because the language of pure moral justification does not sit comfortably in the conventional business lexicon.

If, however, I approach people by saying 'can we discuss how CSR can help you achieve your commercial objectives', the reception is much warmer. This means first understanding what those objectives are and second establishing how CSR risks and opportunities fit in. Together, these two factors deliver an effective 'business case' for sustainable development.

That is not to say for one minute that one 'dumps one's morals' in favour of an amoral business case. As Jonathon Porritt and I state in *Just Values* (2003: 29):

> The business case for sustainable development won't work unless it generates real, lasting trust with all a company's principal stakeholders. And a company can't build trust on an amoral basis. Acting in more socially and environmentally responsible ways for purely instrumental, profit-maximising reasons threatens to undermine rather than build trust. You can't add value without values.

So, the message is that we all need to see matters better from the other's point of view. Civil society is best placed to give guidance to business, but let me venture a few suggestions from the business side:

- Involve business from the very start.

- Avoid scattergun approaches. Don't expect every business to be interested in every initiative simply because it's a 'good thing to do'.

- Understand the sector, and match initiatives to sector players.

- Understand the commercial, CSR and brand proposition strategies of the company being approached—not all operate everywhere in the world for example, or address the same market segments.

- The world's big challenges (e.g. the Millennium Goals; see Appendix A) will not be solved through philanthropic programmes. New millennium partnerships need new ways of engagement and new ways of making a profit.

- Establish initiatives that will become self-sustaining in a financial sense.

12.4 How the Global Compact made a difference in BT

In a number of Global Compact-related forums non-business participants have challenged businesses to disclose what they have done differently as a result of signing the Global Compact commitments. This is often tricky to handle. The Global Compact is definitely one of the more significant of a number of commitments BT has made over the years to support sustainable development and the company often refers to it when explaining to managers why action needs to be taken on a variety of issues. This is not difficult as it is frequently complementary to and supportive of BT's own stance and stated values concerning human rights, the environment and labour relations.

Although BT has connected its support for the Global Compact to many of its CSR activities, as the company website clearly shows, I'm not sure it's possible to say that BT has done anything uniquely specific as a result of signing. That's not to say it does not see the Global Compact as important, but rather that it sees it as synergistic. And that is not to say the Global Compact has not made a difference; it has in terms of further embedding the ethos of CSR into BT.

BT's supply chain activities are a good example. Its Sourcing with Human Dignity (SWHD) initiative was launched in April 2001. The initiative seeks to ensure that the working conditions in BT's supply chain meet international norms. The initiative consists of a set of standards and principles based on the UN Universal Declaration of Human Rights[4] and the International Labour Organisation (ILO) Conventions.[5] It goes beyond legislation in these areas and covers issues such as child labour, forced labour, health and safety, discrimination, working hours and fair remuneration.

This was successful because there was a good match between societal need (improved working conditions) and business benefit (brand protection). However, there is not always such a comfortable match between Global Compact principles and business rationale.

Probably the biggest sustainability challenge directly linked to the ICT industry is the digital divide in the developing world. The Global Compact has further highlighted this, and many approaches to BT on digital divide matters make reference to the Global Compact.

4 For the Universal Declaration, see www.un.org/Overview/rights.html.
5 For details of the ILO Conventions, see www.ilo.org.

For BT this issue more than any other dramatically highlights the distinction between corporate philanthropy on the one hand, and market-led forces making a societal difference on the other. The sheer scale of the investment needed to address the international digital divide means that philanthropic (social investment) gestures, although laudable in their own right, are inevitably just a drop in the ocean.

At the height of dot.com mania BT had global ambitions and, like many others, was investing in new markets, including in some developing countries. Following the market crash of Internet stocks and the massive debts incurred in the auctions for third-generation mobile licences, a retrenchment took place to more traditional markets.

Today, outside the United Kingdom, BT essentially serves only large multi-site organisations. In other words, there is no longer any synergy between BT's commercial strategy and infrastructure investment for mass telecommunications provision in LDCs. This is a classic case of where the 'business case' for CSR runs out.

The inspiration behind the Global Compact commitments is described on the Global Compact website as follows:[6]

> Through the power of collective action, the Global Compact seeks to advance responsible corporate citizenship so that business can be part of the solution to the challenges of globalisation. In this way, the private sector—in partnership with other social actors—can help realise the Secretary-General's vision: a more sustainable and inclusive global economy.

In most instances one can achieve a degree of progress against the Global Compact commitments within the confines of today's business case for sustainable development. Yet, it is almost definitely the case that even if the majority of big global companies were to adopt and meet the Global Compact principles it would be insufficient to deliver a sustainable society. A 'more' sustainable society, perhaps, but not a fully sustainable society.

To achieve this we must adapt our economies to extend today's business case for CSR into new territory, and this needs a much stronger partnership to develop between governments and the business community. In *Just Values*, Jonathon Porritt and I offer some insights into what might need to be done to make this happen (see Fig. 12.2).

12.5 Making the Global Compact a two-way deal

The Global e-Sustainability Initiative (GeSI) is a partnership between ICT companies and the UN in the form of UNEP and the ITU. In many ways it embodies the partnership aspirations of the Global Compact.

Its association with the UN gives it status, but this also ties it down. There has been the usual UN bureaucracy and administrative inefficiency, which makes it

6 See www.unglobalcompact.org.

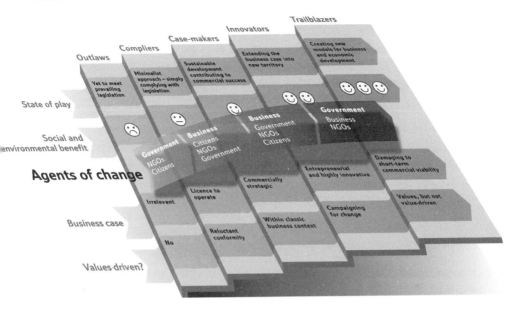

Figure 12.2 Agents of change

© BT

Source: Porritt and Tuppen 2003

frustrating for business people who may be accustomed to quick and empowered decision-making processes, and although the UN links have attracted some companies to join GeSI they have also put many off, especially US companies.

Over the past two years GeSI has been investigating issues surrounding mining of a tantalum ore known as coltan in the Democratic Republic of the Congo (DRC). Tantalum is a metallic element, twice as dense as steel, highly resistant to heat and capable of storing and releasing an electrical charge, making it ideal for miniature capacitors. It is found in several countries, including Australia, Thailand, Nigeria, Canada, Brazil, Malaysia and the DRC.

In the DRC, people are able to make good money by surface-mining coltan, the local tantalum ore, by using shovels and sieves. When demand for tantalum peaked in 2000, DRC miners were able to earn what for them was a staggering US$80 a day. Unfortunately, most of the miners found their coltan deposits in national parks, located in rebel-held areas where warring factions have been responsible for humanitarian atrocities, deforestation, illegal hunting and the wholesale killing of endangered species.

In the past five years, poachers have killed all but two of the 350 elephants that once roamed the Kahuzi Biega National Park. The story is the same for gorillas in the eastern Congo: the population of gorillas was 17,000 in 1999 but is now estimated at no more than 1,000.

Although tantalum has many applications in the electronics, aviation, chemical and medical industries, campaigners have focused on its application in mobile phones. In response, some ICT companies have declared a boycott on the use of Congolese coltan. However, due to smuggling and the nature of the commodity market, it is almost impossible to guarantee that coltan purchased on the 'spot' market is not from the DRC. Furthermore, a blanket boycott may have adverse effects on the DRC, which desperately needs economic investment and support to alleviate poverty.

GeSI, which published a report on the matter in 2003, supports the view that a long-term, sustainable, solution is required (Hayes and Burge 2003). This may involve the establishment of a regulated Congolese coltan market, comprising a buyers' collective that would pay a fair price for ethically mined coltan. Although not the easiest solution, this could contribute significantly to the peace process by providing much-needed economic support to the DRC.

Achievement of this objective will require support from, and more particularly partnership between, all parties of the tantalum supply chain—from refiners to end-users, as well as international institutions and appropriate NGOs.

Members of GeSI have declared their readiness to play a part in such an initiative and have called on an appropriate international organisation, independent of any particular industry sector, to take the lead in making this happen. To many of the members of GeSI the Global Compact seems like a natural choice for this role, though at the time of writing this looks rather unlikely.

12.6 Where next for the Global Compact?

The Global Compact has brought sustainability principles to an increasing number of companies around the world. It has supplemented and re-enforced many other voices and adds weight to the pressure to change.

Up to now, businesses have mostly been at the receiving end of requests of support and involvement, but for those in the ICT industry the coltan issue has turned the tables and it will be interesting to observe the way in which the Global Compact responds to this call for help.

Overall, the challenge remains one of global governance. How can we create the right kind of socioeconomic frameworks that make it profitable for business to deliver significantly greater social and environmental benefit?

13
Learning from company engagement with the Global Compact
The First Global Compact Learning Forum, Denham, UK, November 2001*

Malcolm McIntosh
Independent Commentator

*Ruth Thomas***
Sustainability Researcher

The Global Compact is evolving, the participants are learning and there are many beneficial spin-offs from a process that has been set in motion by this attempt to directly marry market activity and international development. As the number and

* This analysis of company engagement with the Global Compact in phase one of the Learning Forum is based on submissions to the Global Compact from July 2000 to October 2001. It draws on the theory behind the Global Compact and company engagement in the Global Compact Learning Forum as evidenced by submissions to the Global Compact website (www.unglobalcompact.org) during that period. All parties learned from this initial phase and the lessons were applied to the subsequent Learning Forums in Berlin, Germany (2002) and Nova Lima, Brazil (2003). A much longer analysis was published in January 2003 in *Living Corporate Citizenship*, by Malcolm McIntosh, Ruth Thomas, Deborah Leipziger and Gill Coleman and published by Financial Times Prentice Hall. Since the research was carried out on which this chapter is based, the requirement for Global Compact signatories to submit reports has been removed.

   This report was written in December 2001; the company case studies can be found on www.unglobalcompact.org under phase one of the Learning Forum.

** Since 2002, Ruth Thomas has been a Senior Sustainability Advisor, Defence Estates, Ministry of Defence, UK.

scope of global corporate citizenship initiatives increases, it is important to take time out to consider how these new social partnerships between the private, public and civil sectors are evolving. That is the aim of this chapter, which presents the findings from the first phase of the Global Compact. These findings have been presented at a number of public forums, and the ensuing energetic discussion led to a refinement of the data and lengthy debate on a number of distinct topics. It may not have been the intention of the architects of the Global Compact to focus attention on some of these topics but the learning process is possible only if all parties stand back from their entrenched positions. Here are the main topics that have arisen in open discussion:

- The varied nature of company engagement, represented by quality, self-analysis, sector and topic

- The nature of learning on the part of companies *and* the UN

- The reaction of the UN to the findings of this research

- The learning lessons drawn from the data presented by the first wave of companies in their submissions

It is crucial that the information presented here is taken as a starting point for discussion of a central dilemma elucidated by Kofi Annan, the UN Secretary-General, in Davos, Switzerland, presented on 31 January 1999 (see Chapter 1 of this book). It is perhaps the *leitmotif* for the 21st century. He called for a compact 'on the global scale, to underpin the new global economy' (Chapter 1, page 29), asking business 'to embrace, support and enact a set of core values in the areas of human rights, labour standards and environmental practices (page 29). The first phase of the Global Compact was an attempt to engage with business on these principles based on a new approach to change, based on shared learning.

13.1 The Global Compact: a different approach to change

According to John Ruggie (Chapter 2, page 206), one of the architects of the UN Global Compact, the Global Compact has:

> explicitly adopted a learning approach to inducing corporate change, as opposed to a regulatory approach; and it comprises a network form of organisation, as opposed to the traditional hierarchic/bureaucratic form.

It is worth spelling out this approach, which, like the original call to the business community, had received little substantive thinking before being articulated by Ruggie and others in the UN Global Compact Office. First, it says that we must learn as we proceed. In effect, it is saying: 'we don't know what is going to happen; we have high expectations, and we are praying that business engages fully'. Second, it sees a form of organisational learning that breaks metaphysical boundaries between business and non-business communities so that an open enquiry can take place. In doing so it suggests that an outdated mode of learning (the hierarchic or bureaucratic form) has not taught us enough, or is not adequate in a new 'global' age where the challenges have new characteristics.

This has been as much of a challenge to the non-business community as it has to the business community. Although management literature may abound with references to network organisations, horizontal organisational forms and flat management structures, in reality there still seem to be hierarchical forms of management for the gathering and dissemination of information and for public relations.

Originally, supporting companies were asked to present one submission a year to indicate their implementation of one or more of the original nine principles of the Global Compact. This chapter reports on an analysis of the first 33 such company submissions that arrived, prior to the first Global Compact Learning Forum conference in Denham, England, in October 2001. There were several double submissions, and the number of participating companies after 15 months was 30 from a possible 43 that had attended the opening session in New York on 26 July 1999.

Each of the companies submitting reports received a written commentary from a team, led by Malcolm McIntosh and Ruth Thomas, which endeavoured to engage in a dialogue with each company on their submission. The intention of these commentaries was to stretch the information provided, to seek clarification and to aid in the interpretation of the original submission. The companies were asked to resubmit their reports after taking into account the commentaries. A few did resubmit and, of these, there were some significant changes made to their submissions. In January 2002 all commentaries, which by that time numbered 43 from 41 companies, were posted on the Global Compact website, with a caveat that the UN took no responsibility for the contents. In November 2001 all companies received written commentaries on their submissions that had been received up to that date.

The aim of the analytical research exercise reported here was that companies would engage in the learning process and reassess their submissions. In reality, most companies did not resubmit their reports in the light of the commentaries provided for them by the expert team. The revised and the original company submissions can be found at the Global Compact website, www.unglobalcompact. org, under 'Phase One', 'Case Studies'.

It should also be mentioned that the Global Compact acts as a useful, global, convening platform, bringing together business, government and civil-society organisations in regional meetings. Many of the early meetings, particularly in Brazil and Scandinavia, encouraged companies to make submissions to the learning network such that by April 2002 many hundreds of companies had indicated their desire to make a submission to the UN.[1]

1   At the end of 2002, the Global Compact discontinued the formal requirement for companies to submit examples of how they enact the principles. The initiative now encourages companies to publish their progress in annual financial reports or in separate sustainability reports. The web portal contains links to these documents in order to promote transparency and public accountability.

13.2 Analysis of company submissions to the Global Compact, 2000–2001

The two most important findings arising from an analysis of the company submissions are as follows:

- There is a significant amount of information on outcomes (on what had been achieved) but much less on the processes the companies went through to achieve these outcomes. There is an urgent need to study these processes and to share these stories with other companies.

- There is a need for further research, particularly for in-depth, long-term studies of processes. These would enable researchers to assemble a comparable dataset that would describe the rich nuances of organisational change and learning.

Other key issues that emerged across the submissions were as follows:

- It was unclear in many cases whether organisations were aiming to achieve specific standards (such as those set down by the International Organisation for Standardisation [ISO]) rather than to address the nine principles.

- It was evident that many organisations faced difficulties in assessing the priority of corporate social responsibility (CSR) issues in relation to their wider portfolio of activities.

- Lessons of operating successfully in networks need to be assimilated and learned in these sample organisations. There is a great deal of research knowledge about networks that did not appear to have been utilised in the sample studied.

Other issues that arose from a reading of the submissions included:

- Different approaches to dealing with social and environmental issues

- A lack of clarity on the definitional issues

- Convergence between different corporate citizenship initiatives

- The relationship between new initiatives, such as the Global Compact, and local, regional and national law

- The creation of a local context for global initiatives

There are also some problems that arose from the submissions:

- Some issues were ignored by the Global 8.

- There was a bias in favour of large companies.

- The development impact was not addressed.

- There was no analysis of the compensation of the losers from these new initiatives.

- Corruption was not mentioned as an issue.

13.3 Patterns and themes within and across all the cases

It was clear from the submissions that there was a concerted effort on the part of these organisations to engage in CSR generally and to address the Global Compact's principles more specifically. However, in virtually all the submissions there was a need for more detailed and richer information. One common theme emerging from the cases is that CSR was perceived as being closely linked to the way in which businesses are run in general and that companies remain very suspicious about publicly and widely revealing how they enact CSR. As in any other form of business research, the question of business confidentiality was raised. On the more positive side, if companies are seeing CSR as being integrated with their main business activities, this points to a substantial degree of integration between CSR and the perceived everyday 'business of business'.

Given the willingness of these companies to write such cases, however, one can deduce that the companies held great expectations regarding the UN Global Compact as a means of improving commercial relations whether within the local region or at a more global level. As the UN principles are broad and far-ranging, it is encouraging that companies were interested for 'their own sake' to address what can be broadly labelled as CSR. The data indicates that a fundamental criterion of engaging in CSR, even at the most general level, is predicated on firm managerial belief and commitment. It is also worth noting that case studies alone will be unlikely to fully convince any single member of the companies participating in the Global Compact to implement the principles. To do this requires answers to specific questions and to the broader issues of organisational design, learning and strategic change. But the cases do reveal that they are a 'good' means of building stories regarding what it takes to adopt mechanisms sustaining the principles. It is also worth noting that in none of the cases is there any evidence of organisations being critical of the principles.

13.3.1 Generally observed factors, patterns and themes

As noted above, the submissions cannot provide all the data required to answer all questions of interest and further data would have been needed to increase the richness and depth of the case studies. However, some important patterns emerged across the cases that resonate with a wider body of organisation theory. In summary, these patterns concern:

- Organisational design

- The understanding of processes as well as outcomes
- Learning and communicating

13.3.1.1 Organisational design

A common feature of nearly all the cases was an emphasis on working through partnerships with other organisations and agencies. Nothing, it seems, can be achieved by single organisations working alone. They have to ally themselves with others. This resonates perfectly with changes we can observe more generally in organisations worldwide. CSR would seem to be following similar lines to the general trend toward working in networks rather than through hierarchies and to favour alliances rather than organisations working alone. Many terms have been used to describe these forms of inter-organisational working. For example, in existing literature, they have been described as 'networks' (Castells 1996), 'postmodern' (Volberda 1998), 'federal' (Handy 1992) and 'cellular' (Miles *et al*. 1997). In this chapter, for convenience we use the term 'networks', but recognise that the term can cover a wide range of inter-organisational forms.

The basic premise of this radical shift in organisational design is that firms such as DuPont (responsible for one of the current submissions), General Motors and other organisations established in the late 1920s had been advised that the multi-divisional (M form or Fordist) type of design was the best way to achieve both efficiency and effectiveness, especially when undertaking strategic growth by expanding internationally (see Chandler 1963). Until the 1990s this vertical, hierarchical and firm-centric view prevailed. The advent of information technology, increased globalisation and greater awareness of social values and ethics rendered this form of organisation largely obsolete (that is not to say that many do not persist in retaining the M form—they do, in all countries of the world) and triggered the search for organisational designs that emphasised flexibility, knowledge creation and collaboration. Such a design is the network form (N form or post-Fordist) of organisation.

However, managing in networks places different demands on organisations. Studies have revealed that there are broadly similar demands placed on organisations of all types when they operate in networks (Whittington *et al*. 1999). The main demand is to ensure that processes as well as structures change and interrelate. Old, contingency perspectives on organisational design (where one variable such as organisational size was associated with another variable such as organisational structure) have made way for configurations of variables where structures, processes and boundaries have to be simultaneously managed. It has been demonstrated beyond doubt that performance benefits accrue only to those organisations that co-align structures, processes and boundaries (Whittington *et al*. 1999). The main features of each are as follows:

- Structures. There is a need for widespread de-layering and decentralisation to remove the expense of hierarchy and many layers of management. There is a focus on decentralisation of strategic decision-making and a greater emphasis on small organisational units and project-based approaches to organising.

- Processes. The requirement is now for intensive interaction both vertically and horizontally in organisations. The flow of information should include all organisations in the network (such as suppliers, customers and collaborators) and requires some investment in electronic data interchange.

- Boundaries. The emphasis is away from the organisation as a fully self-contained unit and toward a view that asks: 'What are the core competences of this organisation?' Having defined these, organisations can redraw their boundaries around these core competences. Outsourcing and the abandonment of non-core activities are examples of this process.

The main point about the configurational approach is that organisations will succeed to the extent that they change, adapt or pay attention to structures, processes and boundaries simultaneously rather than approaching them in a piecemeal fashion.

13.3.1.2 Organisational processes

Broadly, processes describe the various ways in which outcomes are achieved. They include the 'hard' factors of measuring performance, setting targets and financial benefits as well as the 'softer' issues of developing people as a key resource. An analysis of processes also is to 'tell the story' of how initiatives or changes were initiated, sustained and finally 'locked' into the organisation's infrastructure.

This story over time is something missing from the majority of the cases in the sample. There is a wealth of information about outcomes (what was achieved) but very little about *how* such outcomes were achieved. Future research will need to concentrate on the processes. Some cases come close to providing some process data, but much more detail will be needed from a range of cases if advances are to be made in 'knowing how' organisations implement CSR and engage with the principles. It may be helpful for companies to consult recent research on organisational change and the successful implementation of strategic initiatives.

Change is unlikely to happen unless it is actively locked into place in the organisation. This means that, whatever the initiative, it becomes a natural way of conducting business. A great deal of effort and time may have been spent on getting changes started and keeping them alive in the organisation, but successes come from ensuring that they are locked into place in the organisation. Paradoxically, this means that what began as an innovative and completely new initiative becomes a day-to-day operation. From the perspective of the principles, the challenge is to render the changes into 'everyday' activities in organisations rather than letting them remain as innovations or novel ways of doing business.

Success in implementation is closely linked to two factors. The first is the achievement of high levels of agreement among all stakeholders that the new approach is the right way to proceed. The second is to ensure that strategic initiatives (such as the principles) are clearly prioritised in the overall strategic portfolio of the organisation. There needs to be a clear indication of exactly how important this initiative is in comparison with other strategic decisions.

The majority of the cases in the study sample reveal little evidence of such processes, preferring instead to concentrate on reporting outcomes. For example, the fostering of collaboration among stakeholders is reported only when outcomes have already been consolidated within the organisation and when the hurdles of collaboration have been largely overcome. Outcomes are important, but they do not tell the whole story.

Finally, it is a truism to say that 'what gets measured gets done', but the cases seem to indicate that we should not overlook the importance of assessing success, specifying targets, measuring outcomes and giving resources to strategies. For example, in cases such as that of Unilever we would need to know the proportion of overall investment in the principles in relation to the rest of the organisation's investment portfolio. We would also need to know the steps taken and assessment processes (measures) used in cases such as that of UBS, Storebrand or Statoil. These are cases where further data would have been useful.

13.3.1.3 Learning and communicating

It is clear that an immense amount of organisational learning took place during the time-periods covered by the submissions. It also seems that organisations had to forget and 'unlearn' some of their embedded types of behaviour. The older organisations in the sample (not surprisingly) seem to have had most need for unlearning, whereas the younger organisations had most need to build in CSR as an integral part of their strategic portfolios. In any further analyses of company reports, it may be useful to sample organisations on the basis of embeddedness and/or age.

Communicating is an integral part of learning, especially when this is across networks of organisations. As far as the Global Compact is concerned, one of the primary tasks for the UN will be to maintain the discussion and to continue giving feedback to companies on any sustainability reports they may produce. Without such interest, companies will be discouraged from creating further reports and thus other companies will be unable to learn from example.

Along the same theme of communication, it is vital to examine the ways in which self-reports from companies are presented. In this chapter the data as presented has been taken at face value, but a further issue of data collection would relate to validation and verification (in the spirit of good research). It would also be useful, from an analytical perspective, if the way in which data is collected and the ways in which reports are constructed were standardised, as far as possible. In some of the cases studied there was something approaching standardised reporting under headings such as 'lessons learned', 'costs' and 'benefits'. In others cases, such as that of Nexen, the whole discourse of the case is relatively loose and unstructured. Although companies are no longer required to submit case reports such as those analysed in this chapter, it is worth noting that any further phase of data collection from these or other organisations would benefit from the use of more standardised research tools and validation procedures. It is also essential to place the changes demanded by the adoption of the principles in the wider context of changes taking place in the world of organisations generally.

14
Learning from experience
The United Nations Global Compact Learning Forum 2002*

Sandra Waddock
Boston College, USA

In December 2002, representatives from more than 100 companies, labour and non-governmental organisations (NGOs), government, and about 30 academics convened in Berlin for the second Learning Forum of the United Nations Global Compact initiative. The strategy devised by the Global Compact staff to move toward realisation of this goal involves five major elements operationalised through a network structure of companies, NGOs, governments and academics. The first element of the strategy is **leadership**, which requires signatory companies to get top-management commitment to the principles. A second is multi-stakeholder **dialogue** processes that can help companies and others involved in the Global Compact identify and solve problems together. The third strategy involves **learning** through various forums, such as the one convened in Berlin, which strengthens and reinforces dialogue by developing and disseminating knowledge and good practice related to the principles. The fourth mechanism involves encouraging networks of companies and other stakeholders to develop **partnership projects and action** related to the Global Compact and implementation of its principles, which can provide guidance and support for the Global Compact but at the national or regional level. Much of the work of making the Global Compact real will be done through evolving **local networks**, the fifth strategy (Global Compact Office 2002).

* This chapter first appeared in *The Journal of Corporate Citizenship* 11 (Autumn 2003): 51-67.

14.1 Bridging the gulf: companies that care and those that don't

The Global Compact evolved rapidly in its first three years into a network structure, comprising loosely connected companies and other institutions bound by the common agreement to adhere to the Global Compact's original nine principles (see page 12). The success of the Global Compact and the level of interest by the business community is remarkable, particularly in light of the limited number of staff associated with its implementation and the need for action steps to be taken by members of the network rather than by central staff. By December 2002, some 800 enterprises (600+ companies and numerous trade unions, international NGOs, business schools and corporate responsibility organisations) from through-out the world had already signed on to uphold the principles.

14.1.1 Spreading the Global Compact word

Numerous speakers at the Learning Forum pointed out that there is considerable distance to go before a 'tipping point' (Gladwell 2000) for full integration of the Global Compact's principles into corporate practice is reached. For example, although more than 800 total participants worldwide have now committed to the Global Compact, this number is but a drop in the bucket compared to the nearly 70,000 multinational companies (MNCs) in the world. And this number does not include the millions of small and medium-sized enterprises (SMEs) that have yet to become involved with (or even aware of) the Global Compact. Some of these smaller companies are connected to MNCs because in today's disaggregated, networked world the production and distribution processes in many MNCs have been out-sourced to smaller companies, frequently found in developing nations. Other SMEs are independent, local companies, frequently operating on shoestring budgets.

The tendency toward outsourcing production and distribution operations has created fuzzy boundaries between sourcing companies and their suppliers and distributors. So undefined are boundaries that external actors such as corporate critics—environmental, labour, anti-corruption and human rights activists—frequently do not distinguish between the sourcing company and its network of suppliers and distributors when exposing problems related to implementation of the principles. As some MNCs have discovered, a multinational's reputation can be tainted by the failure of companies within its supply and distribution networks to live up to the standards or agreements it has pledged to uphold, such as the Global Compact. A number of implications (or learning gaps), raised by participants at the Learning Forum, arise from the realities of the global business environment today:

- Over the next years, it will be important to gain the commitment to the Global Compact and its principles of *many more high-visibility multi-national companies*. Large MNCs need to demonstrate their leadership and commitment to the Global Compact principles through initial CEO com-mitment, followed by the driving-down of the principles into strategies, management systems and operating practices.

● The leadership and involvement of large companies in the Global Compact is important; however, supply and distribution chain companies today make up a large part of the systems that create goods and services. The implication of this reality is that large companies will need to begin working with companies in their own supply and distribution chains to adopt the principles and drive them into practice throughout the supply and distribution systems, not just within the MNC itself. As happened with the quality movement, large MNCs may need to require commitment to and implementation of the Global Compact principles within supply and distribution chain companies if they are to avoid being tainted with problems found within smaller supplier or distributor firms.

● The involvement of large companies in the Global Compact will be insufficient to address the Global Compact's goals of inclusiveness and sustainability. Over the next years, it will be important to bring many more SMEs, whose businesses comprise much of the new employment opportunity and new ventures in today's world, into commitment to and alignment with the Global Compact principles. Large companies' commitment alone will be insufficient to achieve the long-term goals of the Global Compact.

14.1.2 Dynamics of commitment

As well as the necessity to bring in more companies as Global Compact signatories, there is important learning still to be done related to why some companies are willing to make the commitment to sign up to the principles and others are not, no matter what their size. Brand-name and global companies, of course, are increasingly aware of the need to establish and defend their reputation in the eyes of customers, investors, NGOs, trade unions and communities. But what of those companies whose name is largely unknown because, perhaps, they are business-to-business companies or suppliers to larger entities, companies that, in the words of one participant, just 'don't care'? It is not yet clear what forces, dynamics, competitive, consumer or investor pressures will motivate these companies to become Global Compact signatories and to begin operationalising the principles.

Further, although companies from more than 20 nations have signed up to the Global Compact, there is a notable gap in (particularly large) companies from the US signing on, which is ascribed to fear of legal reprisals, among other reasons. Although a number of large US companies have recently become signatories, many more European and developing-nation companies have signed the principles. Global balance in terms of economic power distribution, developed and developing nations, rich and poor nations, and regional distribution of signatories, will increasingly be important to the credibility of the Global Compact and its efforts to achieve its goals. The following implications arise from the foregoing:

● More needs to be learned about the reasons why companies do or do not sign up to the Global Compact and what can be done to encourage non-signatories to become signatories. The structure of incentives, business reasons and motivations for joining (or not joining) the Global Compact needs to be elaborated so that strategies can be developed for bringing more companies into the Global Compact fold.

● More needs to be learned about differences between brand-name and unbranded companies' rationales for committing to the Global Compact.

● More needs to be learned about why so few US companies have signed the principles and what can be done to encourage them to become signatories.

14.1.3 Transparency and integrity: a tenth principle?

The question of whether there should be a tenth principle, on transparency—and, if so, what that principle should encompass—pervaded the Learning Forum meeting. Through multiple discussions and workshops, it became clear that most participants supported the notion of a transparency principle, though a couple of people stated a preference for the simplicity of the current nine principles. The concept of transparency, as expressed in the Learning Forum, went well beyond that of anti-bribery and anti-corruption measures to encompass broader issues of accountability, responsibility and integrity. The most frequently stated view seemed to be that 'Sunlight is the best disinfectant', and that a transparency principle could be a useful mechanism for helping to achieve organisational integrity.[1]

With respect to the transparency/integrity principle, participants at the Learning Forum raised the following issues and implications:

● A transparency principle, if adopted, should encompass issues of responsibility, accountability and integrity: that is, it should be more broadly oriented than a simple anti-corruption or anti-bribery measure. Core values with respect to transparency seem to involve honesty, and openness with respect to innovation and development.

● A transparency principle applies to organisations in all spheres, political/governmental enterprises, non-governmental and activist organisations, civil-society organisations, educational institutions and so on, as well as to business; thus a transparency principle should apply not just to business but to all enterprises.

● If a transparency principle is adopted, work needs to be done to determine and define what is legitimately confidential (proprietary) and what is legitimately transparent.

● Transparency implies responsibility and accountability, which creates a need for credible (internal *and* external) auditing, monitoring and assurance systems.

● If a transparency principle is adopted, companies (and other enterprises) will need to determine how to create and sustain competitive advantage within a transparent framework that levels the playing field for all.

● The adoption of a transparency principle will necessitate development of new implementation policies within companies with accompanying

---

1 See Appendix D for the results of the 2004 consultation process on the introduction of a tenth principle on corruption.

needs for training programmes, incentives/reward structures and possibly enforcement mechanisms to create a level playing field.

- Indicators and measures of transparency, identification of good practices across industries as well as sector-specific measures, and establishment of priorities related to transparency implementation will be needed if a transparency principle is adopted.

- Transparency is inherently linked to public policy and regulation. The creation of a transparency principle may necessitate closer examination of what needs to be regulated and what does not, and some refocusing on the role of government in establishing a level playing field.

14.2 Learning: a central focus of the Global Compact

Learning is a central focus of the Global Compact Learning Forum. Beyond the general implications and learning gaps raised by the level and type of participation in the Global Compact, described above, specific learning came from workshop sessions at the forum. Among the possible **learning structures** already in place or discussed at the forum are:

- **Local Learning Forums, dialogue groups, and conferences or meetings** in which companies and other stakeholders share common frameworks, application of principles to practice, systematic understanding of the processes that work effectively for adoption and implementation of the Global Compact principles, and sharing of lessons learned.

- **A 'User's Guide' to the Principles**—that is, a manual that illustrates in simple terms how the principles are translated into practice—would be a useful tool for companies, as would wider dissemination of the research and cases, and more analytical case studies, as well as additional analysis of the cases already created.

- **Training and development programmes** related to management systems and processes used successfully by different actors for adopting and implementing the Global Compact and its nine principles. Companies that gain experience with successful adoption or implementation of the entire set of Global Compact principles or individual principles may be willing to share their strategies and tactics with other signatories by sharing their training and development programmes.

- **Generalisable frameworks, theories, application tools and systemic management approaches** derived from company experience and/or systematic study of individual or multiple companies' experiences will be useful adjuncts to case studies.

- **Newsletters, online reports and studies**: published research studies that report effective results and practices related to the Global Compact can provide a foundation for common understanding of what works and what does not work in adopting and implementing the Global Compact's principles.

- **Cases** should be developed with specific purposes in mind: that is, as descriptive stories, teaching cases or research cases, and used accordingly. All types are likely to be needed.

- **Fundamental research** by academics, consultants and other researchers into what does and does not work in the adoption and implementation of the Global Compact principles also needs to be undertaken. Research published and 'translated' for practising managers can provide important insights into and development of application tools and methodologies, evaluation instruments, processes and problem-solving approaches.

- **The Global Compact Web Portal**[2] offers a unique possibility for social vetting and public discussion of the case examples and company practices as they relate to the principles because it supports a worldwide, Web-based dialogic process that fosters development of a common under-standing of principles-based (good) corporate practices.

14.3 Driving principles into practice

The Global Compact sets out principles that are framed at a fairly high or abstract level (see page 12). Driving these principles into practice, as became clear at the Learning Forum meeting, requires a wide range of actions and initiatives at the micro, meso, and macro levels.

14.3.1 Micro level

Driving the principles into practice involves systemic change for many companies, at least in the ideal realisation of the principles that drove the conversation at the forum. Although some 600+ companies had signed up to the Compact at the time of the meeting, there was a clear recognition that CEO commitment needs to be supplemented by other processes that can involve significant organisational change. CEO commitment is in and of itself insufficient to drive the principles into practice. Significant work needs to be done on the translation process, possibly on a principle-by-principle basis to ensure that companies understand what needs to be done to bring the principles alive. Learning more about this *integration* process will be a critical component of the long-term success of the Global Compact in achieving its goals of a sustainable and inclusive society, as businesses begin to redefine their relationship to and within the societies where they operate. But, again, as far as the learning agenda embedded in the forum goes, even integration needs to be supplemented by a feedback loop that allows for continual *improvement* on what has been done in the past.

2 www.unglobalcompact.org/Portal

The Global Compact performance model presented by Claude Fussler (2002) at the Berlin meeting starts with the Global Compact principles at the top. Like the three 'Is' of inspiration, integration and improvement in a total responsibility management (TRM) approach (Waddock and Bodwell 2002; Waddock *et al.* 2002), the Global Compact performance model is analogous to the processes of total quality management (TQM). Driving the principles into practice requires all three elements of inspiration (vision setting, values and stakeholder engagement), integration (into strategies, employee practices since employees carry out strategies, and management systems across multiple functions and units) and improvement (measurement, feedback and transparency/accountability) in a plan–do–check–act systemic approach modelled on Deming's (1982) approach to quality (see Fig. 14.1).

14.3.1.1 Inspiration and vision

Gaining CEO commitment and willingness to state publicly the company's commitment to the Global Compact's principles is the key to the vision/inspiration process; however, according to forum participants, there is a gap between the 'high-level politics' of signing a set of principles and the realities of day-to-day practice that clearly needs to bridged. Participants in the forum noted consistently that CEO commitment is simply the first step in what amounts to a long-term process of commitment, implementation, recommitment, continual improvement and transparency. Essential to the inspiration process is what one participant termed 'creating a culture of accountability and responsibility' within the firm, which inevitably involves being explicit about the company's values, especially as they link to the Global Compact's core principles as well as to the company's own code of conduct and stated values. As the Global Compact performance model illustrates (Fussler 2002), enablers for implementing the vision include leadership, empowerment, having sufficient resources that are related to policies and strategy, and integration into processes and ongoing innovations. Key implications of the inspiration and visioning process as raised by participants at the Berlin Learning Forum were:

- Companies need to be explicit about their commitment to the Global Compact principles and articulate that commitment from the top, communicate it widely internally and externally, and be aware that significant systemic changes may be necessary to operationalise the principles.

- There is a continuing need to make the business case for adopting the Global Compact principles, at the large- and small-firm level, and provide assurance that integrity is not simply a 'luxury of competitive advantage'.

- Companies adopting the principles need to be aware that significant organisational change may be necessary to create a culture of accountability and responsibility to people (human rights), employees (labour standards and conventions) and the natural environment (sustainability).

- Should a tenth principle around transparency be added, companies will also need to develop a culture of transparency (see Appendix D).

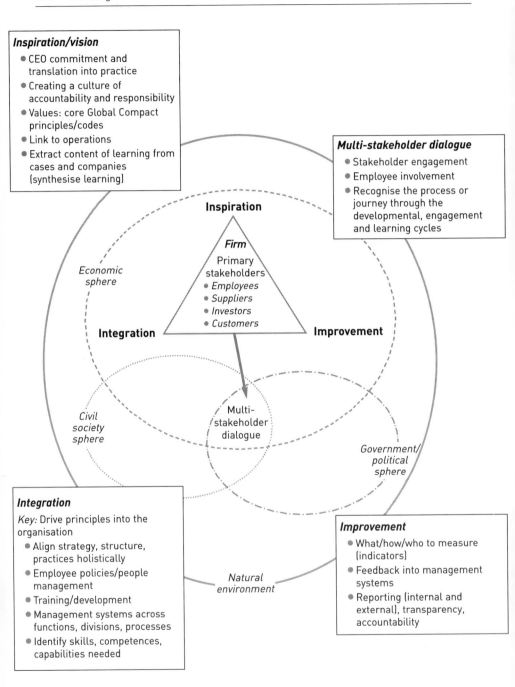

Inspiration/vision
- CEO commitment and translation into practice
- Creating a culture of accountability and responsibility
- Values: core Global Compact principles/codes
- Link to operations
- Extract content of learning from cases and companies (synthesise learning)

Multi-stakeholder dialogue
- Stakeholder engagement
- Employee involvement
- Recognise the process or journey through the developmental, engagement and learning cycles

Inspiration

Firm
Primary stakeholders
- *Employees*
- *Suppliers*
- *Investors*
- *Customers*

Economic sphere

Integration   Improvement

Civil society sphere

Multi-stakeholder dialogue

Government/ political sphere

Natural environment

Integration
Key: Drive principles into the organisation
- Align strategy, structure, practices holistically
- Employee policies/people management
- Training/development
- Management systems across functions, divisions, processes
- Identify skills, competences, capabilities needed

Improvement
- What/how/who to measure (indicators)
- Feedback into management systems
- Reporting (internal and external), transparency, accountability

Figure 14.1 Micro-level learning and learning gaps

- Practical examples, tools, methodologies, frameworks and processes are needed to translate principles as articulated by the CEO or Global Compact into practice and make corporate responsibility real for line people and throughout the company's distributed network of related companies (for example, the supply and distribution chain).

- Implementation of the Global Compact principles needs to be viewed through at least three lenses: content, structure and processes.

Content
Specific details about the content associated with adopting and implementing the Global Compact principles is needed: for example, What is being done? What are the results? What kinds of strategies, programmes, policies and practices are related to the implementation of each of the principles?

Structure
Specific details about the structures that emerge to make the principles real are needed: for example, By whom are the principles being implemented? How is the implementation organised? What structures and systems have evolved that work effectively?

Processes
Specific details about the processes used in translating principles into action are needed: for example, What is involved in translating principles into action? What organisational or system change methods work best and under what circumstances?

14.3.1.2 Integration toward results
The integration process is the implementation process. Integration means making the principles come alive in the organisation, which means making them integral, not separate from, corporate strategies, employee practices (since employees carry out strategies) and management systems. The Global Compact principles are aspirational, in that they set high and meaningful targets for companies to achieve. Empowering people, and recognising the impacts of change on people, the value chain and society are core elements of the Global Compact performance model for which specific tools and practices that can be broadly applied in companies have been developed (Fussler 2002). Among the implications of the integration process discussed by participants at the Leaning Forum meeting were:

- Companies need to take a systemic or holistic perspective on the implementation of the Global Compact principles. Programmes overlaid on top of existing practices and structures will be insufficient to provide for true integration of the principles into practice. Systemic approaches to integration of the principles into policies and strategies, empowerment of employees, and resource allocation are needed.

- Global Compact principles need to be incorporated into management systems in all disciplines, especially employee practices, but also marketing, operations, finance and accounting, and information systems. To accomplish this integration, employee training and development programmes, reward and incentive systems and structures, and information and communication systems will need alignment with Global Compact principles.

- Global Compact principles also need to be linked to product design and production processes, as well as to resource allocation.

- There is a need to incorporate Global Compact principles into people management. To accomplish integration of the Global Compact principles into practice requires engaging employees in a real way, sharing power with them, and engaging them in the process of creating responsibility, transparency and accountability loops. Similar structures with respect to external stakeholder engagement, input and feedback will likely also be necessary.

14.3.1.3 Improvement

The improvement process necessitates a process of continual in-organisation measurement, assessment and analysis, learning, innovation, and improvement where problems are found (Fussler 2002; Waddock and Bodwell 2002). The Global Compact has linked itself to the reporting and auditing standards of the triple-bottom-line-oriented Global Reporting Initiative (GRI), which is an important step in developing adequate measures for arenas that some observers believe to be highly qualitative, and also advocates measuring improvement through other tools such as activity-based accounting, risk and opportunity assessment, internal audits, life-cycle assessment, eco-design, SA8000, AA1000, ISO 14000 and related tools (Fussler 2002). With respect to creating continual improvement systems within companies, participants at the meeting raised the following issues:

- The Global Compact staff will need to clarify the link between the Global Compact and the GRI, focusing on developing easily used measurement and reporting instruments that provide for transparency and accountability. Reporting to external and internal stakeholders (for example, employees) is a critical element of the Global Compact performance model (Fussler 2002).

- Simple, practical measurement tools to assess the implementation and effectiveness of Global Compact principles are needed. Such tools need to be communicated widely, be relatively easy to use, and assure a degree of credibility to the data, linked to measurement, transparency and accountability systems, and directly tied into specific principles of the Global Compact.

- Specific information about the skills, competencies and capabilities that are needed to adopt and implement the Global Compact principles within the context of large and smaller enterprises needs to be developed, along with appropriate training and development models and tools.

- Credibility is important to integrity assurance, meeting Global Compact standards and principles, and consideration of enforcement mechanisms. The issue of credibility raises important considerations: for example, Should standards be voluntary or mandated? Who should gather, analyse and report data? Are internally generated and voluntary reports sufficient? Do reports need external verification? Does Global Compact principle implementation need external monitoring and verification?

● To the extent that external monitoring, verification and certification with respect to implementation of the principles is undertaken, questions remain about what type of enterprise is best suited to carry out this type of work. Large accounting firms, NGOs, or social-audit-specific enterprises are among the possibilities, although each brings to this task a particular set of issues that will need to be addressed.

● For many companies, there is still a need to use measures and reporting systems to 'make the business case' for responsibility and living up to the principles. In this regard, some 'worst-case' as well as 'good-practice' examples may be useful to highlight what can happen when principles are abrogated, because it is otherwise hard to convince managers to undertake action to avoid some kinds of outcomes.

14.3.1.4 SME-specific tools, frameworks and approaches

A major topic of conversation in many of the workshops was the difference between large multinational enterprises and small and medium-sized enterprises, both in their capacities and resources and in their knowledge of the meaning of signing on to the Global Compact principles. Specific information, tools and techniques for adopting and implementing the Global Compact principles with the needs of SMEs held clearly in mind are needed. SME objectives and requirements for signing on to and living up the Global Compact's principles are considerably different from those of global or very large firms, which may have more resources to commit to initiatives such as the Global Compact. SMEs, in contrast, tend to be more entrepreneurial, have simple structures, operate beneath the radar screen of many corporate critics because of their small size, and thus have fewer incentives to adopt Global Compact principles. Although SMEs can be (and often are) values-driven as a result of their founder/owner/ entrepreneur's values, they are frequently severely constrained in terms of managerial capacity, time limitations and resources. These constraints and differences between smaller and larger enterprises suggest an important set of learning gaps identified by participants at the forum:

● Specific information, examples and studies of SMEs adopting the Global Compact principles are needed.

● More examples of SME-specific learning, skills, competences, capacities and specially focused tools are needed to help SMEs understand how to commit to and live up to the Global Compact's principles.

● The more limited resource, managerial and time capacities of SMEs may necessitate simplification of processes of implementation, accountability, transparency and reporting with respect to implementation of the principles.

Starting in 2003, the United Nations Industrial Development Organisation (UNIDO) will take over leadership for SME-related activities within the Global Compact, in conjunction with the UN's Institute for Leadership Development (ILD),[3] which specialises in supporting SMEs globally. ILD has incorporated materials on how to integrate the Global Compact principles into its training kits and developed a specific agenda with respect to the Global Compact and SMEs, so that the Global Compact can:

> promote the nine principles of the Global Compact within the world community of small and medium enterprises (SMEs) so that they too could become not only a timely partner to the Global Compact but also define, shape and influence the larger implementation of these nine principles. SMEs in the UN GC enhance a unique mechanism of learning by doing by utilising knowledge sharing, knowledge creation and active dialogue. This initiative brings forth specific principles for SMEs (led by case studies, lessons learnt) and design and implement interactive toolkits to integrate these principles internationally. SMEs in the UN GC also provides a knowledge network which is an ongoing support and learning tool—the Global Mentoring Service—to respond to challenges faced by SMEs in emerging and developing economies. It is a programme that promotes responsible effective business principles by providing a global framework for constructive action learning (ILD 2003).

14.3.2 Meso level

Participants in the Learning Forum identified the meso or industry, local multi-stakeholder, and regional level as important to the long-term success of the Global Compact. Issues of competitive advantage, proprietary information and free-riders can make an association of companies within an industry group or pact, or a regional business community, an important player in implementing principles such as those of the Global Compact. Figure 14.2 shows some possibilities for the emergence of industry pacts or agreements through industry or regional business associations to live up to some standards, as well as the possibilities for change represented by multi-stakeholder dialogue.

Industry and regional business associations, according to forum participants, have the potential to create a context in which principles such as those of the Global Compact can become reality. The Global Compact performance model illustrates the need to look at external impacts of companies on society in general as well as the business value chain in thinking through the implementation of the principles (Fussler 2002). Industry and regional associations can create agreements for member companies that provide for generalised codes of conduct and industry self-regulation (though issues of credibility and free-riders may remain). Such associations, according to forum participants, can potentially accomplish some of the following objectives:

● Peer business organisations and industry associations can create voluntary and self-regulatory standards and guidelines that generate significant peer pressure on member and even non-member companies for enforcement.

3   See www.ildglobal.org.

Industry pacts can:
- Develop industry association, multi-stakeholder agreements
- Create self-regulatory standards, guidelines using peer pressure (e.g. grey-zone principles, avoiding free-riders)
- Define boundaries between public, private, societal organisations
- Develop mechanisms for pressuring non-branded companies and including supply chain companies in principle adoption/implementation

Government(s)

Industry(ies)

Industry pacts

MSD

NGOs

Multi-stakeholder dialogue (MSD) can:
- Bridge to credibility: real engagement, involvement, shift of mind-set and power dynamics
- Frame issues, bring multiple perspectives, insights, advice to bear
- Create accountability structures, practical indicators and processes to generate collaboration, transparency
- Link global to local ('glocal') standards, practices and groups
- Provide insight into how SMEs can/do apply Global Compact principles
- Communicate transparency (and accountability) within or outside industry
- Create exemplars (highlight individual company/system integrity)

△ *Company*   ⬡ *NGO*   ⬭ *Government*

Figure 14.2 Meso-level learning and learning gaps

- Peer business organisations and industry associations may be able to help companies negotiate in 'grey areas', where application of specific principles needs clarification or elaboration.

- Peer business organisations and industry associations can enhance boundary definition between public, private and social responsibilities.

- Peer business organisations and industry associations may be needed to pressure non-branded or less visible companies into conformance, or may be able to set industry standards that provide minimal norms for compliance, including norms of practice for supply chain companies in developing nations.

- Expertise is needed to help businesses understand their roles with respect to human rights, labour rights, environmental issues and, should the transparency principle be added, transparency. Industry associations can play a pivotal role in identifying needed areas of expertise and translation, and even in helping to identify or develop appropriate experts with industry-specific knowledge.

- Sector-based associations can be a source of sector-specific working groups that can create and communicate shared understanding of the Global Compact principles as they apply to that sector.

Multi-stakeholder dialogue involves bringing together actors from different sectors or spheres of influence around areas of common concern: for example, the Global Compact's principles. Such dialogues can occur at multiple levels, including local, regional and international (for example, the dialogues already established by the Global Compact). Because they help to link the global with the local, and because they inherently bring multiple perspectives together, such multi-stakeholder dialogues (MSDs) can provide what one participant characterised as a bridge to credibility. MSDs create a natural link between global standards such as those of the Global Compact and local norms.

At the time of the Berlin meeting, the Global Compact had sponsored two main multi-stakeholder Policy Dialogues explicitly focused on issues related to the Global Compact, one on the role of the private sector in zones of conflict and the other on business and sustainable development. Policy Dialogues provide a forum where representatives of companies, trade unions and NGOs can share perspectives and, it is hoped, come to innovative solutions regarding very tough issues. The conflict prevention Policy Dialogue, for example, has explored several topics, such as transparency, multi-stakeholder initiatives, revenue-sharing regimes, and guidelines for conflict assessment and risk management for businesses, all of which are now available online.[4] The second Policy Dialogue, launched in 2002 to complement the Johannesburg Summit on Sustainable Development, has produced several reports also available online.[5] Additional Policy Dialogues on HIV/AIDS in

---

4   See www.unglobalcompact.org/Portal → Policy Dialogues → Conflict Prevention, for copies of related publications.
5   See www.unglobalcompact.org/Portal → Policy Dialogues → Sustainable Development.

the workplace, freshwater resources, conflict prevention, and internalisation/integration of the principles were under consideration.

Among the purposes for MSDs that participants discussed are:

- MSDs can create a 'bridge to credibility' by creating a context for real intersector engagement and involvement by all parties with an interest in a given issue. By bringing parties to the table with equal opportunity for voice and input, they can create a shift of mind-set among participants (and their home organisations) as well as potentially changing some existing power dynamics simply by providing for views to be expressed.

- MSDs can help to frame issues, principles and ideas in new ways because they bring multiple perspectives, insights and advice to bear on the problem. They are useful in situations where interdependent organisations need to co-operate to resolve a problem.

- MSDs can be credible agents for creating accountability and measurement structures, evolving practical indicators and reporting results of initiatives, as well as developing integrative processes of collaboration and transparency.

- MSDs can potentially provide insight into how SMEs can and do apply the Global Compact principles by being a source of examples, cases and understanding. They can simultaneously develop studies of exemplary companies and/or collaborations that can provide role models for others.

- MSDs can use their credibility and multi-sector perspectives to communicate transparency and accountability within and outside a given industry or region. In doing this, they can help bridge any existing gap between individual, company, local and international cultures and standards.

- MSDs can enhance understanding of the boundaries of responsibility for private-sector, public-sector and non-governmental organisations, and develop appropriate assessment, auditing, measuring and verification models for all sectors.

14.3.3 Macro level

The Global Compact gains its credibility from the global reach and moral authority of the United Nations, which is made up of the nation-states of the world and brings a multilateral perspective on problems into its activities. One of the benefits of the Global Compact is the relative simplicity of the principles. Because the nine principles are derived from internationally agreed UN documents, they represent a set of core foundation values (or what Donaldson and Dunfee term 'hypernorms' [1994, 1999]) that most nations have agreed, in theory, should be applicable. At the societal level, then, the Global Compact principles (at least in theory) span the boundaries of the three spheres that make up human civilisation: economic, political/governmental and civil society (see Fig. 14.3) (Waddock 2002a). Resting as they do on the health of the natural environment, the Global Compact principles also speak to the issue of sustainability—ecological, social, as

Inter-sector collaboration can:
- Solve long-term, unstructured problems that no individual enterprise can solve
- Create relationships and trust across sectors over time
- Create a context for the tenth principle, 'transparency' (including integrity, responsibility, accountability, as well as lack of corruption)
- Put 'sunlight' on practices
- Enhance knowledge about how to create competitive advantage in a transparent context
- Put 'sunlight' on all social actors, not just businesses

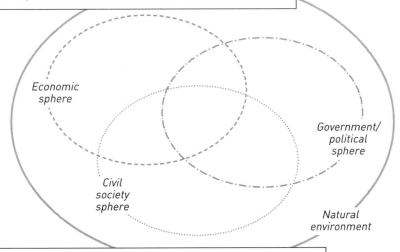

Focus on societal issues/problem-solving
- Failed governance/government. *Define:* What should the role of government(s) be?
- Assess the viability of voluntary standards
- Focus on issues of sustainability (environmental, societal, economic)
- Create an inclusive global economy (developed/developing nations)
- Reduce the learning and knowledge gap globally, and the poverty–social justice gap.
- Determine what form of capitalism will prevail
- Shift the conversation to societal health, welfare, social justice, income, access and resources

Figure 14.3 Macro-level learning and learning gaps

well as economic (a reflection of the triple-bottom-line approach to reporting popularised by Elkington [1997]).

In addition to multi-sector dialogues at the meso level, the Global Compact provides significant opportunity for multi- or inter-sector collaboration at the global level, especially in resolving global or boundary-crossing problems that no single social actor can resolve (Ackoff 1974). Although organisations in the major spheres of society have historically tended to operate independently of each other, many of today's problems have no natural boundaries (for example, HIV/AIDS, climate change or global warming, businesses operating in zones of conflict) and demand multilateral action for their resolution. Multi-sector collaborative processes, though difficult to manage because of large gaps in point of view, not to mention differences in operating goals and styles (Waddell and Brown 1997; Waddell 2000, 2002b) may be 'society's' only hope for resolving complex problems without easy boundaries. As Klaus Leisinger (2002) pointed out in his presentation at the Global Compact Learning Forum, different societal actors have 'different normative answers to the core question—*to whom, for what, and to what extent is a corporation responsible?*' As Leisinger pointed out, it is important to determine what responsibilities are required by society of business, or are 'must do' elements, what responsibilities are expected or the 'ought to do' dimensions, and what are desired or 'can do' dimensions, deserving of public praise but not attracting blame if left undone (see also Chapter 5).

The following points and implications for societal level learning through collaborative mechanisms raised at the forum included:

- There is a need to bring multiple organisations and perspectives to bear on issues where interdependence exists, issues that cross social and national boundaries, and highly complex issues, to have any hope of resolving such long-term, unstructured social problems.

- The Global Compact could use scenario planning, future search, open space and related techniques to help companies and other stakeholders deal with complex issues. Such techniques could also be used to help companies determine their participation in the Global Compact and for resolving (or facing) specific issues that affect companies as well as countries.

- Collaboration across sectors can create relationships and trust among actors in different sectors over time, especially if results are achieved.

- Cross-sector collaboration could create a context in which the tenth principle on transparency and integrity can be supported and, ultimately, adopted.

- Cross-sector collaboration can create a context in which 'sunlight' is brought to bear on organisational practices, can enhance knowledge related to competitive advantage in a context of transparency, and create pressures for organisations in all sectors to have to live up to the same set of principles and standards.

Social problem-solving through the lens of the principles raises many other issues, including private-sector knowledge and practices in dealing HIV/AIDS in the workplace, the role of the private sector in zones of conflict and conflict prevention, issues related to fresh water, social and ecological sustainability, and the internationalisation of the nine principles. Other issues include determining the viability of voluntary (as opposed to mandated) standards, establishing an agreed framework for the role of government and governance, assessing the appropriate roles of the public and private sectors, and reducing the learning, knowledge and resource gaps globally. Underlying much of this discussion is tension about what form of capitalism will prevail and whether principles—and humanity—can be built into the prevailing form.

Thus, key insights related to the Global Compact's role in social health and well-being, from participants at the Learning Forum, include:

- In the interests of simplicity, it is important that social issues raised within the Learning Forum and through the dialogue process be viewed through the lens of (one or more of) the Global Compact's principles.

- The proliferation of standards, codes and related mechanisms in the world today needs simplification, analysis and rationalisation (along the lines of the Global Compact principles). The Global Compact could play an important role in fostering research to determine what are really core or foundational values and standards, and what the common framework is that unites the range of emerging codes, values statements and standards.

- The Global Compact has an opportunity to make the business case while simultaneously recognising the 'integrity' case, by fostering measures and methods, practical solutions, and simplified approaches to implementing basic principles. Both long- and short-term frameworks are needed.

14.4 Lea(r)ning toward a tipping point

The Berlin meeting of the Learning Forum provides significant evidence of progress toward understanding what it will take to create a global context in which the principles of the Global Compact become 'on-the-ground' reality in companies and in other types of enterprises. The principles matter. The fact that they are aspirational also matters in that they provide inspiration and meaning to companies attempting to define their places in a complex and changing world. But the forum makes clear that aspiration or vision alone is insufficient to long-term success: understanding how to drive the principles into practice—in large and small firms alone, in MNCs and in small companies in developing nations, in supply and distribution companies, and throughout the functions that make up a company's management systems—is also important.

The tipping point (Gladwell 2000) for integrity through adopting and implementing the principles of the Global Compact within companies—and, indeed, within all sorts of enterprises that make up the context of today's complex societies—has yet to be reached. Still, the Learning Forum highlights that progress, though difficult to achieve and happening in fits and starts, can be and is being made. Right now that progress is on a case-by-case basis, but, as knowledge and understanding increase, learning will proceed toward more in-depth knowledge of how to apply what has been learned in a far wider range of situations and how to analyse effectively what is really good practice, separating it from practices that harm stakeholders or the natural environment. Processes of dialogue and engagement within sectors, within companies, between companies and internal and external stakeholders, and across sectors of society, can create new structures that support responsible practice and adherence to the principles. Such structures, very likely network structures, built on the moral authority and platform provided by the Global Compact's universal principles, may be the best hope there is for creating that tipping point toward transparency, responsibility, accountability and, ultimately, integrity.

15
Learners and leaders
Evolving the Global Compact in North America

Sandra Waddock
Boston College, USA

> The perfect is the enemy of the good.
>
> *Voltaire*

Dateline, Palo Alto, California, 29 April 2003. A group of 40 or more North American companies, academics and staff of the United Nations Global Compact—an innovative effort to encourage companies to live up to a set of foundational principles—gathered to discuss experience with the Global Compact to date, as well as the pro and cons of involvement. Hosted at Hewlett-Packard's headquarters (other lead companies were Pfizer and Deloitte & Touche), the meeting brought together current North American participants (mostly US companies) in the Global Compact and potentially interested companies to discuss in a safe environment their experience. This chapter reports the learning derived from the meeting, which followed Chatham House rules in that specific attributions are omitted. It synthesises the benefits experienced by those companies already participating, the concerns raised by those not yet involved and by participants as they considered whether to become signatories or not and concludes with a section on what has been learned to date.

15.1 Background

The UN Global Compact was established in 1999 after UN Secretary-General Kofi Annan, speaking at a meeting of the World Economic Forum, called for companies to join in an international initiative that supported nine fundamental and internationally agreed principles on human rights, labour rights and the environment (for the principles, see page 12; for a transcript of Annan's speech, see Chapter 1). Since that time more than 1200 companies, international labour organisations and civil-society enterprises around the world have joined the Global Compact global network, with signatories committing to uphold the principles through multi-stakeholder engagement and dialogue, leadership commitment, learning, partnership projects and participation in local networks as well as the global network that constitutes the Global Compact and that is increasingly vital in the boundary-less world that is rapidly evolving.

In addition to the principles and policy dialogues, one of the hallmarks of the Global Compact is an annual Learning Forum, where participants come together to share their experiences in relation to the Global Compact and learn from each other. It was at this annual meeting in Berlin in December 2002 that the few representatives of North American companies realised that of the more than 800 Global Compact signatories at that time, only 44 were US companies, four were Canadian, and one was Mexican. Only three large US companies of the many thousands of companies in North America were represented in Berlin. The Palo Alto meeting evolved from the recognition of the need to raise the profile of and commitment to the Global Compact and its principles in North America as well as to create a forum in which learning could be shared and where questions and concerns about the Global Compact could be raised.

15.2 Why sign the Global Compact? Benefits and expectations

The Global Compact is nothing if it is not aspirational. It focuses attention on good (not perfect) company practice around a few core principles that provide for respect for human dignity in both social and work settings and for the natural environment. The Global Compact is an effort to build a better world by involving businesses directly in the development of healthier societies, by emphasising a relatively simple set of ideals. The Global Compact is simple, clear and relies on 'universal' principles that have already been widely agreed on by the world's nation-states. In its simplicity and aspiration, the Global Compact focuses attention on fundamental ethical principles that give guidance on how people should treat each other and the natural environment, without the overly complex codification of rules, norms or expectations sometimes found in codes of conduct.

Conference participants identified a number of important benefits that they saw deriving from participation in the Global Compact, as summarised below.

15.2.1 The importance of aspiration

The aspiration integral to the Global Compact involves the establishment of a core set of principles that, when implemented, will provide a foundation of trust among businesses, civil society and non-governmental organisations (NGOs) and governments. Especially in the context of the explosion of corporate scandals in the USA in the early 2000s, enhancement of public trust is acknowledged to be essential by current participants in the Global Compact. In signing up to the Global Compact, companies recognise the moral authority, credibility, convening power, inclusiveness and global reach of the UN and are able to participate in the world's only truly global corporate citizenship initiative. They are also acknowledging the importance of the universality of the principles to which their home countries have also agreed as aspirations about how we as human beings working as a part of companies should behave. This engagement positions business squarely as part of the solution to today's social and ecological issues, not the source of problems. The multi-stakeholder design of the Global Compact recognises inherently that economic development, in which large enterprises as well as small and medium-sized enterprises (SMEs) play a significant role, is at the core of healthy societies over the long term and that businesses can be positive actors in such economic development.

15.2.2 Leadership in the global context

CEO and other top-management commitment to the Global Compact is essential. The process of signing up to the Global Compact involves the CEO of the company sending a letter to the UN Secretary-General in which the company's CEO and, if possible, board express support for the principles. The very process of signing the Global Compact therefore provides an opportunity for the company's leaders to open up dialogue on the important issues embedded in the Global Compact with the top-management team. In addition, signing the Global Compact places companies in a forward-thinking leadership position with respect to issues on which they might otherwise be criticised.

Because important social issues embedded in the nine principles of the Global Compact can be raised within the company during the signing and implementation processes, the Global Compact is more likely to provide a framework for continued company leadership as well as constructive interactions with key stakeholder groups than if the company simply developed an internal code of conduct. Further, the principles are global in scope; hence they can help signatory companies avert nationalistic sentiments and a 'go it alone' mentality that has the potential to create conflict in settings beyond national boundaries.

15.2.3 A simple, clear framework for action

One of the important appeals of the Global Compact is the simplicity and clarity of the principles, which provide general and pragmatic, but not overly specified, guidance (note that there is a possibility that a tenth anti-corruption and transparency principle may be added if global agreement is achieved; see Appendix D). This simplicity provides coherence about the 'rules of the game', combined with clear guidelines regarding practices and acceptable behaviour. The principles designate a 'floor' for practice below which actions and behaviour become problematic, as well as a forum for proactive and interactive collective action on important issues by companies themselves.

Although particular reporting standards are not mandated, the link with the Global Reporting Initiative (GRI;[1] which, in turn, is linked to the SA8000 labour standards[2] and the AA1000 accountability standards[3]) provides a potential roadmap for companies interested in meeting external demands for greater transparency about their social and ecological impacts. In a world that has exploded with a confusing array of standards, principles, codes of conduct and guidelines for corporations since the early 1990s, the principles of the Global Compact are straightforward, easy to grasp and reasonably simple to implement. The principles are, as company representatives suggested, a good place to begin a complex, long-term process of specifying and implementing core values in corporate practice. Further, the principles are voluntary and, from a North American perspective, voluntary adoption may help to forestall governmental regulation, which is often considered onerous.

Another benefit provided by the Global Compact is an already-constructed infrastructure or framework for multi-stakeholder engagement on difficult issues. This infrastructure can provide a forum for interaction that helps avoid possible future problems and reduces future liabilities. For SMEs as well as large companies, the ability to become part of such a larger network can be important because it means that other companies may be able to offer insights, learning and experience, thus averting the reinventing-the-wheel problem that might otherwise be faced.

15.2.4 Alignment

The Global Compact can help companies align their own internal values with internationally accepted values, in part by making those values and the company's adherence more explicit and transparent and by fostering discussion on the nature and implementation of core values. This alignment happens not only in conjunction with external standards such as the Global Compact principles but also internally, across divisions and sub-units. Values that are consistent and coherent can be particularly helpful in highly complex and decentralised companies operating in many divisions and geographical settings, serving as a sort of 'glue' that holds a company's culture together in these diverse arenas.

1 See www.globalreporting.org.
2 See www.cepaa.org.
3 See www.accountability.org.uk.

Additionally, social expectations of companies have risen in the past few years. Many demands are being made on companies to 'give away' their products, technologies and services, particularly in developing nations. Companies in widely disparate industries face similar social and stakeholder expectations. The Global Compact can provide a helpful framework for working out what to do in the face of such expectations which if met could make the current business model quite unworkable.

Further, there is credibility to be gained from companies working in conjunction with the UN, which itself has a good deal of standing in the world today, despite questions that surround the 2003 US-led war in Iraq. In a world full of conflict and divisiveness, where the motives of large multinational corporations (MNCs) are frequently questioned, alignment with the core principles of the Global Compact potentially provides a degree of credibility to corporate actions that is otherwise questionable in the minds of corporate critics.

15.2.5 Opening up the conversation

One of the clear benefits that current signatories saw as they considered whether to sign on to the Global Compact and after signing was that even the process of consideration allowed for the possibility of opening up a conversation within the company about specific issues that were previously off the table, undiscussable or simply not in the corporate mind-set. Issues such as human and labour rights, child labour, living wages, facilitating payments, supply-chain management, freedom of association and the meaning of sustainability itself all become topics of discussion as the company makes its decision to join the Global Compact and determines how to support the principles once it has signed up. These conversations can surface potential problems of which the company had previously been unaware, make them discussable and move the company forward on actions to resolve potential pitfalls before they are made public in ways that damage company reputation. Further, the need for CEO and senior management commitment to the Global Compact makes such issues discussable at top levels within the company, not just within traditional arenas of corporate citizenship and responsibility.

15.2.6 A catalyst for learning

The Global Compact in many ways serves as a catalyst for learning both within and across companies. The framework provided by the Global Compact includes the Learning Forum, processes of multi-stakeholder engagement and dialogue. These meetings and engagements, as well as the research process that goes along with the development of cases, provide a 'safe space'. Internally, cases and experiences in implementing the principles can be used for communication and management development purposes. Externally, company experiences can be shared and mutual learning generated, where pitfalls experienced by others can be explored and potentially avoided by companies newer to the process of supporting global standards or engaging with NGOs, governments and civil-society organisations.

Although activists have been 'hammering' companies for years about human and labour rights and environmental sustainability, these issues have not yet become prominent in many North American companies. Participation in the Global Compact provides an opportunity to raise up such topics as human rights, labour rights and sustainability (or others issues covered by the Global Compact dialogue process, such as: HIV and AIDS in the workplace; water resources; the boundaries of public and private enterprise; or participation in zones of conflict). They can then be dealt with proactively rather than reactively.

Internally, learning is generated within companies as new topics of conversation open up and executives are exposed to areas that previously were not discussed. Opportunities to create new training instruments and processes associated with a more professional approach to internal capacity-building are also generated as the company begins to discuss how to implement new practices related to Global Compact principles, particularly if they are in areas such child labour, sustainability or human rights, that have previously not been in the forefront of management's attention.

15.2.7 Engagement: a forum for dialogue

One of the things that the Global Compact provides is a ready-made forum where two things can happen. First, companies can engage with each other to share their experiences around issues related to the Global Compact (e.g. human rights, the boundaries between the public and the private sector, demands by activists and related issues) and other important issues relating to business in society. Interactive learning, becoming or learning from a role model and engagement on important issues are all possible outcomes of involvement in the Global Compact.

Second, the Global Compact provides the possibility for engagement in multi-stakeholder dialogues about important issues in a safe, reflective forum that is focused on mutuality and learning rather than adversarial tactics. Through these dialogic processes new alliances can be forged, challenges identified and lessons learned shared. Multi-stakeholder engagement provides a new way for companies to explore the views of potential critics in settings where common goals and concerns can be expressed as well as underlying issues shared, thus providing a mechanism for gaining connections, insights and perspectives that might otherwise be lacking. This interaction provides a useful way to move forward action on important social issues not readily resolved by organisations in a single sector through an emerging type of multi-stakeholder alliance called 'global action networks' (Waddell 2003a; see also Chapter 20).

15.2.8 Risk management

Participants in the Global Compact believe that it is better to be part of the process of creating the rules by which companies will live than to be an outsider in that process. Such involvement in creating the 'rules of the game' has a practical benefit in that participants can shape the very rules by which they will live, rather than later having to adapt to rules shaped by others, thereby reducing risks (Mahon 1989).

15.3 Concerns and responses

Why have so few US or other North American companies become signatories to the Global Compact? Other than a general lack of visibility of the Global Compact, what drawbacks might companies perceive to agreeing to uphold principles that are already well-established foundational norms in the international community, as evidenced by the fact that they are drawn from internationally agreed documents that most of the nation-states have signed? Concerns generally revolve around several specific Global Compact principles and the litigiousness that is particular to US culture and society.

15.3.1 Let's show it to legal counsel

In the US context, in particular, what can 'kill' the capacity for company involvement in the Global Compact is the phrase 'Let's just pass this idea by legal counsel'. To overcome the issues that legal counsel raises related to liability, the Global Compact has worked closely with the American Bar Association to work up language for the commitment letter that does not subject the company to potential lawsuits.[4] Basically, the CEO's letter simply states the company's commitment to aspire to living up to the principles without making any attestations to the particular implementation of any principle. There is no commitment to performance or success implied in a commitment to aspire to the principles, nor any interference implied with existing national laws.

Participants agreed that there is no 'silver bullet' to deal with legal considerations except the power of leadership. One thing that has become clear to signatories is the important role that the CEO plays in establishing a company's vision and commitment to the Global Compact. When the CEO is visionary enough to recognise the importance of the aspirations embedded within the Global Compact, the objections of legal counsel can be overcome.

15.3.2 What is in the fine print?

This question surfaced more than once, yet the Global Compact is simple, clear and straightforward. There is no fine print that anyone has yet uncovered. Thus, for example, companies can aspire to and support the precautionary approach (importantly, it is *not* the precautionary principle, which is far more stringent in its implications, that is written into the Global Compact) without having to be environmentally sustainable at this point in time. Or they can support the right of employees to free association without necessarily committing to a union in the company, in the recognition that employees demand a union as a tool for getting something else that they want (such as better working conditions) that the company could potentially voluntarily supply. One important point is that the

---

4 For information on this letter, see the UN Global Compact website, www.unglobalcompact.org.

Global Compact does not oblige companies to endorse unions but rather to behave lawfully, civilly and respectfully with employees.

15.3.3 Vulnerability: 'no good deed goes unpunished'

One of the challenges of the Global Compact is for participating companies to evidence a bit of vulnerability in sharing not only good practices but also those that may not have worked so well. Yet the 'safe space' provided by the Learning Forum and multi-stakeholder dialogues provides an opportunity for this sharing and mutual learning to occur. The other source of possible vulnerability is the risk that companies taking leadership on Global Compact principles may become targets of activists, particularly when internal problems do arise, as they almost inevitably will in large, complex and inherently human organisations. But size alone is frequently a basis for being targeted, so companies that are already in leadership positions by virtue of their size may find benefits in participation in the aspirations set by the Global Compact, especially when the values of the Global Compact are consistent with those already established within the company.

Charges of 'greenwashing' or 'bluewashing' (wrapping a company in the blue flag of the UN) by ideologically oriented NGOs can make stepping out in front on some of the Global Compact's principles seem risky indeed. One response to this concern was raised in the question: what is the risk of *not* becoming involved with the Global Compact? To the extent that the Global Compact succeeds in putting the issues embedded in the principles into the public arena, companies that are recalcitrant could find themselves subject to even greater scrutiny by NGOs and civil-society organisations.

What happens when a company does not conform to the principles of the Global Compact is a serious issue. The Global Compact has no powers for sanctioning companies, nor does the UN or the Global Compact have enforcement powers (indeed, this is a primary criticism directed against the Global Compact by some observers). The primary 'power' of the principles is the moral authority and weight of public opinion associated with them. Basically, the power of persuasion for the Global Compact is that power associated with the UN's 'bully pulpit' combined with the peer pressure that comes from other signatories making a sincere commitment of collective intention to support the principles.

15.3.4 Effectiveness: these things take time

One of the charges levelled at the Global Compact is that it has not yet achieved much. What it has done is to create a global network of companies focused on the principles, yet the cases developed to date suggest the validity of a common statement about organisational and social change: these things take time. Immediate results, even internal company changes, that require systemic attention and new ways of thinking do, in fact, take time, as acknowledged by the Global Compact staff.

15.3.5 Reporting and transparency

External demands on companies for greater transparency and broader reporting of corporate activities and impacts (seen in the growing popularity of triple-bottom-line reports, which report not only on economic and financial performance but also social and ecological performance) are creating uncertainty about how far to go. Although the Global Compact does not require triple-bottom-line reporting or monitoring of corporate activities, questions arise about reporting, including what, when, how often, and how. Further, concerns exist about whether third-party verification and certification will eventually be demanded. Should that happen, Global Compact companies may well be at an advantage because they will have already had some experience with reporting and transparency that may not be embedded within competitors.

Measures of progress with respect to implementation of the principles still need to be developed and can provide an important indicator of success, as well as becoming a source of needed credibility. At some point, the issue of data and reporting comparability across companies in different nations also needs to be addressed. Because many companies desire voluntary reporting standards, one of the incentives, conceived as a political strategy (Mahon 1989) aimed at greater participation in the Global Compact, may be to avert mandated reporting guidelines at some future point. Minimally, measurement can prepare companies for future demands for greater transparency.

15.3.6 The 'glocal' problem

The principles of the Global Compact carry a certain integrity and focus around core issues of human rights, labour rights and environmental sustainability. The principles are widely accepted by nations globally, even though they may not always be fully enforced. There are considerable differences, however, between espousing 'universal' principles and implementing them in the specificity of local contexts around the world. The benefit of universal principles is that they have the effect of providing a level playing field, especially as standards are more widely promulgated. The drawback comes from the fact that not all companies have yet voluntarily agreed to support these principles and standards. This tension is particularly highlighted when supply chain management is under scrutiny. If all companies were expected to apply consistent and high labour and human rights standards, for example, then local suppliers would feel considerably less exposed and have to exert far less effort to meet different standards from different customers or work through the implementation of standards independently.

15.4 Lessons learned so far

If one theme pervaded the launch of what it is hoped will become the North American Global Compact Learning Forum it is embodied in the quotation from

Voltaire that opens this paper: 'The perfect is the enemy of the good.' The Global Compact aims at good practice in companies. The principles provide guidance for company practice with respect to treatment of people, civil society, governments and the natural environment. The Global Compact supports an important set of fundamental principles that if fully implemented would enable all of us to live better lives—and companies to be successful operating within healthy and effective societies. There is no expectation in the Global Compact that any human enterprise, business, NGO or government will achieve perfection. The aspiration is rather simpler. It is that by working together around a set of common agreed values we, including businesses, can build a better world.

Many of the current signatories view the time and management energy that they invested in the decision process to sign the Global Compact as good long-term investments. The summary lessons to date can be found in three 'Cs' that were repeatedly discussed at the Global Compact meeting in Palo Alto:

● **Coherence.** The principles provide a coherent, simple and straightforward set of commonly agreed and (hoped-to-be) consistently applied principles around which practice can be established; they represent the basis of an agreed set of global 'rules of the game' that can make participation in the global economy fairer for all.

● **Co-ordination.** The Global Compact network structure, Learning Forums and dialogue processes provide an infrastructure in which companies can learn from one another's practices and engage in productive and useful conversations with stakeholders in other sectors, such as NGOs, civil-society organisations and governments.

● **Credibility.** The global reach and moral authority of the UN, the universality of the principles and the convening power of the UN create a context of credibility and the potential to develop trust among institutions in society that lends credibility to participation in the Global Compact.

Perfection may never be achieved in the human enterprise of which business is one important manifestation; however, good practice and good intentions are possible. The Global Compact demonstrates both of these qualities in its aspiration to improve the ways in which businesses participate in the global economy. This meeting represents but a start for North American companies in playing their part in developing the 'good'.

16
Pfizer
A new mission in action

Nancy Nielsen
Pfizer Inc. USA

US business—known for its innovation, competition and speed of action—has been slow to embrace the UN Global Compact. In July 2003, when the Global Compact celebrated the third anniversary of its founding, only a handful of major US companies could be counted among the nearly 1,000 firms around the world that had signed it. Pfizer Inc., a US pharmaceutical company headquartered in New York City, was among the early adopters.

Despite the fact the Global Compact is a voluntary initiative, many corporate CEOs did not sign up. The Global Compact's original nine principles for corporate behaviour include language on human rights, labour and the environment. 'Why invite unnecessary attention or potential trouble when one doesn't need to?' argued many corporate advisors.

Some US companies were concerned about attaching their corporate reputations to perceptions of the UN. Others worried that signing would invite litigation, labour problems or unwarranted public scrutiny.

On 4 October 2002, Pfizer announced it had signed the UN Global Compact. A few days earlier, Dr Henry A. McKinnell, the chairman of Pfizer, sent a letter to UN Secretary-General Kofi Annan affirming Pfizer's support for the Global Compact. In doing so, Pfizer became the first US-based pharmaceutical firm and the first top-ten company on the New York Stock Exchange to join the Global Compact.

McKinnell told colleagues:

> Some companies may fear that if they sign the Global Compact, they'll be held to a higher standard of corporate citizenship. That's a challenge we frankly welcome, because being a good global citizen has long been at the core of how we do business. That's why after

careful deliberation we determined that joining the Compact is in our business interest.

Unlike any other industry in the world, the pharmaceutical industry sits at the crossroads where the global interests of business, science, government, religion and the general public can collide over issues of life and death. In 2002, it seemed like collision was more the norm for the industry than the exception.

The AIDS crisis brought into sharp relief the changing expectations that society has of multinational companies such as Pfizer. AIDS issues blurred the boundaries between the public and private sectors and the healthcare priorities of the developing and developed worlds. People wanted new breakthrough medicines and they wanted them at affordable prices.

Pfizer alone certainly cannot ensure everyone gets the medicines they need. But it can understand its stakeholders' needs and build partnerships that make progress. How well Pfizer and the other pharmaceutical companies do this may spell the difference between an industry with the freedom to operate and one threatened by controls that stifle innovation.

This chapter is a reflection on how and why Pfizer's chairman and leadership team decided to sign the UN Global Compact when most other major US companies would not. Intermittently, over six months, Pfizer management weighed the risks and benefits of the Global Compact relevant to their area of expertise, and then the leadership team unanimously decided to support it. The next challenge was to introduce the Global Compact across a decentralised company of 122,000 employees in more than 100 countries, and for colleagues to begin assessing how to operationalise the Global Compact in their own business units. Like any new path, there were unexpected twists and turns.

At time of writing, the Global Compact recently passed its 18 month anniversary at Pfizer. Has it made any difference in how the company sees its role in the world, identifies and engages with stakeholders or thinks about its business? Where is Pfizer headed? Last, has the Global Compact effort been worth it?

Michael Useem, author of *The Leadership Moment* (1998), says his single most important finding about leadership is 'the overwhelming significance of vision and action' (1998: 263). Useem, Director of the Wharton School's Center for Leadership and Change, said, 'Leadership decisions and the development of good leaders are important in any age, but the changing face of business and government makes both more important today than perhaps ever before' (1998: 7). Further, he said, 'Leadership matters most when it is least clear what course should be followed' (1998: 8).

The leadership vision for Kofi Annan, as he said at the World Economic Forum in 1999 (see Chapter 1), is to foster global stability and prosperity and to share the benefits of globalisation with all people, and so he launched the Global Compact. Hank McKinnell has a vision for advancing sustainable health that builds on prevention, disease management and discovering new medicines, and he spearheaded a new mission for Pfizer in support of this vision. The two visions are related. Good health is a key component in creating stability and prosperity, which brings with it a virtuous cycle of longer lifespans. Neither the UN nor the business community can create that alone.

When Pfizer signed the Global Compact, McKinnell said:

> We have learned that no single entity—whether business, government or NGO—can alone bridge the deep divides between poverty and affluence, health and disease, growth and stagnation. As the world's foremost pharmaceutical company, we have an important obligation to take a global leadership role. Multilateral partnerships are one of the best means for achieving those ends, and there is no greater or more effective platform to forge such partnerships than the Global Compact. Signing the Global Compact is another way we can be part of the solution.

In 2002 many companies worldwide had signed the Global Compact, including BP, Royal Dutch/Shell, BMW and DaimlerChrysler. But in the USA the only major companies that had signed were Cisco, DuPont, Hewlett-Packard and Nike. Pfizer's signing—as the world's largest pharmaceutical company in one of the most important and contentious industries—was an important signal for both the Global Compact and Pfizer stakeholders.

16.1 Pfizer's evolution: a modest beginning

Pfizer was founded by two cousins in 1849 in Brooklyn, New York, as a small retail speciality chemicals shop. Today it is the number one research-based pharmaceutical company, by revenue,[1] in every major market in the world, with 14 of the top-selling prescription medicines.

Pfizer's main line of business is to discover, develop, manufacture and market new medicines for humans. Pfizer's medicines currently cover most major therapeutic areas: asthma and allergies, cardiovascular disorders, high cholesterol, central nervous system disorders, depression and anxiety, diabetes, HIV and AIDS, inflammatory diseases, metabolic disorders, oncology, ophthalmics and women's health. That means Pfizer serves patients along a continuum of healthcare, starting with products for well-being, moving to medicines for chronic conditions and ending with the most advanced therapies for life-threatening conditions.

In addition, the company invests heavily in biomedical research and development (R&D). Pfizer manages the world's largest privately funded pharmaceutical research effort, with more than 13,000 scientists worldwide and with an R&D expenditure of US$7 billion annually in 2003 (Pfizer 2003). In all, Pfizer now has 130 new molecules in its pipeline of new medicines, along with 95 projects to expand the use of therapies currently offered.

The pharmaceutical business is the epitome of a high-risk, high-reward business. Scientists test thousands of molecules to develop a single marketable medicine, which takes 10–15 years and costs an estimated US$800 million.[2] Medicines that

1 'Performance report', Pfizer press release, 22 January 2004.
2 Tufts University Centre for the Study of Drug Development, press release, 30 November 2001.

make it to market have to cover the costs of all those that don't 'pan out'. Unfortunately, compounds that were on-track to be suitable to reach their final destination (the patient) can get derailed very late in their development. Pharmaceutical companies cannot gauge the success of a new medicine until it is fully developed, approved by regulatory authorities, prescribed by doctors and in the marketplace long enough to identify the full range of side-effects.

The challenges of managing this complex business in today's quickly changing environment require a leader who knows business, science and government and who has a worldwide view with much experience 'on the ground'. In short, that person must thrive on the new realities of global leadership.

Hank McKinnell joined Pfizer in 1971 in Tokyo and later served as country manager in Iran and Afghanistan. He later led all of Pfizer's Asia operations. He came equipped with a BA in business from the University of British Columbia and both an MBA and PhD from Stanford University's Graduate School of Business. He has held many senior management positions at Pfizer, including executive vice president, chief financial officer and president of Pfizer Global Pharmaceuticals. He is currently chairman and CEO.

16.2 Pfizer's internal revolution: a new mission

In 1997, Pfizer launched a mission of becoming the world's premier pharmaceutical company by 2001 as measured by revenue. Pfizer reached that goal two years ahead of schedule. The company took its first step toward a new mission in November 2000, when McKinnell convened 25 senior leaders from throughout Pfizer to identify and address the most significant issues facing the company. The need for a new mission quickly emerged as an area of focus. Internal focus groups were conducted at a number of Pfizer sites, during which colleagues were asked to 'think out loud', not only about a new mission for Pfizer but also about the company's purpose and reason for being.

Two crucial ideas were committed to paper. First, Pfizer would measure itself on a combination of financial and non-financial measures, reflecting stakeholders' changing expectations of business. Second, Pfizer would no longer measure itself solely against others in the pharmaceutical industry, but against all other companies in all industries.

McKinnell unveiled the new Pfizer mission in June 2001 at a meeting of 400 top executives from all of Pfizer's businesses from around the world. He said:

> Our new mission is: We will become the world's most valued company to patients, customers, colleagues, investors, business partners and the communities where we work and live.

Then he added:

> This is our shared promise to ourselves and to the people we serve.

The mission was supported by Pfizer's purpose and values. Pfizer's purpose is to:

> dedicate ourselves to humanity's quest for longer, healthier, happier lives through innovation in pharmaceutical, consumer and animal health products.

Pfizer's values are integrity, leadership, innovation, performance, teamwork, customer focus, respect for people, community and quality. McKinnell also introduced the Pfizer Leader Behaviours: to sustain the focus on performance, to create an inclusive environment, to encourage open discussion and debate, to manage change, to develop people and to seek alignment of ideals across Pfizer. Since then, the values and leader behaviour expectations have been continually communicated to colleagues and reinforced by the leadership team.

The new mission was significantly different from anything Pfizer had done before. For the first time, Pfizer would intentionally measure itself against other companies on non-financial measures, along with the traditional financial measures. This would mean using all of the company's resources—whether in R&D, manufacturing, marketing or corporate functions—to improve society and satisfy investors. In other words, Pfizer's mission was an early platform on which to advance sustainable health.

With an eye on the business, McKinnell said:

> We all know of companies that made it to the top and then declined. We must learn what it takes to go beyond number one. That journey includes a self-imposed transformation. Companies that endure in leadership work to build on their best qualities. However, they also lead an internal revolution to instill behaviours that foster change . . . Ultimately, every one of our colleagues must join the revolution, and step up to new concepts of leadership. Everyone must find a way to lead.

Leadership was clearly the watchword of the meeting. But rather than celebrating Pfizer's current leadership position, the bulk of the meeting was spent taking a hard look at the things that needed to change at Pfizer if it were to sustain and extend its leadership.

In addition to a new array of medicines that will compete with many of Pfizer's best sellers, McKinnell added that competitors were

> also banking on a less obvious threat to our leadership. That's the threat of our own arrogance, of complacency, of the belief that number one is now our birthright. They [Pfizer's competitors] are banking on us to let up and resist change . . . to continue to focus on individual heroics and not team interaction. They hope that we will keep ourselves trapped in functional silos.

How could Pfizer go beyond number one? The solution would be in extending the new realities of global leadership throughout the company.

McKinnell said that leadership at Pfizer used to mean 'a small group of senior executives at the top'. Going forward, he said, 'every colleague must be a leader'.

In addition to calling for a revolution in the 'who' of leadership, McKinnell also called for dramatic changes in the 'how' of leadership. McKinnell said he was making it his personal priority to:

> build a more inclusive environment where we benefit from diversity of background, thought, and experience. We need a company where people can talk openly and candidly. Where we confront problems before they become larger. And where people feel confident that their ideas will get a fair hearing and prompt action.

16.3 The UN Global Compact and Pfizer

With that as McKinnell's call to action, one might think the decision to sign the Global Compact would have been simple for Pfizer. Not so. The leadership team, with input from Pfizer colleagues across the company, evaluated the Global Compact from its own areas of expertise. The team is made up of McKinnell and the top executive from R&D, science policy, manufacturing, pharmaceutical marketing, corporate finance, legal affairs, corporate affairs and human resources.

Chuck Hardwick, who was Vice President of Corporate Affairs at the time, brought the Global Compact to the attention of McKinnell around April 2002. McKinnell asked numerous questions about the principles and why other US companies had not signed. There wasn't much of a track record on the risks and benefits of the Global Compact for a US company as only a few had already signed. Dawn Rittenhouse, Director of Sustainability at DuPont, was instrumental in answering Pfizer's many questions from the risks involved to the nuts and bolts of implementation.

After McKinnell was satisfied that the Global Compact was worth putting on the agenda for the leadership team to discuss, more questions arose from the team that revolved around risk assessment, which implied legal or business difficulties:

- How does Pfizer's performance rate compare with the principles? Do we have that data?

- Will signing the Global Compact ever pit Pfizer against foreign governments?

- How do the human rights principles apply to Pfizer?

- Could Principle 3, on freedom of association and the right to collective bargaining, encourage barriers to discussion between management and non-management employees?

- How would Principle 7, on supporting the precautionary principle toward environmental challenges, affect our application of the precautionary approach?

The leadership team resolved their questions one at a time:

Question: How does Pfizer's performance rate compare with the principles? Do we have that data?

Answer: Georg Kell, Executive Head of the Global Compact, said all companies had the same concern. He replied that it was unlikely any company fulfilled all the principles before they signed. He said, 'If a company were perfect, it wouldn't need the Global Compact. The point is to aspire to meet those principles and take actions to get there'.[3]

Question: Will signing the Global Compact ever pit Pfizer against foreign governments?

Answer: There was no evidence of that, even among companies based in other countries. The goal of the Global Compact was to work with governments and civil society.

Question: How do the human rights principles apply to Pfizer?

Answer: As the term 'human rights' has begun to enter the business environment, Pfizer is engaging stakeholders to learn more about it. We support and respect fairness and safety for individuals and communities. Pfizer already had strong compliance with local and international laws, promoted the rule of law, provided safe and healthful working conditions, supported diversity and worked with communities and governments to improve society.

Question: Could Principle 3, on freedom of association and the right to collective bargaining, encourage barriers to discussion between management and non-management employees?

Answer: The leadership team was confident that Pfizer's working conditions around the world were very good and met or surpassed local standards and laws. McKinnell's sign-on letter to Kofi Annan said:

> Pfizer abides by all of the laws and regulations of the countries in which we do business, including the laws and regulations governing an individual's right to associate and collectively bargain. At Pfizer, we provide all of our employees with a competitive compensation and benefits package and maintain working conditions in line with our values, especially Respect for People, even in the absence of an organised labour group and without the need for a collectively bargained agreement. Our goal is to create an inclusive environment and one that encourages open discussion and debate. We do not want anything that prevents us from maintaining this environment or limits colleagues from dealing directly with leaders of the organisation. Pfizer also conducts all of its operations with the highest care for protection of our environment, employing the same high standards worldwide.

3 Conversation with author, New York, September 2002.

Pfizer posted McKinnell's letter on the company's Internet site to be transparent about Pfizer's commitment to the Global Compact.

Question: How would Principle 7, on supporting the precautionary principle toward environmental challenges, affect our application of the precautionary approach?

Answer: The precautionary principle or approach is a concept that has been or could be employed by government or industry decisions that involve potential risk to the environment or human health. There is no one definition, but rather many definitions or interpretations that reflect the user's view of what is an acceptable risk.

One of the most widely quoted definitions is from the 1992 United Nations Rio Declaration on the Environment and Development:

> In order to protect the environment, the precautionary approach shall be widely applied by States according to their capabilities. Where there are threats of and development of serious or irreversible damage, lack of full scientific certainty shall not be used as a reason for postponing cost-effective measures to prevent environmental degradation.[4]

The Pfizer leadership team recognised that Principle 7 was fully consistent with the way Pfizer does business. As a research-based pharmaceutical company, Pfizer routinely develops extensive datasets on its proprietary compounds. Using this information, Pfizer applies state-of-the-art scientific risk assessment technologies to assure the safety and efficacy of its human and veterinary products. Pfizer's identification of the development of health, physical and environmental hazards and exposure data also provides the scientific basis for understanding and minimising the occupational and environmental impacts during product manufacture, transport, use and disposal. In effect, Pfizer employs the precautionary approach in the development and manufacture of its products. Participation in the Global Compact would provide Pfizer with another opportunity to engage in dialogue with interested stakeholders on the appropriate application of the precautionary approach by government, industry, academia and others.

Finally, with those questions answered, the leadership team asked whether the Global Compact would support Pfizer's strategic vision. What was in it for Pfizer that could help support its mission to become the world's most valued company to its stakeholders: patients, customers, colleagues, investors, business partners and the communities where Pfizer lives and works, which includes governments, NGOs, multilateral organisations, academia and the media?

The Global Compact staff replied that the UN is a truly global organisation with far-reaching power to convene. It encourages fact-finding and debate among disparate parties. The Global Compact, which is not a UN agency but an extension

4   See www.un.org/documents/ga/conf151/aconf15126-1annex1.htm.

of the UN Secretary-General's Secretariat, has the flexibility to bring together business, governments and civil society for informal discussions without getting entangled in the slow-moving UN bureaucracy.

Pfizer is a global company with sales or operations in about 150 countries. All of Pfizer's major stakeholder groups were represented in the UN system in one form or another. Whether it was in the form of ambassadors from 191 member-states or in the agencies such as the World Health Organisation (WHO) or World Trade Organisation (WTO), many of Pfizer's interests were present at the UN. It was almost like one-stop shopping to engage some stakeholders. And many of these stakeholders would see Pfizer being attuned to the interdependent nature of society and business if the company publicly aspired to and acted on the principles of the Global Compact.

Although Pfizer had good relationships with many stakeholder groups, it had a reputation for being unwilling to engage with some critics, such as NGOs. Some, but not all, NGOs and civil-society organisations viewed Pfizer and other multinational firms as arrogant, unapproachable and uncommunicative. The pharmaceutical industry itself was under attack for its focus on 'Western diseases' and the price of its prescription medicines. The industry's position wasn't getting through the media or other channels. McKinnell knew that, in order for Pfizer to fulfil its mission and sustain a productive business, it needed to engage these critics. The Global Compact was a network Pfizer could enter and immediately get to work learning from others, discussing issues and explaining how medicines are discovered and brought to market. The goal would be to find common ground and new solutions.

Around that time, a corporate citizenship position was created to initiate and co-ordinate corporate responsibility across the company with each business unit deciding how best to operationalise it. Nancy Nielsen, who had experience in the public and private sector, undertook the role of launching the initiative.

Her first action as Senior Director of Corporate Citizenship was to create a global, cross-divisional team to actively involve all operating and support divisions. This team includes about 25 management-level colleagues from different functions throughout the company. The team's inaugural meeting was a free-wheeling discussion on what corporate citizenship should mean at Pfizer. The team quickly realised it had to first establish a common vocabulary on corporate responsibility. It ended with a discussion on how to align corporate citizenship with Pfizer's mission statement, purpose and values.

Next, that team benchmarked Pfizer's performance to the Global Compact principles. Given Pfizer's global operations and decentralised structure, collecting the data was difficult. Colleagues in human resources, legal affairs, corporate governance, corporate affairs, marketing and environment, health and safety reached out to other colleagues and pooled information. Throughout the process, colleagues asked what the principles really meant in terms of Pfizer's day-to-day operations.

This analysis provided a functional framework to understand the Global Compact within Pfizer's operations and provided ideas that directed the evolution of Pfizer's corporate citizenship role. In many ways, Pfizer does align with the Global Compact principles. As the team imagined, there were many examples of good alignment and there were areas that needed improvement.

One of the strengths of the Global Compact is that it is broad enough to apply to all industries. It is also structured as a positive incentive rather than as a set of rules of 'thou shall not'. The Global Compact's literature says:

> [It] is not a regulatory instrument—it does not police, enforce or measure the behaviour or actions of companies. Rather, the Global Compact relies on public accountability, transparency and the enlightened self-interest of companies, labour and civil society to initiate and share substantive action in pursuing the principles on which the Global Compact is based.[5]

From Pfizer's perspective, this encourages companies to raise the bar for high standards of corporate behaviour.

Critics of the Global Compact may not appreciate the power of positive incentives. If the Global Compact had been a list of rules and regulations, Pfizer would not have joined. Although regulatory bodies are necessary for society to function, the Global Compact fills a crucial gap in fostering dialogue, best practice and public–private relationships.

As has often been said by critics of the Global Compact, this broad approach also allows companies to sign the Global Compact and then ignore it. Although some have done so, they are the ones that will be left behind.

16.4 Pfizer focuses externally

The main tools of the Global Compact are multi-stakeholder dialogue, Learning Forums and public–private partnership projects, with which companies determine on an individual basis precisely how they will implement the principles of the Global Compact. Like many other companies, Pfizer focused its Global Compact activities on projects that benefited external stakeholders.

Pfizer already had its Diflucan Partnership Program under way.[6] That programme donates Diflucan, an anti-fungal medicine, to treat HIV/AIDS-opportunistic infections. The programme is now running in 18 African countries and in Haiti and Cambodia. In addition to providing free medicine, Pfizer partners with the International Association of Physicians in AIDS Care (IAPAC) to train healthcare professionals in the diagnosis and treatment of opportunistic fungal infections. Nearly 18,000 professionals have been trained to date.

In 2002, the year McKinnell signed the Global Compact, Pfizer was rated by the newspaper *Chronicle of Philanthropy*[7] as 'the world's most generous company'. That year the company donated US$447 million in the form of cash and its own medicines valued at wholesale prices to non-profit organisations around the world to people who lived in medically under-served areas. Although the Global Com-

5 www.unglobalcompact.org
6 www.diflucanpartnership.org
7 25 July 2002

pact is not about philanthropy, Pfizer's philanthropy has played an important role in helping Pfizer to understand the needs of society and to build new relationships while helping non-profit organisations become stronger members of society.

A new example of how Pfizer is living the principles was its announcement in June 2003 on important research results in malaria, SARS (severe acute respiratory syndrome) and smallpox. McKinnell said, if the results were positive, Pfizer would work with national and international bodies to deliver medicine to patients in need. He said to colleagues:

> We are getting into this battle because the human cost is so high and because we believe that corporate citizenship and expanded access to basic healthcare are also central to Pfizer's performance.

These R&D projects are not likely to result in the next billion-dollar medicine, but they could potentially improve the lives of millions of people around the world and make a strong statement about what Pfizer means by its mission to be the world's most valued company.

McKinnell serves on George Bush's Presidential Advisory Council on HIV/AIDS, along with leading scientists, physicians, activists and patients representing a broad spectrum of the AIDS community. The Council's role is to provide the President, as well as the Secretary of Health and Human Services, currently Tommy Thompson, with recommendations regarding programmes and policies intended to promote the highest quality of research, prevention and treatment.

16.5 The Global Compact encourages companies to focus internally

In 2002 when the Global Compact took stock of its impact on business, it realised it needed to put more emphasis on how companies internalised and operationalised the principles rather than on how companies undertook projects. The goal was to incorporate the principles into the way a company routinely does business.

To that end, Pfizer focused on internal education and alignment through regular cross-divisional meetings. The education process of colleagues has included executive memos, stories about the Global Compact on Pfizer's online worldwide news service for employees and a two-day global meeting of senior corporate affairs employees that focused on stakeholder engagement. In addition, the company's mandatory education for all employees on Pfizer's Policies on Business Conduct[8] included segments on corporate citizenship, with reference to the Global Compact. When Pfizer acquired Pharmacia in April 2003, an in-house video called *Day One* marked the beginning of the 'New Pfizer'—and the unifying theme was

---

8 www.pfizer.com/are/mn_investors_corporate_policies.cfm

corporate citizenship, which included the underlying principles of the Global Compact.

Education to employees recently hit a tipping point. Colleagues are now initiating contact with the Senior Director of Corporate Citizenship to offer ideas or ask for help in supporting the principles. Recently, the Global R&D division held an internal symposium on environmentally friendly 'green chemistry'; Global Manufacturing included a discussion of the Global Compact principles with the division's colleagues; and the Intranet Communications Council discussed translating corporate citizenship information into languages other than English. A Corporate Citizenship intranet site is presently under construction which will provide tools to assist colleagues in integrating corporate citizenship into their strategic plans; it is scheduled to launch in autumn 2004. In addition, an Internet site is scheduled to launch in summer 2004.

16.6 Pfizer merges internal and external focus

Pfizer is now at the point of integrating the Global Compact's internal and external focus. Pfizer's Global Health Fellows—otherwise known internally as 'Hank's Peace Corps' because it was McKinnell's idea—was launched in late 2003. Jon Levine, an independent case writer, describes it like this:

> Pfizer sends fellows to fight against HIV/AIDS. The programme sends skilled Pfizer medical and managerial volunteers to help NGOs develop the health and social infrastructures required to combat the disease in developing countries. The Fellows programme, still in pilot testing, is an innovative response that goes beyond conventional industry donations of cash and drugs. In its attempt to scale the programme to include volunteers from throughout private industry, Pfizer is undertaking a challenging experiment in large-scale international development.[9]

Another kind of integration was aimed at investors. Pfizer's 'quarterly earnings report' was renamed the 'quarterly performance report'. It now includes not only a financial report but also regular updates on the company's actions in corporate citizenship and in improving access to medicines to people who cannot afford such medicine. This is one way Pfizer communicates its priorities to crucial stakeholder groups.

---

9   This summary was submitted at the UN Global Compact Learning Forum on 10 December 2003 in Brazil. The actual case can be found at www.unglobalcompact.org.

16.7 Moving forward

A study in October 2003 by the International Institute for Management Development in Geneva (Eckelmann 2003: 5) found that stakeholders expect more social responsibility from the pharmaceutical sector than from any other industry. That came as no surprise to Pfizer.

Looking ahead, McKinnell sees how the different business units are interpreting the new realities of leadership by aligning Pfizer more closely with the needs and interests of its stakeholders. Pfizer is examining ways to 'partner, operate and communicate differently'. This is Pfizer's general roadmap for the future, and business units around the world will operationalise it to align better with the needs of patients, physicians and caregivers and with other stakeholders.

Partnering differently means listening to what stakeholders are saying, finding common ground and together seeking new solutions to healthcare issues. Operating differently means taking a clear-eyed look at how Pfizer's policies and operations may need to change to align better with stakeholders' needs. Communicating differently means looking at new ways Pfizer can support its efforts to operate and partner differently.

This is part of McKinnell's plan on how Pfizer can advance his vision of sustainable health built on prevention, disease management and discovering new medicines. His aim is for Pfizer to play a key role in refashioning healthcare systems in the 21st century to better meet stakeholder needs. As he has often said, even the best medicines are of no use to people who cannot obtain or afford them.

Michael Useem says that leadership is about 'improving and perhaps even transforming what we have inherited from others without subverting the organisation's mission or making the organisation the slave of our egos' (1998: 263). McKinnell says his father taught him 'the best way to say thank you for something you borrow is to return it in better condition than when you borrowed it'.

McKinnell said he has been asked numerous times whether he really thought that Pfizer could fulfil its mission of becoming the most valued company in the world. He said:

> Here's my answer, and it may surprise you. I don't know. I believe that we should never take on a mission we absolutely know how to do. The satisfaction comes in proving to ourselves that we can do it— that we can move beyond number one, and build a company like no other.

16.8 Has the Global Compact been worth the effort?

The Global Compact has contributed to Pfizer's mission in many ways. It was the catalyst for creating a global cross-divisional team to define and co-ordinate issues of corporate responsibility. It has served as an external framework of principles on corporate behaviour. The Global Compact has been crucial in opening the door for

Pfizer to build new relationships with civil-society organisations. Socially responsible investors welcomed Pfizer's participation in the Global Compact. And the Global Compact has helped Pfizer acknowledge to all its 122,000 employees that Pfizer is truly a global company.

Finally, it helped focus the cross-divisional citizenship team. Corporate citizenship at Pfizer is about the company's role in the local and global community and the way it strives to do business responsibly. Operationally, it means improving access to medicine and health information, incorporating stakeholder perspectives in all aspects of Pfizer's business and making ethical and sustainable business decisions. Or, as McKinnell would say, 'Good corporate citizenship is the road to most valued company'.

17

Learning from doing
The Third International Global Compact Learning Forum Meeting in Belo Horizonte, Nova Lima, Brazil, December 2003*

Malcolm McIntosh
Independent Commentator

As evidenced by the 2003 UN Global Compact Learning Forum in Brazil this annual meeting is developing into one of the more useful annual conferences on corporate responsibility among the many that are now held around the world. Its strength lies in three areas: the unifying moral authority of the UN, the cross-sectoral convening platform that the principles of the UN Global Compact provide and its global remit.

The Global Compact Learning Forum has succeeded in engaging global corporations and local small and medium-sized enterprises (SMEs). There is no doubt that the case studies presented at this conference, and on which much of the legitimacy of the Global Compact rests, are a great improvement on those presented at the conferences in London (2001) and Berlin (2002). In phase one up to November 2001 companies were encouraged to engage honestly in the learning process and submit examples of engagement with the principles of the Global Compact in order that there could be better collective understanding of how organisations can embed human rights, labour standards and environmental protection in the heart of their operations. The model proposed after phase one of companies' engaging 'independent researchers' in the preparation of presentations and written material raised the quality of engagement by companies with the Global Compact Learning Forum, but there are some lessons to be taken from this process which, if learned,

---

* This report was written in December 2003 and the case studies referred to can be found at www.unglobalcompact.org under 'The Learning Forum'.

will further strengthen the role that the Global Compact can play in providing a global learning forum for corporate responsibility.

17.1 The UN Global Compact Office

It is remarkable that this event, and others during the year, was launched and run by such a small core staff in the New York Global Compact Office. It was a testament to their hard work and dedication as well as their ability to build close working relationships with local organisations. The Global Compact Office is the holder of the flame; the 'Olympic runner' with the core principles; the values co-ordinator and enforcer. The flexibility and smallness of the Global Compact Office provides flexibility and allows for innovative thinking and creativity. It is a lesson to other members of the UN 'family' of agencies, many of which are significantly larger but perhaps less effective in facing the challenge of the globalisation process at the start of the 21st century.

For those who wish this initiative to live beyond the tenure of both the current Executive Director, Georg Kell, and the current UN Secretary-General, Kofi Annan, and those companies, non-governmental organisations (NGOs) and UN agencies that may be 'nailing their futures to its mast', the 'bedding-down' process or institutionalisation, and perhaps de-UNisation, of the Global Compact is of great importance. Can and should the UN Global Compact establish itself as an independent initiative in the way that the Global Reporting Initiative (GRI)[1] has?

The 3rd Global Compact Learning Forum conference received significant and much-needed help from Instituto Ethos, a business association, and private companies who are corporate members of Instituto Ethos. In such a setting it was perhaps no surprise that some corporations dominated the first full day of the conference. The cultural context may be relevant in understanding the relationship between the corporate sector, government and civil society in Brazil, but, in working with business, this highlights one of the issues at the heart of the global–local nature of the Global Compact.

The location and the December date of the 3rd Global Compact Learning Forum conference in Belo Horizonte, Brazil, militated against many people from attending owing to cost and time of year. In this case non-corporate participation (NGOs and academics) was diminished for these reasons, which lessened the continuity from the Berlin conference in 2002. Many corporations now have CSR (corporate social responsibility) personnel in place who, due to lack of seniority and lack of institutional learning, find it difficult to engage in deep reflection on the learning that has taken place in the organisation on CSR. The notable exceptions were the senior representatives from Pfizer, BP and Hewlett-Packard, who provided context, reflection, humour and some humility.

---

1   For details of the GRI, see www.globalreporting.org.

If the Global Compact is to engage globally and locally, the local cultural context will always present a dilemma. The possibility of a future conference being held in some other countries raises all sorts of questions about freedom of speech, human rights, corporate involvement and free entry to the country for all those who want to attend—particularly from NGOs.

The Global Compact Learning Forum is always going to encounter the dilemma of two conferences in one. Many of the participants at the Brazilian event, particularly on the first full day, were local business people for whom this was a first meeting with the learning process—and the Global Compact. The second full day, which focused on human rights, was not dominated by local companies. For the Global Compact Learning Forum to graduate to becoming part of a culture of learning and participation in a public–private process requires a conference format that promotes real engagement.

A possible solution to this particular problem is to have a three-part programme:

● Day one: Local Day, followed by an opening international dinner

● Day two: International Global Compact Learning Forum conference

● Day three: Research Day, particularly for those interested in theory and practice

Delegates could then decide to participate in one or more days.

The programme will always have to cope with local dignitaries and some public-relations grandstanding from companies and government, but this can be kept manageable if located within the first 'Local Day' and if all sessions are incisively chaired.

17.2 The UN Global Compact Learning Forum: case studies, 2003

There was an overall improvement in the case studies presented to the Global Compact Learning Forum.[2] The Global Compact Learning Forum guidelines clearly say that the case studies must be written independently and that no payment shall be made (apart from travel and other expenses) to the researcher. In fact, a significant number of researchers had been paid, and many companies reported that they had received useful consultancy in this regard. A way needs to be found between the ideals of the current guidelines and the reality of the current situation. That reality is as follows:

● Very few of the 'case studies' have been inspired by the Global Compact, but the Global Compact has been instrumental in bringing them to light.

2 Case studies are no longer a criterion for becoming a signatory of the Global Compact. This came as a result of companies having a greater awareness of their commitment to the Global Compact and as a result of collaborative writing between companies and 'researchers'. Companies have been creative in their relationships with researchers.

- The Global Compact Learning Forum is a great place to air these 'case studies' and to provide commentary through open conversation in the break-out sessions and on the website.

A possible progression, and a significant learning point for the Learning Forum, could be to rewrite the guidelines so that they are based on action research and to use postgraduate students, supervised by research tutors, to write the case studies.[3] Corporations would engage with university departments, sometimes management and business schools, and pay them for this service. This mechanism needs early negotiation but has several merits:

- It engages corporations and universities.

- It cuts out the obvious charge of interested consultancy.

- It brings learning institutions into the Global Compact Learning Forum process.

- It provides university teaching programmes with real action research related to business engagement with the Global Compact.

- It allows funds to flow between corporations and universities—to build private–public partnerships.

17.3 New sessions

As well as the need for the application of an action research methodology, succeeding conferences will need break-out sessions on:

- The Global Compact as a global network, linking it to network theory, complexity and other new ways of seeing globalisation (as highlighted in this book)

- The Global Compact and education, particularly in relation to business and management schools

- The Global Compact and research, particularly aimed at PhD and other researchers

Future international UN Global Compact conferences could also make provision for an 'open-space' agenda. The democratisation of the agenda calls on participants to suggest titles or areas for possible sessions. Out of this normally emerges themes that have risen spontaneously or have been missed by conference organ-

---

3   On the way in which action research might be a way forward for the Learning Forum, see Chapter 26.

isers. It requires conference organisers to be confident enough to allow for flexibility, spontaneity and surprise.

Also, there is much to be gained by asking: 'What is the UN Global Compact: an idea whose time has come, a conversation among friends, a "bowl of cherries" or a new neural network?' Various speakers would raise the intellectual level of the conference above the public-private partnership debates, corporations-government-civil society debates and would put forward alternative ways of seeing the world as envisaged in Annan's, Ruggie's and Kell's earlier postulations at the birth of this initiative.

Given the lessons that arise from the contributions to this book we need to find a way of exploring the various levels at which the UN Global Compact can be approached. The conference in Brazil had two major themes, human rights and corruption, but it would also be possible to theme future conferences around the issues of 'the business *not* as usual', 'education and training for a networked world' and 'business for the common good'.

Above all, there is a necessity for the Global Compact to help participants envision what the world might look like if the Global Compact principles were implemented globally and if it were to help in achieving some arrival at the Millennium Development Goals (see Appendix A). This means attempting to map the system that it is trying to organise, because, as Steve Waddell suggests in his contribution to this book (Chapter 20), this map is necessary to identify the critical leverage points for the Global Compact to take action and avoid being overwhelmed by the scale of its challenge. As he says (page 301):

> The change that the Global Compact implicitly aims to achieve is very profound. A global society that integrates the principles will look very different from the one that we have today. The structures, processes and organisations needed to support them are still not well understood, and the Global Compact is doing the hard work of giving shape to them. The depth of the work suggests that it is critical for the Global Compact to develop some profound, deep-change, initiatives that will be long term and require an interpersonal and inter-organisational intimacy that goes beyond the intellectual and into the emotional-spiritual dimension where stakeholders can 're-vision' their future.

This could be the theme of a future Learning Forum conference, with business being asked to make contributions to these overarching themes rather than providing siloed case studies focused on a single company.

18
Shaping the future by walking together
Novo Nordisk's promotion of human rights and good environmental management, with specific reference to an evaluation of suppliers in 2002/2003

Malcolm McIntosh
Independent Commentator

Annette Stube
Novo Nordisk

> To shape the future, we must learn from the past. So why don't we? . . .
>
> The path to sustainability isn't smooth, and our destination is not around the corner. Still we see no other way. Let's walk it together.
>
> *Lars Rebien Sørensen, President and CEO, Novo Nordisk A/S, 2003*[1]

Novo Nordisk, a Danish pharmaceutical company, became a signatory to the UN Global Compact in 2001. The story told in this chapter is one of three from the global pharmaceutical industry, the others being Novartis (see Chapter 5) and Pfizer (see Chapter 16).

In this chapter we look at the work being conducted by Novo Nordisk within the interpretation of Principles 1 and 2 of the UN Global Compact on understanding

1 Quoted in Novo Nordisk 2003a: 1.

and influencing their 'sphere of influence' through an ongoing dialogue with stakeholders, particularly those in their downstream supply chain.[2]

For companies beginning the engagement process with the UN Global Compact the lessons learned by Novo Nordisk are lessons for everyone. This company allowed itself to learn in public and, as Claude Fussler explains in this book (Chapter 19), such transparent public learning benefits the company and its stakeholders as it increases trust through reflective transparency. It is, in a sense, a very real form of accountability in a dialogic world.

Novo Nordisk is promoting basic labour rights and good environmental management in its supply chain worldwide. The approach is systematic and entails not only suppliers for production but also research and development (R&D), marketing, engineering, services and stationery. To ensure an ongoing commitment to the programme, it has been integrated into Novo Nordisk's corporate governance system. The company promotes human rights and good environmental management with all its stakeholders and therefore engages with all Global Compact principles. This engagement with the principles of the Global Compact is discussed in the context of an ongoing evaluation of the company's first tier of suppliers. This process is evaluated and information provided on processes and outcomes.

There are two aspects discussed. First, there is a general discussion of the role of Novo Nordisk in relation to its 'sphere of influence' and its engagement with human rights, labour and environmental issues with its stakeholders. Second, specific data is discussed on one aspect of the company's overall performance in these areas: namely, that of promoting human rights and good environmental management with its first-tier suppliers.

18.1 The Novo Nordisk approach

18.1.1 Systemic and systematic issues

In order to interpret the language of Principles 1 and 2 of the UN Global Compact in the context of one company's performance it is necessary to look at both systemic and systematic issues. The global system in which the company operates provides the context in which strategic, or systematic, implementation can take place. A **systematic process** is one that has been planned and is characterised by consistency and ongoing management. A **systems perspective** contextualises the activities of the company in a wider sphere and provides linkages to relationships with stakeholders and wider processes that may be beyond the company's cognisance. The company cannot know all the connectivities and convivialities it has, as seeing the whole is rarely possible for any of us. It can, however, try to be open to its responsibilities and impacts and, through its stakeholder engagement strategy, this is what Novo Nordisk is attempting to do.

---

2   The principles of the Global Compact are listed on page 12.

Novo Nordisk's approach has been to develop policy at a systemic level while implementing policy in a systematic way. Here we look at one aspect of its strategy and acknowledge that the next steps for the company will be to further develop the systematic implementation of that systems approach. The Global Compact is explicit in recognising the need for business to be engaged in the development of global governance but it has not been explicit in endorsing a systems approach to problem-solving.

The link between systems and strategy is acknowledged by Novo Nordisk in its recognition of the challenges and opportunities presented in attempting to understand the global context in which they operate. As it states in its 2002 sustainability report, 'social responsibility extends beyond the company's grounds. It reaches throughout the supply chain and to the global agenda of sustainable development' (Novo Nordisk 2003a: 23). This is an important acknowledgement that positions this company as 'an agent for positive social change' (McIntosh *et al.* 2003b: 34) if it can be shown that its actions create both private and public wealth. For Novo Nordisk, 'sustainable development is part of its strategic business agenda' (Novo Nordisk 2003a). In theory, this means that the public good is a private necessity and that the 'strategic business agenda' cannot be satisfied without a shared public–private determination to work towards sustainable development. The President and CEO, Lars Rebien Sørensen, has clearly articulated the company's position: 'I believe that corporations—big and small—can bring into play their collective creativity and expertise to help solve issues of social injustice and inequality' (Novo Nordisk 2003a: 1).

18.1.2 Vision and values

According to the company's vision and values, 'the aim of the company' 'is to eradicate diabetes'. If this were to happen the company would have to diversify or die. Its mission could, therefore, be seen as putting itself out of business! This is a rational and natural consequence of seeing a company, any company, as a public, not a private, entity. In order to reach the goal of a more sustainable society there must be certain activities, and therefore companies, that become obsolete.

Lise Kingo, appointed as Executive Vice President for Stakeholder Relations (reporting to Lars Sørensen) portrayed Novo Nordisk's 'Utopian' scenario in a slide-show, giving an indication of the company's understanding of sustainability (Kingo 2003). According to Kingo, by 2020, the average economic global growth rate will be at 4%; technology will have advanced in the areas of information technology (IT), fuel cells, nanotechnology and biotechnology; a resource consumption tax will have replaced income taxes; and even food companies will be selling predominantly healthy products and promoting exercise. All in all, there will have been a 'mind change' towards buying from sustainable companies and living a healthier, more eco-friendly, life.

Most of these ideals might well be beyond the scope of a relatively small pharmaceutical company, but Novo Nordisk, through putting its values into practice and turning vision into reality, is playing its part in developing and promoting the ethos of corporate responsibility.

18.1.2.1 Governance

The protection of human rights that forms the basis of the case study examined in this chapter is just one aspect of Novo Nordisk's corporate responsibility programme. The company also works along a defined governance model. This involves putting the vision of accountability, responsibility and engagement with stakeholders into practice in three ways: through the use of triple-bottom-line reporting, through the use of a balanced business scorecard and through facilitation (Stube 2003).

18.1.2.2 Human rights

Human rights came onto the agenda at Novo Nordisk during 1998 when a review established the company's stance on and commitment to human rights. The following year this was made formal through the official commitment to the UN Declaration of Human Rights.[3] In 2001 Novo Nordisk became a signatory to the UN Global Compact, which has helped in the specification of values as well as the identification of priorities in the company. Priorities for the company centre around access to health, equal opportunities and the right to privacy.

18.1.3 Company profile[4]

Novo Nordisk is a company focused on healthcare, holding 48% of the global market in insulin, which represents 71% of the company's business. It also produces products for haemostasis management, growth hormone treatment and hormone replacement therapy. The financial turnover is divided geographically as 44% in Europe, 24% in North America, 16% in Japan and Oceania, and 16% in the rest of the world. Headquartered in Denmark, it is represented in 69 countries and its products are sold in 180 countries. Some 99% of sales are outside Denmark, but production is concentrated in the home country, with other production sites in the USA, France, Japan, China, South Africa and Brazil. Of the total workforce of 19,241 people, 60% live and work in Denmark. The Novo Nordisk Foundation owns all A shares which represents 65.4% of the entire voting power of the company. B shares are quoted on the Copenhagen, London and New York stock exchanges. In 2003 the turnover of the company was DKK26.5 billion (EUR3.6 billion).

The company is registered in Denmark as a public limited liability company with a board of directors and executive management. In accordance with Danish law, three (out of a total of nine) board members are elected by the employees, and these board members serve in that post for four years (Novo Nordisk 2003b: 6). The company accords with current regulations and recent recommendations on the Copenhagen, New York and London stock exchanges (Novo Nordisk 2003b: 8-9).

Novo Nordisk is ranked number 26 among the world's pharmaceutical companies, measured by sales, and is dwarfed by companies such as Pfizer, the world's

3   For the Universal Declaration, see www.un.org/Overview/rights.html.
4   For more information, see www.novonordisk.com.

largest such company (see Chapter 16), and other competitors. However, Novo Nordisk has a focused product line supported by an intense R&D programme.

18.2 Industry and country profile

18.2.1 Industry context

Lise Kingo, Executive Vice President for Stakeholder Relations, says that the pharmaceutical industry faces a number of industry-specific challenges in the 21st century. In a presentation to the European Academy for Business in Society in Copenhagen in September 2003, she proposed that the dilemmas revolved around the following key points:

- Intellectual property rights are being challenged.

- Pricing is questioned and under consistent pressure.

- Declining R&D has led to and/or is a result of few real innovations.

- Clinical trials are increasingly biased towards sales.

- There are issues over business ethics, especially in the areas of sales and marketing.

The result is that there has developed a general distrust towards the pharmaceutical industry.

18.2.2 The Danish context

Lise Kingo exemplifies a Danish attitude when she says (Novo Nordisk 2003a: 16):

> Collaboration rather than confrontation is an innate attitude on which Novo Nordisk bases its business conduct. Novo Nordisk has been systematically engaging with stakeholders for decades now . . . Increasingly we move from dialogue to partnership built on mutual respect and trust.

The company hired a UK stakeholder consultant, Vernon Jennings, because it 'wanted to gain a non-Danish perspective'. Indeed, the company would like to think that its perspective is global rather than Danish, but, as one senior company employee mentioned:

> The truth is somewhere between the two. Danes talk so much that the consensus model can mean going nowhere, whereas the UK/US model is too confrontational. The company wanted to find a way between these two models.

The Danish attitude (see also Quote 18.1) embodied in Novo Nordisk's corporate vision, values and culture may not be apparent to those who work for or in close association with the company in Denmark. As one of the clear findings of this case

> *The Nordic Partnership, of which Novo Nordisk is a co-founder and main sponsor, builds on the best of Nordic values: democracy, transparency and openness. As a WWF-led initiative, supported by Danish thinktank Monday Morning together with 17 companies based in Nordic countries, it aims to integrate sustainability into core business.*

Quote 18.1

Source: Novo Nordisk 2003a: 17

study is that 98% of first-tier suppliers originate in Denmark or other European countries, this participative model of social democracy may not be so easily found either in second-tier and third-tier suppliers or in upstream relationships.

In seeking to promote labour rights and environmental management down the supply chain the issue for Novo Nordisk is one of promoting what are everyday norms of behaviour in the company in Denmark. However, the interesting and more difficult application of this policy is tested when applied outside advanced social democracies; in places where the rule of law is not paramount, where there is a deficit of regulatory enforcement or where there is no regulation covering issues related to labour rights and environmental protection.

18.3　The project: supplier evaluation, April 2003

18.3.1　Background

Novo Nordisk has made a public commitment to the UN Universal Declaration of Human Rights, the Global Compact and the International Chamber of Commerce (ICC) Business Charter for Sustainable Development.[5] This means that the company is actively seeking to promote social responsibility and good environmental performance throughout its business, not only in its own organisation but also with its business partners. This proactive approach includes working with suppliers and contractors to support human rights standards and to promote improvements to environmental practices in the supply chain.

18.3.2　Objectives

Managing potential risks in the supply chain, such as human rights violations, is important for a company such as Novo Nordisk that has a high ethical profile and attracts substantial attention from non-governmental organisations (NGOs) and media. The greatest risk factor at this stage is estimated to be in the company's licensed production, as this is located mainly in the developing world and is tightly associated with the company brand name.

5　For details of the ICC Charter, see www.iccwbo.org.

The objective of the supplier evaluation project is therefore to manage these risks to the brand name through the more effective application of International Labour Organisation (ILO)[6] standards and good environmental management, which will ultimately improve standards. Through this process the company also aims to learn from different stakeholders:

> Consultants provide an interpreted, higher-level opinion; NGOs remind the company of the heart of it all, purchasers reiterate the business aspects while suppliers inform us of the 'other' perspective (Stube 2003).

18.3.3 History

1999 Novo Nordisk had been evaluating its suppliers on environmental issues for some time, but with significant variations in the way the process was implemented internally. Global trends indicated a new focus on corporate responsibility in supply chain management.

2000 A team was set up representing all major purchasing functions in Novo Nordisk. Desk research and international consultation informed the project group in terms of trends and best or worst practices as well as gaining an overview of the supply chain regarding geographical spread (risk) and spend (risk and impact).

2001 It was decided to take a self-evaluation approach through a questionnaire. This followed the original environmental approach—asking questions rather than incorporating a code of conduct. Recognising the shortcomings of this approach, the company used the opportunity to actively notify suppliers of its position and expectations and possibly to identify risks without jeopardising business.[7] A pilot project carried out in seven countries, involving seven different industries (a total of eight workshops), showed that this approach could push development and still maintain a positive atmosphere. Learning from the workshops, the company amended the programme and an evaluation procedure, criteria and a follow-up process were established.

2002 The evaluation programme was launched:

> – January: all purchasers, including purchasers from production sites in France and the USA, as well as some auditors, were invited to an information meeting with top-management representatives, underlining management commitment.

6 See www.ilo.org.
7 A change of supplier is in many cases a very costly and time-consuming process because of the high quality demands. A cautious approach was therefore recommended. When unsatisfactory behaviour was found, Novo Nordisk preferred (as it still does) to work with the suppliers to improve performance rather than to terminate the relationship, although there may be exceptions to this rule.

- A one-day training day followed: 64 people were trained and awarded certificates. The training focused on environmental and social issues as well as on the practical elements of carrying out the actual evaluation.
- A toolbox on supplier evaluation was launched internally, both for new employees and for reference purposes.
- Update meetings, with all purchasers invited, were held to discuss issues arising from the evaluation.
- By the end of 2002 the target of evaluating 90% of key suppliers was reached; 86% of the evaluated suppliers were rated as satisfactory.

2003   The project will expand into the purchasing areas of R&D and sales and marketing. Furthermore, an audit system has been developed. The project group has been changed to a co-ordination group, as new subgroups working directly with the above areas have been established.

18.3.4 Summary of outputs and outcomes

During 2002 Novo Nordisk undertook the first social and environmental evaluation of 289 (90%) of its key suppliers. The results show that:

- In the first instance, 1% of the results were unsatisfactory in social areas because of insufficient answers.

- 11% proved unsatisfactory in environmental areas, largely because of a lack of knowledge concerning impact, policy and training.

- No serious violations of social or environmental issues were identified in the first tier of the supply chain covered by the evaluation.

- Implementation of the evaluation has been successful, with a questionnaire covering issues relevant to the scope of the project.

- The majority of answers are of high quality, providing quite detailed responses, which suggests that suppliers have taken the questionnaire seriously.

- In 2003–2005 the project will focus on assurance (audits) and expansion of the evaluation programme to R&D, sales and marketing.

Novo Nordisk performed purchases with external suppliers to a value of DKK12.3 billion in 2002. This covers transactions with 5,000 suppliers ranging from flower shops to suppliers of raw materials. Less than 200 suppliers deliver 80% of the value purchased. Geographically, 93% of Novo Nordisk's suppliers are located in the European Union or in countries in the European Free Trade Association (EFTA), with 5% in North America, Japan, Australia and New Zealand. Only 2% by number (or 0.4% by value) are located outside these regions.

18.3.5 Key leaders in the company

The board of the company has been insightful in supporting radical engagement with the world through stakeholder dialogue. It was influenced by the work of the New Economics Foundation[8] in the United Kingdom and latterly by Account-Ability.[9] On an individual level members of the board have for many years employed John Elkington from SustainAbility[10] as a consultant and Vernon Jennings as Vice President in Stakeholder Relations. At a senior level, Lise Kingo has driven policy and strategy.[11]

18.3.6 Stakeholder pressure

The key stakeholder group was not external. The beginning of the story is really written in the history of the project (see Section 18.3.3). The 1999 Social Report was in the process of being written and the company wanted to look at its suppliers because they were a relevant close-to-the-company stakeholder group. One of the authors of this chapter, Annette Stube met with the company's purchasing managers, who, independent of her initiative, said that they had been waiting for something to happen in this area. In their words, 'We knew something needed to be done here.' Other internal conversations relayed the feeling that there was 'no particular group or pressure, just a sense that we needed to do it'.

18.4 Analysis of the results

There are two issues. First, Novo Nordisk would clearly like to be seen as 'an agent for positive social change' by remaining both a profitable and an ethical entity. Not only does it try to 'do no harm' but it would like to be seen as contributing to, and possibly creating, common wealth. As already reported in Section 18.1.1, the company says (Novo Nordisk 2003a 23):

> Social responsibility extends beyond the company's grounds. It reaches throughout the supply chain and to the global agenda of sustainable development.

Second, the company has adopted a strategic, or systematic, approach to its role in fulfilling this social mission. On this basis the company has put significant effort into promoting labour rights and environmental good practice in most of its stakeholder relations. This includes first-tier suppliers—the focus in this chapter. The company have correctly pointed out, '[our relationship with suppliers] is where we can have an effect; this is where we have some influence'. It points out

8   See www.neweconomics.org.
9   See www.accountability.org.uk.
10   See www.sustainability.com.
11   One of the authors, Annette Stube, has carried out the day-to-day work along with the Purchasing Manager and has managed the ongoing process.

that it has a range of types of engagement, all of which involve pushing forward the sustainability agenda.

But, it also seems to be the case that everywhere the company looks to extend its social influence there is work to be done. In other words, pushing at its own values boundaries is often more akin to building doors in walls than swimming across a smooth sea looking for like-minded islands of people with a shared philosophy. Swimming may take strategy but building doors takes planning, strategising and construction. In terms of strategy, the company has correctly looked at the world beyond its own culture and adopted a 'softly softly' approach lest it offend and thereby lose business.

It might be thought that suppliers downstream would be smaller than Novo Nordisk and more vulnerable to pressure to meet the preferences of a larger purchaser—in other words that they could not afford to offend—but, in fact, there is evidence that this company is part of a social and strategic movement in smaller *and* larger companies. Some companies, larger and smaller, are swimming in the same pool when it comes to the new role of business in society, and other companies seem to understand the strategic advantage in understanding and sharing values within the supply chain. In other words, in both cases, there seems to be evidence of the supply chain being as much a social values network as a purely goods-driven supply chain. Management of the supply chain is then driven to a higher level where purchase and supply managers are required to talk values as well as quality, cost and delivery. This is an excellent example of the normalisation of the human rights conversation globally, albeit in this case mainly within Europe.

18.4.1 Reconstructing the process

How is it possible to reconstruct the change that has taken place over the past few years in Novo Nordisk? Having decided on a policy, the company's strategy was first to change the culture in which its own purchasers operated. Many purchasers were initially opposed to sending out the questionnaire because they assumed that it would upset the relationships they had with their suppliers. As in many supply chain situations these relationships had taken many years to establish, and maintenance of those relationships was seen as a priority. Some Novo Nordisk purchasers thought that their suppliers might be offended by being asked about issues such as child labour and forced labour. As several suppliers said: 'Of course we don't employ children; why do they need to ask us?' Novo Nordisk's purchasers also thought that completing the questionnaire might be too time-consuming for suppliers. For Novo Nordisk this meant a two-year programme of workshops and training to increase understanding among the group that comprises supply chain managers and purchasers. Perhaps because there were already good relationships between purchasers and suppliers, two years later the completion of the questionnaires is increasingly 'taken as standard'.

In December 2003, a survey, protecting the identity of the respondents, undertaken by an external agency, asked suppliers what they thought about the programme. The response rate was 61%. In general, suppliers agreed that they have a good dialogue with the contact person at Novo Nordisk; 56% of suppliers believed that the evaluation of suppliers on social and environmental issues has had a positive impact on the way they operate internally; only a small percentage believed the evaluation to be negative. As noted below, there were mixed feelings about the ease of providing information for the evaluation.

An internal report for the company by an external consultant, titled 'Social Responsibility in the Supply Chain', published in March 2003, found that there needed to be greater emphasis on 'improving the dialogue between supplier and purchaser, based on trust'. The report recommended that there was a real opportunity for Novo Nordisk to have an impact on the improvement of suppliers and on environmental issues 'through extensive communication, dialogue and relationship management'.

For the suppliers, the initiative was as new to them as it was to Novo Nordisk's in-house purchasing managers . One supplier from a company significantly larger than Novo Nordisk said the arrival of the form was a complete shock. A supplier from a smaller company said that it had caused a great deal of work and had been a challenge but was consistent with the way his company worked anyway. Their stories are told below.

18.4.1.1 Story 1: larger supplier

The larger company cited here, 'Company A', is a supra-territorial company, global in its operations and quoted on stock exchanges around the world. Novo Nordisk's questionnaire landed on the desk of a chemist whose normal day-to-day job was to supply technical support to the pharmaceutical industry. Never before had he had to interest himself professionally in human rights or sustainability issues. In his words: 'The form fell on my desk and I said "Oh my God! I am a chemist; how would I know?" ' He had no warning and, as he said, 'there was no foreplay—we just had to do it!' His first question up the line was: 'What reference has this to the supply of [our product] to Novo Nordisk?' He said it caused 'some anger and frustration but also great conversation among the 12 people in [his] office'.

He had no training and no expertise then, but now two years later he is an expert in these issues. But first he had to ask his line manager if this was a priority, given that this company was much bigger than Novo Nordisk and that his day was full of other tasks anyway. His line manager said that Novo Nordisk's approach was in line with his company's approach to human rights and the environment; that Novo Nordisk was an important customer and that the information was easily available. The last comment proved to be less than true, and completing Novo Nordisk's form took several weeks as 'despite the company's pioneering efforts in promoting the Global Compact there was no co-ordination on the collecting and collation of data related to human rights, labour or the environment company-wide'. Of greatest learning to the supplier was the cross-functionality of the form— 'Who should fill it in?' Novo Nordisk wanted a local person, a site-based official, but the form asked questions that related to the company as a whole.

Two years later this major global company, many times the size of Novo Nordisk, has co-ordinated its information systems on its website. This particular supply chain manager, a chemist by training and a technologist in his job, has been able to practice at work what he believes at home. Now he can feel that the company's values are aligned with his own. It is one man's salutary story of personal empowerment and organisational change, but most of all it is a sign of the growing conversation in organisations about multidisciplinary issues relating to business and values.

18.4.1.2 Story 2: smaller supplier

The second story comes from a small, family-owned business supplying plastics, 'Company B', with an international market specialising in niche products based in Germany. For this company this was not the first challenge to supply value statements as well as quality and quantity in plastics. A previous questionnaire had come from a major US-based company with sourcing arrangements in Asia. The content required by Novo Nordisk is regulated in Germany when it comes to labour issues, and on labour rights and the environment the greatest challenge had been in processing the information. This had involved issues for Company B as a company of 'quality, time and costs' in completing the questionnaire.

The owner saw no competitive advantage within Europe for his company engaging in this values-based conversation as much of it accorded with regulatory norms, but he did think that there was significant advantage for his company when dealing with, and competing against, companies in Asia. This was because there was clear differentiation between those companies in Asia that had adopted a proactive stance on human rights, labour and environmental issues and those that had not.

'This' he said 'is the future. Will we have regulations or fights? Will we have the old battles between capital and labour or will we have regulations that force companies to report on human rights, labour and environmental issues?' Most pertinently, he argued that a more comprehensive and contextualised approach to supply chain management, and therefore relationships 'keeps stability in the supply chain'.

18.5 Conclusions and next steps

18.5.1 Specific conclusions on first-tier supplier evaluation

The specific outcomes of the promotion of labour and environmental issues with Novo Nordisk's first-tier suppliers were satisfactory enough for the company to feel encouraged to continue to push up the standards in its supply chain. For instance, an internal report on this first phase stated that 'no serious violations of social or environmental issues were identified in the first tier of the supply chain covered by the evaluation' and that 'the majority of answers were of high quality, providing quite detailed responses which suggest that suppliers have taken the questionnaire (and the issues) seriously'. The next steps in this specific project will be to 'focus on assurance (audits) and expansion of the evaluation programme to R&D, sales and marketing'.

18.5.2 General conclusions

The most important conclusion from Novo Nordisk's own internal work on emphasising respect for human rights along the supply chain is that this is just a beginning, and the company can feel greatly encouraged to move forward with its dialogic strategy.

Despite the extensive rhetoric of the corporate responsibility movement, aided and abetted by some companies that would like to see themselves as leaders in this field, the process of making business more socially and environmentally aware and responsive has only just begun. A cursory investigation in support of this company's case study, provided for the UN Global Compact Learning Forum, of promoting 'basic labour rights and environmental protection' in its supply chain shows that the internal and external conversation has just started. People in business are learning to talk about something other than cost efficiency, profit maximisation and shareholder value. Novo Nordisk sees itself as being at the forefront of this global change. Specifically, the next steps for Novo Nordisk's work in this area are:

- To comprehensively map its 'sphere of influence' as envisaged by Principle 1 of the UN Global Compact

- To further extend its promotion of basic labour rights and environmental protection, upstream and downstream

- To encourage its suppliers to extend their endorsement (where it exists) of the standards to *their* suppliers

- To extend its engagement to second-tier suppliers

These moves will necessarily carry an even higher risk than has accompanied the first steps described in this chapter. In moving upstream and further downstream the company will have less influence and therefore less leverage, and other strategies for engaged conversation are being devised. In moving away from the company's core supplier relationships one suspects there will be less clarity, responsiveness and engagement. Coupled to this there are likely to be significant non-compliance issues—or perhaps not, but the company won't know until it looks.

Part 5
The unfolding world of the UN Global Compact

19
Responsible excellence pays*

Claude Fussler

I should be counted as a 'Compactophile' of the first hour. In my view the universal principles provide the shared reference to all corporate citizenship initiatives. In the early discussions around corporate social responsibility business quickly came to the conclusion that 'one size cannot fit all'. But it must also accept that it is not 'do as you please'. Business needs a set of robust co-ordinates to stimulate alignment towards a shared purpose of progress. The principles presented in the Global Compact are precisely this non-negotiable underpinning to any corporate citizenship approach.

Of the 1,000 and more companies that have now signed up to the Global Compact how many have yet to rethink their business model in the context of this commitment? After four years of campaigning, the Global Compact, as a project, will soon face a test of performance. Is it like a comet, with all the energy concentrated in a few companies, deeply engaged, with the larger number dragging in the tail? With the foresight of this test of performance the Global Compact has initiated a dialogue around a model for implementation that should rather change the comet into a plain but growing snowball. This dialogue among early adopters and other experts has resulted in the design of a 'performance model' closely aligned to the practice of total quality and business excellence in order to start from a familiar discipline. The Global Compact performance model is now described in a practical handbook (Fussler *et al.* 2004), detailing a set of tools and examples of practices that can link what managers must do 'on Monday morning' with what the Global Compact and society also expect them to deliver.

---

* The author worked closely with Alois Flatz, Colin le Duc and Urs Schön of SAM Research, Zurich, on the background data for this chapter.

While I was working on the 'how to' and the performance model the questions of 'why?' and the 'business case' kept raising their heads. Much has been written in recent years about the business case. The list of business benefits is for example well summarised in a SustainAbility and UNEP (2001) study: a value matrix highlights the following main factors:

- **Human capital.** It is easier to attract and retain talented people—motivation, creativity and focus run high in the company.

- **Risk management and licence to operate.** By going beyond the obvious risks and setting radical goals for improvement the business disruptions are reduced—frequent information and consultation with stakeholders avoid delays in building and operation permits.

- **Cost savings and productivity.** Eco-efficiency programmes and process control reduce the consumption of energy, water and raw materials and save waste and emissions costs.

- **Revenue growth and market access.** Product and service innovation, a new-ventures approach to the huge potential of basic-needs and low-purchasing-power markets create new growth.

- **Brand value and reputation.** A proactive social responsibility and sustainability strategy opens many doors—to public authorities and procurement, green consumers and the media.

- **Access to capital.** A convincing risk management and a high brand reputation attract investors and reassure bankers.

Such a list always creates the impression that there are no limits and no downsides to this business case. Every business to the last should have been on-board for some time now. What is still holding so many up? The answer is: two things. First, implementation requires a will to change and a wilful co-ordination of practices and resources to enable that change. The majority of people prefer to ride the waves. They change only under pressure or because of a great inspiration. Second, there are a number of discouraging market conditions and institutional failures that raise the uncertainty of success and demand even greater courage and creativity to move and 'lean out of the window'.

However, on balance, the advantages are convincing when one analyses the financial performance of those who have mustered this courage, taken the step and declared their commitment to the Global Compact and now allow the public to track their progress on social responsibility and sustainability.

To get the facts, I turned to the research team at SAM Sustainable Asset Management: SAM produces, from its Zurich base, the Dow Jones Sustainability Index (DJSI), which enables many financial institutions to create equity funds on the basis of a sustainability filter. With the SAM team we asked ourselves how a fund solely based on Global Compact supporters would reward its investors compared with a fund of non-supporters. We also wondered if we could detect a number of practices that could account for better performance. We were curious to see if it would make a noticeable difference. I was even apprehensive that it could turn out to be worse; it would be out of character to cover up the evidence, but certainly awkward to explain in a text composed to show companies how to implement the Global Compact through openness and dialogue! Fortunately, the analysis shows rather robust advantages.

SAM has developed a thorough process to evaluate companies through a comprehensive set of criteria based on sustainability. Based on a best-in-class hypothesis and methodology, the proprietary process selects sustainability leaders and creates a group of companies that can be tracked for performance in the form of an index. The founders of SAM started their work in 1995 as asset managers at the early stage of the socially responsible investment wave that in the meantime has grown to a US$2 trillion business worldwide. Their methodology to screen and select a distinct portfolio of companies proved successful and robust. They could demonstrate that this selection consistently outperformed the Morgan Stanley Capital Index (MSCI) therefore bringing a positive risk–value profile.

This was a very strong research finding concerning the objective correlation between shareholder value and a sustainability strategy. At last the advocates of the business case were vindicated by this clear divergence between the peaks and troughs of two stock market charts. In 1999 the SAM selection was adopted into the Dow Jones family as the Dow Jones Sustainability Index (DJSI). It is now the basis for a number of specific variations and facilitates the design and delivery of customised financial products based on equities screened for sustainability.[1]

Every year SAM takes the largest 2,500 companies, by market capitalisation, from the Dow Jones Global Index. In order to avoid comparing a mining company with a bank or a food producer, it sorts the companies into market groups by their respective major activity—an allocation that is based on Dow Jones & Co.'s mainstream allocations. Although all companies are invited to take part in the evaluation, 487 responded to a detailed questionnaire in 2003. Another 284 were evaluated from publicly available data. The SAM evaluation competes for time with more and more questionnaires from other rating agencies and research groups. Invariably, such questionnaires land on the desk of the same person who may already be grappling with the internal process of the company's own sustainability report. This is not likely to change. There are ever more specialised analysts looking for insights on the social responsibility side. Mainstream analysts are also looking for additional indicators of a company's management quality. Companies usually have more staff to cultivate the traditional financial analysts through yearly group briefings, monthly conference calls, special interviews and continuous news lines. It may be time to think also about the opportunity for their investor relations staff to master the issues of sustainability.

The SAM questionnaire is tailored to each market sector. It probes for key performance elements in the environmental, social and economic domains under the aspects of risk and opportunity management. It is practically SAM's version of a yearly performance report, as comprehensive as the Global Reporting Initiative (GRI) guidelines in several aspects but also more focused on elements that have a material impact on the financial bottom line.[2] SAM carefully scores each element

1   For the latest DJSI charts, consult www.sustainability-index.com.
2   For details of the GRI Guidelines, see www.globalreporting.org/guidelines/2002.asp.

of the questionnaire for each company in each market sector. It also assesses the information from other sources for complementary evidence of performance. As a result it gets a league table of companies ranked by total sustainability scores; it retains in each sector the leader and the top 10% of companies (it may select a few more), with the aim of including at least 20% of the market capitalisation of that sector.

In the 2004 vintage, 317 companies qualified for the index, with a leader in each of the 18 market sectors (see Table 19.1). Some have maintained the lead obtained in previous years, whereas others have lost or gained in a remarkable new race to the top.

Sector	*Year*		
	2001	**2002**	**2003**
Automobiles	Volkswagen	Volkswagen	Toyota
Banks	UBS	Westpac	Westpac
Basic resources	Dofasco	Dofasco	Dofasco
Chemicals	Dow Chemical	DuPont	DuPont
Construction	Skanska	Lafarge	CRH
Cyclical goods and services	Sony	Teijin	Philips Electronics
Energy	Shell	Shell	BP
Financial services	ING	Land Lease	British Land
Food and beverage	Unilever	Unilever	Unilever
Healthcare	Bristol-Myers Squibb	Novozymes	Novozymes
Industrial goods and services	3M	3M	3M
Insurance	Swiss Re	Swiss Re	Swiss Re
Media	Granada Media	Pearson	Pearson
Non-cyclical goods and services	Procter & Gamble	Procter & Gamble	Procter & Gamble
Retail	Ito Yokado	Marks & Spencer	Marks & Spencer
Technology	Intel	Intel	Intel
Telecommunications	British Telecom	British Telecom	British Telecom
Utilities	Severn Trent	Severn Trent	Severn Trent

Table 19.1 Dow Jones Sustainability Index leaders, by market sector

The yearly SAM corporate sustainability assessment includes a good number of Global Compact supporters. There were 99 assessed in detail in 2003, and 76 made it to the index (see Table 19.2). This is a good sample but represents only large market capitalisation companies that are included in the Dow Jones and STOXX markets. Small companies, privately held companies or state companies are, of course, not included. With this limitation in mind we found that the group of 76 signatories—let's call it the GCS76—clearly outperformed the mainstream Morgan Stanley Capital World Index (MSCI World) by 3.4% over the two-year period between January 2002 and January 2004 analysed in terms of US dollars (Fig. 19.1)

Global Compact signatories in the DJSI 2004 (the GCS76)

- ABB Ltd
- Accor
- AGF
- Allianz AG
- Asahi Breweries Ltd
- Aventis
- Aviva plc
- Banca Monte Dei Paschi Di Siena
- Banco Bilbao Vizcaya Argentaria
- Banco Itaú Holding Financeira SA
- BASF AG
- Bayer AG
- Bayerische Motoren Werke AG (BMW)
- Bhp Billiton Ltd
- Bnp Paribas
- BP plc
- BT Group plc
- Carrefour
- Coloplast
- Credit Suisse Group
- Danisco A/S
- Deutsche Bank AG
- Deutsche Lufthansa AG
- Deutsche Telekom AG
- Dexia
- Diageo plc
- DuPont De Nemours & Co.
- Electrolux AB
- Endesa SA
- Groupe Danone
- Groupe Société Générale
- Grupo Ferrovial SA
- Grupo Iberdrola
- Grupo Santander Central Hispano
- Henkel KGaA
- Hennes & Mauritz AB
- Hewlett-Packard Co.
- Holcim
- HSBC Holdings plc
- Inditex SA
- ISS A/S
- L.M. Ericsson
- Lafarge
- Li & Fung Ltd
- Nestlé SA
- Nexen Inc.
- Nike Inc.
- Nokia Corp.
- Norsk Hydro ASA
- Novartis AG
- Novo Nordisk A/S
- Novozymes A/S
- Pearson plc
- Pfizer Inc.
- Reed Elsevier plc
- Ricoh Co.
- Rio Tinto plc
- Royal Dutch/Shell Group of Companies
- Saint-Gobain
- SAP AG Pfd
- Schneider Electric SA
- Serono
- STMicroelectronics
- Statoil ASA
- Stora Enso Oyi
- Storebrand ASA
- Suez
- Technip-Coflexip
- Telenor ASA
- UBS Group
- Unilever
- UPM-Kymmene Oy
- Veolia Environnement
- Volkswagen AG
- Volvo AB
- Westpac Banking Corporation

Global Compact signatories assessed but not in the DJSI 2004 (included in the GCS99)

- Air France
- Aracruz Celulose
- AXA
- Cisco Systems Inc.
- DaimlerChrysler AG
- EPCOS AG
- France Telecom
- ICI
- L'Oreal
- LVMH Moet Hennessy
- Norske Skogsindustrier Free
- Rabobank
- Renault
- San Paolo-IMI
- Sanofi-Synthelabo
- Sasol
- Skanska AB
- Sodexho Alliance SA
- Telecom Italia Mobile
- Telecom Italia SPA
- Telefonica SA
- Titan Cement Co.
- TotalFinaElf

Table 19.2 **UN Global Compact supporters that are included in the SAM Corporate Sustainability Assessment™**

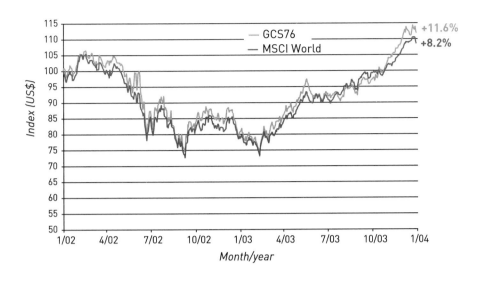

Figure 19.1 Two-year stock performance of the 76 Global Compact signatories (GCS76) compared to the Morgan Stanley Capital Index (MSCI)

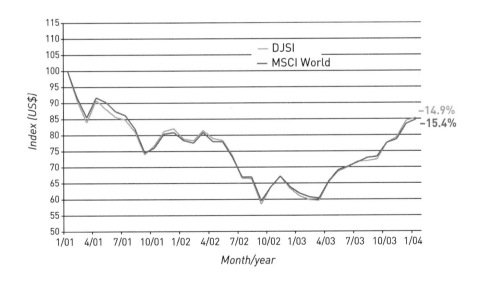

Figure 19.2 Three-year performance of the Dow Jones Sustainability Index (DJSI) compared to the Morgan Stanley Capital Index (MSCI)

Furthermore, the DJSI also outperformed by 0.9% the mainstream market, as measured by MSCI World in US dollars, over a three-year period between November 2000 and November 2003 (Fig. 19.2). Colin le Duc, former Head of Research Operations at SAM, points out that:

> Furthermore, the degree of uncertainty of return on an asset, in this case the equity of the Global Compact Signatory companies was 26.43% for the GCS76 compared to 20.99% for the MSCI. This is an extremely interesting risk profile for an investor. Excess return is achieved at relatively low risk, even though only 76 companies are part of the GCS76, compared to approximately 1,500 companies in the MSCI. One would usually expect a much higher risk for such a small selection of companies. Thus, a broad conclusion is that Global Compact Signatories and members of the DJSI create premium shareholder value at acceptable risk levels. They definitely do not carry a handicap for shareholders relative to the mainstream market.[3]

In theory, an investor takes more risk in reducing investment options to a portfolio that covers only a fraction of the market opportunities, but experience shows that a sustainability criterion is an efficient method to pick investments. It produces rewards that clearly outweigh the risks. Of course, it is not the only method to pick a winning group of stocks. Warren Buffet's focused Berkshire Hathaway portfolio is a resounding example (Hagstrom 1999). Nor is the sustainability portfolio failsafe: in 2000 the sharp simultaneous fall of Dell, Intel, AOL and Lucent stock values was such that it caused the whole DJSI to underperform the market average for several months before rebounding to the lead. The sustainability premium goes only so far.

Can we really speak of a Global Compact market premium? It is a fact that if I had bought the 76 shares of the GCS76 at the end of December 2001 instead of the 1,500 shares of the larger MSCI group I would be 3.4% better off in January 2004 (in the context of a declining market). As a group, the Global Compact signatories created more value. We have yet to understand why.

The first answer is that over that period there were more bidders than sellers for their shares and that the bidders were prepared to offer a premium so that sellers let go of their shares. This is why markets move up—the bulls outnumber the bears. Why did the bidders behave like this? Obviously, they felt that this purchase was a safe use of their money and they speculated that it would return more than inflation, treasury bonds or whatever else they could use it for. They expected the companies in that group to do better in the future. One always buys shares for future returns, in the short or long term.

What did the Global Compact bring to this speculative move? Is it a magic wand that boosts stock appeal? Of all investors trading in and out of those equities none is likely to trade purely on the basis of a Global Compact criterion, or even know anything about it. A few, the socially responsible investors, definitely select shares on the basis of principles that include human rights, corruption, labour standards and environmental responsibility. They have leverage but not to the extent of

3   Private communication with the author.

pushing this kind of premium in the highly traded, large market capitalisation stocks of the GCS76.

So, why is there a premium? The more realistic influence on this premium lies finally in the overall quality of each company that composes this group. It is their credibility as paragons of management excellence and responsibility and the resulting portent of future returns that draws the investors to these companies. This same responsible excellence opens and moves the leadership of those companies to support the Global Compact and even use it to trigger and focus further improvements. In the first instance, engagement with the Global Compact is an effect of managerial dedication to responsible excellence with all the reinforcing potential to become a key performance driver by means of strategic integration.

I need to temper these conclusions with a reminder of the uncertainties, or risk profile, of such a comparison. Beside the assumed value of the sustainability commitment of the GCS76 there are a number of other biases, such as geography, currency and market mix, in the comparison with the MSCI. These could well be the main cause for the value differential, but I lean toward the sustainability explanation, for two reasons. One is the growing body of research in this area, in particular a recent study by Hendrik Graz and Claudia Volk of WestLB; in *More Gain than Pain* they clearly establish the value of a sustainability investment style, giving a detailed discussion of its risk profile and statistical confidence for various traditional investment categories (Graz and Volk 2003). The second reason is that, when it comes to a large number of managerial practices that are driving business excellence, the group of Global Compact signatories demonstrates a clear difference from non-signatories. This hypothesis of a difference was actually the starting point of the inquiry reported in this chapter. It was only after I found such a clear difference in practices that I thought you, the reader, would also wonder about a stock value correlation; it is a simple way to confirm the business case and to catch the attention of business readers.

Let's get back to the principal enquiry: I looked at the SAM database for tangible practices that underpin the elements of business excellence in the area of corporate citizenship. A number of indicators enabled a reliable comparison between two groups of companies—those 99 companies that have signed the Global Compact and the 436 that had not (see Table 19.3). I have also included in the comparison the 308 companies that made it to the 2004 DJSI. This index actually includes 76 of the Global Compact signatories. The other 23 signatories have still some way to go to move into the index—a proof, if needed, that support for the Global Compact is not a magic wand for top performance but the start of an interesting journey. But all three groups are already remarkable for the fact that they qualified for the SAM corporate sustainability assessment. The differences therefore become a clear sign of leadership and excellence. They provide further evidence that it is possible to live up to responsible excellence without an economic penalty but, on the contrary, a market value premium. It must be noted that 90% of the Global Compact sample have headquarters in Europe.

For instance, the leaders take a stand on the boundaries and the scope of responsibility: they clearly influence the behaviour of their suppliers and contractors; they show a stronger customer orientation and their engagement with stakeholders has moved beyond communication and dialogue to partnerships on

Parameter	Percentage		
	SAM436	DJSI308	GCS99
Have guidelines for suppliers on:			
Human rights	28	43	65
Environment	68	82	90
Labour practices	46	58	68
Occupational health and safety	53	63	73
Audit suppliers performance	36	40	39
Corporate environmental policy covers impacts of:			
Products and services	77	84	95
Suppliers and service providers	66	75	83
Other business partners	23	28	26
Measure customers' satisfaction	28	33	37
Engagement with external stakeholders:			
Engage with shared projects	36	50	64
Key stakeholders are prioritised	51	55	67
Seek feedback from stakeholders	52	56	58
Provide regular briefings	75	81	75
Spend more than 1% of EBIT for social investments and philanthropy	23	29	31
Employee survey show a trend for:			
Higher satisfaction	20	28	38
Constant satisfaction	26	24	20
Lower satisfaction	3	3	1
Specific job training covers 90–100% of employees	23	28	35
Over 80% of employees covered by knowledge management system	38	43	44
Long-term success of human resources policies is measured	84	86	95
Performance indicators are used and published for			
Diversity	25	38	54
Environment, health and safety	40	49	66
Layoffs	9	14	24

GCS99   UN Global Compact signatories
DJSI308   group of companies selected for the Dow Jones Sustainability Index 2004
SAM436   group of companies that have not signed the UN Global Compact

Table 19.3 SAM Corporate Sustainability Assessment™: selected performance
parameters (continued opposite)

Parameter	Percentage		
	SAM436	DJSI308	GCS99
Performance indicators are used and published for (cont.)			
Discrimination	11	16	25
Freedom of association	6	9	17
Forced labour	10	11	8
Child labour	12	13	9
Have a certified environmental management system for over 90% of business	22	24	20
Publish a certified sustainability report with strong social component	14	23	36
Publish corporate environmental targets	41	52	56
Have set a greenhouse gas reduction target	37	52	40
Have a greenhouse gas inventory for over 80% of operations	66	80	72
Have a corporate governance policy	74	80	84
The code of conduct covers			
Environment, health and safety	85	92	92
Discrimination	84	90	90
Corruption and bribery	84	89	83

Table 19.3 (continued)

projects (2 out of 3 companies [64%]). Their investment in employee skills and knowledge and satisfaction is deeper—as a result, more than 1 in 3 (38%) could measure progress in employee satisfaction. Every second company has set public environmental targets (56%) and 2 out of 5 have greenhouse gas reduction objectives (40%). One out of 3 gets its sustainability report certified (36%). When it comes to codes of conduct, all companies in the assessment obtain similarly high scores. The differentiation is in implementation. The set of key performance indicators tackles a number of Global Compact principles, but issues such as child and forced labour are still low on the radar screens for all the groups analysed.

Are such differences enough to create value? The answer is: not on their own, but they evolve from a broader base of value drivers. There is no simple equation or a mathematical model that enables one to calculate the market value of the 'soft' dimensions of performance such as having a diversity target, the certification of a sustainability report or even the more tangible targets of waste and emission reductions. A few logical chains, however, link social and environmental responsibility to financial value. It is easier to argue the links to the value of traded shares, but this should not leave out all those companies that are not publicly traded. At some point in time state companies could be offered to public investors, private companies acquire, merge, pass to successors or secure credit lines; they too need to be concerned about value and how to enhance it for the long run.

Share value is a reflection of a company's worth through a complex prism—the economy at large, the news, the cash flows of investors, the situation of the company's sector and the investors' reading of the relative risks and opportunities of all the other choices in the market, to name a few. The market is a real-time approximation of the company's worth and, as many painful corrections have shown, its own nervous dynamics can carry it away. The market actually does not create value like a product or service business. It creates value through arbitrage between investors who have different views and expectations about the value of the titles they are prepared to sell or buy. But what finally counts in the long run is the quality of earnings of the company behind the traded security.

What creates a premium is the expectation of excess returns compared with other options to invest money. These excess returns depend on the competitive advantage of the company and, particularly, on the sustainability of its competitive advantage over time. Thousands of financial analysts continuously screen the universe of companies to assess company strategies and future earnings in relation to the companies' current market value. Are companies undervalued in relation to their business opportunities? Are they overvalued in relation to their business risks? Alois Flatz, head of SAM Research, observes that:

> Investors are once again looking for returns in excess of a general risk premium caused by exceptional costs that the economy must absorb. While throughout the '90s the economy benefited from the peace dividends of the end of the Cold War, we had to cope in the few past years with the costs of ecological disasters of a new magnitude, anti-terrorism, pre-emptive wars, country reconstruction and major corporate failures. In many ways the lack of sustainability raises the hurdle or risk premium that earnings must exceed to reward investors in absolute terms and create real financial value.[4]

This financial value premium is based on strategy—hardly big news but sometimes taken lightly in the more extreme moods of the stock market—and strategy is the effective and efficient combination of resources and business processes, employee creativity and empowerment towards a shared vision, in ways that are difficult to imitate by competition.

Are the Global Compact signatories, then, better at strategy than others? I think so; at least I believe that they continue to be better than many others. The goals of sustainability, the challenges of social responsibility and leadership's inspiration by principles higher than the sole profit motivation all foster business excellence. I like to call this **responsible excellence**, in the broadest sense of each word. The Global Compact brings an additional aspect: voluntary exposure to public scrutiny. The majority of business leaders shy away from such an exposure because they just hate to admit that they don't quite have their act together on all issues. In the absence of a common framework that encourages proactive corporate transparency and accountability, engagement with the Global Compact is therefore a strong indication of confidence by a company in its own performance. It is even a bet that, for a certain number of issues, it is more interesting to get one's act together through public exposure and stakeholder dialogues than behind closed

---

4   Alois Flatz, private note to the author; paper to be published in 2004.

doors with like-minded, or like-confused, colleagues. As Professor Gary Hamel (1998: 82) has written:

> If a company is interested in understanding the future, most of what it needs to learn about the future it is going to learn outside of its own industry.

Plain signs of this confidence to interact on sustainability issues can be read from the SAM Corporate Sustainability Assessment table (Table 19.3): the GCS99 are the companies with the highest proportion of reporters, verification, public improvement targets and depth of interaction with selected stakeholders.

Managing plantations, drilling platforms, extruders, clean rooms, warehouses, truck fleets, computers and bank accounts is one thing—and is complex enough. If that were the only source of value a good accountant would quickly establish book value: end of story. Yet companies are valued at several multiples of their book value. The difference is 'goodwill' made of many layers of 'intangible' assets—intangible but essential to generate earnings, starting with the strategic savvy, the managerial competence and the know-how, creativity and motivation of the personnel. Goodwill is also the art of relationships, of building credibility, commitment and loyalty, not only with commercial partners but also with public authorities, communities or new consumers, such as the poor, who have needs that no one has yet cared to satisfy adequately. We are back in the area of the Global Compact and sustainable development. And we are at a major source of the future cash flows and the excess returns investors are looking for. Brand strength and reputation are all about this art of relationships and vision.

In the long run, I believe that strategies and actions consistent with the principles of the Global Compact exercise and enhance a number of intangible assets that drive value. Although causality is hard to prove it may be just as well to believe it and manage accordingly. Investors expect excess returns, and it is for managers to make them happen. This brings the management of intangible assets into focus and the necessity to understand how they drive value.

As society recognises the vital role of business in wealth creation and economic development, transparency and accountability have come to the forefront of the qualities expected from business management. A Global Compact performance model is part of the answer (see Fussler *et al.* 2004). Those who embrace it beyond the declarations and token documentation, to effectively drive progress towards sustainable development, do not lose out. On the contrary, the evidence grows that they also do well on the financial scorecard.

The metaphor of the triple bottom line is now popular to describe how value is a composite of economic, social and environmental performance. Beware of the simplistic maths: it is not a sum; social and environmental progress will not offset an economic loss. Milton Friedman was justified in his claim that the primary social responsibility of business is to make profits; he should not have stopped there, however. We need some higher maths to better encapsulate how responsible excellence drives value. An appropriate formula may be:[5]

---

5   Proposed by the author, Claude Fussler, in a keynote speech at the launch of the EDF Sustainability Chair of Ecole Polytechnique de Paris, February 2003.

$$P = me^i$$

The share's market price, P—and hence the market capitalisation—is the multiple, m, of expected earnings per share, e; the exponent i stands for an important cluster of **impacts** (social and environmental), **innovation** and the **intangible** drivers of reputation discussed above. The power of this index will enhance value when it is positive and growing, but, as algebra and business life has taught us, when it turns negative it slashes value with a vengeance. The power of i rises from vision, leadership and a wilful, creative co-ordination of the elements of responsible excellence.

20
The Global Compact as
a new organisational form
A global action network

Steve Waddell
Global Action Network Net, USA

Global action networks (GANs) are a new type of organisation that is arising in response to complex global issues that traditional organisations cannot successfully address (Waddell 2003a, 2003b). In fact, they are an important emerging form of global governance that includes business, government and civil-society organisations as participants. They are related to Oran Young's concept of 'international regimes' (Young 1999a, 1999b) but without the emphasis on the role of governments; to Wolfgang Reinicke's concept of 'global public policy networks' (Reinicke 1999; Reinicke and Deng 2000; Witte *et al.* 2000) but without the political science framework and with a deep-change focus; and to Jean-François Rischard's concept of global issue networks (Rischard 2002) that require collaboration between business, government and civil-society organisations. The Global Compact is an example of a GAN.

The concept of a GAN is grounded in several frameworks that can be applied to the Global Compact to better understand its distinctive characteristics, evolution, potential and core challenges. In this chapter, three of those frameworks are applied to the Global Compact. One framework is the core elements that make a GAN a distinct organisational type (Section 20.1). A second framework concerns development stages (Section 20.2). A third framework is the core competences that are needed to create an effective GAN (Section 20.3). To deepen understanding of the Global Compact, these frameworks are applied with the core challenges that they present with respect to the Global Compact.

20.1 The Global Compact and core global action network elements

There are five qualities of GANs that, as a set, make them a distinct type of organisation. In the following sections, each is raised with respect to the Global Compact and a particular challenge that the quality presents.

20.1.1 A global approach: transforming international into global approaches

GANs address issues that cross national boundaries and are recognised as being global in nature. This includes issues such as: corruption, which has produced the GAN of Transparency International; the environment, which has produced numerous GANs such as the Forest Stewardship Council; peace and security, which led to the Ban the Landmines initiative; and healthcare, which is the focus of the Anti-Malaria Campaign.

The Global Compact is the creation of the United Nations and gains its legitimacy from international agreements that have been ratified by most nations of the world. Imbalances and inequities of globalisation were pointed to by the UN Secretary-General as the focus of the Global Compact. A global orientation brings with it significant issues about cross-cultural action in highly diverse contexts and resource bases. Simply communicating across the linguistic barriers is one particular challenge that comes with global aspirations—one the Global Compact has particular difficulty with as almost all of the Secretariat's work is in English.

A global orientation highlights the problematic structure of the government sector. Governments and the United Nations are international structures rather than global structures—that is to say, governments' legitimacy rests within their geographic boundaries. National governments are not accountable for the interests of the whole and do not have a global perspective. Intergovernmental organisations, such as the United Nations, are the creatures of national governments and also reflect this quality.

Civil-society and business organisations also commonly organise along national lines. Organisations that operate around the world most often have sub-units organised along national lines, and organisations very often create coalitions and associations that are national in character. The Global Compact reflects this in the national network structure that it is developing. These organising structures reflect a view that national boundaries are the appropriate ones for organising—and that national governments are *the* critical structure to respond to.

However, global issues by their very nature cannot be dealt with at national government levels, and, very often, national government structures actually inhibit development of truly global solutions. A global world is organised around such things as issues, markets, class, ethnicity, geographic communities, eco-regions, language and shared traditions. We are still at a difficult stage of development where most nation-states jealously guard their powers and tend to behave as though national governments should be unilaterally setting global rules. This is a problem even within government as subnational and regional governments assert their roles, and the national government focus ignores the important role of other types of organisations in fashioning solutions to global issues.

All this reflects a bit of a dilemma. If the Global Compact is to truly support development of a global future it must somehow honour the nation-state tradition that reflects its UN creator and yet clearly move beyond that tradition. The Global Compact is making an important contribution to creating 'global' action through its structures that reflect issues, learning and projects that cross national boundaries. It must guard against the historical vortex pulling it to organise along national boundaries, and its success will be determined in part by its ability to be truly global.

20.1.2 A focus on complex issues of the common good: reframing corporate activities to encompass concerns with the common good

The issues that GANs deal with are classic messes where no one institution is clearly responsible for addressing them (Ackoff 1974). These are issues of the commons, where the traditional public and private interests overlap, and without the creation of a collaborative solution a disaster will result and everyone will suffer. The Marine Stewardship Council (MSC) aims to address the consequences of the resource common of ocean fish by engaging many stakeholders to develop sustainable approaches to fisheries that go well beyond traditional intergovernmental agreements as a way to manage fisheries.[1] Through its comprehensive triple-bottom-line (social, environmental and economic) approach with joint action from civil society and business, the Global Reporting Initiative (GRI) is rewriting 'the rules of the game' with respect to business practice to reflect sustainability imperatives.[2]

The issues of the Global Compact—human rights, the environment and labour—are classic commons concerns that are traditionally associated with government action through rules and regulations. However, the government-based approach has not produced the desired impact—evidenced by continuing non-compliance with the principles. The problem of regulation between nations is particularly complex, and the traditional government-based approach of international agreements and conventions has proven insufficient even with expenditure of immense amounts of effort such as with the climate change negotiations. The Global Compact can be seen as both a supplement to the traditional convention processes that gives life to international agreements and as a potential replacement for them in development.

'Corporate responsibility' and 'corporate citizenship' are key concepts used by the Global Compact as it strives to engage business more deeply in giving life to the principles. The norms-changing and learning strategies that are core to the Global Compact suggest that these are sufficient to give life to these concepts and to the principles. However, encroachment on the commons and historic levels of business engagement do not simply reflect an attitude of business or lack of knowl-

1   See www.msc.org.
2   See www.globalreporting.org.

edge—they also reflect an economic system and rules embedded in a larger social-environmental structure. The system and rules are based on 'carrots and sticks'. To achieve success, eventually the Global Compact will have to get involved in changing the carrots and sticks used in order to fully engage business in application of the principles.

20.1.3 Systems thinking: defining stakeholder boundaries

The complexion and strategies of GANs reflect a systems thinking approach to bring all stakeholders together to take effective action. This is in contrast to traditional intergovernmental approaches where governments get together and write the rules of the game. It is also in contrast to the traditional advocacy coalition strategies of non-governmental organisations (NGOs) where NGOs attempt to force their own standards on others. And it is in contrast to the lobby strategies of traditional business associations. These might be considered constitutional law and unisectoral norm-making strategies that reflect Young's (1999a) term of 'collective action' strategies.

In contrast, GANs focus on what Young calls 'social practice' strategies (1999a) and what Global Compact architect John Ruggie (see Chapter 2) calls 'learning-based approaches' that can be likened to a common law tradition. In this approach, stakeholders with an interest in a common issue gather together to jointly learn through experiment how to address that issue, and they develop among themselves a network system that combines the competences and resources needed to address the issue effectively.

Of course, there is already much learning going on when a GAN emerges, and stakeholders typically already have organisations and initiatives addressing the issue in which they are interested. GANs are important because they build 'system consciousness'—that is to say, they raise awareness among stakeholders of one another's activities. More importantly, GANs raise stakeholders' attention to the priority action for creating an effective system, in contrast to the typical focus on the priorities of an individual organisation or project (Waddell 2003a, 2003b).

The definition of 'system boundaries' is an ongoing challenge for GANs, and who the stakeholders are changes as GANs' knowledge about the issue evolves. If the boundaries are too limited, important stakeholders will be left out and the system organising will be undermined, under-resourced, or simply marginal. If the boundaries are too expansive, there will be lack of focus and inability to achieve coherence. System mapping is critical. This means literally drawing out global relationships to identify the system gaps and key interventions that are necessary.

The Global Compact commenced with a vision of

> bring[ing] together all the relevant social actors[:] . . . governments, who defined the principles on which the initiative is based; companies, whose behaviour the Global Compact seeks to shape; labour, in whose hands the concrete process of global production takes place; NGOs, representing the wider community of stakeholders; and the United Nations, the world's only truly global political entity (Ruggie, Chapter 2, page 42).

Ruggie's boundaries are much too expansive to operationalise, and critical microcosms of stakeholder groups must be identified. Within this expansive vision, the goal was to have 1,000 corporations participating within three years, but the level of participation of other entities was not specified. However, the focus was naturally on other international organisations, and a priority subset quickly evolved. Close relationships have been established with the International Chamber of Commerce (ICC), the International Organisation of Employers (IOE), the World Business Council for Sustainable Development (WBCSD) and the Global Reporting Initiative (GRI). Major international corporations were priorities. Ruggie's NGOs became mainly international organisations that were willing to engage in dialogue. Academia was added as the importance of being a learning organisation was more readily appreciated, and the United Nations Industrial Development Organisation (UNIDO) was added to the original four UN agencies engaged[3] as the focus expanded to include small and medium-sized enterprises (SMEs).

However, whether this shifting definition of critical stakeholders represents the critical microcosms from a systems thinking perspective is unclear. Of course, the Global Compact cannot hope to engage everyone, and it must carefully choose high leverage points. At least some reviewers feel the Global Compact has missed out on some critical sub-groups of Ruggie's vision (RING Alliance 2003; see also Section 20.3.1).

A major challenge for GANs and one that will continue to exist for the Global Compact is to balance an expansive global vision with highly strategic system interventions based on a clear definition of 'the system'. For the Global Compact, the definition of the system is not entirely clear. It could be related to corporate responsibility and corporate citizenship, but the Global Compact is functionally a UN agency and that is hardly the appropriate vehicle for organising a corporate vision. It could be a 'nine-principle' system, which seems more appropriate but comes with its own challenges. Giving life to the principles means engaging all levels of government and other organisations that are part of such a system, and that makes the scope so broad that it could become unmanageable; it also emphasises the importance of understanding the system and of carefully identifying and prioritising critical leverage points and projects. It is easy to get carried away by what seems easiest or most exciting, rather than identifying and focusing on what is most needed for the system to evolve.

20.1.4 Boundary spanning: building and maintaining diversity

Given their global nature, their focus on complex issues and a systems thinking approach, GANs typically bridge problematic traditional divides such as those between organisational sectors (business, government and civil society), cultural divides, disciplinary divides, a North–South or a rich–poor divide, and divides along functional lines between ministries and departments. With such complex-

---

3 The original four agencies were the International Labour Organisation (ILO), the United Nations Environment Programme (UNEP), the United Nations High Commission on Human Rights (UNHCHR) and the United Nations Development Programme (UNDP).

ity, a significant challenge is to ensure that the diversity of the system is reflected in the GAN and its actions and that the diverse parts can work together effectively.

One aspect of boundary spanning concerns the creation of network relationships and communications functions and the emotional, physical, intellectual and spiritual capacity of individuals to communicate across boundaries. Take for example the Partnership for Principle 10 (PP10),[4] which is giving life to Principle 10 of the Earth Charter regarding participation in environmental decision-making. It was initiated by NGOs by creating a global network of national groups of NGOs with competences in writing laws, in environmental measurement and in participatory practices. They had to build among themselves a common understanding and language across the cultural and professional boundaries. These NGOs then had to help national governments organise themselves across ministerial and departmental boundaries, as the issue of environmental decision-making relates to many ministries and departments. PP10 was then organised as a place for intergovernmental agencies, donor agencies and other stakeholders for building the required systems globally and for creating a joint learning space for all the participating national governments; it plans to open participation to corporations as it develops.

The Global Compact has been struggling with the complexities of crossing numerous divides, but learning how to do this in an effective way is a critical task. One obvious problem is linguistic, as Global Compact activities are comprehensively available only in English. Its major vehicle of exchange is intellectual, as demonstrated in its meetings, and it is tackling 'head on' the need to integrate distinct bodies of knowledge that have developed around the various principles. In addition, it brings together organisational sectors. However, the Global Compact as a GAN is challenged to substantially deepen mutual understanding and actually to build the capacity of people to communicate more profoundly across divides. Unfortunately, this includes a range of emotional, physical and spiritual communication that most people are reluctant to explore because of the need to make oneself personally vulnerable, to free significant time to engage in such communication and our general weak capacity for undertaking such exchanges. It includes discussing really difficult issues, such as the meaning of equity and integrity as values when one person at the table is earning millions of dollars and another a few tens of thousands of dollars or less (Waddock 2001).

20.1.5 Agents of large system change: getting everyone to change

This last point leads directly to the property of GANs as agents of large system change. A core task is to generate deep change by creating new consensual knowledge, relationships and actions that move in a coherent direction. The scale of this change reflects Thomas Kuhn's (1962) concept of 'paradigm shift' and the scale of change in South Africa that accompanied the ending of apartheid (see Bartunek 1988; Tushman and Romanelli 1985).

4 See www.PP10.org.

GANs deal with change that involves realignment between the three core systems of society—economic (business), political (government) and social (civil society). This is societal learning and change (Brown *et al.* 2000; Waddell 2001, 2002). As long as environmental degradation is seen as the fault of business, because of the short-term perspective of business, or as the fault of government, because of lack of regulatory commitment from government, the degradation will continue. Change by a part of the system is insufficient; the whole system and usually all its stakeholders must change.

In addressing the issue of corruption, Transparency International brings together business, government and NGOs. Addressing corruption is not simply a matter of business ceasing to pay bribes; in many countries, an end to corruption will also require governments to raise salaries of government officials to adequate levels. Addressing corruption also requires vigilant NGOs and media to report such corruption and legal systems that work effectively. Basic change and capacity-building of all stakeholders and their relationships is necessary.

Societal change is a core product of the Global Compact (see Kell and Levin, Chapter 3 in this volume). For many stakeholders, particularly in civil society, this requires shifting from a position of finger-pointing and saying someone else is to blame to realising that giving life to the principles of the Global Compact requires changing one's own behaviour and capacity. For many in business, the Global Compact requires shifting from a 'it's not my responsibility' position to working with others to give life to the principles, and, for governments in particular, the deep change requires shifting from a 'we're in charge' position to one of working collaboratively as peers with others to co-produce solutions.

The Global Compact is highly innovative for the UN because it reflects change in its traditional way of operating. According to Ruggie (Chapter 2, page 33):

> [It] has explicitly adopted a learning approach to inducing corporate change, as opposed to a regulatory approach; and it comprises a network form of organisation, as opposed to the traditional hierarchic/bureaucratic form.

However, it still does not reflect a full shift to a collaborative model that most GANs find necessary to be effective. The Global Compact remains a creature of the UN, although it does have an impressive cross-sectoral advisory council. This means that 'ownership' is not fully embedded in the emerging system and that government weaknesses remain (such as its rule-driven nature, which can be overcome in more categorical collaborations).

The Global Compact is challenged to move beyond negotiated change and conflict-resolution approaches to build and maintain a goal of deeper visionary change to a future where everyone has changed and is working collaboratively to give life to the principles. Emphasising learning at this point is a good strategy, as people have to learn about each other as well as about the issues. But can the scale of change needed be produced?

20.2 Development stages

The question about scale of change relates directly to questions about how to move GANs through development stages. The development stages of GANs combine characteristics of those for other multi-sectoral collaboration processes and for public policy development processes. These have been analysed to identify half a dozen and more distinct development stages, but they can be condensed into three:

- The first stage may be labelled as **issue definition**. Stakeholders must be able to agree on a framing of the problem or opportunity to a sufficient degree to move ahead. For example, with the issue of climate change an important step in consensual definition occurred with development of the concept of 'ecological footprint' in the early 1990s (Rahman *et al.* 1998). Before this, the population growth of developing countries was considered a major source of the climate change problem, but the footprint concept demonstrated that, in fact, the industrialised countries are the major source of the problem.

- The second stage may be labelled **solution design**. Once the key characteristics and conceptual framework for describing the issue are agreed, stakeholders must define what they are going to do about it. In the case of the climate change issue, this stage was represented by a painful decade of negotiations that resulted in what is popularly thought of as the Kyoto Protocol.[5]

- The third stage may be labelled **implementation**. With the stakeholders agreed on their roles in addressing the issue, they must actually play them out. Whether this will occur with the Kyoto Treaty is still unclear, but failure can result from poorly defining the problem or from developing a solution design that is impractical or too weak or for which there is insufficient political will to apply.

Of course, given the complexity of GANs and their global work, the stages interact—that is to say, they are all going on to some extent at the same time. However, the challenges of one stage tend to dominate at any one time.

The Global Compact may be thought of as representing the second time the world has gone through this development cycle with respect to its principles. The first time through was with the collective action approach, where governments created international conventions as the design solution, but this never moved to meaningful implementation. Failure of the first cycle has become both obvious and so problematic that it can no longer be ignored.

Therefore, this time around, the problem definition has two dimensions. One concerns the definition of the principles themselves. The first attempt at their definition left their qualities too vague and theoretical, skipping over the problematic questions about cultural and other contextual differences which, if addressed,

5   http://unfccc.int/resource/convkp.html

would create robust and rich definitions. The second dimension of the issue definition arises from the fact that there is little evidence of a relationship between the international conventions on the principles that governments signed and their actual practice. This was the proverbial elephant in the UN, which, under the glare of economic globalisation and anti-globalisation protests, finally became an open topic of discussion with the broader community with the forming of the Global Compact. The Global Compact must bridge this theory–practice gap. Therefore, the Global Compact must deepen our understanding of issue definition and design the processes that will lead to implementation.

The Global Compact is based on the assumption that there is widespread agreement about the value of the principles and represents a new approach to solution design. However, the issue definition and solution design are still in the making. Participants are deepening their understanding about the implications of the principles to better define the key issues. They are experimenting with projects and are learning collaboratively about what can be done to give life to the principles. Pieces of the solution design are emerging bit by bit, such as in the creation of global labour agreements.

Maintaining the participation of the stakeholders—business stakeholders, in particular—during this process of learning and solution design is a particularly daunting challenge. Business is notorious for its short attention span, and the work of the Global Compact can easily appear to be low-return and long-term and requiring heavy investment. This suggests that, rather than trying to engage any particular corporation in a broad range of activities with respect to implementing the principles, the Global Compact should identify a narrowly defined experiment with any particular corporation or group of corporations with issues that are highly salient to financial performance. Of course, the collective learning potential of the Global Compact promises to help reduce the costs for any one participant and to aid in the spread of leading practice to change relatively quickly the underlying problematic rules of the game.

20.3 Core competences

Building on two 'gaps' identified in global governance processes (Reinicke and Deng 2000) Global Action Network Net (GAN-Net) (thanks in particular to Tariq Banuri) has identified four competences that GANs must develop if they are to be effective (Waddell 2003b). These represent the distinctive contributions that GANs must make if they are to be of value. Each of these competences has multiple aspects, and in the following sections I highlight only one critical point in relation to the Global Compact.

20.3.1 Participation: achieving the 'tipping point'

GANs must influence a sufficient number of system stakeholders to achieve their missions of creating deep societal change. How many this means in practice is not easily defined. Anthropologist Margaret Mead suggested that a handful of committed citizens can change the world.[6] Gladwell refers to the 'tipping point' as a process of social epidemics just like outbreaks of infectious disease that obtain sufficient momentum, scale and adherence that they result in what Kuhn referred to as a paradigm shift (Kuhn 1962; see also Gladwell 2002).

This competence emphasises the importance of creating highly participatory development processes that engage all parts of the system. Rather than traditional intergovernmental top-down or expert-driven processes, the Global Compact must develop competence in meaningfully engaging all the critical system stakeholders. This means vertical system integration, from every local shopfloor employee up to the top of the corporation, from all citizens up to intergovernmental agencies and from individual members up to international civil-society associations. It means horizontal system integration, including business, government and civil society and whole supply chains.

Although this seems like a daunting challenge on the global scale, it emphasises the importance of identifying key system leverage points where projects will be undertaken in ways that produce widely disseminated learning. An additional reason to engage network organisations is that one of their major functions is to share information. The Global Compact must be able to tie together these pieces, as it is aiming to do through its Learning Forums, partnership projects and policy dialogues.

Attaining sufficient participation is a substantial challenge, of course. A 2003 report identified four weaknesses in the Global Compact with respect to the meaningful participation of:

- Non-OECD countries, even though more than half of the participating companies come from developing countries

- Governments, which have often been indirect participants—as donors, or as deliverers of political support, rather than being placed as key actors at the centre of the Global Compact

- Uni-national SMEs, which are a key engine of growth in middle-income and low-income countries

- Co-operatives, informal-sector enterprises and entrepreneurs, where participation has been almost non-existent

- Some major civil-society-based organisations, among them some of the most significant drivers of equitable development 'on the ground'— community-based organisations (RING Alliance 2003)

The Global Compact must develop competence in creating and supporting a number of different types of network, including information networks, communities of practice and, most importantly, networks that generate change. Networks

6 She stated that: 'Never doubt that a small group of thoughtful, committed citizens can change the world; indeed it's the only thing that ever has.' This quote appeared on a poster shown at the 2003 Business and Human Rights seminar of the Business Leaders Initiative on Human Rights, London, 9 December 2003.

that generate change are common to all GANs and involve the identification and undertaking of key system interventions that optimise influence. In the context of the Global Compact, there is a need for such influence to ripple out to organisations that are not even participants in the Global Compact. The Ethical Trading Initiative (ETI) is a GAN that does this by focusing on supply chains as systems that will carry the 'infectious disease' of ethical imperatives.[7]

20.3.2 Ethics and values: integrating the principles into participants' actions

Often, a change process begins with clear articulation of values, but these get lost along the development path. Article 3 of the climate change convention of 1992 clearly articulates a commitment of developed nations to take the lead and to financially support developing countries to adapt to the climate imperative on the basis of the value of equity (Climate Change Secretariat 1999). After ten years of negotiations, however, the solution design failed to meaningfully honour this commitment. The founding document of the World Trade Organisation (WTO) emphasises the value of sustainable development, but few would claim that the value has played an important role in implementation of the WTO accord.

The Global Compact is distinguished by the fact that it is all about ethics and values. The challenge of integrating them into participants' actions is central and at the forefront of concerns. However, many NGOs have raised reasonable scepticism about the ability of the Global Compact to do this and about the degree of commitment of corporations to the principles (Judge 2000). By the very nature of its mission the Global Compact requires an open-ended approach. The principles have never been integrated into business activity in a comprehensive way and therefore the Global Compact represents a grand experiment. The issues of monitoring, accountability and transparency are all part and parcel of the competences that the Global Compact must develop for itself and for its participant corporations as they strive to integrate the principles into their operations and actions.

Some suggest that, in fact, the principles must be further refined to incorporate more categorically the values of transparency (Waddock 2003) and sustainable development (RING Alliance 2003; Waddock 2003), reflecting a critique that, in fact, the principles are cobbled together in a rather ad hoc manner that lacks a comprehensive framework. For example, it has been argued that the value of sustainable development should result in each principle being accountable to the themes of reducing poverty, building social capital and enabling responsible entrepreneurship (RING Alliance 2003).

20.3.3 Operations: developing useful data and transforming it into action

As learning organisations, information centres and experiment initiators, GANs generate enormous amounts of data that must be transformed into information,

---

7   See www.ethicaltrade.org.

knowledge and action. They face the enormous danger of generating vast amounts of data and information without successfully connecting that data to change. Social Accountability International (SAI)[8] or the GRI, for example, could simply become a GAN that stimulates the production of reports from corporations, without ever resulting in meaningful change. The Global Compact might degenerate into a growing list of participating companies and country networks without ever generating meaningful change. Indeed, the lack of usefulness of the initial commitment required of companies to provide examples of how they are implementing the Global Compact was discontinued in favour of more disciplined ways of generating, organising and disseminating the data.

GANs, as global networks to generate change, can never reasonably aspire to know or be in touch with everything that is going on in the system they are helping to develop. However, they must be able to point to outcomes valued by their participants within a reasonable period of time. For GANs, a period of three to five years is a common lag between conception and the start of realisation of the originally envisioned valued outcomes. The Global Compact is just now at the end of that period, and there are some outcomes that it appears to have supported that are indeed valued by participants.

Outcome attribution in complex networks is always difficult—would the international labour agreements have been produced without the Global Compact? Did the Global Compact increase the number and speed of production of these agreements? Has the Global Compact's promotion of the GRI helped advance the principles beyond what the GRI would have done on its own? Although a large part of the Global Compact's success will depend simply on whether participants 'feel' that their connection with the Global Compact is producing meaningful results, the Global Compact has to become adept at chronicling the results in the various ways that its various stakeholders value. At the end of 2003 the website[9] still appears to be more of a list of ideas, speeches and events rather than giving details of valued impacts where the Global Compact has played a critical and clearly articulated role.

20.3.4 Communications: developing strategies to connect

When governments reach international agreements, one of the first questions to arise is about enforcement. What is the process for ensuring that governments abide by the agreement? Typical responses feel evasive, with reference to peer pressure, the impact on prestige if there is abrogation, the ability for others to take retaliatory action (that will simply worsen the situation for everyone) or reference to a panel that may issue a finding. A critical weakness with these traditional approaches is that they do not involve the whole system and therefore there is little room for a system response. GANs, by involving the whole system, have a much greater capacity to develop a powerful system response to the failure of a stakeholder to meet its obligations. However, this depends to a large extent on the ability to create a strong network to generate change.

8   See www.sa-intl.org.
9   See www.unglobalcompact.org.

Critical to creating such a network is the Global Compact's ability to stimulate communities of stakeholders that build mutually reinforcing ties and commitment to one another's success. These communities must be able to communicate effectively among themselves and between other Global Compact communities and to ensure that their learning and actions are disseminated through their respective networks. The Global Compact's role in all this is one of facilitator and creator of a culture that functions in a highly communicative way. The Global Compact itself can never hope to be responsible for broad dissemination but rather must inculcate a culture among its participants so that they understand the importance of dissemination and do it automatically. Of course, this requires an understanding of the bigger picture of change behind the Global Compact and the tipping-point strategy. For, in the end, just as most citizens obey a nation's laws because they understand and agree with them, so, too, signatories to the Global Compact must understand why the principles are important and how they may give life to those principles.

20.4 Conclusions

The Global Compact faces classic challenges that are associated with many GANs, but it also faces some distinctive challenges. Unlike many GANs where principles are foundations for achieving a core GAN objective, such as improved healthcare or the end of poverty, the Global Compact is all about values. The connection of values to the full range of business activity makes the work of the Global Compact particularly diffuse and complex. This heightens the importance of the Global Compact having a good understanding of 'the system' that it is trying to organise, the relationships between stakeholders in the system and their core competences with respect to the principles. This map is necessary to identify the critical leverage points for the Global Compact to take action and avoid being overwhelmed by the scale of its challenge.

The change that the Global Compact implicitly aims to achieve is very profound. A global society that integrates the principles will look very different from the one that we have today. The structures, processes and organisations needed to support them are still not well understood, and the Global Compact is doing the hard work of giving shape to them. The depth of the work suggests that it is critical for the Global Compact to develop some profound, deep-change, initiatives that will be long-term and require an interpersonal and inter-organisational intimacy that goes beyond the intellectual and into the emotional–spiritual dimension where stakeholders can 're-vision' their future. These types of approach are under development, and if the Global Compact can focus on development of its own organisational capacity as well as change among its participants it has a rich base of knowledge on which to build.

21
Learning by doing
The Global Compact and the ethic of corporate citizenship

James E. Post and Tanja D. Carroll

Boston University, USA

21.1 Introduction

The UN Global Compact is a practical mechanism for integrating the business and social strategies of multinational corporations (MNCs). It may, in time, influence all businesses because it urges an ethic of global corporate citizenship that is appropriate to the global economy of the 21st century.

Modern corporations have become extended enterprises, with long supply chains, complex market channels and extensive networks of voluntary and involuntary stakeholders. There is interdependence, and risk, at every point in these networks, creating a pressing need for effective business and social strategies.

Extended enterprises are 'learning by doing' in their efforts to develop a robust, practical approach to corporate citizenship in the 21st century. No theory guides companies toward 'optimal' outcomes. The norm is still trial and error, yielding some successes and many failures. The Global Compact now provides a template against which corporate policies can be tested, measured and improved. It also provides a dynamic system for co-operating with others and for learning from a broad range of participants. This chapter assesses how the Global Compact facilitates these relational and learning goals in business. In so doing, the Global Compact is propagating a new ethic of global corporate citizenship.

21.1.1 Context: where are we going?

There is a saying that roughly translates as, 'If you don't know where you are going, any road will do.' In the 21st century, people of many cultures realise that 'any road' will *not* do when it comes to the intricate relationship between economic activity, people, the ecological environment and communities. The days of economic 'free-riders' and unchallenged externalities are over, as they must be. It may well take decades to fully define the road that must be taken, but the Global Compact is an important mechanism to advance that understanding.

To grasp the importance of the Global Compact in the modern world, and the importance of the human commitments it contemplates, it is important to consider the context in which 21st century commerce exists:

● We are one world—6 billion human beings inhabiting one planet.

● The ecology of the planet Earth is fragile.

● Human beings have the capacity to seriously damage the Earth; it is unknown whether—or to what extent—they also have the ability to correct the damage done to the biosphere.

● Economic activity is a nearly universal activity of human beings, and it produces many of the externalities that threaten the ecology of the planet.

● There is growing understanding of—and commitment to—concepts of development and economic activity that do not compromise the rights of future generations to a comparable quality of life on this planet.

● Human beings must reassess how the world's resources are used if they are to enable all of the world's people to have an opportunity to exercise their universal human rights.

● Global peace and international security are essential to the future of the human race. Economic status is entwined with peace and security issues.

These propositions are accepted in large measure by most people and by many national governments. The operative question is whether critical institutions—businesses, political bodies and non-governmental entities— can be encouraged to behave in ways that conform to these imperatives. The Global Compact is one means of helping that process to occur.

21.1.2 Corporate citizenship

Corporate citizenship is defined in many ways by academics and practitioners (see Wood and Logsdon 2002). Such definitions converge in their recognition that an organisation has a core set of responsibilities to its various stakeholders. Some of these stakeholders are voluntarily 'in relation' to the organisation, gaining some benefit from the association. Others are involuntarily related to the organisation, bearing a risk that flows from the activities of the entity. Their 'stake' is the risk of harm (e.g. communities that bear the risk of pollution) whereas the 'stake' of the voluntary stakeholders is the benefit they will enjoy when the organisation achieves success.

The nature of the organisation's obligations to its voluntary and involuntary stakeholders has been addressed in numerous statements of principles, codes of conduct and policy documents. Important precursors to the Global Compact included the Principles of Business of the Caux Round Table (1994), developed by a consortium of business leaders and advisors, and the 1999 Clarkson Principles, named for the Clarkson Center in Toronto, Canada, drafted by a community of scholars and practitioners (see Post 2002). These statements recognise the benefit–risk relationship of the enterprise and its stakeholders and the business importance of these responsibilities.

The principles of the Global Compact incorporate conceptual principles of citizenship and stewardship and apply them to the unique challenges of multi-national businesses in the global economy. The principles, listed on page 12, cover the areas of human rights, labour and the environment. In a recent report, the United Nations (2003c: 10) stated:

> Good corporate citizenship can be defined as embracing the Global Compact's universal principles within a company's sphere of influence and making them part of a company's strategy and operations, while at the same time contributing positively to the society where the company operates . . . These two dimensions of good corporate citizenship—internalising the principles within corporate domains of operations and contributing proactively in support of broader societal goals, especially with respect to development—are complementary and inseparable.

21.1.3 The extended enterprise

The idea of the 'extended enterprise' refers to firms for which network relationships are extensive and include resource-dependency relations, competitive relationships and sociopolitical relations. Originally defined in terms of its complex logistics and manufacturing requirements, the extended enterprise is now understood to be characteristic of firms with global product and service orientations. The complexity of the networks that support such an enterprise is the signal feature of the extended enterprise and its principle vulnerability. The extended enterprise depends on elaborate flows of information, money, knowledge and physical resources. Because the firm is highly dependent on resources, competitive presence and predictable sociopolitical dynamics, management of these relationships is a vital business activity: These relationships are the key to sustainable business success in both the short term and the longer term. This is the essence of the new stakeholder view of the firm (Post *et al.* 2002a).

To achieve sustainable success, a company needs to develop both a sophisticated business strategy and an appropriate citizenship strategy. Competitive success earns the firm its economic legitimacy and the support of investors. Social and political successes are the key to societal legitimacy and earn the firm its public credibility. In the modern business environment, the extended enterprise needs both economic and societal legitimacy, because such enterprises are so powerful and interconnected in the global economy.

The extended enterprise is the nodal element within a network of interrelated stakeholders that create, sustain and enhance the firm's value-creating capacity. 'Relationships rather than transactions . . . are the ultimate source of organisational wealth . . . Survival and success of a firm are determined by its ability to establish and maintain relationships within its entire network of stakeholders' (Post *et al.* 2002b: 7). This view of stakeholder management as a key to organisational success clearly emphasises the important role of partnerships. The Global Compact provides a framework for the enhancement of these relationships through partnership projects.

21.1.4 Aligning the business and citizenship models

Social and economic success is achieved when a firm's business and citizenship models are combined, or made compatible, and positive externalities are leveraged. This has been demonstrated at the local and national levels; the ultimate goal is to attain this balance at the global level. Public policy in the form of 'hard' or 'soft' government involvement is vital to facilitating business citizenship at the national level. What public policy has done at the local and national levels needs to be done by the Global Compact in order to reach a win–win outcome at the global level, where supranational government has few powers of enforcement. Without formal regulations, there is a need for a framework to encourage voluntary corporate action to address externalities. The Global Compact does not guarantee a win–win scenario but it does help guarantee that the win–lose balance is not too extreme.

The case for avoiding win–lose situations can be made at many levels. The UN Secretary-General has highlighted the case in terms of global socioeconomic and political dynamics, stating: 'History teaches us that such an imbalance between the economic, social and political realms can never be sustained for very long' (see Chapter 1, page 29). In 1999, UN Secretary-General Kofi Annan urged business leaders to voluntarily comply with international standards in the form of nine principles, based on labour, human rights and environmental practices

> even when not obliged to do so by states within which operations were occurring. He pledged UN collaboration in such efforts and seemed to be proposing such action as a move toward the negotiation of a global social contract based on a novel idea of private sector 'global citizenship' (Falk 2002: 194).

If corporations fully implemented these nine principles, there would be a balance between the economic, social and political worlds, ensuring a win–win situation.

Jane Nelson, in her report, *Building Partnerships: Co-operation between the United Nations System and the Private Sector*, states that 'The Global Compact's overall goal is to make markets more stable and inclusive' (2002: 135). The vision is appealing:

> weaving universal social and environmental values into the fabric of corporate activity everywhere, will help to advance broader societal goals and address some of the downsides of globalisation, while giving open markets a social dimension (Nelson 2002: 135).

In a paper written for the Global Corporate Citizenship Initiative of the World Economic Forum, Roberts *et al.* (2001) defined eight areas in which business benefits accrue to being a good corporate citizen:

- Reputation management

- Risk profile and risk management

- Employee recruitment, motivation and retention

- Investor relations and access to capital

- Learning and innovation

- Competitiveness and market positioning

- Operational efficiency

- Licence to operate

They write:

> While there may be a lack of consensus as to the extent of a company's moral responsibility for corporate citizenship, the range of business benefits that that can result should be sufficient to make any forward-thinking organisation see increasing corporate citizenship as an integral part of good business management (Roberts *et al.* 2001: 7).

21.2 Developing an ethic of global corporate citizenship

These formulations of good practice for modern corporations are an extension of thinking that has evolved for nearly 40 years in Europe, the USA and in Asia–Pacific nations, notably including Japan and Australia.

Throughout the global economy, serious conflicts have strained the relationship between business and society and have required the imaginative engagement of government, business and community leaders. From these experiences, we have discerned a developmental model that recognises the uneven process through which most organisations—public or private—pass as they encounter new challenges.

21.2.1 Decades of learning

The ethic of global corporate citizenship has evolved over many decades. MNCs have moved from a 'when in Rome, do as the Romans do' mind-set (*circa* 1950s) to a modern 'glocal' (global and local) mind-set that recognises the need for a global approach that builds on deep local understanding. Three evolutionary trends have helped lay the foundation for the Global Compact:

● The 1970s and 1980s: concepts of corporate social responsibility (CSR)

● The 1980s and 1990s: the power of quality management

● The 1990s and 2000s: global risk, responsibility and action networks (the era of the Global Compact)

21.2.1.1 The 1970s and 1980s: concepts of corporate social responsibility

Core concepts of CSR emerged as business and society worked out practical answers to the question, 'To whom, and for what, is the modern corporation responsible?' European and North American companies were pressured to respond—simultaneously—to critical environmental, employment, consumer and community concerns. Crises, public outrage and regulatory activism by governments pressured companies to replace narrow, tactical approaches with more holistic, strategic thinking. Market incentives also emerged and reinforced responsive business practice. A 'market' for socially responsible companies and investment began to form.

21.2.1.2 The 1980s and 1990s: the power of quality management

Asian, European and North American companies faced intense price and quality competition during this period. Product quality, customer focus and internal-external responsiveness were intensely measured and managed for overall corporate performance. Concepts such as 'six sigma', 'best practice' and 'best in class' supported radical innovation. The employment and community dislocations of transformational change were severe, however, and whole industries were wracked by major change. A major reconceptualisation of the employer–employee and company–community 'social contract' took place under duress. Companies in many industries developed quality improvement programmes and perfected their 'learning by doing' methodologies. Training, organisational learning and external standards (e.g. the ISO 9000 series) contributed to a highly demanding approach to measurement and statistical evaluation of performance. Corporate environmental performance was also advanced through the adoption of the ISO 14000 series standards.[1]

---

1 For details of standards from the International Organisation for Standardisation (ISO), see www.iso.org.

21.2.1.3 The 1990s and 2000s: global risk, responsibility and action networks (the era of the Global Compact)

Media, non-governmental organisations (NGOs) and governments focused on the global externalities of MNC behaviour, especially in emerging economies where asymmetrical power structures created market conditions that permitted exploitation of vulnerable populations. Economic and political pressures to expand free trade were constrained by the need to reconcile labour and environmental concerns with economic freedom. International agreements expanded the formal recognition of ecological, labour and human rights concerns. 'Sustainability' became an operative concept in the international business and political community. Global activism increased and NGOs became legitimate parties at the table of international negotiations. Expectations of—and commitments to—responsible corporate behaviour in the global economy were manifested in numerous voluntary codes, statements, principles and reporting initiatives. The Global Reporting Initiative (GRI) evolved as a successor to earlier reporting schemes.[2] The Global Compact is promoted as a conceptual framework of global principles and corporate action.

21.2.2 Lessons learned

Four broad lessons can be drawn from this reservoir of experience. First, effective responses to social and political issues occur in stages. There is a universal corporate response model that describes critical phases through which an organisation passes as it responds to social and political issues. These phases include:

- Awareness (i.e. cognisance)

- Learning (i.e. technical learning about the problem and administrative learning about organisational barriers)

- Policy commitment (i.e. from executive leadership)

- Implementation (e.g. in systems, culture and evaluations)

Second, there is a knowledge-management process through which individual organisations capture existing information and create new understandings of the substantive issues and the barriers and enablers of organisational change. There is both a learning curve and a performance curve in each organisation; learning drives performance.

Third, organisations in the same industry do not respond to specific issues in the same way or at the same rate. Therefore, a normal distribution of innovators, early adopters and late adopters will emerge over time.

Last, innovation cycles develop as companies and industries respond to social and political challenges, as in dealing with economic and organisational challenges. Several cycles of innovation and adoption may need to take place before transformational change occurs in an industry.

---

2   For details of the GRI, see www.globalreporting.org.

21.2.3 Learning by doing

Learning is a process, not an event. The organisational capacity to learn is the characteristic that most clearly separates successful from unsuccessful organisations. Learning involves the ability to extract information, understanding and insight from experience; and the ability to accumulate and transfer knowledge is the distinguishing characteristic of 'learning organisations'. Organisations learn both their negative and their positive experiences. Effective organisational learning integrates knowledge about internal and external change processes with prevailing assumptions about an organisation's strategy, structure and culture. As a result, these basic organisational characteristics may change—along with the policies and procedures created to implement them. The ultimate result is a change in the way in which an organisation pursues its fundamental goals of survival, value creation and growth.

There is an extensive body of research on organisational learning (Senge 1990; see Post *et al.* 2002a), with numerous theories and data, ranging from the anecdotal to the systematic:

- Single- and double-loop learning. Of central importance is the fundamental distinction between single-loop and double-loop learning. Single-loop learning occurs when there is a mismatch between the organisation's action and intended outcome. These mismatches are corrected by changing actions, but without a critical examination of governing variables for action. Only when underlying assumptions are also examined does double-loop learning take place.

- Lower- and higher-level learning. Others differentiate between lower-level and higher-level learning. Lower-level learning involves developing cognitive associations that facilitate incremental organisation adaptation, but without questioning norms, assumptions and frames of reference. Higher-level learning occurs when these norms, assumptions and frames of references are challenged and altered, producing a more accurate understanding of causal relationships

- Adaptive and generative learning. Peter Senge, in particular, has emphasised the distinction between adaptive and generative learning (Senge 1990). Adaptive learning is incremental and involves coping within an existing frame of reference, whereas generative learning is about being creative and requires new ways of perceiving the world.

Our own research reveals that the organisational learning processes involving stakeholders involve many elements of the types of learning listed above. External change imposes different degrees of pressure on an organisation to respond and, in so doing, promotes different kinds of learning. A corporation's interaction with its stakeholders typically involves a 'responsiveness process' that includes the generation of organisational awareness of the issue and stakeholders involved; learning about the technical and administrative factors affecting the issue; policy commitment by senior management to a course of action; and efforts to institutionalise change (Post *et al.* 2002a: ch. 8).

The learning process creates path dependences within organisations. Learning is a link between two states of knowledge—one that exists before a particular event or experience occurs, and another that exists afterwards. The second state is different from the first state, but its specific characteristics depend significantly on the conditions that prevailed in the earlier state as well as on the character of the event or experience that stimulated the learning.

The companies we have studied manifest three distinct forms of organisational learning about stakeholders. We refer to these as adaptation, regeneration (renewal) and transformation:

- Adaptive learning involves adjusting routines and practices to avoid known mistakes and to take advantage of recognised opportunities. Processes and behaviours are modified within an essentially unchanged configuration of corporate strategy, structure and culture. Adaptation is typically single-loop learning, although the Cummins Engine experience reveals an example of double-loop learning within an adaptive learning process.

- Regenerative (or renewal) learning involves both evolutionary and consciously proactive behaviour, including the re-examination of assumptions and cognitive frameworks. Basic values and goals may be pursued in new ways, involving noticeable changes in strategies and structures. Learning that is focused on renewal and regeneration can involve a mixture of single-loop and double-loop learning.

- Transformational learning involves substantial change within the organisation to increase its probability of success within a changed environment. This type of learning may lead to substantial, even disruptive, change within an organisation, including some degree of change in the core culture. Significant discontinuities, or 'new realities' (as Peter Drucker called them [Drucker 1989]), can force such learning and lead to major changes in the firm's strategy, structure and culture. This type of learning must involve double-loop processes, as the organisation addresses the disrupted equilibrium that once prevailed.

These ideas are directly relevant to the Global Compact process. For example, Novartis, one of the world's largest pharmaceutical companies, has successfully integrated the business and citizenship models at the global level. As one of the first companies to commit to the Global Compact, Novartis faced many challenges in adhering to the nine principles, both internally and externally. Sandoz, one of Novartis's predecessor companies, lived through an environmental accident because of failures in its environmental management system 15 years earlier (Wynhoven 2002: 5). Lessons learned from this incident served as a model that Novartis could use for initiating additional corporate responsibility principles into its business practices (Wynhoven 2002: 5-6).

In the case of Novartis, corporate citizenship was not a completely foreign notion. The Novartis Foundation for Sustainable Development was established before the Global Compact emerged.[3] In her case study of Novartis, Ursula Wynhoven (2002: 6) observed that:

> Working on these and other development issues meant that people within Novartis had first-hand knowledge and experience of the realities of poverty and poor health in many of the world's countries.

But, she noted, Novartis recognised that 'it was no longer enough for a company to concern itself with just maximising the return to shareholders' (Wynhoven 2002: 6). In fact, Novartis went as far as to state that 'the guiding philosophy was both that corporate citizenship was the right thing to do and because it made good business sense' (quoted in Wynhoven 2002: 14). Most significant to the commitment of Novartis to the Global Compact is their assertion that (quoted in Wynhoven 2002: 17):

> if compliance with the Corporate Citizenship policy and guidelines is genuinely incompatible with meeting another business target . . . the other business target will have to be revised, as corporate citizenship is not to be compromised.

As emphasised by Kofi Annan at Davos in 2001 (quoted in Wynhoven 2002: 2):

> The focus of Novartis's corporate citizenship initiative is on making its core business operations compliant—via the *integration* of business and social goals—rather than merely engaging in philanthropic acts unrelated to its regular activities [emphasis added].

Novartis used the Global Compact as a springboard to develop an implementation strategy designed to manage compliance with all of its corporate citizenship obligations, not merely those that it assumed under the Global Compact. Novartis made two points to its managers, explaining the interconnection between corporate citizenship and other business objectives 'so that they understand that corporate citizenship can be a business opportunity rather than a threat' (quoted in Wynhoven 2002: 18):

1. Employees would rather work for 'an ethical company with a good reputation'

2. 'Governments concerned about their own reputation are more likely to do business with a company that is known for ethical behaviour than with a less reputable company'

In addition, it was expressed that making the business case is important to the business sectors within Novartis as well as to the shareholders and other groups in society.

To get ahead of the issues, Novartis devised its own policies on corporate citizenship, based on the nine Global Compact principles (Wynhoven 2002: 19). Novartis also set standards intended to hold its major business partners to the same norms (Wynhoven 2002: 22). They recognised that 'citizenship policy . . . commits the

---

3 For details of the Novartis Foundation for Sustainable Development, see www.foundation.novartis.com.

company to giving priority to business partners, suppliers and contractors who share their societal and environmental values' (quoted in Wynhoven 2002: 22).[4] Roberts, Keeble and Brown (2001: 5) reiterate this point:

> Companies with the most direct relationships to consumers are working hard to ensure that their suppliers demonstrate high standards of corporate citizenship. As more and more retailers and brand owners commit themselves to environmental and social standards, their suppliers face increased pressure to comply with similar standards.

Adhering to the principles of the Global Compact means that the corporation is complying with a minimum set of standards for sustainable development. The experiences of Global Compact companies such as Novartis demonstrate that a company can be a good corporate citizen and also engage in activities that set the context for innovation and creative collaboration of the business and citizenship models. Today's company needs to understand stakeholder issues that are internal, and under a firm's control, as well as those issues outside their control (Roberts *et al.* 2001: 3).

Some guidelines on implementing the Global Compact are given in Box 21.1.

21.3 Learning and partnering

The Global Compact principles are drawn from official international documents such as the Universal Declaration of Human Rights,[5] the Fundamental Principles on Rights at Work of the International Labour Organisation (ILO)[6] and the Rio Declaration on Environment and Development.[7] The mission of the Global Compact is to have companies implement these principles in their businesses and to share lessons learned with other companies. As Nelson (2002: 135) has written, these principles were selected on basis of (1) their operational and strategic relevance to the private sector; (2) their having been developed through international intergovernmental agreements; and (3) their being of crucial importance to give the open global market and multilateral system a social underpinning.

Learning and partnering are two of the most important capabilities that corporations must implement to be successful. These activities are vital to harmonising economic and societal goals because the integration of business and citizenship goals requires significant partnership and learning components. The Global Compact's progress report (United Nations 2002c: 17) emphasises that

---

4 Novartis has approximately 50,000 business partners and recognises that it cannot investigate the compliance of all of them; it has decided instead to focus on the 'major' partners (see Wynhoven 2002: 22).
5 For the Universal Declaration, see www.un.org/Overview/rights.html.
6 For the ILO Principles, see www.ilo.org/public/english/standards/index.
7 For the Rio Declaration, see www.un.org/documents/ga/conf151/aconf15126-1annex1.htm.

These guidelines were developed for a group of companies at a meeting hosted by ABB in Zurich in November 2000 and produced by the Prince of Wales International Business Leaders Forum (IBLF):

- Management commitment. Companies that have committed to the Global Compact at the international and headquarter level should bring this to the attention of country directors.

- Review business activities and practices against the principles. Management should review its business activities and practices against the principles, identifying where there is compliance and where there are areas of doubt or risk, and how standards are measured.

- Integration with business principles. Best efforts should be made to integrate the Global Compact principles with business principles, thereby demonstrating convergence with the universal norms and values agreed by the UN system.

- Feedback. Management should provide feedback on the results under key headings of business activity, including dealings with the supply chain.

- Companies should communicate the results of this exercise in the company, more publicly and to the UN Global Compact Unit.

Proactive initiatives. Companies can take three initiatives to promote the UN Global Compact more proactively:

- Businesses supporting the Global Compact can, at the location level, work with key companies, business partners and organisations in their supply chain, possibly through the holding of briefing and review sessions, to encourage suppliers to adopt the Global Compact principles and to measure performance.

- Businesses can encourage their business membership organisations to adopt and promote the Global Compact in their countries of operation.

- Businesses can identify suitable business projects where they actively promote action that advances the goals of the UN in terms of human development and environmental protection. The following is a checklist encompassing the type of activity that might result:
  - Select a business location or operation, particularly in a developing country, where the business operation can contribute to local development.
  - Review how the activity can contribute to human resource development (education, training, knowledge transfer) in the location through proactively engaging partners that can help transfer knowledge and resources.
  - Review how business health promotion and social service activity might be shared with other stakeholders in the community.
  - Review how communities might be assisted through job, work experience, training subcontracting and enterprise opportunities from the company activities.
  - Review how management expertise and skills can be shared with local institutions to assist problem-solving and to improve service delivery.
  - Review how the company's know-how in business standards, corporate governance and environmental protection can be shared with other businesses in the community.
  - In conflict-prone countries actively engage in activity with civil society and others to prevent conflict and to promote social cohesion.
  - Encourage employees to be actively involved in community initiatives through advice and volunteering initiatives.
  - Engage in partnerships with public authorities and civil-society organisations to promote and support social development initiatives.
  - Measure and report on results and impacts.

Box 21.1 Suggested guidelines for implementation of the UN Global Compact

Source: Prince of Wales International Business Leaders Forum, www.iblf.org

> In an era of globalisation and economic interdependence, the private and public sectors—along with increasingly influential stakeholder communities of civil society—must share information and communicate effectively.

Partnerships and structured learning processes (e.g. the Learning Forum) are critical ways for corporations to do this.

Dialogue with labour and civil-society groups enables corporations to exchange experience and information. This enables firms to discuss measures regarding strategy, management and operations, with the objective of better aligning their business activities with the principles of the Global Compact. The central premise is a belief in the necessity for collective learning among labour, civil society, business and development, environment, and human rights movements. Hence, the Learning Forum advances the goal of institutionalising learning across the Global Compact's main participatory platforms (United Nations 2002c: 17).

21.3.1 Learning Forum

The evolution of a technology and method for working toward the learning objectives outlined above began with a pilot phase in 2001. The Learning Forum is neither an instrument for monitoring companies nor a regulatory regime to oversee or control corporate behaviour. Rather, the goal is that the Learning Forum will become an information bank of experiences describing company efforts to implement the principles (United Nations 2002c: 17).

The pilot phase involved 44 companies that agreed to submit reports of corporate efforts to advance the Global Compact's nine principles within their enterprise. A conference was held in November 2001 at the conclusion of the pilot phase. None of the reports conformed to the guidelines suggested by the Global Compact Office, and half of the 30 reports considered at the meeting did not directly address the implementation of the nine principles (United Nations 2002c: 18; an in-depth analysis of the 30 reports is provided in Chapter 13). Changes were recommended, and the next phase reflected lessons from the initial phase. Participants had learned that they had to undergo major organisational change to implement the Global Compact principles. The older companies, in particular, and those in mature industries, had difficulty deviating from established practices in order to embrace the principles (see Chapter 13, Section 13.3.1.3). Many firms faced difficulties assessing the priority of corporate citizenship responsibilities relative to their profit-seeking business activities. Company reports were posted on the website, and reviewers read the submission and even provided feedback to the Global Compact. This process is a critical aspect of the efforts to share information and to build a shared database.

The future is likely to involve broader learning networks. By the end of 2002, the Global Compact Learning Forum Meeting attracted almost 200 participants, representing business, civil society, labour, academia and the United Nations. Georg Kell (United Nations 2003e), Executive Director of the Global Compact Office, commented that:

> This is the first time that so many global stakeholders—all experts in their respective fields—came together under the umbrella of the Global Compact to share practices and engage in broad social vetting . . . This meeting clearly contributed to a better understanding of responsible corporate citizenship, thereby building real issues leadership.

More than 100 companies shared their experience on how to integrate the nine principles into core business practices. Case studies of corporate involvement included Novartis's presentation on the integration of the principles, Daimler-Chrysler's presentation on HIV/AIDS in the workplace and Statoil's experience addressing human rights issues in managing its supply chain (United Nations 2003e). The Learning Forum provided a wide array of stakeholders, corporations, universities and intergovernmental organisations the opportunty to learn from, and work with, one another to share ideas and lessons learned and 'to leverage the power of research' (United Nations 2003e).

The legitimacy of the Global Compact system appears to be growing in the view of experts. According to John Ruggie (United Nations 2003e) of Harvard University's Center for Business and Government:

> Large multinational companies are beginning to understand that they are at the receiving end of rapidly escalating social expectations about their responsibility to society, at home and abroad. The Global Compact is the only set of principles that chart a vision of global citizenship by the corporate sector which have been endorsed by all the world's countries, and thus represent the aspirations of the international community as a whole.

21.3.2 Partnership projects

As stated in Section 21.1.3, the extended enterprise of the 21st century is the nodal element within a network of interrelated stakeholders that create, sustain and enhance its value-creating capacity. Relationships, rather than transactions, constitute the ultimate source of organisational wealth. The survival and success of a firm are determined by its ability to establish and maintain relationships within its entire network of stakeholders. This new stakeholder view clearly emphasises the important role of partnerships, and the Global Compact provides a framework for the enhancement of these relationships through formal partnership projects (Post *et al.* 2002b). The partnership projects fostered by the Global Compact focus on behavioural learning:

> The emphasis in these projects rests on the collective action taken, rather than the formation of common understanding . . . All learning and policy-setting around best practices and methods to address critical social problems must be followed by effective and sustained action (Kell and Levin 2002: 17).

The ultimate objective is to promote concrete and sustained action by participants, in alignment with broad UN goals and the international Millennium Development Goals (see Appendix A). Individual companies have launched partnerships with UN agencies and civil-society organisations aimed at addressing a range of development issues. The Global Compact website clearly states that (United Nations 2002d):

> Through partnership projects, Global Compact participating companies can pool their knowledge and expertise with development organisations, be they UN agencies, state agencies, labour or NGOs. The objective of Global Compact partnership projects is to help develop the host country of a Global Compact firm's operation, by using the UN Millennium Development Goals and the nine Principles of the Global Compact as guidelines.

Many of the Global Compact companies had partnership projects in place prior to joining the Global Compact. However, aside from encouraging an even greater number of projects, the Global Compact 'offers companies a communication platform and the organisational and technical services of UN agencies—particularly the United Nations Development Program (UNDP)' (United Nations 2002d).

There are five key actors in these partnership projects:

- The initiating company. The initiating company is expected to inform the Global Compact Office that it is committed to the principles. A description of the project is then posted on the Global Compact website and subsequent reports are also posted to the website. An initiative can also emanate from a UN agency, development agency, NGO or local government where the project is going to take place.

- A Global Compact partner. Again, this can be a development agency, labour organisation, NGO or an agency associated with the Global Compact with expertise in sustainable development. It will help draft the partnership project.[8]

- The actual implementing agency. This may be a UN agency, an NGO (national or international), a local government entity or a private firm. In some cases the corporation initiating the project implements it too. Responsibilities include project execution and the delivery of results that match the goals and objectives of the project.

- The UN resident representative. This representative must verify that project objectives are in harmony with country strategies; he or she is responsible for securing the agreement of the government for the project to go ahead.

- The Global Compact Office. The Global Compact Office is responsible for promoting the partnership project on its website. The Global Compact also facilitates the relationships among the numerous players.

As the format of the partnership initiative becomes clearer, the Global Compact is successfully linking with other associations. In January 2003, an agreement was

---

8   According to the website (United Nations 2003), 'partnership project documents indicate overall goal and objectives, assess opportunities and risks, determine who is the implementing agency and clarify who will monitor and evaluate'.

announced between the Global Compact and the World Business Council for Sustainable Development (WBCSD),[9] itself a network of multinational enterprises:

> The WBCSD believes that the spirit of partnerships between the UN and the business community as promoted by Secretary-General Kofi Annan should be encouraged and supported . . . The very distinct nature of the two organisations presents considerable scope for building on complementary strengths and creating synergy—the Global Compact being an open action and learning network and the WBCSD being a membership-based organisation dedicated to sustainable development and engaged in such programmes as Sustainable Livelihoods, Advocacy and Communications, Accountability and Reporting and the Regional Network (quoted at United Nations 2003d).

21.4 Conclusions

The Global Compact is encouraging MNCs to develop new linkages with societal actors to harmonise the economic, social and political realities of the 21st century. The future of the Global Compact depends on how widely the global community embraces its missions of bringing multinational businesses, national governments and NGOs together amid myriad global threats of war, insecurity and terrorism. For now, the Global Compact appears to be an experiment that has the promise of teaching business, government and NGO leaders how to create new partnerships that serve society through common purpose.

The evolution of ever-larger enterprises may lead to an age of institutional dinosaurs, great in size but lacking the mental faculties to survive a changing environment. The same can be said of governments and NGOs whose agendas are premised on immunity from the ecological, human rights and labour requirements that most of the world recognises. Global peace, security and harmony require more co-operation in all of those areas that affect human well-being. The environment is changing for all institutions, and the need for change-management skills could not be more apparent.

The preferred alternative is an extended enterprise that possesses the mental capacity to understand its environment, relate to its stakeholders and meet the complex demands of economic, social and political change. That is the ultimate ethical challenge of corporate citizenship in the 21st century. Helping leaders to understand that challenge, and respond effectively to it, is the mission of the Global Compact.

9 See www.wbcsd.org.

22
The living world of
the UN Global Compact*

Malcolm McIntosh

Independent Commentator

The UN Global Compact has been variously described as 'the most creative reinvention of the [UN] to be seen yet' (*CSM* 2000) and that it 'fills a major lacuna in the discussions and evolution of global governance' (RING Alliance 2000). Further descriptions can be found throughout the pages of this book.

For Leisinger (2003: 116) the implementation of the principles of the Global Compact throughout the global pharmaceutical company Novartis is an 'open-ended process' (and not a programme) (2003: 116) of 'uncertain complexity' (2003: 117). For Teller (Chapter 23, page 330), at the City of Melbourne, the global conversational characteristics of the Global Compact mirror the 'pre-developed and complex "neural networks" ' of cities.

Not all the commentaries on the Global Compact have been positive, however, and there are some in the world of activist non-governmental organisations (NGOs) who have said that corporate engagement with the UN Global Compact amounts to 'bluewash' (see e.g. Bruno and Karliner 2000). Friends of the Earth in the United Kingdom have asked: 'Could it by any chance be a public relations vehicle for companies?' They called the picture of Nike's Phil Knight shaking hands with Kofi Annan at the UN launch of the Global Compact in 1999 a 'photographic coup' for Nike (Juniper 2002).

Let us step back, however, and apply some perspective to the noisy debate around the Global Compact. There have been a number of explanations about the

---

* The author is grateful for the comments of participants of the first annual CSR in Asia Conference, held in Kuala Lumpur, 26–27 March 2003, by Nottingham University in Malaysia and Deakin University, Australia, where the contents of this chapter were first presented.

theory that supports the origins of the Global Compact—from the originators—and some useful contextualisations of an initiative that has quickly become part of the landscape of the globalisation debate.

The real merit of the Global Compact is in acting as:

● A values-based social partnership

● A global social network for supraterritoral conversation

● A local or regional boundary-breaking convening platform for meetings

22.1 The United Nations: a temple of peaceful conversation?

On 5 March 1946 Winston Churchill spoke in Fulton, USA, on the need for 'the English-speaking peoples' to maintain 'an overwhelming preponderance of power . . . until the highroads of the future will be clear, not only for our time but for the century to come'. The UN, he said, must become 'a true temple of peace' and not 'merely a cockpit in the Tower of Babel'.

The UN Global Compact was born at the World Economic Forum in Davos on 31 January 1999 (see Chapter 1) and has quickly added to the noise of Babel by advocating partnerships for progress between corporations, states and communities. This progress may still be accounted for by the postwar consensus outlined by Churchill. His host that day in 1946 was US President Truman who three years later was to talk of US 'moral certainty' and the modernist mission:

> We must embark on a bold new program for making the benefits of our scientific advances and industrial progress available for the improvement and growth of underdeveloped areas. The old imperialism—exploitation for foreign profit—has no place in our plans. What we envisage is a program of development based on the concepts of democratic fair dealing (Truman 1949).

It is no accident that the UN Charter begins with the words: 'We the peoples of the united nations' and echoes the US Constitution, which begins: 'We the people of the United States'. The UN Charter preamble continues (United Nations 1945):

> We the peoples of the united nations determined to save succeeding generations from the scourge of war, which twice in our lifetime has brought untold sorrow to mankind, and to reaffirm faith in fundamental human rights, in the dignity and worth of the human person, in the equal rights of men and women and of nations large and small, and to establish conditions under which justice and respect for the obligations arising from treaties and other sources of international law can be maintained, and to promote social progress and better standards of life in larger freedom.

As those commentators opposed to the Global Compact have pointed out, at no point does the UN Charter mention business or corporations or envisage any links between the UN and market-based organisations. At this time a statist world saw governments as the sole legitimisers of global organisation. More than 50 years after the inauguration of the UN Charter one commentary on the UN Global Compact suggests changing the opening words of the Charter to: 'We the corporations . . .'

There are several frameworks for understanding global social change since 1946 and linking them to the Global Compact. The first framework is that of the post-1945 'grand social bargain'. The authors of the Global Compact, Kell and Ruggie (see Ruggie, Chapter 2) make reference to 'the embedded liberal compromise', and Donaldson (see Chapter 4, page 70) refers to the idea that the very language of a Compact suggests 'a hypothetical, implicit [global] social contract'.

The second framework is based on the deconstruction of the nation-state—the 'collective biopolitical world' of Hardt and Negri (2000), based on Foucault's analysis of the dispersion of power.

The third framework is that the Global Compact has simply added another social layer to the idea of the world as a complex adaptive system. This is a plea for the Global Compact to be seen as two symbiotic processes requiring a multidisciplinary intellectual approach *and* a cross-sectoral partnership (McIntosh 2003). This accords with some of the theories on global public policy networks, global neural networks and international organisational networks if they are viewed as contributing to the complexities of global social space.

These three approaches are not necessarily discrete. Indeed, theories on global public policy networks and on global neural networks draw on each other in their analyses; theories on global neural networks and on international organisational networks recognise the symbiotic relationship between people and planet; and the theory of international organisational networks recognises all aspects of the other two theories.

22.2 The grand social bargain, embedded liberalism and globalisation

John Ruggie, as Assistant Secretary-General at the United Nations,[1] along with his colleague Georg Kell, now Executive Director of the Secretary-General's Global Compact Office, were the two main drivers of the Global Compact. Ruggie has written that the Global Compact represents a significant piece of the postwar 'grand social bargain'. In this bargain, or negotiated compromise:

> all sectors of society agreed to open markets . . . but also to share the social adjustment costs that open markets inevitably produce (Chapter 2, page 34) . . .

1   John Ruggie is now Director of the Centre for Business and Government at the Kennedy School at Harvard University, Cambridge, MA.

. . . That was the essence of the embedded liberalism compromise: economic liberalisation was embedded in social community (Ruggie 2003).

The grand social bargain of the past 50 years (and more) learned from the first wave of globalisation in the 19th century when European powers, and particularly Britain, were to the fore, and from what can be seen as the ensuing collapse of civilisation that led to two world wars in the space of one generation. The social compromise has variations, depending on historical, cultural and climatic conditions. In countries such as the United Kingdom it led to the introduction of universal healthcare free for all at the point of delivery and to the introduction of compulsory secondary education for all. By 1978 Britain had become as egalitarian as it had ever been, with a low level of wealth disparity, full employment and significantly high measures of happiness and life satisfaction (see e.g. Toynbee 2003).

Other European countries, particularly in the North and Scandinavia, had achieved similar or better states of social democracy. The end of the 1970s saw a significant tilt back towards market capitalism and away from social community, with the election in the USA of President Ronald Reagan and in the United Kingdom of Prime Minister Margaret Thatcher. Since that time, although 70% of the world population can claim higher standards of living, and in some cases a higher quality of life, there is now a greater gap between the top 70% and the bottom 30% than ever before in the history of humanity. This is true in the USA, the United Kingdom *and* globally.

Many of the 'Tiger economies of South-East Asia' managed to achieve relatively stable economic and social growth through the latter half of the 20th century, with countries such as Japan establishing enviable levels of economic equality and social stability.

The second wave of globalisation, in which the world economy acts as one system, has speeded up and become continuous over the past 30 years through developments in communications technology. At the same time, humanity has reached a better understanding of the global ecosystem on which the globalisation project is reliant. But, as Nobel Prize-winning economist Joseph Stiglitz says in his book, *Globalisation and its Discontents* (2002: 248):

> If globalisation continues to be conducted in the way it has been in the past, if we continue to fail to learn from our mistakes, globalisation will not only not succeed in promoting development but will continue to create poverty and instability.

There is an inevitability about the globalisation project, because it is driven largely by economics and trade made possible by communications technology. This is recognised by those such as Will Hutton (2002) who wish to see the project facing up to social and environmental challenges, as well as by those such as Thomas Friedman (1999) and John Micklethwait and Adrian Wooldridge (2000) who think that whatever happens it is inevitable.

Hutton (1996: xxvii) says that 'the attempt to isolate economics from other disciplines has fatally disabled its power to explain what is happening in the world', and Micklethwait and Wooldridge (2000: 335) are positive about the benefits of globalisation, stating, 'the bulwark of our defence [of globalisation] has been economic' and that 'the simple fact is that globalisation makes us richer, or makes enough of us richer to make the whole project worthwhile'.

In an effort to explain some of the complexities of globalisation, and to dispel some of the polarisation and inflamed passion that has taken place around the subject, Jan Aart Scholte (2001) has categorised the elements of globalisation into five types:

- Internationalisation
- Liberalisation
- Universalisation, or Westernisation
- Modernisation, or Americanisation
- Deterritorialisation, or supraterritoriality

This analysis is most helpful as it forces all those engaged in the debate for and against globalisation to recategorise existing arguments. For example, let us take the ephemerality of a popstar such as Britney Spears. Which of Scholte's categories can be applied to this description of her in London's *Sunday Times* in 2002?

> She's global capitalism in a micro-mini. She's junk food. Britney is the triumph of America made flesh—one more time (Conrad 2002).

The same may have been true for the Beatles in relation to the United Kingdom in the 1960s and 1970s, it may be true for Nintendo in relation to Japan now, and for BMW and Mercedes in relation to Germany for several decades. Do we have all five of Scholte's categories in each example?

In essence, Scholte supports the idea that we are now talking about social space as much as territory when we refer to globalisation. As he says (2001: 15):

> Globalisation is understood as transformation of social space marked by the growth of supraterritoral connections between people. This reconfiguration of geography has far-reaching implications for governance. No longer can public affairs be managed through the territorialist framework of sovereign statehood.

So it was that in an effort to promote global values, and develop universalisation by putting some checks and balances on economic liberalisation, the UN Secretary-General announced the UN Global Compact. As he said, we have a choice: 'Let us choose to reconcile the creative forces of private entrepreneurship with the needs of the disadvantaged' (Annan 1999d). This can be read as liberalisation and development going hand in hand.

22.3 The Global Compact as strategy

The idea that the Global Compact is a chance happening is not credible. It is true that it was an adventure waiting to be born, and the invitation to the UN Secretary-General to speak at the 1999 Davos World Economic Summit provided the maternity suite. Georg Kell (2001b) has said that 'we really did not know where we were headed when we started talking about the Global Compact [in 1999]. The truth is that we had no intention of actually doing anything.'

But Kell also says that the UN Secretary-General's 'overriding objective was to offer a framework for filling the governance void at the international level for social and environmental issues that were being bundled up with trade, and to protect the open global market from protectionism'.

As Erroll Mendes has written in Chapter 6 of this book (page 101):

> The first major attempt by the United Nations to develop a code of practice for what were termed transnational corporations (TNCs) began in 1977, and a draft code was completed in 1990. Within two years it was dead, killed by the TNCs and Western governments that fiercely opposed it.

So, at one level, the Global Compact is part of a long-term strategic plan to embed the social in the grand *social* bargain and to reinforce embedded liberalism in global governance frameworks. At the instrumental level it was designed to decouple corporate standards and operating practices from the self-interest of the structural adjustment programmes of the International Monetary Fund (IMF) and the trade liberalisation agenda of the World Trade Organisation (WTO). In other words, there is no desire to limit free trade or to deny the benefits of the global economy, but there is a concern to make corporate bodies operate with the social community in mind. In the long term this could lead from the voluntarism of corporate citizenship to the closer regulation of corporate activity and behaviour.

The Global Compact can be seen as one step in this direction. Perhaps the most important pupil in this extraordinary operation is not business or member-states, but the United Nations and its agencies themselves. They are on a voyage of discovery to see if they can manage the next phase of the grand social bargain. First, they need to learn how global business operates; second, they need to learn how the UN agencies can work together and how to operate to the same standards that the Global Compact demands of business; and, third, they need to learn how to manage new social partnerships between corporations, states and civil society. An essentially statist-oriented organisation that ostensibly derives its legitimacy from member-states now has supraterritoral legitimacy as *the* major player in the new global governance order operating alongside, and sometimes in opposition to, the only current hyperpower, the USA.

But, continually, and most importantly, they are reminded that all UN agencies have a moral mission—embedded in the UN Charter. The Global Compact can be seen as a synopsis of that Charter and all other agreements, charters, conventions and declarations since the UN Charter's adoption. In a sense, with its simple admonitions it is like the pop song that sings: 'All you need is love'.

The devil is in the detail, perhaps? But perhaps the devil is also in the universality of the principles prescribed at a global level but enacted at the local level. So the very wording of this new ideational code sets it up as an easy target for attack. 'Global' is beyond the capacity of most individuals and communities to understand in terms of how it relates to the ways they share their daily lives, and 'compact' suggests some agreement between us all.

While political philosophers such as Martin Shaw[2] have called for the development of a global social democratic movement, so others such as John Gray (1996) have argued that it is a mistake to believe that there is a single goal of social justice or equality. Gray contends that global communitarian liberalism is what is now needed, in a form that recognises diversity and distinctiveness and the connectedness and convivialities of local development, history and culture.

The problem, as ever, is the link between the global and the local; between what we can handle and what we can hypothesise about. We have seen through the globalisation project the expansion of the local 70/30 wealth disparities of advanced industrial social democracies writ large on the global landscape. And what can be done?

Francis Fukuyama (1992) argued that the events of 1989 and the 'triumph' of economic liberalism meant 'the end of history'. There was no other system that worked. The political left were angry, and since then there have been massed demonstrations against global capitalism around the world, in Seattle in 1999, Prague in 2000, Genoa in 2001, London 2002 and Los Angeles in 2003. In a similar way, global television has brought us together across the world to hold vigils and march against the war in Iraq (both in 1991 and in 2003). People have been united through the mechanism of the Internet—communications flowing randomly across borders. In this context some local political leaders have instantly become global.

The UN Global Compact derives its legitimacy from the UN's moral mission, from its provenance in assorted UN charters, declarations, conventions and agreements and from member-state participation in the UN. But it also derives legitimacy, as I have argued above, from the supraterritoral status of the UN—a legitimacy that it has earned as a 'brand' in its own right. In other words, the whole is greater than the sum of its parts. However, its efficacy is in its ability to be transformed or adapted at the local level. In other words, its instrumentalist characteristics are both its strength and, possibly, its weakness. If there is a general acceptance that liberal economics is as good as it gets, and Fukuyama's hypothesis in *The End of History and the Last Man* (1992) is endorsed, and it is argued that global social democracy is mostly concerned with ameliorating the downside of capitalism, then the vision becomes blurred and uninteresting. In which case, the Global Compact will engage global publics only at the angry margins where it is clear that injustice is being seen to be done: 70% of the world's population will be left to Galbraith's hypothesis that richer nations tend towards 'the politics of affluence and apathy'.

---

2 See www.theglobalsite.ac.uk/martinshaw.htm.

In order to believe in a vision, it is necessary to have faith and passion (which, post-Enlightenment, is irrational), but there are some who see that the Global Compact, if it is not to be seen simply as the management of the social in the grand social bargain, will wither if there is no sense of transcendence. What the Global Compact needs is some sense of its ability to give us a better world, to uplift the human spirit, to make people believe that there is another way. Let us be honest: the language of corporate citizenship is often anything but uplifting, mired as it is in arguments for the business case for corporate social responsibility, the certification and assurance of social auditing standards and the development of global guidelines in nine or ten easy principles. How, then, can the Global Compact help provide 'a human face to globalisation'?

22.4 Deconstructing the nation-state, and the dispersion of power

Another way of seeing the world and helping to contextualise the Global Compact draws on the work of Michel Foucault (Danaher *et al.* 2000). He argued that modern social science and technology enabled power to be exercised by the state and others over individuals because it knows so much about them and because it conditions the individual to play an acquiescent part in the use and abuse of power. Essentially, it is a reciprocal arrangement that has developed since the Enlightenment that concerns the relationships that individuals have with themselves, with each other and with organisations, institutions, states and corporations.

In their book, *Empire* (2000), Hardt and Negri talk of the 'new collective biopolitical structuring of the world', by which they mean that power is exercised at all levels from the personal to the global and through a variety of mechanisms. They say (2000: 150):

> As the world market today is realised ever more completely, it tends to deconstruct the boundaries of the nation-state. In a previous period, nation-states were the primary actors in the modern imperialist organisation of global production and exchange, but to the world market they appear increasingly as mere obstacles.

Hardt and Negri (2000: 153) recognise that organisations with 'rigid boundaries and homogenous units are not adequate for doing business in the modern world' and that what is needed for 'postmodern management' is for organisations to be 'mobile, flexible and able to deal with difference'.

The world into which the Global Compact has been born is one in which the global exchange process is dominated by some 500 global corporations—multinational, transnational and supraterritorial—operating in a financial system that is characterised more by discontinuity and non-linearity than by order, control and boundaries. When it comes to commercial activity and marketing expertise, these corporations know the world better than governments and are fleet of foot, light of touch and flexible to the point of being more water-like than granite-based.

22.5 The living world of the UN Global Compact

In *The Emperor's Nightingale* Robert Monks (1997) has written that until recently he saw the corporation as

> a machinelike system increasingly based on non-dynamic, non-living, non-human principles: a profit-seeking missile of unlimited life, size and power operating under the stealth of human guise.

Now, with the advent of various innovative local and global governance initiatives he has come to find hope in a re-analysis of corporations as living complex adaptive systems—as agents that can have the potential for enhancing humanity.

There is a link to be made between seeing the world as a complex place and the power we have vested in some of our largest economic institutions—private corporations and nation-states. If we can just stand back we can see the world as being characterised not so much by near entropic chaos but as being adaptive and dynamic. Within this rich picture our institutions can be seen as social systems that could work within an inclusionist view of 'life in space' and on Earth (McIntosh 2003), for Earth is currently home to humanity.

New organisational forms linked to reputation and brand management have a direct bearing on the developing social bargain at the beginning of the 21st century. Without an analysis of these features any discussion of accountability, governance and partnerships will tend towards confusion. If we begin with the premise that classical organisational forms are disintegrating, or that there are a multiplicity of organisational forms, then we can perhaps begin to unravel the relationship between human activity and the planet.

There is now a digression from hard boundaries of organisations to looser, more informal working arrangements between empowered knowledge workers. It applies to all organisations, across all sectors (see e.g. Salaman 2001: 172). It is not post-industrial in the sense that industrial workplace settings continue and range from thousands of workers sitting in serried ranks sewing sweatshirts in Asia–Pacific to thousands of workers sitting in serried ranks in call centres in the United Kingdom and India.

The development of network organisations as global phenomena is not limited to business. The growth of international non-governmental organisations (INGOs) is well documented (see e.g. McIntosh *et al.* 2003b: ch. 4). Many INGOs with a media presence may actually operate with a handful of individuals working on an informal, voluntary basis. Some NGOs draw funds from public and/or private sources, whereas others are founded on a substantial membership base.[3] Their account-

---

3   See the website of the Royal Society for the Protection of Birds (RSPB), an NGO that now has over a million members (www.rspb.org.uk).

ability and governance structures span the entrepreneurial–institutional spectrum, with an increasing number demonstrating the resources and organisation of professional organisations.

22.6 Conclusions

The UN Global Compact is in its infancy, as a quick read of its website will attest. The issues for Asia are not radically different at the macro level from those in North America, South America or Europe. It is at the meso and micro level that the real work arises. If one checks the number and type of companies from different parts of the world that have become supporters of the UN Global Compact up to June 2004 one finds the issues are similar throughout the world. In some countries, such as India and the Philippines, the Global Compact has hundreds of corporate supporters. In the lists there are companies of all sizes and in all sectors. The unifying feature across the world is that countries with significant corporate support often have a business association that has encouraged members to send personal letters of support to the UN Secretary-General.

To repeat: the real merit of the Global Compact is in acting as:

- A values-based social partnership

- A global social network for supraterritoral conversation

- A local or regional boundary-breaking convening platform for meetings

But:

- The UN Global Compact is a process-based, not a programme-based, initiative that is part of an expanding view of the dynamic patterning of social life on Earth.

The rigorous application of the triple-bottom-line concept in business leads inexorably to an enhanced (sustainable) single bottom line. In the same way, a multidisciplinary examination of the complexities of social and ecological interactions at the local and global levels can lead to a new awareness of the limits, challenges and opportunities of life on Earth. With the moral legitimacy of the UN Secretary-General and of the United Nations itself, the Global Compact has the potential to be an innovative use of global social space made open by global telecommunications technology.

23
The UN Global Compact Cities Programme
The Melbourne Model: solving the hard urban issues together

David Teller
Committee for Melbourne, Australia

By 2010 over 50% of the world population will be living in cities (UNPD 2003). Urbanisation and the effects of urbanism present a growing challenge to governments, institutions and communities. Complex economic, social, environmental and cultural issues face virtually every city and are often becoming more intractable as urban populations increase. The availability of affordable food, potable water, housing, education and health services, environmental degradation, unemployment, rising crime rates and the erosion of cultural and social identity are a sample of the issues typifying the failure of existing frameworks to deal effectively with the process of population migration to and concentration within cities.

It is proposed in this chapter, however, that, beyond their negative impact, cities are also an under-utilised resource for the creation of solutions to the very problems they have created. As highly networked focal points of economic wealth, skilled labour, learning, government and infrastructure, urban centres are prolific incubators of new ideas, technologies and skills. If effectively captured and co-ordinated, these outputs have the potential to provide solutions to otherwise intractable problems. However, owing to the 'silo mentality' and poor communication that often characterises relationships within and between organisations, such opportunities are often lost. The Melbourne Model, at the centre of the Global Compact Cities Programme, is a new mechanism designed to identify, focus and facilitate the constructive capacity present in any given city—regardless of its economic, social or cultural structure. The Model puts the principles of the Global Compact into practice by providing a framework within which business, government and civil society, in a city, combine their inherent resources, ideas, knowledge and experience in order to develop effective solutions to pressing local problems. Once validated, these solutions are made available to other cities facing similar issues by way of a Global Compact Cities Learning Forum.

23.1 The UN Global Compact: background

In 1999, at the World Economic Forum in Davos, Switzerland, UN Secretary-General Kofi Annan highlighted the critical role that business can and must play to ensure that globalisation develops as a force for positive change rather than as a catalyst for backlash and protectionism (see Chapter 1 of this book). Corporations were receptive to the warning and encouraged the UN Secretary-General to create a formal programme designed to include business in the traditional government–civil society nexus. As a result, the UN Global Compact, based on shared values and principles in the areas of human rights, labour standards and environmental practices, was officially launched at the UN Headquarters in New York on 26 July 2000.[1] Since its inception, participation in the Global Compact has grown rapidly, with several hundred companies, labour groups, academic institutions and civil-society organisations from around the world engaging in the programme.

23.2 The Global Compact Cities Programme

In early 2001, the Committee for Melbourne[2] developed the value proposition that cities, as well as companies, should be allowed and encouraged to engage in the Global Compact. The Committee for Melbourne argued that for a city to do so would make a clear statement of its civic, cultural and corporate character, as well as motivating positive change and participation in international dialogue focusing on issues surrounding the principles of the Global Compact. The Global Compact Office generously accepted the proposal and the City of Melbourne subsequently became the first city in the world to engage in the Global Compact, in June 2001.[3] Following this process, Melbourne recognised that an opportunity existed to develop a new framework specifically designed to add value to cities engaging in the Global Compact. The resulting Melbourne Model, launched in April 2003,

---

1   See the 'Guide to the Global Compact: A Practical Understanding of the Vision and Nine Principles', at www.unglobalcompact.org.
2   The Committee for Melbourne is a private, non-profit network of business, academic and civic leaders based in Melbourne, Australia; see www.melbourne.org.au.
3   The cities of Bath, UK, San Francisco, CA, USA, Nuremberg, Germany, Porto Alegre, Brazil, Jamshedpur, India, and Amman, Jordan, followed suit in 2003.

proposes a simple framework that catalyses and combines the resources of government, business and civil society in order to find concrete solutions to seemingly intractable urban social, economic and environmental problems.

Following the launch of the Model, four Australian-based socioeconomic and environmental projects were instigated with the use of the Melbourne Model methodology. In late 2003, the Committee for Melbourne, as co-ordinator of these projects, was invited by the Global Compact Office to lead an international pilot programme, with the objective of determining the effectiveness of the Model in a variety of socioeconomic environments. In March 2004 Amman, Jordan, became the most recent city to formally agree to participate in the Global Compact Cities Pilot Programme. It is planned that by early 2005 Tianjin, Chicago and Nairobi will join Porto Alegre, Jamshedpur, Melbourne and Amman to complete the network of cities constituting the Cities Pilot Programme.

23.2.1 The case for the Global Compact Cities Programme

The world today faces an unprecedented rate of urbanisation. In 2000, the world's urban population accounted for 47% of humanity, or 2.9 billion people (UNPD 2002). By 2030, this number is expected to grow to 60%, representing 5 billion people (UNPD 2002). Urbanisation is exacerbating existing, as well as creating new, urban environmental, economic and social problems. Including poverty, personal safety, illiteracy, drug misuse and land, air and water pollution, urban issues impact far beyond the geographical limits of the city itself and, in many cases, become more intractable the longer they are left partially or entirely unaddressed.

Cities are also inherently dynamic and creative. As a focus of infrastructure, technology, political power, labour and capital they play a vital and strategic role in the development of the community's social, economic, environmental and cultural life. They are a crucible for the creation of negative societal phenomena while containing the ingredients with which to tackle the very issues they have created. The proposed Cities Programme therefore aims to harness the implicit experience, knowledge and intellectual capital present in cities in order to develop solutions to overcome the challenges of urbanisation. This process will be facilitated by the shared characteristics of cities that enable the efficient identification, qualification, quantification and development of projects and solutions around complex problems:

- Based on shared language, experience, geography, culture and economies, cities have their own pre-developed and complex 'neural networks'. Rather than attempting to create new national or international networks around given issues, significant time, effort and resources can be saved by tapping into these pre-existing local networks to develop innovative solutions to urban issues.

- Many complex issues are already being addressed by government, business and civil society either independently or in loose coalitions. An opportunity therefore exists, using the Melbourne Model, to more effectively facilitate and catalyse existing work for a given desired outcome.

- Urban issues in similar cities can have common root causes, impacts and ramifications. Therefore, there exists an opportunity for solutions developed in one city either to be directly applied in or to be adapted to other cities facing the same or similar issues.

- Hypothesis testing around an identified problem and proposed solution can be rapidly and effectively carried out in a discrete geographic urban area. Results can be compiled and the proposed solution altered as required until an optimal solution is developed.

- The direct impacts of problems and their proposed solutions on government, business and civil society can be readily qualified and quantified in a limited area.

23.2.2 The added value of the Global Compact Cities Programme

A great variety of urban-based public and private programmes already exist to address issues of importance to the community. However, these programmes often maintain a narrow focus and are often characterised by limited resources, differing agendas and the imperfect exchange of information between the various sectors involved. The Global Compact Cities Programme proposes a novel approach whereby traditional inter-sector silos are broken down and scarce public and private resources harnessed and focused in order to bring business, local government and civil society together to develop action-oriented projects with perceivable outcomes of clear benefit to the city. The programme also provides a rallying process with which to bring together disparate groups, projects, ideas, experience and information. It constitutes a clear message from city leaders to their populations regarding their vision for a sustainable future. In addition, as the programme is based on the principles of the Global Compact, it illustrates a collective willingness to adhere to a set of fundamental values and principles over and beyond those stated and adhered to at a local and national level—the concept of global citizenship at its most constructive.

23.3 The Melbourne Model

The Melbourne Model (Fig. 23.1) is the central component of the Global Compact Cities Programme—an urban-specific subset of the business-oriented Global Compact. It is designed to develop real solutions to intractable urban problems by facilitating and co-ordinating the ideas, knowledge, experience and resources inherent in business, government and civil society. The Model overcomes traditional organisational insularity by providing a neutral ground on which those most capable and willing to develop new ideas and solutions, regardless of their sector of activity, organisational agendas and seniority, can work together to

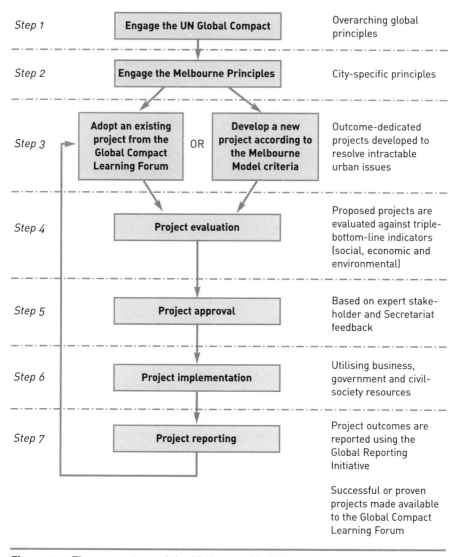

Figure 23.1 The seven steps of the Melbourne Model

develop, prove and communicate significant and viable solutions (Fig. 23.2). The Melbourne Model is purposely rigid in its approach. It is entirely outcome-focused. It is not designed as a forum for debate but as a process to develop, test and implement outcomes. Maintaining constant involvement from public, private and nongovernmental stakeholders ensures that the process is self-vetting and does not open itself to accusations of bias or lack of transparency. Multi-sector involvement further ensures that scarce project resources are used effectively and that stakeholders are engaged and working effectively together.

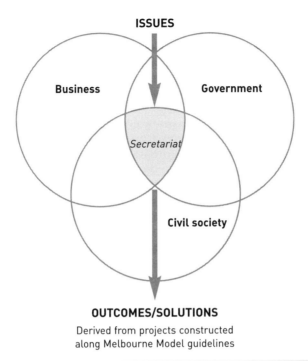

Figure 23.2 Outcomes through partnerships

The Melbourne Model (Fig. 23.1) seeks to ensure observable outcomes by ensuring stakeholder engagement by way of sustained involvement in objective-oriented projects. The Model consists of seven steps that ensure engagement, evaluation, concept testing and reporting.

23.3.1 The Seven Steps of the Melbourne Model

Step 1: Engage the Global Compact principles

The Global Compact principles are the overarching, universal principles under which all Business and Cities Programme activities take place. Cities and Cities Programme stakeholders will be asked to engage in the Global Compact if they are to take part in any Cities Programme project. The engagement process for government and civil-society organisations is the same as that for businesses engaging the Global Compact: a letter is simply addressed to UN Secretary-General Kofi Annan stating the city's or organisation's support for the principles of the Global Compact. The letter is signed by the CEO of the company or by a senior officer of the city.

Step 2: Engage the Melbourne Principles

Developed to assist cities that wish to achieve sustainable development objectives, the Melbourne Principles for Sustainable Cities list ten urban-related social, economic, environmental and cultural value propositions.[4] It is proposed that the Melbourne Principles be positioned as a city-specific subset to the overarching principles embodied in the Global Compact itself. Companies, organisations and governments will be expected to engage in both the Global Compact and the Melbourne Principles if they wish to be involved in Cities Programme projects. In addition, all proposed Cities Programme projects will be measured against these values to ensure they fit within the desired outcome parameters: that is, to ensure they:

● Provide a long-term vision for cities based on sustainability, intergenerational, social, economic and political equity and on individuality

● Achieve long-term economic and social equity

● Recognise the intrinsic value of biodiversity and natural ecosystems and the need to protect or restore those systems

● Enable communities to minimise their ecological footprint

● Build on the characteristics of ecosystems in the development and nurturing of healthy and sustainable cities

● Recognise and build on the distinctive characteristics of cities, including their human and cultural values and their history and natural systems

● Empower people and foster participation

● Expand and enable co-operative networks to work towards a common sustainable future

● Promote sustainable production and consumption, through the appropriate use of environmentally sound technologies and effective demand management

● Enable continual improvement, based on accountability, transparency and good governance

---

4   The Melbourne Principles for Sustainable Cities are the product of the United Nations Environment Programme (UNEP) International Workshop on Building Urban Ecosystems, held in Melbourne. The Principles were launched by the Lord Mayor of Melbourne at the 2002 UN World Summit on Sustainable Development in Johannesburg and were subsequently incorporated into Local Agenda 21—the international sustainable development implementation framework for local government. The Melbourne Principles may be found at www.melbourne.vic.gov.au (including translations into French, Spanish, Russian, Chinese and Arabic). A full English version of the Melbourne Principles for Sustainable Cities is available at www.melbourne.vic.gov.au/upload/melbourneprinciplesenglish.pdf.

Step 3: Adopt or develop projects

The project component is the central platform of the Global Compact Cities Programme. By combining resources from business, government and civil society, projects can be developed and solutions subsequently found to intractable social, economic and environmental issues.

The project opportunity

- The aim is to use minimal resources to co-operatively resolve long-standing and intractable economic, social and environmental issues.

Choosing a project

- Option 1: adopt an existing and proven project from the Global Compact International Learning Forum. It is proposed that successful city projects be placed within a Global Compact International Learning Forum database specifically set up for cities. This database will be run by and located at Global Compact headquarters in New York. Participating cities will have the option of choosing projects from the database to apply to their own cities. Using the Global Compact principles and the refined city-based principles (i.e. the Melbourne Principles), the adopted project will be tailored to suit the specific needs of the city.

- Option 2: develop a new project according to Melbourne Model project criteria. Cities will also have the option of developing new projects that target previously unaddressed (or unsuccessfully addressed) issues, or of promoting a new approach to sustainable development. New projects must conform to the new project criteria.

New project criteria

- Projects must be based around an issue that impacts directly on *each* of the following:
  - Business
  - Government
  - Civil society

- Projects should be used *only* where the problem can be resolved efficiently and effectively by the involvement and implication of *all* three sectors listed above.

- The nature, scope and outcome of projects should be able to be qualified or quantified: that is, the objectives of the project should be SMART (sustainable, measurable, achievable, realistic and timely).

- The project should be unique.

- The conclusions, lessons and outcomes should be able to be directly applied and of immediate benefit to:

-   The city of origin
-   Other cities facing similar issues

Note

●   Participants will be chosen for their specific relevance and expertise to a given project. Participants will be expected to engage in the Global Compact prior to or during the project.

Testing the project mechanism in Australia

As of 2003, three major socioeconomic and environmental projects were being developed utilising the Melbourne Model mechanism. The projects are the Debt Spiral Prevention Project (socioeconomic), the Zero Net Emissions by 2020 project (environmental and economic) and the WaterMark Campaign (environmental and economic). These are described in Boxes 23.1, 23.2 and 23.3, respectively.

Commenced in May 2003, the Debt Spiral Prevention Project was the first project to utilise the Melbourne Model methodology. Its success is measured in the continued participation of 25 companies, non-governmental organisations (NGOs) and government departments working together (many for the first time) in order to develop innovative solutions to an intractable socioeconomic problem. The project illustrates the potential of the Model to have a significant impact on government policy, corporate behaviour and community involvement.

In Melbourne every month approximately 15% of customers are unable or unwilling to pay their utility bills. Of those that are unable to pay their bills a great number represent the most fragile and vulnerable members of society. These include pensioners, youth at risk and the short-term and long-term unemployed. The inability of these individuals to pay utility bills often starts or exacerbates the debt cycle, leading, potentially, to the poverty trap. Besides the obvious negative impact on the individuals and families concerned, the poverty trap also impacts directly on business, government and civil society:

●   The bottom line of business is negatively impacted because of costs incurred in debt write-offs, legal pursuit of individuals, debt servicing, disconnections and connections, and the counselling of affected individuals.

●   Government expends resources on related departments, projects and funding.

●   Multiple NGOs work in assisting those people who have fallen into the poverty trap.

The desired outcome of this project is therefore to remove non-payment of utility bills as a significant contributing factor to individuals falling first into the debt cycle and subsequently into the poverty trap. It is planned that this outcome will be achieved by catalysing the resources and expertise of utility companies, government and NGOs in order to develop sustainable solutions with local, national and international applicability.

Box 23.1 The Debt Spiral Prevention Project

The Zero Net Emissions by 2020 strategy of the City of Melbourne, endorsed by APEC (Asia–Pacific Economic Co-operation), seeks to unite government, commercial and residential interests to shift mainstream business investment in buildings, plant and power generation to superior energy-efficient design over the next two decades. This will be achieved by:

- Using market mechanisms and regulation
- Aligning with local, state and federal government programmes and policies
- Tapping the growing interest and support for 'green' products and work practices

Global Compact signatories can contribute to the achievement of this target by participating in the proposed municipal carbon-trading market, by investing in the triple-bottom-line sequestration project and by joining city-led buying consortia for renewable energy.

Box 23.2 Zero Net Emissions by 2020

Through the WaterMark project the City of Melbourne aims to:

- Drive improvements in the efficiency of water consumption
- Seek alternative water supplies to replace potable water consumption where potable water is not required (e.g. for irrigation)
- Maximise opportunities for water recycling

The Campaign will involve residential, industrial and commercial sectors of the municipality as well as the City Council's own operations. Each sector will be assigned a reduction target relevant to the sector's water usage profile and its potential for efficiency gains. Global Compact signatories can contribute to the achievement of the efficiency targets through participating in a city-led water-efficiency programme.

Box 23.3 The WaterMark Campaign

Step 4: Evaluate the project

Once the nature and objectives of the project have been clearly identified, the process and implications of the project must be evaluated. It is proposed that the triple-bottom-line (TBL) toolkit be adopted as the official vetting mechanism for Global Compact Cities Programme projects. The TBL 'is used as a framework for measuring and reporting corporate performance against economic, social and environmental parameters'.[5] The evaluation process will take into account environmental, social and economic performance indicators.

---

5   Read more about the TBL at www.sustainability.com/philosophy/triple-bottom/tbl-intro.asp.

Step 5: Seek approval for the project

Based on the TBL evaluation report, the project is either approved by the stakeholders and secretariat to be implemented or those proposing the project are asked to rework the project and then submit it again for another evaluation. This process continues until the evaluation panel is satisfied with the project.

Step 6: Implement the project

Work will commence once the project is approved by stakeholders. Every attempt will be made to put in place time-lines, responsibilities and clear milestones to be reached.

Step 7: Report on the project

A project will be developed and refined within the city of origin. 'Only successful and completed projects will be placed on the Global Compact Cities Programme database.' It is proposed that, using the Global Reporting Initiative[6] (GRI) guidelines, a complete report be made on completion of the project. In addition to being a partner organisation to the Global Compact, GRI is a common reporting framework that defines the guidelines for sustainable reporting.

23.4 Roles within the United Nations Global Compact

23.4.1 The secretariat

The Global Compact secretariat is the 'multi-function neural hub' that plays a critical and central role in, first, facilitating the engagement process of organisations, companies and cities and, second, translating the Global Compact and Melbourne Principles into action.

It is proposed that the secretariat play a co-ordinating and communication role for all activities within the city, and an official linking role with Global Compact headquarters in New York (Fig. 23.3).

The role of such a city secretariat would be to:

- Encourage business, government, civil society and companies to engage in the Global Compact
- Disseminate information to all stakeholders
- Provide forums for debate around the policy dialogues and Learning Forums
- Centralise all local activities relating to the Global Compact
- Disseminate condensed information to external stakeholders

6 Read more about the GRI at www.globalreporting.org.

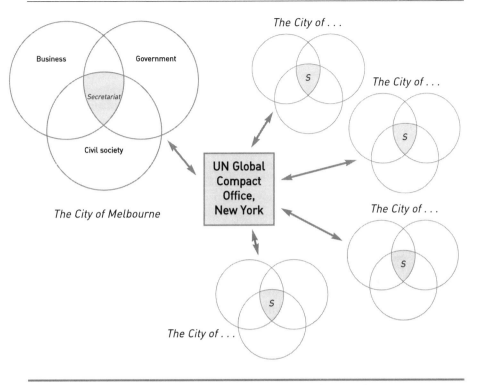

Figure 23.3 Proposed structure for the Global Compact Secretariat

- Vet project ideas
- Form project groups
- Provide a forum to match projects relating to the Global Compact with resources to implement them
- Facilitate the report-back mechanism to New York by way of the compilation and communication of project reports

Note: It is important that a non-political, independent organisation with strong networks within business, government and civil society be chosen in each city to perform this role.

23.4.2 The Global Compact New York headquarters

The role of headquarters is to:

- Serve as the central co-ordination point between regional Cities Programme centres

- Maintain the Global Compact Learning Forum as a central repository of proven city projects

- Ensure communication of all new Global Compact Cities Programme policies and practices

- Develop the Cities Programme as an important and effective component of the Global Compact programme

23.5 Conclusions

In support of the Global Compact principles, the Global Compact Cities Programme presents an opportunity to develop and share real and sustainable solutions to intractable economic, social and environmental urban problems. The Melbourne Model—the core methodology of the Cities Programme—facilitates this outcome by providing neutral ground on which business, government and civil society can openly communicate the ideas, knowledge and experience present in their discrete sectors. Detailed solutions are generated by participants and are tested for effectiveness. If validated, solutions are implemented in the city of origin and made available to other cities around the world that face similar issues.

24

The Global Compact

Promoting convergence in corporate responsibility

Deborah Leipziger
Consultant, Corporate Responsibility

The field of corporate responsibility faces several significant challenges. First, in order to maintain momentum, convergence between initiatives and standards is necessary. Second, the field of corporate responsibility must deliver progress at the national, regional and sectoral levels in order to 'drill down' strategy and principles into concrete and localised action. The Global Compact is well positioned to address the dual challenges of convergence and localisation.

This chapter describes the linkages and convergence developing between the Global Compact and key initiatives in the field of corporate responsibility, among them the Global Reporting Initiative (GRI),[1] the Norms on Responsibilities of Transnational Corporations and Other Business Enterprises with Regard to Human Rights (Norms),[2] Social Accountability 8000 (SA8000)[3] and the Organisation for Economic Co-operation and Development (OECD) Guidelines for Multinational Enterprises (OECD Guidelines).[4] (For details of these and other codes and initiatives, see Leipziger 2003[5] and McIntosh *et al.* 2003b.) These bilateral examples of convergence are solidifying the field of corporate responsibility by assisting companies seeking to become more socially responsible. The Global Compact is to

1 See www.globalreporting.org.
2 See www1.umn.edu/humanrts/links/commentary-Aug2003.html.
3 See www.sa-intl.org/SA8000/SA8000.htm.
4 See www.oecd.org/department/0,2688,en_2649_34889_1_1_1_1_1,00.html.
5 This code book reproduces the text of the values, principles, norms, codes and standards discussed within its pages.

be commended for promoting convergence and, as a result, clarity in the field of corporate responsibility.

To provide an analogy, this chapter focuses on the Global Compact as the hub, with linked spokes to four other corporate responsibility initiatives. The reader should bear in mind that some of these 'spokes' have strong bilateral relationships between them, in addition to those forged with the Global Compact. For example, GRI has developed a formal partnership with the OECD Guidelines for Multi-national Enterprises.[6]

The Global Compact provides a framework for understanding corporate responsibility; it provides a template for action, accessible to companies from both North and South in all sectors. Where it succeeds brilliantly is in providing an umbrella large enough to cover companies across the globe. However, the simplicity of the Global Compact is both a strength and a perceived weakness. Its simplicity is part of what makes the Global Compact appeal to a critical mass of companies—to beginners in the field of corporate responsibility as well as to companies with an extensive track record in social and environmental issues. The Global Compact can gain both depth and momentum by promoting convergence with other initiatives in the field of corporate responsibility that extend beyond principles.

Initiatives in the field of corporate responsibility can be differentiated by their focus on performance and/or process (see Table 24.1). The Global Compact is an initiative geared towards performance, setting general principles for what companies should do or refrain from doing. Process standards, on the other hand, focus on management systems, and the 'how' of corporate responsibility, including such issues as reporting, training, and controlling suppliers. As such, it is useful for companies to adopt the Global Compact and complement it with process standards such as the GRI, SA8000, AccountAbility 1000 (AA1000)[7] and others. It is also useful to combine the Global Compact's principles with more specific performance-oriented principles, such as the OECD Guidelines.

First a word on convergence—what it is and what it is not. For the purpose of this chapter, convergence represents a commitment to work together towards a common vision. The goal of convergence is not necessarily harmonisation but understanding how the various corporate responsibility initiatives interrelate and can provide leverage for one another. Convergence begins with mutual recognition and continues with the formation of durable alliances to develop and explain the linkages between initiatives. This chapter examines bilateral forms of convergence between corporate responsibility initiatives.

There are two types of convergence: procedural convergence and convergence of performance standards. Procedural convergence can be described as the convergence of processes such as reporting, external verification and accreditation (see Leipziger 2003: 509). Most of the convergence discussed at this time, and throughout this chapter, focuses on procedural convergence.

The Global Compact is itself a convergence between a range of key UN agreements, including the Universal Declaration of Human Rights,[8] the Fundamental

---

6   See www.globalreporting.org/about/inioecd2.asp.
7   See www.accountability.org.uk.
8   See www.un.org/Overview/rights.html.

Performance focus	Process focus	Process and performance focus
UN Global Compact: www.unglobalcompact.org	Global Reporting Initiative: www.globalreporting.org	Social AccountAbility 8000: www.sa-intl.org
The Global Sullivan Principles of Corporate Social Responsibility: www.globalsullivanprinciples.org	AccountAbility 1000: www.accountability.org.uk	Workplace Code of Conduct of the Fair Labor Association: www.fairlabor.org
OECD Guidelines for Multinational Enterprises: www.oecd.org	ISO 14001: www.iso.org	Norms on the Responsibilities of Transnational Corporations and Other Enterprises with Regard to Human Rights: www1.umn.edu/ humanrts/links/ commentary-Aug2003.html
Conventions of the International Labour Organisation: www.ilo.org		SIGMA Guidelines: www.projectsigma.com
Universal Declaration of Human Rights: www.un.org		

Table 24.1 Initiatives and standards, by focus

Principles and Rights at Work of the International Labour Organisation (ILO)[9] and the Earth Summit's Agenda 21 principles. Many key initiatives share normative principles, making convergence of performance-related initiatives less of a priority than procedural convergence.

24.1 Norms on the Responsibilities of Transnational Corporations and Other Business Enterprises with Regard to Human Rights

The Norms are very comprehensive, addressing the full range of issues facing companies: human rights, labour rights, the environment and development. Unlike

---

9   See the website of the ILO, at www.ilo.org.

the Global Compact, the Norms also address anti-bribery issues (but see Appendix D), consumer protection and war crimes.

Sir Geoffrey Chandler, a well-known expert on corporate responsibility, testified on behalf of the Norms with the following commentary (Chandler 2001):

> The world is rightly asking that companies should be more accountable. And there is today a multiplicity of codes and guidelines reflecting this demand. But none [touches] the totality of what is required. What we need is a comprehensive and authoritative instrument for this purpose. It seems to me that that only the UN can provide this. What we have before us today in the Guidelines [Norms] is such an instrument—it is the logical extension of the Universal Declaration into corporate practice which would be complementary to the Secretary-General's Global Compact.

According to the Lawyers' Committee on Human Rights (LCHR 2002), the Norms

> present the most comprehensive, action-oriented restatement to date of existing human rights laws applicable to global business. Taken as a whole, they confirm in fundamentally new ways (i) the many laws that do indeed apply and then (ii) how they apply and can be implemented with respect to business conduct.

The Global Compact represents an entry point for companies seeking to develop voluntary programmes in corporate responsibility. The Norms serve as a counterpoint to the Global Compact in that they provide a legal framework for the field of corporate responsibility. According to David Weissbrodt (Source 3),[10] a key figure behind the development of the Norms,

> For those companies that want to respect corporate social responsibility, the Norms represent a useful interpretation and elaboration of the Global Compact. The Norms supplement the Global Compact in that the Norms apply to all companies and not just the 1,000 companies that have joined the Global Compact.

The Global Compact and the Norms are complementary (see Table 24.2). Whereas the Global Compact is general, the Norms are highly specific and detailed. According to Georg Kell of the UN Secretary-General's office in the UN, and a leading force behind the Global Compact, the Norms have two roles: to educate and promote awareness on corporate responsibility, and to develop a legal framework for corporate responsibility. This legal framework could one day become a UN Convention (Source 1). According to Kell, voluntarism and regulation aim at the same thing. Change is dialectic, and both regulatory and voluntary approaches are necessary to enact change (Source 1). As I pointed out in *The Corporate Responsibility Code Book* (Leipziger 2003: 107):

> The Norms set an important context for human rights issues, articulating that states have the primary responsibility to promote human rights. This is important, as many codes of conduct leave governments out of the equation altogether.

10 Details of sources are given at the end of this chapter.

Attribute	*UN Global Compact*	*The Norms*
Type and specificity	Principles (general)	Norms (specific)
Administration	By United Nations	By United Nations
Issues covered	Human rights, labour and environment*	Human rights, labour, environment, anti-bribery and war crimes
Nature	Voluntary	Moving towards regulation
Means of starting engagement	Companies sign on	In order for the Norms to gain momentum, governments will need to approve them

* But see also Appendix D on the introduction of an anti-corruption principle.

Table 24.2 **The UN Global Compact and the Norms on the Responsibilities of Transnational Corporations and Other Business Enterprises with Regard to Human Rights: a comparison**

24.2 The Global Reporting Initiative

The GRI defines itself as a 'long-term, multi-stakeholder, international process whose mission is to develop and disseminate globally applicable Sustainability Reporting Guidelines' (GRI 2002). Like the Global Compact, the GRI is a voluntary initiative. The GRI focuses on the process of reporting, whereas the Global Compact focuses on performance.

According to Alyson Slater of the GRI (Source 2), both the Global Compact and the GRI have been growing at a rapid pace and over the same period of time. From the inception of both initiatives, GRI and Global Compact staff have consulted with each other to seek greater alignment. The Global Compact and the GRI have developed a table that links the principles of the Global Compact to concrete indicators drawn from the GRI Guidelines.[11] The table has been approved by all the UN bodies associated with the principles of the Global Compact and has been translated into a wide range of languages (for a version of this table, see Appendix C). According to Slater, convergence between the GRI and the Global Compact promotes increased use of the GRI Sustainability Reporting Guidelines through incremental reporting. The Global Compact also benefits from this process by demonstrating to a cynical public that Global Compact companies are promoting real change.

Table 24.3 is drawn from the GRI website and demonstrates the complementarities between the two approaches.

11   See www.globalreporting.org/guidelines/2002.asp.

Attribute	UN Global Compact	GRI
Core mission	To build the social and environmental pillars required to sustain the new global economy and make globalisation work for all the world's people, based on commitment to universal principles	To elevate economic, environmental and social reporting to routine practice and to the highest standards of rigour and comparability through the development of a generally accepted reporting framework
Governance	• UN Secretary General's office • Global issues network • UN Environment Programme • International Labour Organisation • Office of High Commissioner for Human Rights • UN Development Programme	• Multi-stakeholder board of directors • Technical advisory and stakeholder councils • UNEP Collaborating Centre
Scope	Business operating principles: human rights, labour, environment	• Economic, environmental and social performance • Public reporting
Participants	Participating companies, labour and non-governmental organisations	• Companies • United Nations • Labour, environmental and human rights groups • Accountancy and industry associations • Governments • Investors
Funding	• Government • Foundations	• Foundations • Companies • Governments
Start year	1999	• 1997 • Became an independent institution in 2002
Major difference	It is based on operating principles	It is a disclosure framework based on reporting principles and indicators

Table 24.3 The UN Global Compact and the Global Reporting Initiative: a
comparison (continued over)

Source: www.globalreporting.org/about/inigcompact.asp

Attribute	UN Global Compact	GRI
Major similarity	It is a voluntary effort supported by the UN to promote corporate accountability and sustainability	It is a voluntary effort supported by the UN to promote corporate accountability and sustainability
Key linkage	Global Compact supporters can draw on the GRI indicators to demonstrate accountability to the principles of the Global Compact	It provides Global Compact supporters with an instrument to demonstrate accountability against the principles of the Global Compact

Table 24.3 (continued)

24.3 Social Accountability 8000

SA8000 is a voluntary standard for making the workplace more humane. Developed through a multi-stakeholder process involving trade unions, non-governmental organisations (NGOs) and the private sector and government, SA8000 is a certification standard. As such, it resembles the model used by the International Organisation for Standardisation (ISO) in which companies that are found to comply with the standard through an external audit by an accredited certification body can use the logo of the standard in their publications, on company vehicles and in the workplace. Like the Global Compact, SA8000 is based in part on Conventions of the ILO, although the Compact looks only at the Core Conventions, whereas SA8000 addresses a wide range of ILO Conventions. SA8000 also uses the UN Declaration on the Rights of the Child and the Universal Declaration of Human Rights as normative elements.

The Global Compact and SA8000 are complementary, in that SA8000 provides greater depth in the field of labour rights, whereas the Global Compact is broader but with less specificity (see Table 24.4). The management systems of SA8000 are useful to Global Compact companies seeking process tools. Among the important management systems discussed in SA8000 are: training, control of suppliers, maintaining records, and addressing corrective action.

SA8000 is the only initiative described in this chapter that includes a system for independent, third-party audits. In this way, SA8000 provides an important counterpart to the Global Compact, which, as a UN body, is unable to engage in any kind of monitoring or auditing (for more on the difficulties for the UN inherent in monitoring, see Chapter 2). The Global Compact cites SA8000 as a model for companies seeking to implement the Global Compact.

Attribute	UN Global Compact	SA8000
Nature	Voluntary	Voluntary
Type	Principles	Standard
Focus	Performance	Performance and process
Means of engagement, or outcome	Membership	Certification
Issues covered	Human rights, labour and environment*	Exclusively labour rights

* But see also Appendix D on the introduction of an anti-corruption principle.

Table 24.4 The UN Global Compact and Social Accountability 8000 (SA8000): a comparison

24.4 OECD Guidelines for Multinational Enterprises

The OECD Guidelines are among the oldest and most comprehensive of the corporate responsibility initiatives. Launched in 1976, the OECD Guidelines address human rights, labour rights, environment, taxation, and science and technology, among other things. The OECD Guidelines address a wider range of issues than does the Global Compact (see Table 24.5).

Attribute	UN Global Compact	OECD Guidelines
Type	Principles	Guidelines
Focus	Performance	Performance
Issues covered	Human rights, labour rights and environment*	Human rights, labour rights, environment, science, technology, governance, consumer protection, taxation among other things
Means of engagement	Regional and national forums	National contact points

* But see also Appendix D on the introduction of an anti-corruption principle.

Table 24.5 The UN Global Compact and the OECD Guidelines for Multinational Enterprises (OECD Guidelines): a comparison

The OECD is a membership organisation of 30 governments. The OECD has developed a wide range of guidelines that are accepted very broadly—beyond the membership of the OECD.

The objectives of the Guidelines are (OECD 2000b: 15):

- To ensure that the operations of these enterprises are in harmony with government policies

- To strengthen the basis of mutual confidence between enterprises and the societies in which they operate

- To help improve the foreign investment climate

- To enhance the contribution to sustainable development made by multinational enterprises

The OECD Guidelines are unusual among corporate responsibility instruments in that they assign national contact points (NCPs). The NCPs are individuals assigned from various ministries (and in some cases business or trade unions) to serve as a national point of liaison on the OECD Guidelines. The NCPs raise awareness about the Guidelines through websites, training and the issuing of handbooks.

The OECD Guidelines were reviewed in 2000, and several key issues were added, including them labour standards and sustainable development.

According to Corrine Dreyfus of the European Commission (Dreyfus 2001: 120):

> This is the value added of the Guidelines for all: for enterprises as a useful point of reference, for stakeholders as a high-quality vehicle for dialogue and for developing countries as a partnership and co-operation-building instrument.

The 2001 Annual Report on the Guidelines (OECD 2001b) notes that the OECD Guidelines and Global Compact are complementary. Although the Guidelines contain relatively detailed recommendations on business conduct (compared with the Compact's broad principles) there is an underlying unity of values and purpose.

The distinctive value added of the Guidelines [is] their government-backed implementation procedures—company endorsements are not sought under Guidelines implementation (however, the CIME [Committee on International Investment and Multilateral Enterprises] is grateful when business, trade union or NGO actors publicly express their support of the Guidelines). Guidelines implementation consists of a four-way dialogue (involving the 38 adhering governments, business, trade unions and other civil-society actors) and an associated transparency and reporting mechanism.

This contrasts with the UN Global Compact's implementation procedure, which seeks to create an ongoing relationships with companies that have endorsed the Compact and to promote a learning process involving these companies and other partners to the process.

24.5 Conclusions

The Global Compact is pursuing important bilateral forms of convergence with the GRI, SA8000, the Norms and the OECD Guidelines. These bilateral approaches are mutually reinforcing and lend credibility to each of the initiatives concerned. However, there is a need to move beyond bilateral approaches to develop an overarching consensus on key procedural issues. For example, there are no centralised mechanisms for filing complaints. It would be useful to have a common mechanism where concerned parties, such as workers, NGOs or trade unions, can file complaints.

To embed the Global Compact deeply into companies and to place it firmly into the mainstream, it will be necessary to promote convergence and localisation. By working with the GRI, SA8000, the Norms and the OECD Guidelines the Global Compact is advancing the agenda of corporate responsibility worldwide.

Sources

Source 1 Interview with Georg Kell, 16 September 2003.
Source 2 Interview with Alyson Slater, Global Reporting Initiative, 31 October 2003.
Source 3 Personal (electronic) communication from David Weissbrodt, 3 November 2003.

Part 6
Taking off

25

The Global Compact
Selected experiences and reflections

Georg Kell
UN Global Compact

When United Nations Secretary-General Kofi Annan addressed a plenary session of the World Economic Forum on 31 January 1999 (see Chapter 1), it was neither planned nor imagined that the speech—titled 'The Global Compact'—would mark the beginning of a global corporate citizenship initiative. The idea started to take root rapidly, however, and on 26 July 2000 the Global Compact was launched at UN Headquarters as an operational initiative. At this event, 18 months after the delivery of the Davos speech, about 50 executives from multinational companies, global trade unions and civil-society organisations convened to collectively announce their support and participation. The Global Compact has grown organically over the four years since into a comprehensive, worldwide network of stakeholders. This network comprises several international labour groups, dozens of civil -society organisations and more than 1,000 companies from over 50 countries—all contributing to dialogue, learning and projects that give practical meaning to universal principles on human rights, labour conditions and the environment.

The rapid growth of the initiative took place against a backdrop of significant experimentation and learning. High expectations created by the speech and by subsequent pronouncements created enormous pressure to deliver. The Global Compact Office, consisting of only John Ruggie, myself and Denise O'Brien, had to invent solutions and scramble for operational tools: a challenging proposition given a lack of funding and no in-house expertise. Juggling the conflicting interests of the initiative's participants and racing to 'give globalisation a human face' left indelible marks on the not-so-halcyon early days of the Global Compact.

In this chapter, I would like to share some reflections on this early period in the development of the Global Compact. I will do so not in an analytical mode, as this has been done elsewhere (Kell and Levin 2003;[1] Kell and Ruggie 1999). Nor will I retell the details of the Global Compact's evolution and progress, which is described at length on the website.[2] Instead, I offer a subjective perspective and weave into the story two *leitmotifs* still relevant today.

The first concerns lessons learned regarding the assumption that non-state actors, such as multinational businesses, trade unions and civil-society organisations, are willing and capable of finding solutions to some of the challenges that economic openness poses to societies at large. Questions surrounding the degree to which different actors are willing to co-operate, the existence and extent of self-enlightened motivation and the dynamics of critical masses of first movers are important issues in this context, but, at a more aggregate level, the central issue is whether the Global Compact, as a voluntary initiative, can make a significant contribution and how it relates to regulatory approaches.

The second theme relates to the institutional setting of the Global Compact. As a UN initiative, the Global Compact thrives on the convening power and moral authority of the organisation as well as the universal legitimacy of its principles. However, these strengths come with the liabilities of bureaucracy and cumbersome intergovernmental protocols that stifle innovation. The ability of the historically hierarchical UN to support a diffuse, network-based initiative obviously constitutes an essential determinant of the Global Compact's success. Beyond the matter of organisational constraints, however, lies the more fundamental question of whether the UN member-states are willing to grant the institution a more important role in economic and social issues by bestowing it with sufficient authority and scope to deal with international business.

These two *leitmotifs* simultaneously represent the two basic assumptions defining the viability of the initiative.

Experiences to date suggest that success is far from assured. There is little doubt that the Global Compact will remain an ongoing experiment, testing the limits of self-enlightened engagement and the boundaries of the UN's political and operational spheres. However, I hope that by reflecting on these issues I will be able to provide insights and understanding into the brief trajectory the Global Compact has charted thus far.

25.1 The institutional setting: from code to compact

As an initiative of the UN, the fate of the Global Compact is inextricably tied to the changing relationship between the UN and the for-profit business community—in particular, transnational and multinational companies. Indeed, in institutional terms, the Global Compact's greatest significance as of today may already be its catalytic impact on the UN, fostering a new era of co-operation with business and overcoming the recent past—one of mutual suspicion. Bringing about a funda-

1   Reproduced in this volume, Chapter 3.
2   See www.unglobalcompact.org.

mental change in this relationship has broader political and operational significance, as the following discussion reveals (for more detail on this topic, see Tesner and Kell 2000).

The relationship between the UN and business has undergone radical changes since the UN was created in 1945. Business was present at the historic San Francisco founders' meeting through the supportive International Chamber of Commerce (ICC), the global business association that had long embraced multilateralism and the promotion of trade and investment. The prevailing policy consensus recognised trade and investment as prerequisites to political and social freedoms, as well as bridges to connect common interests across national boundaries. Trade was thus a vehicle for generating shared prosperity, interdependence and peace.

Perhaps the best testimony of the UN-business relationship at the beginning of the UN's life is the telegram that Philip D. Reed, then chairman of General Electric and part of the ICC delegation, sent to the chairman of the US Senate Foreign Relations Committee. Expressing earnest and enthusiastic support for the UN Charter and urging unanimous ratification, he wrote:

> We believe that no finer nor more fruitful gesture could be made towards its successful implementation than for the Foreign Relations Committee and subsequent the Senate itself to ratify the Charter unanimously.

However, there was little time to translate the policy consensus of the founding years of the UN into institutional structures or operational modalities. With the onset of the Cold War, the UN became prisoner to conflicting ideologies and had to adopt a neutral position on the efficacy of markets. Cold War strategic interests produced a normative quagmire in the UN and conditioned many of its operational activities. The ideals of recovery and reconstruction were replaced with a harsh ideological reality and colourful but wasteful debates. Later, in the wake of decolonisation in the 1960s and 1970s, a growing number of developing countries urged the adoption of a new international economic order. The relationship deteriorated further as business adopted an antagonistic attitude towards an international body that, in their view, had little practical relevance. The creation of the former UN Centre on Transnational Corporations, as well as intergovernmental efforts to establish a code of conduct for transnational corporations, fuelled further suspicion and contributed to almost complete alienation.

Within the UN, statist perspectives pervaded institutional thinking and operations alike. The institution was dominated by technocrats focusing on redistribution and central planning rather than on the sources of wealth creation and the incentives required for entrepreneurship to thrive. Such attitudes would prevail within the UN for many years to come, influencing habits, procedures, attitudes and methods of work. The result was mutual suspicion deeply embedded in institutional behaviour and collective memories.

The heated political debates of the 1970s and 1980s came to an end with the fall of the Berlin Wall in late 1989. By then, business instinctively eschewed the UN, but when the UN General Assembly shoved the Code of Conduct for Transnational Corporations into 'deep freeze' in 1992, it began to dismantle the paralysis of conflicting ideologies and seemed to make possible a fresh start. Several years would pass, however, before the UN and business would see a true rapprochement.

A turning point came with the election of UN Secretary-General Kofi Annan in December 1996. The case for approaching business was overwhelming: market liberalisation, technological change and rapid expansion of trade and investment characterised the global economic and social landscape. It became obvious that increasingly interdependent global challenges would be met only if all actors of society contributed, and the rapid growth of foreign direct investment and trade during the 1990s underscored the central role of markets in tackling poverty.

But how could one convince business to pay attention to the UN? What kind of motives and incentives might one establish to ensure the relationship's effectiveness? How could institutional change be brought about when statist bureaucrats with little understanding of the role of business dominated the organisation?

The leadership and pragmatism of Kofi Annan and his familiarity with business issues (he is the first UN Secretary-General with a business management degree) helped to turn the tide. He supported efforts to prove that a strong UN was good for business in a world of growing interdependence. A new institutional focus examined how the UN helped stabilise markets and reduce transaction costs. For example, the UN's contribution to setting technical standards (e.g. in aviation, shipping, postal services, telecommunications, statistics and trade laws) formed an important component of the infrastructure of the global economy, saving many millions of dollars every day for consumers and producers alike (Zacher 1999). Similar arguments explained the benefit of the UN's work for the environment and development and its contribution to fostering mutually reinforcing peace and prosperity. Finally, the case was made that the UN itself had changed, that confrontation had given way to co-operation and that UN organisations were now ready to cultivate partnerships.

At the core of this renewal lay the vital understanding that markets by themselves were not an ideology but rather a tool in the hands of societies. This view afforded Kofi Annan a position above the ideological debates and allowed him to focus on practical, real-world changes. He delivered many speeches on these issues, especially during his first term as UN Secretary-General (Annan 1997, 1999a, 1999c). Meetings were organised with the ICC and joint statements were issued in 1998 and 1999 to herald a new era of co-operation.[3] The message was heard, at least at the level of collective business interests. Global business associations such as the ICC and the International Organisation of Employers (IOE) began to view the UN as an important part of the globalisation debate and acknowledged its constructive contribution. Business associations and individual business leaders started to lobby on the UN's behalf by, for instance, urging the US Congress to pay the nation's outstanding dues. Meanwhile, Kofi Annan had long become an important figure at the World Economic Forum, which he had visited every other year since taking office.

The story of the Global Compact was in many ways the logical extension of these arguments. The emergence of the anti-globalisation movement ahead of the 1999 World Trade Organisation (WTO) meeting and the aftermath of the Asian

---

3 Joint Statement on Common Interests by the Secretary-General and International Chamber of Commerce (ICC) (February 1998); UN–ICC meeting, Geneva, July 1999.

financial crisis of the late 1990s both provided the background for the idea of the Global Compact. The insight that global markets must be embedded in a social consensus of shared values, the basic fact that markets needed an underpinning of rules and laws that transcended the efficiency imperative of economic transactions and the fact that liberalisation, itself the outcome of deliberate policy choices, needed social legitimacy to be sustainable over time all offered useful points of reference. And, as long as governments remained local while markets went global, there was a real gap in global governance that, if left unattended, could be exploited by narrow interests at the expense of many. The idea that the UN could assert itself as a stabilising force, while putting emphasis on market inclusion, seemed both fitting with the mission of the organisation and timely in light of the ongoing leadership vacuums around trade, business and social issues.

These macro arguments gained further momentum as the desire to inject social priorities into the rules of international exchange appeared to become once again a lightning rod in trade negotiations. Moreover, the legitimacy and universality of the Global Compact's principles provided the UN with an institutional advantage in dealing with the burgeoning debate around corporate social responsibility. The world was witnessing changing perceptions about the role of business in society, such that business was experiencing ever-greater pressure to adopt proactive social and environmental policies in order to maintain a licence to operate.

25.2 Voluntarism versus regulation: a false dichotomy

Already during preparatory meetings with business, labour and civil-society organisations ahead of the formal launch of the Global Compact in July 2000 it became clear that a major issue of contention was the voluntary nature of the initiative. The response from business representatives left no doubt that the only way to engage with the UN was on a voluntary basis. Notions such as 'learning', 'dialogue' and 'partnership projects' were acceptable, provided that real value would be added in an already crowded field of voluntary initiatives. Global labour unions shared the view that the Global Compact could add value by promoting social dialogue at the global level, which would complement efforts to establish effective national laws. Participating civil-society organisations, although privately recognising that voluntary approaches could introduce social and environmental principles into corporate strategy and operations, were under pressure from their peers who did not participate in the Global Compact to urge for regulation and external monitoring. These vocal non-governmental organisations (NGOs) argued that the Global Compact was inadequate at best and, at worst, a 'bluewashing' mechanism for companies because of the absence of external monitoring and regulatory enforcement.

Despite numerous explanations about the nature of the initiative and its experimental focus on learning and dialogue, critics soon widely used the argument that the Global Compact was inadequate because it lacked enforcement. The Global

Compact simply was not what some wanted it to be, and explanations to the contrary were simply ignored. Although in recent years a growing number of civil-society organisations have accepted the fact that the Global Compact is not about monitoring and measurement and that engagement through learning, dialogue and concrete actions could complement efforts to improve corporate social and environmental performance the basic issue of voluntarism versus regulation has remained one of the most contentious issues.

For the evolution of the Global Compact, the arguments for and against regulation were, at one level, irrelevant. The Global Compact was, from its inception, an experiment in co-operation based on market-based mechanisms. The experiment would allow the catalytic effects of critical masses, collective action, transparency and front-runner behaviour to set examples that ultimately could become behavioural norms. Although the viability of this approach was and remains far from certain, its distinct and complementary nature *vis-à-vis* conventional regulatory approaches was never in question. Nevertheless, criticism of the Global Compact was instrumental in provoking an ongoing search for the right incentives and methodologies to bring about desired changes while maintaining the integrity of the UN.

Thus, the issues of free-riders and the difficulty of defining 'good practices' posed major conceptual and operational challenges. Initial models of social vetting based on annual submissions by companies on the implementation of the principles proved not to be practical, at least in the short run, for a number of reasons. First, the value of codified information for social vetting or benchmarking is very limited when it comes to generic cross-sectoral performance indications. More often than not, such information is biased in favour of strategic assumptions regarding its use and impact and hence lacks objectivity. Second, examples need to be contextualised to carry analytical meaning beyond the narrow realm of the story itself. Contextualisation, however, presupposes a very large number of cluster examples and the availability of robust analytical capacities. Third, in the absence of performance indicators cutting across all industries and relevant to all companies of all countries of the world, it would not be possible to derive any meaningful comparisons. Fourth, the large variety of languages used around the world and the complexities of information transmission in ways and manners that allow for comparability added processing barriers of great magnitude. For these reasons, we had to abandon the initial model of defining good practices through a centralised social vetting process of large numbers of business examples.

Although the vision of identifying good practice and building a dynamic learning bank remains valid, important adjustments and new strategies had to be employed. There were deliberate efforts to decentralise activities, to align other competent institutions with the Global Compact, to develop a 'performance model' that would offer generic guidance on how to implement the principles, and to promote tools and training materials. The most far-reaching change, however, was the introduction of a 'new strategy', in which companies are asked to communicate progress on the implementation of the Global Compact in their own annual report or other prominent public documents. Supported by a 'guidance note' to foster a coherence of approaches, the publication of progress would henceforth be done in a public manner (presented on the Global Compact website as of early 2004). A maximum degree of transparency would thus be achieved while freeing the Global Compact Office from the impossible mission of providing assurance in a centralised fashion. This approach would also tackle the free-rider issue, as the Global Compact Office will in the future be in a position to indicate on the website which companies did not communicate progress.

The criticism from NGOs has helped to build additional measures to protect the integrity of the Global Compact, beyond the original social vetting process and the new public reporting policy. For instance, the Global Compact Office initiated the formulation of a UN guide on co-operation with business, introduced by Kofi Annan in June 2000 to all UN organisations.[4] These framework guidelines have inspired many UN organisations to develop more specific templates in line with their missions and mandates. They contain strict rules on the use of the UN logo, and lay out basic parameters for engagement, supporting experimentation but safeguarding the integrity of the UN. Additionally, practical procedures have been developed to deal with gross violations of the principles by individual participants. These measures include delisting from the website, referral to the dispute resolution mechanisms of other agencies such as the International Labour Organisation (ILO) and on-the-ground efforts that employ capacity-building and dialogue to find solutions. Still, the Global Compact recognises the need to further develop procedures for dealing with egregious violations of the principles and continues to do so currently.

Clearly, NGO criticism has been instrumental in fostering the formation of governance measures. These procedures protect the integrity of the initiative and elucidate its purpose as a dialogue, learning and action platform. They have helped shape the positioning of the Global Compact not as a membership programme that conveys recognition but rather as an initiative with engagement mechanisms that generate concrete actions, systemic change and convergence around universal principles.

Yet, despite progress made, the relationship between the Global Compact and regulatory approaches is likely to remain contentious. A mantra deeply rooted in the development community still maintains that initiatives can be effective at improving the social and environmental performance of private enterprises only through intense monitoring. Although one may argue that this critique does not apply to the Global Compact as long as it does not convey recognition, the underlying questions are complex.

First, from an efficiency perspective, the real question appears not to be whether regulation or voluntarism is superior but rather which approach produces the greatest impact and under what conditions. The first aspect of this question can be answered only through rigorous comparative studies. Unfortunately, such studies are in short supply, partly because of the complexities of measuring the behavioural change of large organisations. For the Global Compact, the issue of what kind of impact it produces is central not only to the viability of its engagement mechanisms (learning, dialogue and projects) at the operational level but also to the justification of the initiative's very existence.

4   See www.un.org/partners/business/guide

Already, there is much anecdotal evidence that the initiative is producing systemic changes. In-depth case studies of individual companies, available on the Global Compact website, document how the principles of the Global Compact are becoming part and parcel of corporate strategy and day-to-day practices. In addition, several large collective-action initiatives have spawned projects that bring real benefits for people. Moreover, the dozens of local networks that have mushroomed all over the globe, imitating the global engagement functions, produce many positive net effects for workers, communities and the environment. However, at time of writing, no systematic effort has been made to approximate the net impact of these activities. At the Global Compact Office we have long recognised that undertaking a comprehensive study on the impact of the Global Compact is of great importance but the high costs of gathering and evaluating information at very different levels of aggregation has so far made such a study elusive. Clearly, however, the production of more and more comprehensive assessments will in small measures bolster, or undermine, the credibility of the Global Compact.

Second, even if a comprehensive study on the impact of the Global Compact existed, demonstrating that sufficient positive social change has been inspired on a global scale to justify its existence, another question would need to be answered: wouldn't the UN have produced more results if it had tried to establish the Global Compact as a regulatory instrument? Obviously, this question cannot be answered with certainty in the absence of a comparable undertaking, but there are many indications that suggest that a regulatory approach would not have been fruitful. First, the UN has tried previously to regulate transnational companies through its Code of Conduct: 20 years of debate and negotiations yielded no results. Second, any observer of international relations would confirm that in the current political climate it would be impossible for the UN to muster sufficient political will to make such an undertaking possible. Governments simply would not provide the required political support. Third, even if negotiations on a regulatory approach had been initiated, it would have taken years for such negotiations to come to some conclusion, and, even if negotiations were conclusive, the outcome would in all likelihood reflect the lowest common denominator of the UN's 191 member-states.

The importance of flexibility is exemplified by the Global Compact's rapid evolution and stands in stark contrast to the cumbersome nature of establishing regulation. Indeed, it is safe to say that none of the activities that the Global Compact has produced so far would have been possible had the UN chosen a non-voluntary approach. History will be the judge, and the current discussions of the Norms on the Responsibilities of Transnational Corporations and Other Business Enterprises with Regard to Human Rights, as adopted by the Sub-Commission of Human Rights, will offer in many ways a real-time case study on the potential of a regulatory approach at the global level.[5]

The third major concern surrounding the Global Compact's positioning as a voluntary initiative is the current abundance of approaches backed by regulation. The real challenge is not in designing new regulations but in finding ways to make existing regulations effective. The catchword is 'implementation'. The OECD guidelines, for example, are backed by governments and offer many entry points,

5 See www1.umn.edu/humanrts/links/commentary-Aug2003.html.

yet in some of the most important economies of the world the guidelines are barely known or applied. In a similar vein, the ILO has produced nearly 200 conventions,[6] and a superficial review of ratification and implementation reveals the need to improve the effectiveness of these regulations. It is within this context that the Global Compact has been positioned as a complementary tool to explore effective ways of implementing existing norms legitimised by the international community.

The fourth issue relates to the complementarity of voluntary initiatives and regulation. Assuming that the motives for change are dualistic, in the sense that they respond both to positive incentives and to negative incentives, it could be argued that a balance between the two approaches seems almost indispensable to sustain healthy societies. Regulation and the codification of norms usually prescribe what should not be done. As such, regulation defines the minimum floor of performance below which actors are penalised. Such a floor is indispensable, but clearly regulation alone cannot bring about positive change. All too often it merely induces compliance regimes that aim at cost and risk minimisation while failing to provide incentives to stimulate innovation and positive change. And this is where initiatives such as the Global Compact can make a complementary contribution. Assuming that motives for change respond to positive and negative incentives, regulatory and voluntary approaches are indeed complementary.

Last, the nature of voluntary initiatives is poorly understood with regard both to the underlying motives for change and to the relevance of public authority. With respect to motives, corporate activities exceeding the requirements of the law are often driven by market necessities. To the extent that there is a business case for social and environmental responsibility, such actions are hardly voluntary but rather part of corporate competitive strategy. Earning a licence to operate through dialogue; improving productivity through decent workplace conditions; protecting reputation and minimising risks through social and environmental commitments may all be microeconomic imperatives essential for corporate survival.

Even less understood is the relationship between private and public authority. The growth of voluntary initiatives is often seen as the emergence of private authority in global governance, reflecting the diminishing capacity of governments to regulate business. Accordingly, arguments are advanced for more government intervention to curtail the power of the private sector. True, competition policy is indeed the orphan of the corporate social responsibility debate, but such arguments fail to recognise that voluntary initiatives thrive on the basis of a deliberate policy consensus. Moreover, they often reflect a mix of public and private elements, with governments retaining the possibility of intervention at any time. Voluntary initiatives can thus thrive only as long as governments enable them to do so, either by way of tacit tolerance or through more explicit supportive measures. In the case of the Global Compact, governments are intimately involved, both by providing policy space for the initiative within the intergovernmental framework of the UN and by offering funding and other measures of direct support. The Global Compact, like many other national voluntary initia-

---

6 See www.ilo.org.

tives, is thus in essence a mix of public and private authority for which legitimacy is neither mandated nor assured. Governments hold the key. They enable the initiative, but they can also withdraw support and thus instantly bring the experiment to an end, or at least alter its orientation.

The Global Compact has a peculiar and ambiguous design. It promotes voluntarism but is backed by governments and the universal legitimacy of its principles. It is complementary to existing normative frameworks but does not focus not on legal interpretations: it seeks to find practical ways of advancing human rights, social and environmental priorities. From its inception, it was clear that the idea of underpinning global markets with universal principles would require substantial experimentation. No simple answer existed on *how* the Global Compact could significantly contribute to 'making globalisation work for all of humanity'.

25.3 The space for innovation at the United Nations

The United Nations is a bureaucratic and hierarchical organisation. Its board consists of 191 diverse member-states. The operational infrastructure of the UN was designed in 1945, in close resemblance to the administrative bureaucracies of colonial powers. It was thus designed to put a premium on compliance, with cumbersome reporting mechanisms and budgetary rules, while providing little incentive for efficiency and real-world changes. Successive waves of reform have tried to change the nature of the organisation, but the UN remains above all a hierarchical bureaucracy, poorly equipped to provide facilitation and support for new initiatives. The main function of the Secretariat is to implement the decisions, resolutions and agreements of its board members, who exercise strict oversight and who struggle with one another, perpetually seeking more control and political advantages, real or perceived.

The UN is hardly a habitat of innovation, yet the story of the early days of the Global Compact is one of utilising the absolute institutional advantages of the organisation—its international legitimacy, moral authority and tremendous convening power—while avoiding the downsides of the bureaucracy. As an institutional experiment in network-building it challenged the hierarchical boundaries of the UN and provoked suspicion from governments. Clearly, the experiment survived this political gauntlet only because it was an initiative of the UN Secretary-General. His personal involvement and authority as chief administrator of the UN shielded the Global Compact from the rigidities of the bureaucracy and the political suspicions of many governments.

Nevertheless, building the infrastructure for the Global Compact's operations within the UN still proved very challenging. The creation of the Global Compact Office and its influence within the UN system was contested both from within the organisation and by governments, which felt that the Global Compact was not sanctioned sufficiently. The Global Compact managed to overcome these obstacles and to locate its operations in the executive office of the Secretary-General by forming an effective interagency network, involving five UN agencies (see below).

Important lessons were learned in those days, and the quest for institutional renewal was never free of surprise.

At the interagency level, the early days of the Global Compact brought together the the the Office of the High Commissioner for Human Rights (OHCHR), the International Labour Organisation (ILO), the United Nations Environment Programme (UNEP) and the United Nations Development Programme (UNDP). Later, the United Nations Industrial Development Organisation (UNIDO) would join as a 'core agency', and many other UN organisations would be affiliated on an ad hoc basis. The experience of this early formative period produced the following two insights.

First, collaboration among and between different UN agencies cannot simply be mandated but rather must be motivated by shared incentives. The notion of mandated co-ordination has lost significance, as hierarchical order in itself is insufficient in a world where legitimacy must increasingly be earned. In the case of the Global Compact all involved agencies had something to gain. By bringing three dimensions together—human rights, labour and the environment—the sum was much greater than its individual parts. For the ILO, the inclusion of environmental issues and the ability to work directly with companies, as opposed to working with business associations, was an important value addition. For the OHCHR, the learning curve was particularly steep, as UNEP and the ILO shared substantial practical experience on how best to engage business. Additionally, UNDP offered the unique advantage of having comprehensive field-level representation with operational capacities to bring the Global Compact local. Last, for UNEP, the inclusion of social issues was much welcomed, as broader trends have long signalled the need to go beyond the strictly environmental realm when dealing with business.

The second major insight was that tensions within the interagency setting were healthy, spurring a constant search for compromise and improvement. One of the most sensitive issues between the agencies has been the struggle of assigning relative importance to values and principles, on the one hand, and to projects and concrete actions on the other. The struggle in setting priorities—tools and training material for implementing the principles versus efforts to initiate and carry out projects for development—has been a theme of many discussions, leading to sophisticated interpretations of an idealised sequence of good corporate citizenship: commitment to the principles must precede the involvement of partnership projects on the ground.

The collaborative experience also confirmed that, in the end, it is individual people who matter and that UN agencies have a tremendous pool of highly motivated and skilled individuals who are eager to give their best provided they have the opportunity to do so. The core team, Hans Hofmeijer and Michael Urminsky of the ILO, Scott Jerbi of the OHCHR, Jacqueline Aloisi de Larderel and Cornis van der Lugt of UNEP, and Sirkka Korpela and Casper Sonesen of UNDP, have often acted for the Global Compact out of their own conviction and motivation. They have become change agents in their own right within their respective organisations, influencing institutional change in many ways.

A similar experience occurred with many other UN agencies. Several large interagency meetings organised by the Global Compact Office showed that a huge reservoir of mostly young professionals was eager to embrace new methods of work and to experiment with new approaches. The innovative potential of young professionals is impressive and often it is they who drive forward institutional change from the bottom up. Empowering these people, freeing them from unnecessary bureaucratic control and giving them more recognition would surely be the most effective way of renewing the UN from within.

Another key aspect in the formation of the Global Compact was the role of the UN's member-states. Several ambassadors to the UN, from countries such as the United Kingdom, Switzerland, Sweden, Norway and Germany, have offered practical support from the very moment Kofi Annan delivered the speech at the World Economic Forum. Many of them took a very personal interest in the idea and saw in the Global Compact a way of bringing important issues back to the UN and contributing to a rapprochement between business and society in an era of antagonism. These governments would also provide financial support to the Global Compact Office.

In contrast, representatives of developing countries were initially suspicious that the Global Compact would constitute a disguised form of protectionism whereby social conditions would be introduced 'through the back door' into the realm of economic transactions. The ill-conceived effort by former President Clinton at the Seattle WTO meeting in November 1999 to include the social clause in multilateral trade negotiations fuelled such suspicions. In response, the Group of 77, the political platform of developing countries at the UN, called for an intergovernmental oversight of the Global Compact in their Ministerial Declaration of 2000. It took major efforts by European governments to avoid institutionalisation by negotiating a General Assembly resolution, titled 'Towards Global Partnership',[7] in which a mandate for the Secretariat to continue working on the Global Compact was secured.

At the same time, the Global Compact Office undertook major outreach efforts in key developing countries, and business executives in China, India, Brazil, South Africa and many other countries welcomed the initiative as a non-threatening framework for modernising and linking to the global economy. As this occurred, political suspicion was gradually replaced with cautious support. Indeed, it has been one of the greatest privileges so far to witness the readiness of business leaders from developing countries to embrace human rights, labour and environmental priorities, even in situations where their respective governments viewed these issues as Western impositions and, consequently, treated them as political bargaining chips. The motives of business people are straightforward. Coming to grips with these issues is the key to climbing the ladder of value addition as a supplier to large companies or as an exporter to major consumer markets. In addition, as competition for foreign direct investment has intensified, politicians have increasingly discovered that social and environmental issues also factor in to location advantages influencing the decision-making of potential investors.

The drive to convince governments of developing countries that the Global Compact is not about imposing social or environmental conditionalities through their business community was one of the most important developments during

7   GA Resolution A/56/L.33; GA Report A/58/277.

the early days of the Global Compact. It has also made the Global Compact a truly global initiative and broadened the range of needs of its participants. The demand for basic information in many different languages, the desire to foster more business-friendly environments through dialogue and the call for local networks to cultivate inter-organisational learning have significantly shaped the nature of the initiative. Today, more than 50% of over 1,000 participants are from developing countries, and more than half of the functioning Global Compact local networks are located in the developing world.

Despite its widespread acceptance and the fact that the Global Compact has overcome some of the suspicion that typically accompanied previous efforts to elevate social issues in economic transborder activities, important underlying issues remain unresolved. The politicisation of the social clause and of environmental issues as a convenient protectionist tool for short-sighted politicians, or as a tool to divide the world along cultural fault lines, may resurface in the future and threaten the viability of the Global Compact.

To avoid situations in which these issues fall victim to political arguments—such as the 'race to the bottom' or the 'imposition of Western values'—the Global Compact Office has shared with developing countries' representatives the idea of differentiated responsibilities, as developed by trade economist Jagdish Bhagwati (1998). According to this notion, companies from high-standard countries should behave abroad as they do at home. Differentiating responsibility according to capability would ensure that high standards are not watered down and that low levels of development are not penalised. It would help solve the problem that higher standards imposed on domestic companies in developing countries could unintentionally punish the poor, denying them comparative advantages and thus the opportunity to improve their conditions.

25.4 What will the future bring?

The Global Compact has grown rapidly. Mechanisms of engagement have been designed and are today fairly robust. Learning, dialogue and projects are delivering results, and the idea of the Global Compact continues to spread around the globe. However, it remains far from certain whether the initiative will continue to evolve towards making the principles of the Global Compact an integral part of business activities everywhere. Factors both internal to the initiative and factors related to the environment within which the Global Compact functions pose many uncertainties. Will the UN continue to provide the space for innovation that the Global Compact requires to grow, or will control reflexes of the bureaucracy suffocate the initiative and hinder the creation and maintenance of horizontal networks? Will business turn away from the Global Compact or continue to invest time and effort into the idea of a global framework for good corporate citizenship? Will civil society and labour continue to support co-operation, or will they give in to outside pressure and walk away? Will the global economy turn unilateral and thus render the Global Compact, which can make a contribution only in a world that is open and interconnected, completely meaningless, or will governments step in and change the very nature of the initiative?

The Global Compact's relation to global rule-making, and its dependence on the global economic and political milieu, expose it in a direct manner to broader developments, which so far have provided ever greater momentum to the initiative. The debacle at Seattle brought home the message that liberalisation and social issues cannot be separated, revealing the vulnerability of the current system and the exposure of global production systems to public perceptions. Additionally, the corporate scandals in the US have highlighted the importance of a principle-based approach as a necessary complement to regulation—that is, if trust and confidence are to be restored. Finally, terrorist attacks and unilateral military intervention have reminded the commercial world that the construct of an open economy can easily be dismantled and that renewed efforts of dialogue and co-operation are important to safeguard multilateralism.

But, even if external factors continue to favour the evolution of the Global Compact, if participants remain engaged in a co-operative manner and if the UN continues to provide the space for innovation, there are open questions concerning the ultimate shape of the initiative. The scope of possible scenarios for the Global Compact's future is indeed considerable. Several broad directions can already be identified:

● Diffusion and internalisation of the principles. Given that there are by some estimates over 60,000 transnational companies, outreach could become a perpetual challenge. Equally daunting is the challenge to improve the process by which companies make the principles part of their strategy and operations. The demand for tools, benchmarks, information exchange and other microeconomic support measures is endless, and, despite a successful strategy of convergence by which other competent organisations embrace the Global Compact, a focus on micro issues could become an all-absorbing undertaking.

● Collaborative solution-finding. The goal of making the global economy more stable and inclusive cannot be attained by the diffusion and internalisation of the principles alone. However, business, as an integral part of society, can tackle challenges if other stakeholders (e.g. labour, civil society and, above all, governments) are willing to work alongside. Collaborative solution-finding may prove an effective approach to bring about positive change, and the Global Compact could in the future scale up and further develop dialogue functions involving multiple stakeholder groups.

● Global and local governance issues. The goal of making the global economy more inclusive will be attained only if the conditions under which companies operating in the developing world improve. At the global level, this would mean working towards more favourable trade and investment conditions and, at the local level, it would mean tackling the structural deficiencies that hinder business growth, such as corruption, weak institutions and public health crises. Developing a more effective method of improving government governance both at the global level and at the local level would require very different approaches, as developed under the above scenarios.

● Business and society issues in North and South. Priorities vary greatly. In rich countries there is a premium on contributing to a more beneficial relationship between business and society by way of dialogue and the latest 'fads' of the corporate social responsibility debates. Conversely, in many developing countries, inadequate incentives for business operations, weak government institutions and broader societal needs are the overriding issues. Striking the right balance in responding to different needs will become increasingly challenging as the number of participants in the Global Compact continues to grow.

These are just some of the possible substantive orientations that could shape the nature of the initiative in the future. They are not exhaustive, nor are they mutually exclusive. However, clearly, the Global Compact will need to choose and focus on what is achievable. As a pragmatic response to government governance failures, the Global Compact has from its inception embraced the dual goal of promoting the principles at the micro level and building credibility for engagement while recognising that significant improvements towards market inclusion can be attained only through broad-based collaborative efforts. Given that the Global Compact fills government voids, and given that governments continue to hold the key to success, it is probably appropriate now to demand that they 'open the doors' and become a greater part of the collective solution.

26
Vision *and* action
The possibilities of action research

Gill Coleman
University of Bath, UK

The Global Compact has a bold vision: to bring a human face to global capitalism by combining the energies and resources of business, civil society and governments to address major social and environmental problems. Beneath this sweeping vision lies a tangle of difficult detail, requiring real behavioural change on the part of long-established institutions and therefore on the part of individuals. Realisation of the hope embodied in the Global Compact rests on the development of new *practices*, not just new intentions and new policies, and, as most readers of this chapter will know, closing the gap between 'espoused theories' and 'theories in use' (Argyris and Schön 1974) is one of the major puzzles of organisational, as well as personal, life. This is essentially a question of learning to do things differently.

Here sits an opportunity: the Global Compact could opt not only for a bold vision and the establishment of innovative boundary-crossing partnerships but also to seek to underpin these aspirations with a growing body of grounded knowledge generated through an appropriately iconoclastic research approach: that of **action research.**

The Global Compact Office has established a Learning Forum, the goal of which is

> to establish a rich and useful repository of both corporate practice and fundamental research, a platform of knowledge that integrates the views of all relevant stakeholders, while simultaneously increasing the transparency of companies' activities (www.unglobalcompact. org).

Clearly, this is a step in the right direction: activities surrounding the Global Compact currently involve a great deal of experimentation—the 'blueprint' for what it is to be a Global Compact member is not yet clear, and, as the vision intended, organisations in different parts of the world and with different goals and cultures are finding their own ways of working with the principles. Somehow to 'capture' what is going on is therefore worthwhile: it will be helpful to those whose efforts are being recognised, helpful to those who want to know how to get involved and where to start and helpful to those who are watching to see how serious an endeavour the Global Compact might turn out to be.

However, there are some significant methodological and practical difficulties involved in 'transmitting' knowledge—whether in the form of company practices or in the form of more formal academic research. First, let us look at the case of company practices: the concept of 'best practice' case studies is in itself problematic. Passing on good ideas and lessons learned may stimulate ideas on the part of those who read the case studies, but in order to be *useful*—in order to transmit from one set of practitioners to another enough information for them to be able to use a case study as some sort of guide to their own actions—it has to contain a lot of detail, usually of the sort that no one wants published in a case study. Let me give a very simple analogy: if you tell me that you have devised a successful way to persuade your teenage daughter to do her homework, I may be impressed. You tell me that you stopped routine allowances for your daughter and instituted a system of financial incentives attached to homework completion and, after a bumpy transition, it seems to have worked. I may think this is an interesting strategy, *but* . . . in my case it won't work because: my daughter does not spend her allowances, I cannot afford to give her any rewards, I don't approve of bribery, I think it would damage my long-term relationship with my child, etc., etc. In addition, I may think: 'what do you really mean by "bumpy transition"? *How* "bumpy"? What was actually said? And how good is the homework that comes out of this exercise in any case?' The point is, in order for me to really take something useful *for me* from your example, I need to know a lot of the 'fine footwork' of what went on; you need to be really honest with me about the difficulties you were facing (you may not have wanted to tell me that she was about to be excluded from her maths class for non-completion of homework) and why you decided on this particular solution, and I need to be able to quiz you about the similarities and differences between this and my own situation. In other words, we need to have a serious conversation. (In addition, I probably need to be able to come back to you two weeks later to ask you whether your daughter ever tore up her homework book and threw it at you, and, if so, what you did to recover the situation.)

Case studies are not, on the whole, able to give this sort of learning opportunity. What ends up in a 'good practice' case study is an edited construct, a representation of actual events that for all sorts of understandable reasons does not, and will not, contain the 'full' story. Furthermore, probably no one in the company concerned *knows* the full story, because there will have been no collective process of compiling it: all the various actors in the drama will know their own piece and have their own understanding of what has transpired. The 'story' will have been edited at every stage of its construction, both inside the organisation (what the health, safety and environment people will and will not tell the public relations people) and outside. I am not suggesting that this is a deliberate process of presentation management (thought it sometimes may be) but I am suggesting that there is a necessary process of editing and abstraction because of the way in which this 'knowledge' is gathered: it is removed from those who have done things, it is selectively understood by those who compose the case study and it is presented as fact to an unknown external audience. So how *useful* is the version that emerges? In what way does it, or can it, lead to the development of new practice?

The second platform of knowledge is 'fundamental research' generated by the academic network convened around the Global Compact; but here, too, there are problems in relation to the idea of useful knowledge. Universities have well-established ways of judging the quality of research, through peer review processes linked to publication in major journals. Applicability, or practical use, is not one of the criteria of good research, except insofar as something shown to be true in a number of cases is held to be generally true and so applicable at the general level. But the sort of detailed, usable knowledge that manager A needs in company X to help her or him try something that has not been done before is unlikely to be found in academic journals—which may say something about the low regard in which such publications are usually held by business people. The issue of how the 'knowledge' is to leap off the printed page and into people's everyday practice is not one that academia, on the whole, gives much consideration to. In addition, there are now considered to be a number of theoretical difficulties attached to the understanding, representation and transmission of qualitative research (Denzin and Lincoln 1994) which suggest that modelling this work on an objective scientific method is no longer feasible or desirable. It is always, they suggest, relevant to ask *whose* knowledge is being transmitted, by whom and through what interpretative lens?

Action research offers a way of responding to these challenges. It is a cluster of practices that together constitute a general approach to research, rather than a particular method (Greenwood and Levin 1998). It differs from conventional research in that 'it has different purposes, it is based in different relationships and has different ways of conceiving knowledge and its relation to practice' (Reason and Bradbury 2001: 1).

Action research draws on a wide range of intellectual roots, including the social experiments of Kurt Lewin in the 1940s, the work of the UK Tavistock Institute on practices of social democracy and organisational change, the contemporary postmodern critique of disembodied knowledge and the 'view from the top' and work by educationists and development workers such as Freire (1972), Tandon (1997) and Fals Borda (2001) with community-based groups in the South whose voices are routinely muted by the dominating practices of the North.

The particular features of action research that are relevant for the Global Compact are:

- It is concerned with *practical* knowledge, which is useful to those who are the subjects of the research. It seeks validity through practical outcomes (Reason and Bradbury 2001).

- It is concerned *both* with the generation of knowledge *and* with the development of practice: contrary to conventional research that seeks to leave a research site without 'affecting' those who have been research subjects, action research is concerned with ideas of development, improvement and continuous learning—and formulates the research *process* as developmental in its own right.

- It is collaborative. Action research rejects the idea of 'research on' self-determining human subjects and seeks instead to create processes of shared meaning-making. For this reason, it is concerned with the richness of detail, multiple interpretations and minority viewpoints rather than with the sweep of generalisation. Action research holds the voicing of experience as a value in its own right and attempts not to give this power away to the professional researcher.

- It involves a reflective process. Action research is usually conducted over a period of time through cycles of action and reflection in which those engaged in the action carry out disciplined reflection, with others, in order to make sense of what they have been doing and to compare their experience with others. This is can be a powerful developmental process, both for the persons concerned and for their organisation—as reflection is a key part of any learning process. As the organisational theorist Karl Weick says: 'How do I know what I think until I hear what I say?' (1995: 61). In particular, reflective processes allow individuals and groups to notice, and to work on, the gap between intention and action that is so often at the core of efforts to improve organisational functioning.

So, if the Global Compact is concerned both with vision and with action, action research offers an approach that can help in a way that simply 'capturing' knowledge cannot. This means rethinking the role of research in meeting the goals of the Global Compact and will no doubt meet some resistance inside the academic mainstream. But the Global Compact exists to innovate and create a model for leadership in bringing social justice and sustainability into the concerns of corporations, so why not embrace this opportunity?

27
The future

Malcolm McIntosh
Independent Commentator

Sandra Waddock
Boston College, USA

Georg Kell
UN Global Compact

27.1 The grand global social vision

For those of us who believe in the UN Global Compact process it is necessary to remind the world, and ourselves, how we have this faith. This is why we have reprinted in this book both the UN Secretary-General's launch at the World Economic Forum's meeting in Davos on 31 January 1999 (Chapter 1) and John Ruggie's article on learning networks from *The Journal of Corporate Citizenship* in spring 2002 (Chapter 2). We should also heed the UN Secretary-General's words in the Foreword to this book that change cannot happen without leadership and, just as important, that 'behind every leader there are agents of change'. Some of these leaders and agents of change are represented in this book.

There will be some people who, on reading the disparate collection of chapters in this book, leap to point out the ambiguities, confusions and problems associated with this great new thing that is the Global Compact. But that is the strength of the Global Compact: its ability to bring together people from varying backgrounds, disciplines and life experiences to talk about the way forward—a way forward for which there is no existing roadmap. Readers may note that some of the criticism of the Global Compact outlined in this book, some of which is strident, concerns issues of inclusion and exclusion in the development of the form, content and processes of the Global Compact itself. The very structure of the

Global Compact as a network and its orientation toward learning among voluntary participants make it both new and unique.

This is why after just four years of the Global Compact's life it is important to document what is being learned—and how. The Global Compact is at a turning point: we have learned much, so much that perhaps we have not had time to digest it.

First, there is no doubt that crucial to its launch and its success has been the personal leadership shown by the UN Secretary-General, Kofi Annan. His vision and mission to provide bridges between states, corporations and civil society will be one of the legacies of his time in office. Annan's leadership is complemented by the leadership of those progressive companies (and other organisations) that stepped forward to join the Global Compact and make their human and labour rights and environmental practices subject to public scrutiny.

Second, the title of this book was chosen to indicate that this initiative will require new skills that will transform the way in which we relate to the world. Waddell puts it most succinctly in the final paragraph of his chapter (Chapter 20, page 301): 'The change that the Global Compact implicitly aims to achieve is very profound. A global society that integrates the principles will look very different from the one that we have today.'

Among those holding the view that the Global Compact is enormously helpful in helping focus on some essential principles for the corporate responsibility movement generally is Claude Fussler (Chapter 19, page 276): 'In the early discussions around corporate social responsibility business quickly came to the conclusion that "one size cannot fit all". But it must also accept that it is not "do as you please".' Jim Baker, not without strong criticism on the Global Compact's form and process, is nonetheless overall similarly supportive (Chapter 10, page 182):

> The Global Compact is not a 'magic bullet' that can cure the ills of the world. However, dialogue . . . is a process that is indispensable if globalisation is to better serve the interests of the people. And it can and must be used by the global social actors to move the world forward.

27.2 Weaving a tapestry

So how does the Global Compact fit in with the grand scheme of things? In 2003 some 62 countries were considered to be democracies. Is this state of evolution 'the end of history', the 'triumph of liberal democracy' around the world or is it simply one more piece in a long-term and ongoing development of global social democracy with all that this grand vision encompasses? According to UN Secretary-General Kofi Annan, speaking at the World Economic Forum in January 1999 (Chapter 1, page 29):

> Our challenge today is to devise a similar compact on the global scale, to underpin the new global economy. If we succeed in that, we would lay the foundation for an age of global prosperity, comparable to that enjoyed by the industrialised countries in the decades after the Second World War

In 1835 Alexis de Tocqueville, having visited the USA, declared that 'a great democratic revolution is going on among us'. It was, he said, 'an irresistible revolution'. Almost 170 years later, in a world comprised of democracies and dictatorships, with all manner of governance structures in between, it is less clear whether the progress that the fundamental principles of the Global Compact represent are equally 'irresistible'.

Just as business tends towards monopoly, so even the best of democratic societies tend towards cliques and established interest groups, with a balance between the institutions of participation, the rule of law and individual and collective human rights; they have an open and freely participative process and a balance of power among the judiciary, the legislature and the executive. Learning how to participate, building democratic institutions and establishing civil, political and economic rights takes time, patience, forbearance and mistakes, as well as successes. That these processes take time is as true for companies, non-governmental organisations (NGOs) and other social actors as it is for governments. None of these actors by itself can establish freedom, justice and compassion. The holding of fair elections does not make a democracy; it is only a beginning. The construction of a university does not in itself create academic learning. The liberalisation of markets does not establish a good society; it must be accompanied by good laws. Just so, this compact between the UN and business is just the beginning of what is necessarily a long-term process.

The Global Compact is but one strand in the tapestry that is being woven in the expansion of the grand social vision—the global human experiment. It is derivative in that it cannot be understood in its own right, but only by reference to agreements, conventions and declarations of the nations of the world through the UN. It is a mechanism by which the UN Secretary-General can advance human rights, labour standards and environmental protection with the willing co-operation of businesses. The human rights elements of the Global Compact apply to business, but are essentially inviolable; the labour standards have been negotiated and are subject to general agreement among states, labour organisations and employers; and the environmental protection principles of the Global Compact are aspirations, neither rights nor agreed standards. Like many a corporate mission statement, the Global Compact contains mixed messages of determinism, operating practice and aspiration.

The Global Compact will prove its worth only through good actions that are seen to have happened because of it, and such actions can be observed in many ways. First, they can be seen through the Global Compact's power to convene meetings, to bring protagonists and antagonists together and generally to raise the level of global conversation around its principles. Second, they can be seen through its ability to build new social partnerships that help to bring about the Millennium Development Goals. Third, they can be seen through its ability to put pressure on companies and other actors in society to improve their social and environmental performance. Fourth, they can be seen through its capacity to provide forums in which the 'undiscussable' can be discussed: human and labour rights in business, as well as issues of sustainability.

27.3 Globalisation and freedom

According to the World Economic Forum and Gallup International, at the start of 2004 most people in the world felt 'less safe now than before and as individuals they [felt they had] little or no impact on the economic, social and political factors that affect their lives'.[1] Some 43,000 people in 51 countries were interviewed, which the organisers claimed represented the feelings of 1.1 billion people, or just over a sixth of the world population.

The cause of these insecurities is most likely to be that a growing sense of interdependence, by which we mean an understanding of a shared planetary home, coupled with a sense of uncertainty over issues such as global warming, food safety and terrorism, has left many people fearful and uncertain. The increase in global trade, the heart of the globalisation process, has put 10,000 items on the shelves of supermarkets for two-thirds of the world, and little for the remaining third, but also has left many individuals anxious to know 'who is in charge'. In the absence of certainty and equity, many people have turned to 'isms' that provide more surety about one's perspective—creating the potential of an 'us against them' world

The Global Compact is designed to stimulate debate about the way forward, because, according to John Ruggie, an architect of the Global Compact (Chapter 2, page 35), at present we have 'an imbalance in global rule-making' that favours the global market. The idea of initiatives such as the Global Compact is to 'promote equally valid social objectives, be they poverty reduction, labour standards, human rights or environmental quality [which] lag behind and in some instances have actually become weaker' (page 35). These issues, he argues, have produced a global identity crisis in which people are asking: 'Who is in control of the unpredictable forces that can bring on economic instability and social dislocation, sometimes at lightning speed?' (page 35).

For Ruggie the emphasis on free markets created this situation and, as a result, businesses must now help it deliver its promise not just to the privileged few but to the whole of humanity and to the planet. So, as Waddock says (Chapter 14, page 230), the aspirational nature of the principles of the Global Compact is important in that the principles 'provide inspiration and meaning to companies attempting to define their places in a complex and changing world'.

Among the global issues that have increased fear and uncertainty in recent years are the AIDS pandemic, SARS, BSE, bird flu and the terrorist attacks on the USA on 9 September 2001. Each of these has been facilitated through the use of global communications technology, whether that be through global supply chains, ship and air traffic or telecommunications. So there is a very real connection to be made between increased consumerism, increased trade, the increased size of global corporations, global terrorist networks and the transmission of global disease. For most people, their experience of world trade is through the global ubiquity of brand-name products. These products and their corporate owners have deconstructed national boundaries and at the same time have established new connec-

---

1 'Voice of the People', www.weforum.org.

tions among people so that money, time and products flow endlessly round the world 24 hours a day, 7 days a week. The complex trading webs that now exist mirror the network of communications infrastructure. Along these routes travel ideas, innovations and cash, but also accompanying such movement is disease, bad karma, corruption and terrorists. Gore Vidal has pointed out that the terrorists that flew the Boeings into the World Trade Centre towers in New York on 11 September 2001 drove Fords to the airport, were educated at the best universities and paid for their tickets with American Express. It is also worth remembering that in the 15th century the bubonic plague travelled via the world's trade routes from port to port, city to city. Rats, like the tourists of today, 'jumped ship' and travelled the world.

For all these reasons, as Waddell says in Chapter 20 (page 301), it is important for the Global Compact to have 'a good understanding of "the system" that it is trying to organise, the relationships between stakeholders in the system and their core competences with respect to the principles'. He goes on to say that without such an understanding the Global Compact will become 'overwhelmed by the scale of its challenge' (page 301). With just some half a dozen full-time staff in the Global Compact Office in New York, development of a systemic understanding of network interrelationships will be of critical importance. This is the task of the Global Compact Research Network[2]—to map the systems that are the Global Compact as well as the linkages that the Global Compact makes between companies and other institutions in the multiple national contexts of the planet. This difficult task will require a new language and new analytical tools that cross cultural contexts and system levels because, as we pointed out in the introduction to this book, the complexity of many global systems means that they cannot be completely understood at any one level of representation, so that neither a totally holistic nor a totally reductionist approach to modelling will suffice. We need a model that will describe systems over a range of levels of complexity (McIntosh *et al.*, Introduction, page 21).

People have an intuitive understanding of complex systems, but at the moment they do not trust the forces of nationalism, tribalism, religiosity and markets that play around them. It is going to be difficult to move beyond the current paradigm with its political and managerialist view of the world to embrace the complexity of global systems at different levels, but it is exactly this shift of perspective that the Global Compact is taking on.

For Waddell (Chapter 20, page 298), this means:

> vertical system integration, from every local shopfloor employee up to the top of the corporation, from all citizens, from intergovernmental agencies and from individual members up to international civil-society associations. It means horizontal system integration, including business, government and civil society and whole supply chains.

This necessarily requires commitment to change that may challenge the way we all see and interact with the world. It means being able to show humility and to be

---

2 For more information on the UN Global Compact Research Network, see www.unglobalcompact.org.

convivial when confronted with issues of equity and integrity in relation the distribution of wealth and resources.

27.4 Telling stories

The learning in the title of this book connects the idea of the infancy of the Global Compact with the idea of human infancy. However, we could just as easily refer to the idea of unlearning in that a whole collection of actors need to find new ways of conversing, which inevitably requires reflection about and unlearning of old ways. The title is also intended to imply a social element: that there is uncertainty about how, when and where we are to converse, not to mention about what! If there is one common message from all the chapters in this book it is that there is a need to increase the conversation about human rights, labour standards and environmental principles, especially within businesses, where such issues have previously been largely 'off the table'. The Global Compact is fundamentally a way for individuals in large and small businesses, NGOs, governments, labour unions and social activist organisations to find common ground and common meaning about enterprise in today's world. Many people want to use brand-name products and will spend hours working to purchase these items, but they are less keen to discuss the ingredients of those products and the resource acquisition and waste disposal issues that arise from their consumption, not to mention how they were produced, where and by whom. This comparative silence is a paradox in a world of mobile cellular telephones and Internet connectivity, where local and global 'chatter' has increased exponentially over the past ten years and will continue to do so for the foreseeable future

As discussed in Chapter 22, it is not only business and member-states that need to engage in learning but also the United Nations and its agencies. As anyone who has tried to change society knows, the greatest conservatism is often from within one's own peer group. From inside the UN, Kell notes that (Chapter 25, page 361):

> The UN is hardly a habitat of innovation, yet the story of the early days of the Global Compact is one of utilising the absolute institutional advantages of the organisation—its international legitimacy, moral authority and tremendous convening power—while avoiding the downsides of the bureaucracy.

Kell notes the willingness of some businesses to engage with the principles. Perhaps this is exemplified by BT. Chris Tuppen, in Chapter 12 (page 196), explains that

> [BT was] involved in the Global Compact from the very beginning. It participated in the early meetings in New York that formulated the nine principles and felt comfortable from the start that there was a coherence between these principles and the foundations of the company's own management approach to social and environmental issues. It was essentially this coherence of ideology that led the company to 'sign up'.

Pfizer also exemplifies the strategic approach that business takes when it comes to engagement with the fundamentals of global governance. Nancy Nielsen (Chapter 16, page 251) points out that:

> Critics of the Global Compact may not understand the power of positive incentives. If the Global Compact had been a list of rules and regulations, Pfizer would not have joined. Although regulatory bodies are necessary for society to function, the Global Compact fills a crucial gap in fostering dialogue, best practice and public–private relationships.

27.5 Learning and more learning

Learning, learning and more learning are at the heart of the Global Compact, and no more so than in companies understanding the implications of the principles to which they are lending their support. As Leisinger said in Section 5.3.3.1, few companies had a clear idea of what would be involved in supporting the principles of the Global Compact. However, he also pointed out (Chapter 5, page 85), citing Avery (2000: 46): 'Good managers realize that it will be very difficult to be a world-class company with a second-class human rights record—and they act upon this.' How many such 'good managers' are there in companies? How many managers could, without benefit of the Global Compact's auspices, put issues of human rights, labour standards or ecological sustainability in front of their boards and top management teams? How many could make demands of their suppliers without the moral authority provided by the Global Compact's global consensus?

So, with this amount of learning deemed to be necessary and the level of change required it is not surprising that, as Donaldson says (Chapter 4, page 68):

> By announcing the Global Compact, Secretary-General Kofi Annan has set the world a tall, tall task. Indeed, the remarkable ambitiousness of the Compact project is matched only by the remarkable stakes it holds for all of us.

This book contains examples of constructive engagement with the Global Compact, including that of the Danish pharmaceutical company Novo Nordisk (Chapter 18) and the Australian City of Melbourne (Chapter 23). For Novo Nordisk the task is to understand better the company's relationship to the first two principles of the Global Compact. Accordingly, as the case study described in Chapter 18 shows, Novo Nordisk has tried to map the values of it first-tier suppliers through a lengthy process of consultation and engagement.

For the City of Melbourne the Global Compact Cities Programme, and the Melbourne Model, have been used to address what are apparently intractable social, environmental and economic urban problems and to deepen dialogue on the principles of the Global Compact.

The Global Compact requires changes at all levels. It forces all involved—individuals, governments, NGOs, civil-society organisations and all other stakeholders—to confront the idea that it is no longer possible to shift the blame to others, that all must now work together to address the issues.

Therefore, the Global Compact must both deepen our understanding of issue definition and the design processes that will lead to implementation (i.e. to making the Global Compact's principles reality, not just rhetoric). Not only is there a search for dialogue between states, corporations and civil society but also the Global Compact allows for a means whereby the UN can reinvent itself as a mature global body, linked to all of society's important institutions and providing an important values-based underpinning of standards of practice within those institutions. Learning is critical for all of us to grow as human beings, as well as for organisations and societies to prosper. In many ways, it is reflective practice, the unlearning of old ways of behaving, that will be most important as the principles become reality. As Gill Coleman says in the opening paragraph of her chapter (Chapter 26), this requires working between theory and practice. It requires institutional change and therefore change by the individuals who make up those institutions. Let us quote Mahatma Gandhi again:

> You must be the change you wish to see.

The next steps for companies that have adopted the Global Compact are:

- To comprehensively map their 'spheres of influence' as envisaged by Principle 1 of the Global Compact

- To further extend the promotion of human rights, labour standards and environmental protection upstream and downstream

- To encourage suppliers to extend the endorsement of the Global Compact principles with *their* suppliers

In the case of Novo Nordisk, Stube and McIntosh note (Chapter 18) that these next moves will pose an even greater challenge to companies than the first few steps, as companies' influence on upstream and downstream companies decreases as they move beyond the first tier.

At the end of 2002, the Global Compact discontinued the formal requirement that companies submit examples of how they have enacted the principles. The initiative now encourages companies to publish their progress in annual financial reports or in separate sustainability reports. Cases are also being developed by researchers, external to the company, although frequently supported by the company. The web portal will contain links to these documents in order to promote transparency and public accountability.[3]

---

3 See www.unglobalcompact.org.

27.6 A bright future?

Kell and Levin (Chapter 3, page 60) say that:

> Kofi Annan originally conceived of the Global Compact with the recognition that the world's poor will benefit from expanding market access, rather than social and environmental trade clauses that would subjugate them with de facto protectionism. The Global Compact strongly supports the strengthening of existing international social and environmental institutions and the creation of a global marketplace embedded in a framework of shared values. By no means does it promote the status quo or a particular ideology such as neo-liberalism.

In Section 3.3.2, Kell and Levin list some core questions facing the Global Compact, covering company motives for participating in the Global Compact, the confrontational response of some NGOs, the need for the UN to show flexibility and courage in its approach and the future path of globalisation.

One of the respondents to Novo Nordisk's enquiry into its suppliers, the owner of a small, family-owned, factory, commented (Chapter 18, page 272):

> 'This . . . is the future. Will we have regulations or fights? Will we have the old battles between capital and labour or will we have regulations that force companies to report on human rights, labour and environmental issues?' . . . a more comprehensive and context-ualised approach to supply chain management, and therefore relationships 'keeps stability in the supply chain'.

The same theme is echoed by Cornis van der Lugt (Chapter 8, page 145):

> If, ten years from now, we were to look back to the present day we would in all probability conclude that the greatest impact of the Global Compact has consisted in raising the profile of human rights, labour and environmental issues in core business operations.

Jim Post and Tanja Carroll (Chapter 21, page 317) are concerned that

> The evolution of ever-larger enterprises may lead to an age of institutional dinosaurs, great in size but lacking the mental faculties to survive a changing environment. The same can be said of governments and NGOs whose agendas are premised on immunity from the ecological, human rights and labour requirements that most of the world recognises. Global peace, security and harmony require more co-operation in all of those areas that affect human well-being.

It is also clear that the Global Compact's principles need to be applied not only to large-scale businesses, governments and NGOs but also to small and medium-sized enterprises (SMEs) of all sorts as well as to other organisations and stakeholders.

So, how can organisations manage this enlightened change process? The answer is: by bringing employees 'on board' so that they understand the external pressures on the company; by recruiting *i*ntrepreneurs; by listening to and managing employees' feelings and emotional responses to new ideas and change scenarios; by rewarding change; by making sure that it is understood that change is necessary and going to happen and that those who resist might like to reflect on their positions. Above all, there is a need to use the best attributes of a valued workforce (commitment, passion, values, intelligence, identity, pride) in the change process.

The level of change envisaged by the Global Compact requires commitment. Also, the unspoken overriding principles of the Global Compact are those of tolerance, of valuing diversity over fundamentalism, of democracy and participation and of respect for human dignity and the health of nature. Ultimately, the goal is to create a world where 'we' can co-exist securely, peacefully and sustainably rather than a world in which a multitude of 'thems' are fighting against a numerous number of 'us'.

The conditions of humanity improve as more people gain space to breathe, speak and live their lives. So it is that the Global Compact is one more attempt to humanise humanity, to move it beyond what is to what could be. It is a significant attempt at human betterment because it is an initiative of the current UN Secretary-General, Kofi Annan, who has put his reputation on the line in support of the principle that increased co-operation between the market, the state and civil society is a desirable result and will produce increased living standards for all humanity.

As Kofi Annan said at the World Economic Forum in Davos in January 2004, five years after the announcement of the Global Compact in the same place: 'Business has a powerful interest in helping to prevent the international security system from sliding back into brute competition based on the laws of the jungle.' There is a Zen saying: 'Before enlightenment, I chopped wood and carried water; after enlightenment, I chopped wood and carried water.' The Global Compact is so much about the simplicities of chopping wood, carrying water, cooking meals, bathing children, shopping in the supermarket, driving to work and coming home to bed. It is about co-existing, living and loving in a world where we value each other and where everyone has enough.

There are many who believe that we are at a turning point in history. It is argued that the ubiquity and democratisation of communications and transport technologies has led to a more open society where liberalism in varying guises is the established order. The very means by which we might set ourselves free are the same means by which the few wish to impose their tyranny on us all. We can be enslaved by products, by pornography and by blind fundamentalism. There are those who wish to oppress women, to re-establish hierarchy through the abuse of power and to negate the individual and collective freedoms that have been fought for during the history of humankind. As Jim Baker states (Chapter 10, page 171):

> The Global Compact must therefore build on its global dialogue function. That is its 'added value'. This is where it can be most effective. It should drive dialogue and be driven by it, and, dialogue, again, should not simply be defined as meetings that can be then mentioned in reports so that one can tick the right box on a list. It needs to be real dialogue, designed to achieve something.

Everywhere, companies want to extend their social influence; there is work to be done. The Global Compact has already stimulated a much-needed global dialogue and it has the potential to create more. It carries the seeds of success as well as failure. Its future is not assured, but it has promise.

As discussed in Chapter 22, in order to believe in a vision it is necessary to have faith and passion, even though these qualities sometimes seem out of place or out of fashion in the world today. The Global Compact needs to be seen to produce a better world, to lift our spirits and encourage us to believe that there is another way. That is the crucial element of aspiration: it gives hope for the future of us all.

The irony of the Global Compact is that its title seems to herald some agreement and solidity but its purpose is to generate debate and conversational engagement, in other words to normalise the conversation about human rights, labour and environment. The other irony of the Global Compact is that the conversations that it induces sometimes bring out rivalries and often lead people to try to deal with the metaphysical at the level of governance.

The ultimate task is to revisit ourselves while at the same time seeing real improvements in the living conditions of all people on the planet. This requires a better understanding of the global social and ecological systems that today bind us in a shared fate.

As we said in the introduction, the Global Compact is an historic experiment in learning and action on corporate citizenship. By promoting the idea that the corporation earns its licence to operate not only through its ability to remain profitable but also through its ability to engage in meaningful dialogue on human rights principles, labour standards and environmental protection, the Global Compact redefines the definition of corporate citizenship. For this to become a reality we need to see the world as a shared space. It is hoped that this book has contributed to the development of corporate responsibility through the vehicle of the Global Compact. However, we must remember that, as Gill Coleman writes, the Global Compact does indeed have a bold vision. Kell and Levin point out that although it provides added value by promoting global dialogue it does not replace regulations and governmental action.

The world must learn how to navigate the unclear boundaries between belief and bigotry, responsibility and accountability, interventions and interference. Players in the capitalist system—and that is all of us—need to agree on where competition ends and where collective conscience begins. We are all learning to talk.

Appendix A
The Millennium
Development Goals

The Millennium Development Goals are an ambitious agenda for reducing poverty and improving lives that world leaders agreed on at the Millennium Summit in September 2000. For each goal one or more targets have been set, most for 2015, using 1990 as a benchmark.

- Goal 1: Eradicate extreme poverty and hunger.
  - Target for 2015: halve the proportion of people living on less than US$1 a day and those who suffer from hunger.

- Goal 2: Achieve universal primary education.
  - Target for 2015: ensure that all boys and girls complete primary school.

- Goal 3: Promote gender equality, and empower women.
  - Target for 2005 (preferred target year): eliminate gender disparities in primary and secondary education.
  - Target for 2015: eliminate gender disparities at all levels.

- Goal 4: Reduce child mortality.
  - Target for 2015: reduce by two-thirds the mortality rate among children under five years old.

- Goal 5: Improve maternal health.
  - Target for 2015: reduce by three-quarters the rate of women dying in childbirth.

- Goal 6: combat HIV/AIDS, malaria and other diseases.
  - Target for 2015: halt and begin to reverse the spread of HIV/AIDS and the incidence of malaria and other major diseases.

● Goal 7: Ensure environmental sustainability.
  - Targets: integrate the principles of sustainable development into country policies and programmes and reverse the loss of environmental resources.
    • Target for 2015: reduce by half the proportion of people without access to safe drinking water.
    • Target for 2020: achieve significant improvement in the lives of at least 100 million slum dwellers.

● Goal 8: Develop a global partnership for development.
  - Targets:
    • Develop further an open trading and financial system that includes a commitment to good governance, development and poverty reduction—nationally and internationally.
    • Address the least-developed countries' special needs, and the special needs of land-locked and small island developing states.
    • Deal comprehensively with developing countries' debt problems.
    • Develop decent and productive work for youth.
    • In co-operation with pharmaceutical companies, provide access to affordable essential drugs in developing countries.
    • In co-operation with the private sector, make available the benefits of new technologies—especially information and communications technologies.

Further information

Website: www.developmentgoals.org
Source: www.undp.org/mdg
See also: C. Fussler, A. Cramer and S. van der Vegt, *Raising the Bar: Creating Value with the UN Global Compact* (Sheffield, UK: Greenleaf Publishing, 2004).

Appendix B
The Global Compact Advisory Council

The Advisory Council convenes for formal meetings twice a year.

B.1 Business representatives
Mr Robert Hormats, Vice Chairman, Goldman Sachs
Ms Barbara Krumsiek, President and CEO, Calvert
Dr Rolf-E. Breuer, CEO, Deutsche Bank AG
Sir Mark M. Moody-Stuart, retired CEO, Royal Dutch Shell
Ms Marjorie Scardino, CEO, Pearson plc
Mr N.R. Narayana Murthy, Chairman and CEO, Infosys Technologies Ltd
Mr Sam Jonah, Chief Executive, Ashanti Goldfields Company Ltd
Ms Namakau Kaingu, CEO, Kaingu Mines
Dr Wolfgang Sauer, retired CEO, VW of Brazil
Ms Marjorie Yang, Chairwoman, Esquel Group of Companies

B.2 Labour, civil society, academia
Mr Bill Jordan, General Secretary, International Confederation of Free Trade Unions
Mr Fred Higgs, General Secretary, International Federation of Chemical, Energy, Mine and
    General Workers' Unions
Ms Irene Khan, Secretary-General, Amnesty International
Ms Sophia Tickell, former Senior Policy Advisor, Oxfam
Mr Achim Steiner, Director General, The World Conservation Union
Ms Jessica Mathews, President, Carnegie Endowment for International Peace
Professor John Ruggie, Kennedy School of Government, Harvard University

B.3 Observers
Ambassador Jenö Staehelin of Switzerland
Ambassador Paul Heinbecker of Canada
Ambassador Kamalesh Sharma of India

Ambassador Gelson Fonseca of Brazil
Ambassador Dumisani Shadrack Kumalo of South Africa

Appendix C
Global Reporting Initiative indicators for progress on the UN Global Compact

Table C.1 lists a selection of core performance indicators from the 2002 Global Reporting Initiative (GRI) Sustainability Reporting Guidelines. This selection covers the original nine Global Compact principles.

It is not intended to form a comprehensive comparison. Table C.1 does not include, for example, some GRI disclosure elements found in the Guidelines under Report Content (Sections 1–3).

Code and category	GRI core indicator: report content
Human rights	
UN Global Compact Principle 1: Businesses should support and respect the protection of internationally proclaimed human rights within their sphere of influence.	
HR 1 Social Indicators: Human Rights *Strategy and Management*	Description of policies, guidelines, corporate structure and procedures to deal with all aspects of human rights relevant to operations, including monitoring mechanisms and results
HR 2 Social Indicators: Human Rights *Strategy and Management*	Evidence of consideration of human rights impacts as part of investment and procurement decisions, including selection of suppliers and contractors
HR 3 Social Indicators: Human Rights *Strategy and Management*	Description of policies and procedures to evaluate and address human rights performance within the supply chain and contractors, including monitoring systems and results of monitoring

Code and category	GRI core indicator: report content

Human rights (cont.)

HR 4 Social Indicators: Human Rights *Non-discrimination*	Description of global policy and procedures and programmes preventing all forms of discrimination in operations, including monitoring systems and results of monitoring

UN Global Compact Principle 2: Businesses should ensure that their own operations are not complicit in human rights abuses.

HR 2 Social Indicators: Human Rights *Strategy and Management*	Evidence of consideration of human rights impacts as part of investment and procurement decisions, including selection of suppliers and contractors
HR 3 Social Indicators: Human Rights *Strategy and Management*	Description of policies and procedures to evaluate and address human rights performance within the supply chain and contractors, including monitoring systems and results of monitoring

Labour

UN Global Compact Principle 3: Businesses should uphold the freedom of association and the effective recognition of the right to collective bargaining.

HR 5 Social Indicators: Human Rights *Freedom of Association and Collective Bargaining*	Description of freedom of association policy and extent to which this policy is universally applied independent of local laws, as well as description of procedures and programmes to address this issue
LA 3 Social Indicators: Labour Practices and Decent Work *Labour/Management Relations*	Percentage of employees represented by independent trade union organisations or other bona fide employee representatives broken down geographically or percentage of employees covered by collective bargaining agreements broken down by region or country
LA 4 Social Indicators: Labour Practices and Decent Work *Labour/Management Relations*	Policy and procedures involving information, consultation and negotiation with employees over changes in the reporting organisation's operations (e.g. restructuring)

UN Global Compact Principle 4: Businesses should uphold the elimination of all forms of forced and compulsory labour.

HR 7 Social Indicators: Human Rights *Forced and Compulsory Labour*	Description of policy to prevent forced and compulsory labour and extent to which this policy is visibly stated and applied as well as description of procedures and programmes to address these issues, including monitoring systems and results of monitoring

Code and category	*GRI core indicator: report content*

Labour (cont.)

UN Global Compact Principle 5: Businesses should uphold the effective abolition of child labour.

HR 6 Social Indicators: Human Rights *Child Labour*	Description of policy excluding child labour as defined by the ILO Convention 138 and extent to which this policy is visibly stated and applied, as well as description of procedures and programmes to address this issue, including monitoring systems and results of monitoring

UN Global Compact Principle 6: Businesses should eliminate discrimination in respect of employment and occupation.

HR 4 Social Indicators: Human Rights *Non-discrimination*	Description of global policy and procedures and programmes preventing all forms of discrimination in operations, including monitoring systems and results of monitoring
LA 10 Social Indicators: Labour Practices and Decent Work *Diversity and Opportunity*	Description of equal opportunity policies or programmes, as well as monitoring systems to ensure compliance and results of monitoring
LA 11 Social Indicators: Labour Practices and Decent Work *Diversity and Opportunity*	Composition of senior management and corporate governance bodies (including the board of directors), including female–male ratio and other indicators of diversity as culturally appropriate

Environment

UN Global Compact Principle 7: Businesses should support a precautionary approach to environmental challenges.

3.13 Governance Structure and Management Systems: Overarching Policies and Management Systems	Explanation of whether and how the precautionary approach or principle is addressed by the organisation

UN Global Compact Principle 8: Businesses should undertake initiatives to promote greater environmental responsibility.

EN 1 Environmental Indicators: Materials	Total materials use other than water, by type

Code and category	GRI core indicator: report content
Environment (cont.)	
EN 2 Environmental Indicators: Materials	Percentage of materials used that are waste (processed or unprocessed) from sources external to the reporting organisation
EN 3 Environmental Indicators: Energy	Direct energy use, segmented by primary source
EN 4 Environmental Indicators: Energy	Indirect energy use
EN 5 Environmental Indicators: Water	Total water use
EN 6 Environmental Indicators: Biodiversity	Location and size of land owned, leased or managed in biodiversity-rich habitats
EN 7 Environmental Indicators: Biodiversity	Description of the major impacts on biodiversity associated with activities and/or products and services in terrestrial, freshwaster and marine environments
EN 8 Environmental Indicators: Emissions, Effluent and Waste	Greenhouse gas emissions
EN 9 Environmental Indicators: Emissions, Effluent and Waste	Use and emissions of ozone-depleting substances
EN 10 Environmental Indicators: Emissions, Effluent and Waste	Nitrogen oxides (NO_x), sulphur oxides (SO_x) and other significant emissions to air, by type
EN 11 Environmental Indicators: Emissions, Effluent and Waste	Total amount of waste, by type and destination
EN 12 Environmental Indicators: Emissions, Effluent and Waste	Significant discharges to water, by type
EN 13 Environmental Indicators: Emissions, Effluent and Waste	Significant spills of chemicals, oils and fuels in terms of total number and total volume
EN 14 Environmental Indicators: Products and Services	Significant environmental impacts of principal products and services

Code and category	GRI core indicator: report content
Environment (cont.)	
EN 15 Environmental Indicators: Products and Services	Percentage of the weight of products sold that is reclaimable at the end of the products' useful life, and percentage that is actually reclaimed
EN 16 Environmental Indicators: Compliance	Incidents of and fines for non-compliance with all applicable international declarations, conventions and treaties and national, sub-national, regional and local regulations associated with environmental issues
1.1 Vision and Strategy	Statement of the organisation's vision and strategy regarding its contribution to sustainable development

UN Global Compact Principle 9: Businesses should encourage the development and diffusion of environmentally friendly technologies.

EN 17 Environmental Indicators: Energy (additional indicator)	Initiatives to use renewable energy sources and to increase energy efficiency

Source: C. Fussler, A. Cramer and S. van der Vegt, *Raising the Bar: Creating Value with the UN Global Compact* (Sheffield, UK: Greenleaf Publishing, 2004).

Appendix D
Results of the consultation process on the introduction of a principle against corruption

On 10 May 2004 the Global Compact Office in New York issued a statement announcing the results of the consultation process relating to the proposed introduction of a tenth principle on corruption. The statement is reproduced below.

Introduction

On 21 January 2004, UN Secretary-General Kofi Annan initiated a comprehensive, inclusive and transparent consultation process on the possible introduction of a tenth principle against corruption. A formal letter was sent to all participants (1,205, as of 31 December 2003), seeking their views. The Secretary-General stressed that the adoption of such a principle would only occur if there was broad-based support, and that such an addition would be exceptional in nature. The following wording was proposed:

> **Business should combat corruption in all its forms, including extortion and bribery.**

Throughout the consultation process, the Global Compact e-mail newsletter and website provided background information and informed participants about the status of the consultation. Local networks were also mobilised to seek input from their participants.

On 26–27 January 2004, a Policy Dialogue on Transparency and the Fight against Corruption was convened in Paris, France. This event provided the opportunity to discuss the introduction of a principle, addressed issues of both process and substance, and showcased existing initiatives and best practices related to the fight against corruption.

The consultation process concluded on 7 May 2004 (after the original deadline of 21 April was extended). This paper summarises the results of the process and outlines the next steps.

1. Quantitative results of the consultation process

By 7 May 2004, 563 responses had been received—a response rate of 47%. Almost all responses were signed by the chief executives of the companies or organisations consulted, indicating the high level of interest the issue received. Of the responses received, 536 supported the addition of the principle—approximately 95%. In addition, 21 responses included further qualifications. Six respondents opposed the inclusion of a tenth principle.

In addition, 252 new participants, which joined the Global Compact after 21 January, were consulted. None of these new signatories opposed the addition of a tenth principle.

2. Qualitative analysis of replies, by category

Positive responses

Many of the company responses included an in-depth description of the company's own activities in the fight against corruption and thoughtful arguments on the merits of adding the principle. In five countries, all participants supported the addition of the principle (France, Brazil, Nepal, Denmark and China).

Some of the main arguments offered in support of the principles were:

Corruption is bad for business

- Business should be conducted in an environment of fair competition; corruption is against the spirit of competition and meritocracy.

- Business efficiency relies on confidence between business partners; corruption undermines business confidence.

Corruption perpetuates poverty and causes suffering to millions of people

- Government and corporate corruption cost billions of dollars throughout the world that could have been used to improve the lives of countless people.

- Eradicating corruption will facilitate the cascading effect of global economies and contribute to the eradication of poverty.

- A principle against corruption can harness the problem-solving abilities of Global Compact participants to fight corruption.

A principle against corruption reinforces the existing nine principles and company policies

- The aspirational language of the proposed principle is a statement of policy that any company wishing to operate in an ethical manner would support. Such an important principle should be made explicit, rather than being inferred from the other nine principles.

- The other nine principles will be enhanced and facilitated by the corruption principle as corruption has the capacity to erode the gains from implementation of the other nine.

- The corruption principle will reinforce, and will be reinforced by the existing anti-corruption policies, programmes and initiatives of Global Compact participants.

A Global Compact principle will contribute to the broader social movement against corruption

- The corruption principle can lead to a process of awareness, consultations, national conferences and media campaigns to promote positive action.

- The Global Compact can become a neutral platform for governments, business and civil society to exchange and create practical solutions to corruption problems.

- A principle against corruption will provide a bridge between corporate performance and public government accountability.

Qualified responses

There were 21 qualified responses that supported the inclusion of the tenth principle under certain conditions. The key points raised were:

Business should not be singled out, all social actors have a role to play in the fight against corruption

- The tenth principle should not present corporations as solely responsible for the problem of corruption. The role of public institutions, including international organisations, should also be addressed. Likewise, the principle should recognise that global labour and NGOs also have a role to play in combating corruption.

- Participants should be expected to work against corruption 'within their sphere of influence'.

- The principle should express that it applies to both the supply and the demand side of corruption.

Consultation on the inclusion of a new principle must be comprehensive, inclusive and transparent

- Modifications to the Global Compact should only occur after a process has been established for future additions, requiring a certain quorum, perhaps a majority of no less than three-quarters of all participants. Changing the 'rules of the game' could threaten the credibility and solidity of the Compact, and the addition of a tenth principle must remain an absolute exception.

Implementation of a new principle should not undermine efforts to implement the other nine and should not create stringent reporting requirements

- The roll-out and implementation of the other nine principles must continue vigorously and efforts should not be focused only on the new principle. There is much work that remains to be done on the other nine.

- In the same vein, there is unease about the level of expectations on corporations regarding the inclusion of a tenth principle.

Negative responses

There were six responses opposing the inclusion of a tenth principle. The reasons given included:

The fight against corruption is within the realm of criminal law

- The issue of corruption needs to be addressed on a different level than the existing principles. The other nine are derived from international obligations of states and require voluntary co-operation from corporations. Corruption revolves mainly around criminal law and involves legal obligations of corporations.

Fear of a slippery slope to more principles

- Expanding the current nine principles would make the list open-ended and invite other modifications.

- The Global Compact must be viewed as a complete document—not as one that can be amended or modified on an ad hoc basis from time to time by signatories, either by consensus or by vote. Permitting signatories to withdraw if they do not agree with the amendment could be interpreted wrongly as an objection to the substance of the proposed amendment, even though that may not be the case.

A principle against corruption will weaken the other nine principles

- Adopting a principle, like the corruption principle, which cannot be measured, could jeopardise the existing, more easily measurable principles and potentially reduce expectations of their implementation.

- The focus should be on introducing appropriate tools to measure the existing nine principles and to define rules for excluding companies not living up to them, rather than on introducing a tenth principle.

- The fight against corruption is an important means to respect the other nine principles, but is not an end in itself. Anti-corruption could be listed as one the means to promote the nine principles.

- The corruption principle is not based on solid foundations like the ILO standards or UNEP principles, and the wording of the proposed principle eliminates the voluntarism enshrined in the Global Compact.

3. Wording of the principle

There were two main types of comments on the proposed wording of the principle. A large number of responses emphasised the need for the principle to explicitly limit business responsibility to their 'own sphere of influence'. However, the Global Compact Office wishes to stress that this qualification already underlies all existing principles, and would thus automatically apply to a tenth principle as well. The introduction to the Global Compact principles states that:

> The Global Compact asks companies and other civil society organisations to embrace, support and enact, *within their sphere of influence*, a set of core values . . . [emphasis added]

For a variety of reasons, many respondents also expressed discomfort with the phrase 'to combat corruption', which was part of the proposed language. Addressing these concerns, the following wording will be recommended to the Secretary-General:

> **Business should work against corruption in all its forms, including extortion and bribery.**

4. **Next steps**

Based on the results of the consultation process, the Global Compact Office will recommend to the Secretary-General that he formally introduce a principle against corruption at the upcoming Global Compact Leaders' Summit, which he will convene on 24 June 2004. The office will also recommend that the Secretary-General give public assurance that the addition of this principle is exceptional and that the concerns raised will be adequately addressed.

A further recommendation will be that the addition of the tenth principle should not require a new letter of commitment. Participants that do not agree with the principle should be given a period of one year to indicate their wish to withdraw from the Global Compact.

Following the summit, the Global Compact Office will initiate an inclusive process to develop a work programme and to clarify any remaining questions. In the interim, it is worthwhile recalling some of the recommendations made by participants of the first Policy Dialogue on Transparency and the Fight Against Corruption in January 2004. They included: training programmes, internal monitoring of results, and the need to share good examples of company policies. In addition, participants expressed interest in working with the UN towards the implementation of the UN Convention Against Corruption and other existing initiatives (such as the Integrity Pacts of Transparency International), and in developing sectoral initiatives. The local networks will have an important role to play in this work, for many aspects and impacts of corruption are specific to national and regional contexts.

Bibliography

Ackoff, R. (1974) *Redesigning the Future: A Systems Approach to Societal Problems* (New York: John Wiley).

Adams, D., and P. Gunsun (2002) 'Media Accused in Failed Coup: Venezuelan news executives defend themselves against allegations that they suppressed facts as the ousted president returned', *St Petersburg Times*, 18 April 2002, www.stpetersburgtimes.com/2002/04/18/Worldandnation/Media_accused_in_fail.shtml.

AI (Amnesty International) (1996) *Nigeria: Time to End Contempt for Human Rights* (London: AI).

—— (2000) 'Oil in Sudan', AI-Index AFR54/001/2000, www.web.amnesty.org/ai.nsf/index/AFR540012000, accessed June 2001.

—— (2003) *Human Rights on the Line: The Baku-Tbilisi-Ceyhan Pipeline Project* (London: AI).

—— (2004) *The UN Human Right Norms for Business: Towards Legal Accountability* (London: AI).

—— (various years) *Annual Report* (London: AI).

——/PWBLF (Prince of Wales Business Leaders Forum) (2000) *Human Rights: Is It Any of Your Business?* (London: AI/PWBLF).

AI DRC (Amnesty International, Democratic Republic of Congo) (2003) *'Our Brothers Who Help to Kill Us': Economic Exploitation and Human Rights Abuses in the East* (April 2003; AFR 62/010/2003; London: AI).

Andriof, J., and M. McIntosh (2001) 'Introduction', in J. Andriof and M. McIntosh (eds.), *Perspectives on Corporate Citizenship* (Sheffield, UK: Greenleaf Publishing): 13-24.

Annan, K. (1997) Address to the World Economic Forum, Davos, Switzerland, 31 January 1997.

—— (1998) 'Markets for a Better World', address to the World Economic Forum, Davos, Switzerland, 31 January 1998.

—— (1999a) Address to the Chamber of Commerce of the United States of America, Washington, DC, 8 June 1999.

—— (1999b) Message to the Workshop 'Today and Tomorrow: Outlook for Corporate Strategies', United Nations Economic Commission for Europe, Villa d'Este, Cernobbio, Italy, 3-5 September 1999.

—— (1999c) Address to Svenska Dagladet's Executive Club, Sweden, May 1999.

—— (1999d) 'The Global Compact', www.unglobalcompact.org.

—— (2000a) The Secretary-General's Address at the Business Day, WSSD, Johannesburg, 1 September 2002.

—— (2000b) 'Message to the Second International Symposium of the GRI', delivered by K. Töpfer, Executive Director, United Nations Environment Programme, Washington, DC, 13–15 November 2000.

—— (2000c) 'Opening Remarks at the High-level Meeting of the Global Compact', United Nations Headquarters, New York; published as Press Release SG/SM/7495, 'Secretary-General Welcomes International Corporate Leaders to Global Compact Meeting', 26 July 2000.

—— (2001a) 'Address to the World Economic Forum', Davos, Switzerland, 28 January 2001.

—— (2001b) 'Co-operation between the United Nations and All Relevant Partners, in Particular the Private Sector', Report of the Secretary-General to the General Assembly for its 56th Session, Agenda Item 39, 'Towards Global Partnerships', A/56/323*, 9 October 2001.

—— (2002) 'Address at Ceremony of Adherence to the Global Compact', Madrid, Spain, 9 April 2002.

—— (2004) Address to the World Economic Forum, Davos, January 2004.

Argyris, C., and D.A. Schön (1974) *Theory in Practice: Increasing Aprofessional Effectiveness* (San Francisco: Jossey Bass).

Avery, C.L. (2000) *Business and Human Rights in a Time of Change* (London: Amnesty International).

Ayres, I., and J. Braithwaite (1992) *Responsive Regulation: Transcending the Deregulation Debate* (New York: Oxford University Press).

Bagwell, K., and R.W. Staiger (1999) *Domestic Policies, National Sovereignty and International Economic Institutions* (NBER W7293; Cambridge, MA: National Bureau of Economic Research [NBER], August 1999).

Baker, M. (2004) 'The Global Reporting Initiative: Is it Fit for Purpose?', www.mallenbaker.net/csr/CSRfiles/GRI.html, accessed 8 January 2004.

Bartunek, J. (1988) 'The Dynamics of Personal and Organisational Reframing', in R.E. Quinn and K.S. Cameron (eds.), *Paradox and Transformation: Towards a Theory of Change in Organisation and Management* (Cambridge, MA: Ballinger).

BBC (British Broadcasting Corporation) (2003) 'Newshour', BBC World Service, 13 August 2003, 4:00 pm, London; accessed at: www.uscib.org/%5Cindex.asp?documentID=2729.

Beck, L. (2002) 'Election Dysfunction', *Brazzil*, August 2002, www.brazzil.com/p20aug02.htm.

Bellamy, C. (1999) 'Statement to Harvard International Development Conference on "Sharing Responsibilities: Public, Private and Civil Society"', Cambridge, MA, 16 April 1999.

Bendell, J. (ed.) (2000) *Terms for Endearment: Business, NGOs and Sustainable Development* (Sheffield, UK: Greenleaf Publishing).

—— (2001) *Towards Participatory Workplace Appraisal: Report from a Focus Group of Women Banana Workers* (occasional paper; Bristol, UK: New Academy of Business).

—— (2002) 'Greed Inc. or Greed Ltd?', *Lifeworth 2002 Annual Review of Corporate Responsibility*, Spring (April–June) 2002: 1-16.

—— (2004) *In Our Power: The Civilisation of Globalisation* (Sheffield, UK: Greenleaf Publishing, forthcoming).

—— and T. Concannon (2003) 'World Review', *Journal of Corporate Citizenship* 12: 6-20.

—— and W. Visser (2003) 'World Review', *Journal of Corporate Citizenship* 11: 5-19.

—— and M. Young (2003) 'World Review', *Journal of Corporate Citizenship* 10: 7-19.

Bernard, E. (1997) 'Ensuring Monitoring is Not Co-opted', *New Solutions* 7.4 (Summer 1997).

Bhagwati, J. (1995) 'Trade Liberalisation and "Fair Trade" Demands: Addressing the Environmental and Labour Standards Issues', *The World Economy* 18.6 (November 1995): 745-59.

—— (1998) *A Stream of Windows: Unsettling Reflections on Trade, Immigration and Democracy* (Cambridge, MA: The MIT Press).

Brittain, V. (2000) 'Business Rallies to UN Ethics Scheme', *The Guardian*, 26 July 2000: 12.

Brody, R., and M. Ratner (eds.) (2000) *The Pinochet Papers: The Case of Augusto Pinochet in Spain and Britain* (The Hague: Kluwer Law International).

Brown, L.D., S. Khagram, M.H. Moore and P. Frumkin (2000) *Globalisation, NGOs and Multisectoral Relations* (WP-1; Cambridge, MA: Hauser Institute, Harvard University).

Bruno, K., and J. Karliner (2000) *Tangled Up in Blue: Corporate Partnerships in the United Nations* (San Francisco: Transnational Resource and Action Group).

BSR (Business for Social Responsibility) (2000) *Comparison of Selected Corporate Social Responsibility-Related Standards* (San Francisco: BSR).

Buchan, D., and C. Hoyos (2000) 'United Nations: Fight to Regain Respect and Relevance. World leaders meeting for this week's UN Millennium Summit will have much to praise in the organisation's record since 1945—and reasons to look at their own countries' record of support', *Financial Times*, 6 September 2000.

Capella, P. (1999) 'Business Backs Trade Role for UN', *The Guardian*, 6 July 1999: 25.

Castells, M. (1996) *The Rise of the Network Society* (Oxford, UK: Basil Blackwell).

Cattaui, M.L. (1998) 'UN–Business Partnership Forged on Global Economy', *International Herald Tribune*, 9 February 1998.

Caux Round Table (1994) *Principles of Business* (Washington, DC: Caux Round Table, Secretariat).

CCS (Climate Change Secretariat) (1999) *UNFCCC Convention on Climate Change* (Bonn, Germany: CCS).

CEC (Commission of the European Communities) (2002) *Promoting a European Framework for Corporate Social Responsibility* (green paper; Brussels: CEC).

CETIM/AAJ (Centre Europe tiers-monde/American Association of Jurists) (2002) *Will the UN Compel Transnational Corporations to Comply with International Human Rights Standards?* (Geneva; CETIM; New York: AAJ).

Chandler, A. (1963) *Strategy and Structure* (Cambridge, MA: The MIT Press).

Chandler, G. (1997) 'Oil Companies and Human Rights', in *Oxford Energy Forum*, November 1997: 3.

—— (1998) 'Oil Companies and Human Rights', *Business Ethics: A European Review* 7.2: 69–72.

—— (2000) 'Foreword', to *Human Rights: Is It Any of Your Business?* (London: Amnesty International/The Prince of Wales Business Leaders Forum): 5.

—— (2001) Statement regarding the Draft Universal Human Rights Guidelines for Companies, to the Working Group on the Working Methods and Activities of Transnational Corporations, UN Sub-Commission on the Promotion and Protection of Human Rights, Geneva, 31 July 2001.

Chau, N.C., and R. Kanbur (2000) *The Race to the Bottom, From the Bottom* (Ithaca, NY: Department of Applied Economics and Management, Cornell University).

Chisholm, R.F. (1998) *Developing Network Organizations* (Reading, MA: Addison-Wesley).

Chomsky, N., and E. Hernan (1994) *Manufacturing Consent: The Political Economy of the Mass Media* (London: Vintage Books).

Clapham, A., and S. Jerby (2001) 'Categories of Corporate Complicity in Human Rights Abuses', www.amnesty.it/edu/mitw/documenti/Corporate_complicity.doc.

Cohen, J. (2001) 'The World's Business: The United Nations and the Globalisation of Corporate Citizenship', in J. Andriof and M. McIntosh (eds.), *Perspectives on Corporate Citizenship* (Sheffield, UK: Greenleaf Publishing): 185-97.

Conrad, P. (2002) 'The A to Z of Britney Spears', *Sunday Times Review*, 17 February 2002.

CorpWatch (2002) *Greenwash+10: The UN's Global Compact, Corporate Accountability and the Johannesburg Earth Summit* (San Francisco: CorpWatch/Tides Centre, January 2002; www.corpwatch.org).

Crane, A. (1997) 'Rhetoric and Reality in the Greening of Organisational Culture', in G. Ledgerwood (ed.), *Greening the Boardroom: Corporate Governance and Business Sustainability* (Sheffield, UK: Greenleaf Publishing): 129-44.

—— and D. Matten (2003) *Business Ethics: A European Perspective. Managing Corporate Citizenship and Sustainability in the Age of Globalization* (Oxford, UK: Oxford University Press).

Crossan, M.M., H.W. Lane, R.E. White and L. Djurfelt (1995) 'Organisational Learning: Dimensions for a Theory', *International Journal of Organisational Analysis* 3: 337-60.

Crossette, B. (2000) 'Globalisation Tops 3-Day UN Agenda for World Leaders', *New York Times*, 3 September 2000: 1.

CSM (*Christian Science Monitor*) (2000) 'The Monitor's View: A New Global Compact?', *Christian Science Monitor*, 8 September 2000: 10.

Curtin, T., and J. Jones (2000) *Managing Green Issues* (London: Macmillan).

D'Andrade, R.G. (1984) 'Cultural Meaning Systems', in R.A. Shweder and R.A. LeVine (eds.), *Culture Theory: Essays on Mind, Self, and Emotion* (Cambridge, UK: Cambridge University Press): 88-119.

Danaher, G., T. Schirato and J. Webb (2000) *Understanding Foucault* (London: Sage).

Davis, R., and J. Nelson (2003) *The Buck Stops Where? Managing the Boundaries of Business Engagement in Global Development Challenges* (London: International Business Leaders Forum).

De George, R.T. (1993) *Competing with Integrity in International Business* (New York; Oxford, UK: Oxford University Press).

Dell, S. (1990) *The United Nations and International Business* (London: Duke University Press and United Nations Institute for Training and Research [UNITAR]).

Deming, W.E. (1982) *Out of the Crisis* (Cambridge, MA: MIT Center for Advanced Engineering Study).

Denzin, N.K., and Y.S. Lincoln (eds.) (1994) *Handbook of Qualitative Research* (Thousand Oaks, CA: Sage).

Donaldson, T., and T.W. Dunfee (1994) 'Toward a Unified Conception of Social Contracts Theory', *Academy of Management Review* 19.2: 252-84.

—— and —— (1999) *Ties That Bind: A Social Contracts Approach to Business Ethics* (Boston, MA: Harvard Business School Press).

Doyle, M., and G. Kell (2002) 'Letter for the Attention of Mr Kenny Bruno of CorpWatch', 8 February 2002, www.unglobalcompact.org.

Dreyfus, C. (2001) 'Enhancing the Contribution of the OECD Guidelines for Multinational Enterprises: Lessons to be Learned', in *OECD Annual Report 2001* (Paris: OECD): 119-23.

Drucker, P.F. (1989) *The New Realities* (New York: Harper & Row).

—— (1993) *Post-Capitalist Society* (New York: Harper Business).

Duesenberry, J.S. (1967) *Income, Savings and the Theory of Consumer Behavior* (New York: Oxford University Press).

Dworkin, R. (1979) *Taking Rights Seriously* (Cambridge, MA: Harvard University Press).

Dyer, J.H., and K. Nobeoka (2000) 'Creating and Managing a High-performance Knowledge-sharing Network: The Toyota Case', *Strategic Management Journal* 21: 345-67.

Earthrights International (2003) *Total Denial Continues* (Washington, DC: Earthrights International).

Eckelmann, O. (2003) *The Business Case for Sustainability: Pharmaceutical Industry Sector Report* (Geneva: International Institute for Management Development, October 2003).

Economist (2002a) 'The Return of von Clausewitz', *The Economist*, 9 March 2002: 16.

—— (2002b) 'The Dangers of Corporate Social Responsibility', *The Economist*, 21 November 2002.

ECOSOC (Economic and Social Council) (2003) Human Rights, Trade and Investment (E/CN.4/Sub.2/2003/9, 2 July 2003; New York: United Nations).

ECOSOC-CTC (Economic and Social Council, Commission for Transnational Corporations) (1976) *Material Relevant to the Formulation of a Code of Conduct* (New York: ECOSOC-CTC, 10 December 1976).

Elkington, J. (1997) *Cannibals with Forks: The Triple Bottom Line of 21st Century Business* (Oxford, UK: Capstone Publishing).

Evans, P. (2000) 'Counter-Hegemonic Globalization: Transnational Social Movements in the Contemporary Global Political Economy', in T. Janoski, A.M. Hicks and M. Schwartz (eds.), *Handbook of Political Sociology* (Cambridge, UK: Cambridge University Press).

Falk, R. (2002) 'United Nations System: Prospects for Renewal', in D. Nayyar (ed.), *Governing Globalization* (New York: Oxford University Press): 177-208.

Fals Borda, O. (2001) 'Participatory (Action) Research in Social Theory: Origins and Challenges', in P. Reason and H. Bradbury (eds.), *Handbook of Action Research* (London: Sage).

Feltmate, W., B.A. Schofield and R.W. Yachnin (2001) *Sustainable Development, Value Creation and the Capital Markets* (Ottawa: The Conference Board of Canada and the Canadian Center for Business in the Community).

Financial Times (2002) 'Business role is greeted with some suspicion', *Financial Times*, 23 August 2002.

Fiorill, J. (2002) 'USA: Global Compact: NGOs, business differ over initiative's future', www. corpwatch.org/news/PND.jsp?articleid=1588.

Florini, A. (2000) *The Third Force: The Rise of Transnational Civil Society* (Washington, DC: Carnegie Endowment for International Peace Press).

Freeman, R.B. (1994) 'A Hard-headed Look at Labour Standards', in W. Sengernberger and D. Campbell (eds.), *International Labor Standards and Economic Interdependence* (Geneva: International Institute for Labour Studies).

Freire, P. (1972) *Pedagogy of the Oppressed* (Harmondsworth, UK: Penguin).

Friedman, M. (1984) 'The Social Responsibility of Business is to Increase its Profits', in W.M. Hoffman and J. Mills Moore (eds.), *Business Ethics: Readings and Cases in Corporate Morality* (New York: McGraw-Hill): 126-31.

Friedman, T. (1999) *The Lexus and the Olive Tree* (New York: Farrar, Strauss & Giroux).

Fukuyama, F. (1992) *The End of History and the Last Man* (London: Penguin)

Fung, A., D. O'Rourke and C. Sabel (2001) *Can We Put an End to Sweat Shops?* (Boston, MA: Beacon Press).

Fussler, C. (2002) 'Global Compact Performance Model: From Principles to Practice', presented at UN Global Compact Learning Forum, Berlin, 11-13 December 2002; see also: www.unglobalcompact.org/content/CaseStudies/gc_perfmod_1102.pdf.

——, A. Cramer and S. van der Vegt (2004) *Raising the Bar: Creating Value with the UN Global Compact* (Sheffield, UK: Greenleaf Publishing).

Galea, C. (ed.) (2004) *Teaching Business Sustainability. I. From Theory to Practice* (Sheffield, UK: Greenleaf Publishing).

Garz, G., and C. Volk (2003) *Update More Gain then Pain* (London: WestLB AG, October 2003; www.westlb.com).

Gberie, L. (2003) *West Africa: Rocks in a Hard Place: The Diamonds and Human Security Project* (Occasional Paper 9; Ottawa, Canada, May 2003; http://action.web.ca/home/pac/attach/ w_africa_e.pdf).

Geczy, C., D. Levin and R. Stambaugh (2004) 'The Performance of Socially Responsible Mutual Funds', unpublished working paper, University of Pennsylvania, Philadelphia, PA.

GEL (Gallon Environment Letter) (2002) 'Pesticides increase cancer in farm workers', *Gallon Environment Letter* (Quebec), 4 February 2002.

Gereffi, G., R. Garcia-Johnson and E. Sasser (2001) 'The NGO–Industrial Complex', *Foreign Policy*, July/August 2001: 56-65.

Giddens, A. (1984) *The Constitution of Society* (Berkeley, CA: University of California Press).

Gladwell, M. (2000) *The Tipping Point: How Little Things Can Make a Big Difference* (Boston, MA: Little, Brown).

Global Compact Office (2002) *The Global Compact: A More Strategic Approach to Realize the Vision* (working document; New York: Global Compact Office).

Global Witness (1999) *A Crude Awakening* (London: Global Witness).

Gordenker, L. (1996) *NGOs, the UN and Global Governance* (London: Lynne Reiner).

Gordon, K. (2001) *The OECD Guidelines and Other Corporate Responsibility Instruments: A Comparison* (Paris: OECD).

GPF (Global Policy Forum) (2003) 'UN tribunal convicts media leaders of genocide', www.globalpolicy.org/intljustice/tribunals/rwanda/2003/1203media.htm, accessed 9 January 2004.

Grabosky, P.N. (1995) 'Governing at a Distance: Self-regulating Green Markets', in R. Eckersley (ed.), *Markets, the State and the Environment: Towards Integration* (Melbourne: Macmillan Education Australia): 197-228.

Gray, J. (1996) *After Social Democracy: Politics, Capitalism and the Common Life* (London: Fabian Society).

Greenwood, D.J., and M. Levin (1998) *Introduction to Action Research: Social Research for Social Change* (Thousand Oaks, CA: Sage).

GRI (Global Reporting Initiative) (2002) *Sustainability Reporting Guidelines* (Boston, MA: GRI, www.globalreporting.org).

Guardini, R. (1986) *Das Ende der Neuzeit: Die Macht* (Mainz, Germany: Schöningh).

Gunningham, N., and P. Grabosky (1998) *Smart Regulation: Designing Environmental Policy* (Oxford, UK: Clarendon Press).

Hagstrom, R.G. (1999) *The Warren Buffet Portfolio* (New York: John Wiley).

Hamel, G. (1998) 'Reinventing the Basis for Competition', in R. Gibson (ed.), *Rethinking the Future: Rethinking Business, Principles, Competition, Control, Leadership, Markets and the World* (London: Nicholas Brealey): 82.

Handy, C. (1992) 'Balancing Corporate Power: A New Federalist Paper', *Harvard Business Review*, November/December 1992: 59-72.

Hardt, M., and A. Negri (2000) *Empire* (Cambridge, MA: Harvard University Press).

Harker, J. (2000) *Human Security in Sudan: The Report of a Canadian Assessment Mission* (Ottawa, Canada: Department of Foreign Affairs and International Trade).

Hawken, P., A. Lovins and L.H. Lovins (1999) *Natural Capitalism: Creating the Next Industrial Revolution* (Boston, MA: Little, Brown).

Hayes, K., and R. Burge (2003) *Coltan Mining in the Democratic Republic of Congo: How Tantalum-Using Industries Can Commit to the Reconstruction of the DRC* (Fauna and Flora International Conservation Reports; Global *e*-Sustainability Initiative, www.gesi.org/docs/FFI%20Coltan%20report.pdf).

HBS (Harvard Business School) (2000) *Hitting the Wall: Nike and International Labor Practices* (Case Study 9-700-047; Cambridge, MA: HBS).

Hedstrom, P., and R. Swedberg (1998) 'Social Mechanism: An Introductory Essay', in P. Hedstrom and R. Swedberg (eds.), *Social Mechanisms: An Analytical Approach to Social Theory* (Cambridge, UK: Cambridge University Press): 1-31.

Higgs, F. (2002) 'Global Compact: Unions on New Advisory Council', *ICEM Info* 1: 11-12.

Hobbs, J., I. Khan, M. Posner and K. Roth (2003) 'Letter to Louise Fréchette Raising Concerns on UN Global Compact', 7 April 2003, http://web.amnesty. org/pages/ec_briefings_global_7April03.

Hoyos, C. (2000) 'United Nations: Principled Partnership with World Business: The Global Compact: A new role is being carved out as a bridge between big corporations and critics of their impact on society', *Financial Times*, 6 September 2000: 1.

HRW (Human Rights Watch) (2002) *World Report: Cambodia* (New York: HRW, www.hrw.org/wr2k2/asia3.html, accessed 10 October 2002).

—— (2003) 'World Report 2003', www.hrw.org/wr2k3/issues5.html.

Hudock, A.C. (1999) *NGOs and Civil Society: Democracy by Proxy?* (Cambridge, UK: Polity Press).

Hufbauer, G.C., and N.K. Mitrokostas (2003) *Awakening Monster: The Alien Tort Statute of 1789* (Washington, DC: Institute for International Economics).

Hulme, D., and M. Edwards (eds.) (1996) *NGOs, States and Donors: Too Close for Comfort?* (London: Earthscan Publications).

Hutton, W. (1996) *The State We're In* (London: Vintage).

—— (2002) *The World We're In* (Boston, MA: Little, Brown).

Huysman, M. (1999) 'Balancing Biases: A Critical Review of the Literature on Organisational Learning', in M. Easterby-Smith, J. Burgoyne and L. Araujo (eds.), *Organisational Learning and the Learning Organisation* (London: Sage).

IBFAN (International Baby Food Action Network) (2002) 'United Nations Inc.? Nestlé Enters the UN Global Compact', www.ibfan.org/english/news/press/press30oct02.html.

ICC (International Chamber of Commerce) (2001a) 'ICC and the UN: Origins of a Partnership', ICC Internet Section on the United Nations, www.iccwbo.org.

—— (2001b) 'Anti-globalisation Protesters are Modern-Day Luddites: ICC President', press release, 26 January 2001.

——/IOE (International Organisation of Employers) (2003) *Joint Views of the IOE and ICC on the Draft Norms on the Responsibilities of Transnational Corporations and Other Business Enterprises with Regard to Human Rights* (Paris: IOE/ICC, 22 July 2003).

ICHRP (International Council on Human Rights Policy) (1999) *Hard Cases: Bringing Human Rights Violators to Justice Abroad: A Guide to Universal Jurisdiction* (Versoix, Switzerland: ICHRP).

—— (2002) 'Beyond Voluntarism: Human Rights and the Developing International Legal Obligations to Companies', Geneva, 2002, www.ichrp.org.

—— (2003) *Duties sans Frontière: Human Rights and Global Social Justice* (Geneva: ICHRP).

IFG (International Forum on Globalisation) (2002) 'A Better World is Possible: Alternatives to Economic Globalisation', www.ifg.org.

IHT (*International Herald Tribune*) (2000) 'Globalization battle moves to UN', *International Herald Tribune*, 4 September 2000.

—— (2001) 'The Business of Building a Better World', *International Herald Tribune*, 25 January 2001.

—— (2002) 'A World Court on the Environment? Multinationals Object', *International Herald Tribune*, 19 August 2002.

ILD (Institute for Leadership Development) (2003) *SMEs in the Global Compact* (www.ildglobal.org/ newsite/main.htm).

ILO (International Labour Organisation) (2000) *Sustainable Agriculture in a Globalised Economy* (Geneva: ILO, www.ilo.org/public/english/dialogue/sector/techmeet/tmadoo/tmadr.htm).

Jaspers, K. (1949) 'Über Bedingungen und Möglichkeiten eines neuen Humanismus', in *Die Wandlung* (Herbstheft; Heidelberg, Germany: Schneider): 734.

—— (2000) *The Question of German Guilt* (New York: Fordham University Press).

Jenkins, R. (2002) 'Corporate Codes of Conduct: Self-regulation in a Global Economy', in United Nations Research Institute for Social development (UNRISD) (ed.), *Voluntary Approaches to Corporate Responsibility: Readings and a Resource Guide* (Geneva: UNRISD and UN Non-Government Liaison Service [NGLS]).

JIM (Judge Institute of Management) (2003) *Forecasting the Impact of Sustainability Issues on the Reputation of Large Multinational Corporations* (Cambridge, UK: JIM, University of Cambridge).

Johnston, D. (2000) 'A World of Good', *The Globe and Mail*, 1 May 2000.

Judge, A. (2000) 'Globalisation: the UN's "Safe Haven" for the World's Marginalised: The Global Compact with Multinational Corporations as the UN's "Final Solution"', *Transnational Associations* 6: 295-313.

Juniper, T. (2002) 'Smoke Screen: Bringing Corporations to Book', *The Guardian*, 31 July 2002.

Kamyab, N.K. (2001) 'Statement on Behalf of the Group of 77 at the General Assembly on Agenda Item 39, "Towards Global Partnerships"', 56th Session of the United Nations General Assembly, 5 November 2001.

Kapstein, E.B. (2001) 'The Corporate Ethics Crusade', *Foreign Affairs*, September/October 2001.

Karl, J. (1999) 'The OECD Guidelines for Multinational Enterprises' in M.K. Addo (ed.), *Human Rights Standards and the Responsibility of Transnational Corporations* (The Hague: Kluwer Law International): 89.

Karliner, J., and K. Bruno (2000a) 'The United Nations sits in suspicious company', *International Herald Tribune*, 10 August 2000.

Kasky v. Nike (2002) California Supreme Court Decision S087859, Court of Appeal 1/1 A086142.

Kassem, M. (2002) 'Mr Mahmoud Kassem, Chairman of the Panel of Experts on the Illegal Exploitation of Natural Resources and Other Forms of Wealth of the Democratic Republic of the Congo', United Nations Daily Press Briefing, New York, 25 October 2002, www.un.org/News/dh/pages/021025.ram [RealPlayer format].

Kaufman, L., and D. Gonzalez (2001) 'Labor standards clash with global reality', *New York Times*, 24 April 2001.

Kell, G. (1998) 'Strategy Note for Davos Speech', internal note for the attention of Kofi Annan, 19 December 1998.

—— (2001a) 'Dilemmas in Competitiveness, Community and Citizenship', presentation at a business and human rights seminar entitled 'Toward Universal Business Principles', London School of Economics and Political Science, London, 22 May 2001.

—— (2001b) 'Filling the International Governance Void: The UN Global Compact?', speech given at the London School of Economics, 22 May 2001; reprinted in M. McIntosh (ed.), *Visions of Ethical Business Vol. 4* (London: Financial Times Prentice Hall and PricewaterhouseCoopers, 2002).

—— (2003) 'Global Compact Convenes Learning Forum Meeting', www.unglobalcompact. org.

—— and D. Levin (2002) 'The Evolution of the Global Compact Network: An Historic Experiment in Learning and Action', Working Draft of the Academy of Management Annual Conference, 'Building Effective Networks', Denver, CO, 12 August 2002.

—— and J. Ruggie (1999) 'Global Markets and Social Legitimacy: The Case for the Global Compact', *Transnational Corporations* 8.3 (December 1999): 101-20.

Kemp, V. (2001) *To Whose Profit? Building a Business Case for Sustainability* (London: WWF-UK and Cable & Wireless).

Kingo, L. (2003) 'A Business Model for the 21st Century', slide show presented at the annual conference of the European Academy of Business in Society, Copenhagen, 19-20 September 2003.

Kinley, D., S. Joseph and A. McBeth (2003b) 'The Human Rights Responsibilities of Multinational Corporations: A Legal Study', *New Academy Review* 2.1 (Spring 2003): 92.

Klein, N. (2000) *No Logo: No Space, No Choice, No Jobs* (London: Flamingo).

Knight, D. (2000) 'United McNations? The UN's Growing Alliance with Multinational Corporations', *Dollars and Sense*, July/August 2000.

Knight, L. (2002) 'Network Learning: Exploring Learning by Interorganisational Networks', *Human Relations* 55: 427-54.

Kuhn, T. (1962) *The Structure of Scientific Revolutions* (Chicago: University of Chicago Press).

Larsson, R., L. Bengtsson, K. Henriksson and L. Sparks-Graham (1998) 'The Interorganisational Learning Dilemma: Collective Knowledge Development in Strategic Alliance', *Organisation Science* 9: 285-305.

LCHR (Lawyers' Committee for Human Rights) (2002) Statement to the UN Sub-Commission on the Protection and Promotion of Human Rights, 1 August 2002; see www.business-humanrights.org/Lawyers-Committee-1-Aug-2002-statement.htm.

Leipziger, D. (2003) *The Corporate Responsibility Code Book* (Sheffield, UK: Greenleaf Publishing).

Leisinger, K.M. (2002) 'New Social Contract for Globalization with a Human Face', presented at UN Global Compact Learning Forum, Berlin, 11-13 December 2002.

—— (2003) 'Opportunities and Risks of the United Nations Global Compact: The Novartis Case Study', *Journal of Corporate Citizenship* 11 (Autumn 2003): 113-31.

—— and K. Schmitt (2003) *Corporate Ethics in a Time of Globalisation* (Colombo, Sri Lanka: Sarvodaya).

Litvin, D. (2003) 'Raising Human Rights Standards in the Private Sector', *Foreign Policy*, November/December 2003: 68-72.

Luhmann, N. (1989) *Ecological Communication* (Chicago: Chicago University Press).

—— (1995) *Social Systems* (Stanford, CA: Stanford University Press).

—— (1997) *Die Gesellschaft der Gesellschaft* (2 vols.; Frankfurt am Main: Suhrkamp).

Mahon, J.F. (1989) 'Corporate Political Strategy', *Business in the Contemporary World* 2: 50-62.

Margolis, J.D., and J.P. Walsh (2001) *People and Profits? The Search for a Link between a Company's Social and Financial Performance* (Mahwah, NJ: Lawrence Erlbaum Associates).

Matten, D., and A. Crane (2003) 'Stakeholders as Citizens: The Corporate Administration of Social, Civil, and Political Rights', paper presented at the European Business Ethics Network 16th Annual Conference, Budapest, 29-31 August 2003.

McIntosh, M. (2003) *Raising a Ladder to the Moon: The Complexities of Corporate Social and Environmental Responsibility* (London: Palgrave Macmillan).

——, D. Leipziger, K. Jones and G. Coleman (1998) *Corporate Citizenship: Successful Strategies for Responsible Companies* (London: Financial Times Prentice Hall).

——, D. Murphy and R. Shah (eds.) (2003a) 'The United Nations Global Compact', *Journal of Corporate Citizenship* 11 (Special Issue; Autumn 2003).

——, R. Thomas, D. Leipziger and G. Coleman (2003b) *Living Corporate Citizenship: Strategic Routes to Socially Responsible Business* (London: Financial Times Prentice Hall).

Mendes, E., and O. Mehmet (2003) *Global Governance, Economy and Law: Waiting for Justice* (London/New York: Routledge).

Metzl, J.F. (1997) 'Rwandan Genocide and the International Law of Radio Jamming', *91 American Journal of International Law* 628: 630.

Meyer, J., and B. Rowan (1977) 'Institutionalised Organisations: Formal Structure as Myth and Ceremony', *American Journal of Sociology*. 83: 340-63.

Micklelthwait, J., and A. Wooldridge (2000) *A Future Perfect* (London: William Heinemann).

Miles, R., C. Snow, J. Mathews and H. Coleman (1997) 'Organising in the Knowledge Age: Anticipating the Cellular Form', *Academy of Management Executive* 11.4: 7-20.

Mimkes, P. (2002) 'Bayer and the UN Global Compact: How and Why a Major Pharmaceutical and Chemical Company "Bluewashes" its Image', www.corpwatch.org/campaigns/PRT.jsp?articleid=3129.

Moffet, J., and F. Bregha (1999) 'Non-regulatory Environmental Measures', in R.B. Gibson (ed.), *Voluntary Initiatives: The New Politics of Corporate Greening* (Ontario: Broadview Press): 15-31.

Monks, R.A.G. (1997) *The Emperor's Nightingale* (Reading, MA: Perseus Books).

Moody-Stuart, M. (2003) 'The Measure of a Good Company', *International Herald Tribune*, 25 January 2003.

Muldoon, P., and R. Nadarajah (1999) 'A Sober Second Look: The regulatory approach looks better when the context and consequences of voluntary initiatives are taken into account', in R. Gibson (ed.), *Voluntary Initiatives: The New Politics of Corporate Greening* (Ontario: Broadview Press).

Nadvi, K., and F. Wältring (2002) *Making Sense of Global Standards* (INEF Report 58; Duisburg, Germany: Institute of Development and Peace, University of Duisburg).

Nelson, J. (2002) *Building Partnerships: Co-operation between the United Nations System and the Private Sector* (New York: UN Department of Public Information and the International Business Leaders Forum [IBLF]).

Newsweek (1990) 'Clean up their act', *Newsweek*, 19 November 1990: 1.

NFSD (Novartis Foundation for Sustainable Development) (2003) 'Report 2003-2004', NFSD, PO Box, CH-4002 Basel, Switzerland, www.novartisfoundation.com.

Novethic (2003) *Corporate Environmental Responsibility: Synopsis of the Proceedings (G8 Environmental Futures Forum, 27-28 March 2003, Ermenonville, France)* (commissioned by the Ministère de l'Ecologie et du Développement Durable, France; Paris: Novethic, Caisse des dépôts).

Novo Nordisk (2003a) *Sustainability Report 2002* (Copenhagen: Novo Nordisk).

—— (2003b) *Annual Financial Report 2002* (Copenhagen: Novo Nordisk).

O'Reilly, P., and S. Tickell (1999) 'TNCs and the Social Issues. *I*. The Developing World', in M.K. Addo (ed.), *Human Rights Standards and the Responsibility of Transnational Corporations* (The Hague: Kluwer Law International): 274-75.

O'Rourke, D. (2000) *Monitoring the Monitors: A Critique of Pricewaterhouse Coopers (PwC) Labor Monitoring* (Cambridge, MA: Massachusetts Institute of Technology, 28 September 2000; http://web.mit.edu/dorourke/www).

OECD (Organisation for Economic Co-operation and Development) (1976) *Guidelines for Multinational Enterprises* (Paris: OECD).

—— (1999) *Voluntary Approaches for Environmental Policy: An Assessment* (Paris: OECD).

—— (2000a) *The OECD Guidelines for Multinational Enterprises: Revision 2000* (Paris: OECD, www.oecd.org/ dataoecd/56/36/1922428.pdf).

—— (2000b) 'Preface', in *Guidelines for Multinational Enterprises* (meeting of the OECD Council at Ministerial Level; Paris: OECD): 15.

—— (2001a) *Background Paper for the Experts Workshop on Information and Consumer Decision-making For Sustainable Consumption* (unpublished; Paris: OECD).

—— (2001b) 'Guidelines for Multinational Enterprises', in *OECD Annual Report 2001* (Paris: OECD).

—— (2003) *Voluntary Approaches for Environmental Policy: Effectiveness, Efficiency and Usage in Policy Mixes* (Paris: OECD).

OHCHR (Office of the High Commissioner on Human Rights) (1966) *International Covenant on Economic, Social and Cultural Rights* (Geneva: OHCHR): Articles 11 and 12.

Ordzhonikidze, S. (2001) 'Statement of the Russian Federation at the Plenary Meeting of the 56th Session of the UN General Assembly on Agenda Item 35, "Towards Global Partnerships"', 56th Session of the United Nations General Assembly, 5 November 2001.

Oxfam America (2003) *Conflict Diamonds Drive Wars in Africa* (Boston, MA: Oxfam America, www.oxfamamerica.org/advocacy/art826.html, accessed 10 October 2003).

Palast, G. (2002) *The Best Democracy Money Can Buy: The Truth about Corporate Cons, Globalisation and High-Finance Fraudsters* (London: Pluto Press).

Pedersen, M.H. (2003) 'United Nations Global Compact: A Response to Globalisation?' (MSc dissertation; Aarhus, Denmark: Department of Political Science, Aarhus University).

Pfaff, W. (2000) 'Annan's new United Nations is beginning to go its own way', *International Herald Tribune*, 12 September 2000.

Pfizer (2003) *Pfizer 2003 Annual Review: Medicines to Change the World* (New York: Pfizer).

Polanyi, K. (1944) *The Great Transformation* (Boston, MA: Beacon Press).

Porritt, J., and C. Tuppen (2003) *Just Values* (BT in partnership with Forum for the Future, www.bt.com/betterworld).

Porter, M.E. (2002) 'The Competitive Advantage of Corporate Philanthropy', *Harvard Business Review* 80.12 (December 2002): 56-68.

Post, J.E. (2002) ' Global Corporate Citizenship: Principles to Work and Live By', *Business Ethics Quarterly* 12.2 (Special Issue on The Clarkson Principles, April 2002).

——, L. Preston and S. Sachs (2002a) *Redefining the Corporation: Stakeholder Management and Organizational Wealth* (Stanford, CA: Stanford University Press).

——, —— and —— (2002b) 'Managing the Extended Enterprise', *California Management Review* 40.1: 2-18.

Powell, W.W., K.W. Koput and L. Smith-Doerr (1996) 'Interorganisational Collaboration and the Locus of Innovation: Networks of Learning in Biotechnology', *Administrative Science Quarterly* 41: 116-31.

Prahalad, C.K., and S. Hart (2002) 'The Fortune at the Bottom of the Pyramid', *Strategy and Business* 26: 2-14.

Prieto, M., and J. Bendell (2002) *If You Want to Help Us Then Start Listening to Us! From Factories and Plantations in Central America, Women Speak out about Corporate Responsibility* (occasional paper; Bath, UK: New Academy of Business).

Princeton University (2002) *The Princeton Principles on Universal Jurisdiction* (Princeton, NJ: Princeton University).

Rawls, J. (1971) *A Theory of Justice* (Cambridge, MA: Belknap Press of Harvard University Press).

Raynard, P., and M. Forstater (2002) *Corporate Social Responsibility: Implications for Small and Medium Enterprises in Developing Countries* (Vienna: United Nations Industrial Development Organisation [UNIDO]).

Reason, P., and H. Bradbury (eds.) (2001) *Handbook of Action Research: Participative Inquiry and Practice* (London: Sage).

Reinicke, W.H. (1998) *Global Public Policy: Governing without Government?* (Washington, DC: Brookings Institution Press).

—— (1999) 'The Other World Wide Web: Global Public Policy Networks', *Foreign Policy*, Winter 1999/2000: 44-57.

—— and F. Deng (2000) *Critical Choices: The United Nations, Networks, and the Future of the Global Governance* (Ottawa: International Development Research Center).

Reuters (2000) 'Volvo chief says EU–US closer on environment', *Reuters*, 1 May 2000.

Ribanns, E. (2002) 'Measuring Up', *Tomorrow, Sustainable Business* 12.1: 45.

Richter (2003) *Building on Quicksand: The Global Compact, Democratic Governance and Nestle* (Geneva: Third World Centre Europe [CETIM], International Baby Food Action Network [IBFAN] and Berne Declaration, October 2003).

RING (Regional and International Networking Group) Alliance (2000) *Statement to the United Nations Global Compact* (RING, 20 July 2000).

—— (2003) *Development Impact of the Global Compact*, www.ring-alliance.org/pubs.html.

Rischard, J.-F. (2002) *High Noon: 20 Global Problems, 20 Years to Solve Them* (New York: Basic Books).

Roberts, S., J. Keeble and D. Brown (2001) 'The Business Case for Corporate Citizenship', *World Economic Forum's Global Corporate Citizenship Initiative* (www.weforum.org).

Robinson, M. (2002) 'Beyond Good Intentions: Corporate Citizenship for a New Century', RSA World Leaders Lecture, London, 7 May 2002.

—— (2003) 'Foreword', in R. Sullivan (ed.), *Business and Human Rights: Dilemmas and Solutions* (Sheffield, UK: Greenleaf Publishing): 9-12.

Ruggie, J.G. (1982) 'International Regimes, Transactions and Change: Embedded Liberalism in the Postwar Economic Order', *International Organization* 36 (Spring 1982): 379-415.

—— (1998) *Constructing the World Polity* (London: Routledge).

—— (2000a) 'Globalisation, the "Global Compact" and Corporate Social Responsibility', *Transnational Associations* 6: 291-94.

—— (2000b) 'UN's Global Compact', *International Herald Tribune*, Letters to the Editor, 16 August 2000.

—— (2001) 'Globalisation: Shared Risk, Shared Promise', *International Herald Tribune*, 25 January 2001.

—— (2003) 'Taking Embedded Liberalism Global: The Corporate Connection', in D. Held and M. Koenig-Archibugi (eds.), *Taming Globalization: Frontiers of Governance* (Cambridge, UK: Polity Press).

—— and G. Kell (1999) 'Global Markets and Social Legitimacy: The Case of the "Global Compact" ', presented at a conference at York University, Toronto, Canada, 4–6 November 1999 (www.unglobalcompact.org).

Sachs, J. (1996) *Globalisation and Employment* (Public Lectures; Geneva: International Institute for Labour Studies, 18 March 1996).

Sachs, W. (2003) *Environment and Human Rights* (Wuppertal, Germany: Wuppertal Institute for Climate, Environment and Energy).

Salaman, G. (2001) *Understanding Business Organisations* (Milton Keynes, UK: Open University; London: Routledge).

Schabas, W. (2001) *An Introduction to the International Criminal Court* (Cambridge, UK: Cambridge University Press).

Schlesinger, S. (2003) *Act of Creation. The Founding of the United Nations: A Story of Superpowers, Secret Agents, Wartime Allies and Enemies, and their Quest for a Peaceful World* (Boulder, CO: Westview Press).

Scholte, J.A. (2001) 'Globalisation, Governance and Corporate Citizenship', *Journal of Corporate Citizenship* 1 (Spring 2001): 15-23.

Schrage, E. (2003) 'Emerging Threat: Human Rights Claims', *Harvard Business Review* (August 2003): 16-18.

Scott, W.R. (2001) *Institutions and Organisations* (Newbury Park, CA: Sage, 2nd edn).

Sen, A. (1999) *Development as Freedom* (Garden City, NY: Anchor Books).

Senge, P.M. (1990) *The Fifth Discipline: The Art and Practice of the Learning Organization* (New York: Currency Doubleday).

Sengenberger, W. (2002) *Globalisation and Social Progress: The Role and Impact of International Labour Standards* (Geneva: International Institute for Labour Studies, 21 September 2002).

Sethi, S.P. (2003) *Setting Global Standards: Guidelines for Creating Codes of Conduct in Multinational Companies* (New York: John Wiley).

Shue, H. (1980) *Basic Rights: Subsistence, Affluence, and US Foreign Policy* (Princeton, NJ: Princeton University Press).

Simms, A., T. Bigg and N. Robins (2000) *It's Democracy Stupid: The Trouble with the Global Economy: The United Nations' Lost Role and Democratic Reform of the IMF, World Bank and the World Trade Organisation* (London: New Economics Foundation).

Simpson, S. (1990) *The Times Guide to the Environment* (London: Times Books).

Singh, A. (2002) *Global Economic Trends and Social Development* (OP-9; Geneva: United Nations Research Institute for Social Development [UNRISD]).

Smith, A. (1976) *The Glasgow Edition of the Works and Correspondence of Adam Smith* (Oxford/ New York: Clarendon Press; Oxford University Press).

Spar, D. (1998) 'The Spotlight and the Bottom Line: How Multinationals Export Human Rights', *Foreign Affairs* 77.2: 7-12.

Stamler, B. (2001) 'Companies are developing brand messages as a way to inspire loyalty among employees', *New York Times*, 5 July 2001.

Stiglitz, J.E. (1988) *Economics of the Public Sector* (New York: W.W. Norton, 2nd edn).

—— (2000) 'Democratic Development as the Fruits of Labor', keynote address to the Industrial Relations Research Association, Boston, MA, January 2000.

—— (2002) *Globalisation and its Discontents* (Harmondsworth, UK: Penguin Allen Lane).

Stinchombe, A.L. (1965) 'Social Structure and Organisations', in J.G. March (ed.), *Handbook of Organisations* (Chicago: Rand McNally): 142-93.

Strang, D., and J.W. Meyer (1993) 'Institutional Conditions for Diffusion', *Theory and Society* 22: 487-511.

Streeck, W., and P.C. Schmitter (eds.) (1985) *Private Interest Governments* (Beverly Hills, CA: Sage).

Streeten, P. (2003) 'Should Companies Try to Do Good?', background paper to the 'Human Rights and Business' debate of the Novartis Foundation for Sustainable Development, NFSD, PO Box, CH-4002, Basel, Switzerland, www.novartisfoundation.com, February 2003.

Stube, A. (2003) 'Dilemmas in Action: Human Rights in the Supply Chain', slide show presented at the Global Compact Learning Forum Conference in Belo Horizonte, Brazil, December 2003; available from Novo Nordisk, astu@novonordisk.com.

Sullivan, R. (2003) 'Introduction', in R. Sullivan (ed.), *Business and Human Rights: Dilemmas and Solutions* (Sheffield, UK: Greenleaf Publishing): 13-20.

SustainAbility (2003) '21st Century NGO: Playing the Game or Selling Out? International study reveals that more NGOs are shifting from confrontation to collaboration', press release, 26 June 2003, www.sustainability.com.

—— and UNEP (United Nations Environment Programme) (2001) *Buried Treasure: Uncovering the Business Case for Corporate Sustainability* (London: SustainAbility).

—— and —— (2002) *Trust Us: The Global Reporters 2002 Survey of Corporate Sustainability Reporting* (Paris: UNEP-DTIE; London: SustainAbility).

Suter, K. (2000) 'The UN Third Way: Go Corporate', *F2 Network*, 28 September 2000.

Swithern, S. (2003) 'From Bhopal to Doha: Business and the Right to Health', *New Academy Review* 2.1 (Spring 2003): 50.

TADB (Trade and Development Board) (2002) *The Development Dimension of FDI: Policies to Enhance the Role of FDI in Support of the Competitiveness of the Enterprise Sector and the Economic Performance of Host Economies, Taking into Account the Trade/Investment Interface, in the National and International Context* (Geneva: TADB, United Nations Conference on Trade and Development [UNCTAD], 23 September 2002).

Tandon, R. (1997) 'Struggle for Knowledge: A Personal Journey', presentation at the 4th World Congress on Action Research, Action Learning and Process Management, Cartagena, Colombia, 31 May–5 June 1997.

Tandy, H. (2001) 'Business of Chemicals, 2: Bayer Focus is on Growth Areas', *Financial Times*, 25 September 2001: 2.

Ten Brink, P. (ed.) (2002) *Voluntary Environmental Agreements: Process, Practice and Future Use* (Sheffield, UK: Greenleaf Publishing).

Tesner, S., and G. Kell (2000) *The United Nations and Business: A Partnership Recovered* (New York: St Martin's Press).

Tolbert, P., and L.G. Zucker (1996) 'The Institutionalisation of Institutional Theory', in S.R. Clegg, C. Hardy and W.R. Nord (eds.), *Handbook of Organisation Studies* (London: Sage): 175-90.

Töpfer, K. (2000) 'Weaving the Global Compact: The Triple Bottom Line of Economic, Social, Natural Capital, by the Executive Director: United Nations Environment Programme', *UN Chronicle* 37.2 (UN Department of Public Information): 39-41.

Toynbee, P. (2003) *Hard Work: Life in Low Pay Britain* (London: Bloomsbury).

Truman, H.S. (1949) 'Inaugural Address', 20 January 1949; reprinted in *Documents on American Foreign Relations* (Princeton, NJ: Princeton University Press, 1967).

Tushman, M.L., and E. Romanelli (1985) *Organisational Evolution: A Metamorphosis Model of Convergence and Reorientation* (Research in Organisational Behavior 6; ed. L.L. Cummings and B.M. Staw; Greenwich, CT: JAI Press).

UN News Service (2001) 'UN Global Compact Principles Appearing in International Labour Accords', New York, 23 March 2001.

UNCHR (United Nations Commission on Human Rights) (2003a) *Norms on the Responsibilities of Transnational Corporations and Other Business Enterprises with Regard to Human Rights* (E/CN.4/sub.2/2003/12/Rev.2, 26 August 2003; Geneva: UNCHR)

UNCHR (United Nations Commission on Human Rights) (2003b) *Commentary on the Norms on the Responsibilities of Transnational Corporations and Other Business Enterprises with Regard to Human Rights* (Doc.E/CN.4/Sub.2/2003/38/Rev.2; Geneva: UNCHR).

UNCTAD (United Nations Conference on Trade and Development) (1999) *The Social Responsibility of Transnational Corporations* (Geneva: UNCTAD).

UNCTAD-DTCI (United Nations Conference on Trade and Development, Division on Transnational Corporations and Investment) (1996) *International Investment Instruments: A Compendium* (Geneva: United Nations).

UNDP (United Nations Development Programme) (1997) *UN Human Development Report* (New York: United Nations).

—— (2000) *Human Development Report 2000: Human Rights and Human Development* (New York/Oxford, UK: Oxford University Press).

UNEP-DTIE (United Nations Environment Programme, Division of Technology, Industry and Economics) (1998) *Voluntary Industry Codes of Conduct for the Environment* (Technical Report 40; Paris: UNEP-DTIE).

UNESCO (United Nations Educational, Scientific and Cultural Organisation) (2003) *The Universal Declaration on the Human Genome and Human Rights* (Paris: UNESCO).

UNGA (United Nations General Assembly) (1948) *Universal Declaration of Human Rights* (New York: United Nations, www.un.org/Overview/rights.html): Article 25.

—— (2001a) *Co-operation between the United Nations and all Relevant Partners, in Particular the Private Sector* (Report of the Secretary-General, A/56/323; New York: UNGA, 28 August 2001).

—— (2001b) *Business and Development* (Report of the Secretary-General, A/56/442; New York: UNGA, 5 October 2001).

UNICEF (United Nations Children's Fund) (2000) 'Statement to the European Parliament Development and Co-operation Committee: Special Meeting on Standard Setting by European Enterprises in Developing Countries', www.ibfan.org/english/news/press/press23novoounicef.html.

UNIDO (United Nations Industrial Development Organisation) (2002) *Corporate Social Responsibility: Implications for Small and Medium Enterprises in Developing Countries* (Vienna: UNIDO).

—— (2004) *Survey of Small and Medium Enterprises in the Global Compact* (Vienna: UNIDO).

United Nations (1945) *UN Charter* (New York: United Nations, 25 October 1945, www.un.org).

—— (1974) *Charter of Economic Rights and Duties* (New York: United Nations).

—— (1990) *Basic Principles on the Use of Force and Firearms* (New York: United Nations).

—— (2000a) 'Guidelines on Co-operation between the United Nations and the Business Community', issued by the Secretary-General of the United Nations, 17 July 2000, www.un.org/partners/business/otherpages/guide.htm.

—— (2000b) 'Transcript of Press Conference by Secretary-General Kofi Annan at Headquarters, 26 July', press release SG/SM/7596, 26 July 2000.

—— (2002a) *Johannesburg Declaration* (New York: United Nations).

—— (2002b) *Johannesburg Plan of Implementation* (New York: United Nations).

—— (2002c) *The Global Compact: Report on Progress and Activities* (New York: United Nations Global Compact Office, July 2002).

—— (2002d) 'GC Partnership Projects', www.unglobalcompact.org.

—— (2003a) *The Global Compact: Report on Progress and Activities, July 2002–June 2003* (New York: United Nations, www.unglobalcompact.org).

—— (2003b) *Towards Global Partnerships: Enhanced Co-Operation between the United Nations and All Relevant Partners, in Particular the Private Sector* (Report of the Secretary-General; New York: United Nations, 18 August 2003).

—— (2003c) *UN Global Compact Resource Package: Human Rights Presentation* (New York: United Nations).

—— (2003d) 'Global Compact and WBCSD Announce Co-operation', 16 January 2003, www.unglobalcompact.org.

—— (2003e) 'Global Compact Convenes Learning Forum Meeting', www.unglobalcompact. org.

UNPD (United Nations Population Division) (2002) *World Urbanisation Prospects: The 2001 Revision* (New York: UNPD).

—— (2003) *World Urbanisation Prospects: The 2003 Revision* (New York: UNPD).

UNRISD (United Nations Research Institute for Social Development) (1995) *States of Disarray: The Social Effects of Globalisation* (Geneva: UNRISD).

Urminsky, M. (ed.) (2002) *Self-regulation in the Workplace: Codes of Conduct, Social Labelling and Socially Responsible Investment* (Geneva: International Labour Organisation).

Useem, M. (1998) *The Leadership Moment: Nine True Stories of Triumph and Disaster and their Lessons for Us All* (New York: Times Business).

Utting, P. (2000) 'UN–Business Partnerships: Whose Agenda Counts?', paper presented at the Seminar on Partnerships for Development or Privatisation of the Multilateral System, organised by the North–South Coalition, Oslo, 8 December 2000 (Geneva: United Nations Research Institute for Social Development [UNRISD]).

—— (2002) 'Regulating Business via Multistakeholder Initiatives: A Preliminary Assessment', in United Nations Research Institute for Social development (UNRISD) (ed.), *Voluntary Approaches to Corporate Responsibility: Readings and a Resource Guide* (Geneva: UNRISD and UN Non-Government Liaison Service [NGLS]).

—— (2003) 'The Global Compact: Why All the Fuss?', *UN Chronicle*. www.un.org/Pubs/ chronicle/2003/issue1/0103p65.html

Uzzi, B. (1996) 'The Sources and Consequences of Embeddedness for the Economic Performance of Organisations: The Network Effect', *American Sociological Review* 61: 674-98.

Volberda, H. (1998) *Building the Flexible Firm* (Oxford, UK: Oxford University Press).

Von Nell-Breuning, O. (1990) *Baugesetze der Gesellschaft: Solidarität und Subsidiarität* (Freiburg, Germany: Herder).

Waddell, S. (2000) 'New Institutions for the Practice of Corporate Citizenship: Historical, Intersectoral, and Developmental Perspectives', *Business and Society Review* 105.1 (Spring 2000): 107-36.

—— (2001) 'Societal Learning: Creating Change Strategies for Large Systems Change', *Systems Thinker* 12.10: 1.

—— (2002a) 'Global Public Policy Networks: Contested Spaces where the Human Spirit can Triumph', GPPN Research Project.

—— (2002b) 'Six Societal Learning Concepts for a New Era', *Reflections: The SoL Journal* 3.4 (Summer 2002): 19-27.

—— (2003a) 'Global Action Networks: A Global Invention to Make Globalisation Work for All', *Journal of Corporate Citizenship* 12 (Winter 2003): 27-42.

—— (2003b) 'Global Action Networks: Building Global Public Policy Systems of Accountability', *AccountAbility Quarterly* 20: 19-26.

—— and L.D. Brown (1997) 'Fostering Intersectoral Partnering: A Guide to Promoting Cooperation among Government, Business, and Civil Society Actors', *IDR Reports* 13.3.

Waddock, S. (2001) 'Integrity and Mindfulness: Foundations of Corporate Citizenship', in J. Andriof and M. McIntosh (eds.), *Perspectives on Corporate Citizenship* (Sheffield, UK: Greenleaf Publishing): 26-38.

—— (2002a) *Leading Corporate Citizens: Vision, Values, Value Added* (New York: McGraw-Hill).

—— (2002b) 'Learning from Experience: The UN Global Compact Learning Forum 2002', United Nations Global Compact, www.unglobalcompact.org.

—— (2003) 'Learning from Experience: The United Nations Global Compact Learning Forum 2002', *Journal of Corporate Citizenship* 11: 51-67.

—— and C. Bodwell (2002) 'From TQM to TRM: The Emerging Evolution of Total Responsibility Management (TRM) Systems', *Journal of Corporate Citizenship* 7 (Autumn 2002): 113-26.

——, —— and S.B. Graves (2002) 'Responsibility: The New Business Imperative', *Academy of Management Executive* 16.2 (May 2002): 132-48.

Ward, H. (2003) *Legal Issues in Corporate Citizenship* (report prepared for the Swedish Partnership for Global Responsibility; London: International Institute for Environment and Development [IIED] and Globalt Ansvar).

Washington Post (2000) 'Companies, UN agree to rights compact: environmental, labor criteria set', *Washington Post*, 27 July 2000: A06.

Weick, K. (1995) *Sensemaking in Organisations* (London/Thousand Oaks, CA: Sage).

Weiser, J., and S. Zadek (2000) 'Conversations with Disbelievers: Persuading Business to Address Social Challenges', www.conversations-with-disbelievers.net.

Weller, C., and A. Hersh (2002) *The Long and Short of It: Global Liberalisation, Poverty and the Inequality* (Technical Paper 40; Washington, DC: Economic Policy Institute).

Whittington, R., A. Pettigrew, S. Peck, E. Fenton and M. Conyon (1999) 'Change and Complementarities in the New Competitive Landscape', *Organisation Science* 10.5: 583-600.

Wild, A. (1998) 'A Review of Corporate Citizenship and Social Initiatives' (mimeo; Geneva: ILO; prepared for the Bureau for Employers' Activities, International Labour Organisation, 1–2 October 1998).

Williams, F. (2002) 'Prophet of Bloom', *Wired*, February 2002: 60-63.

Williams, O.F. (ed) (2000) *Global Codes of Conduct: An Idea Whose Time Has Come* (Notre Dame, IN: University of Notre Dame Press).

Williamson, H. (2003) 'Making a Commitment to Corporate Citizenship', *Financial Times*, 12 February 2003.

Williamson, J. (1994) 'In Search of a Manual for Technopols', in J. Williamson (ed.), *The Political Economy of Policy Reform* (Washington, DC: Institute for International Economics): 9-28.

Witte, J.M., W. Reinicke and T. Benner (2000) 'Beyond Multilateralism: Global Public Policy Networks', *International Politics and Society* 2.

Wood, D., and J. Logsdon (2002) 'Theorising Business Citizenship', in J. Andriof and M. McIntosh (eds.), *Perspectives on Corporate Citizenship* (Sheffield, UK: Greenfield Publishing): 83-103.

Wynhoven, U. (2002) 'Case Study of How Novartis International AG has Begun the Process of Delivering on its Commitment to the Global Compact', 16 July 2002, www.unglobalcompact.org.

Young, O.R. (ed.) (1999a) *The Effectiveness of International Environmental Regimes* (Cambridge, MA: The MIT Press).

—— (1999b) *Governance in World Affairs* (Ithaca, NY: Cornell University Press).

Zacher, M. (1999) *The United Nations and Global Commerce* (New York: United Nations Department of Public Information).

Zadek, S., P. Pruzan and R. Evans (eds.) (1999) *Building Corporate Accountability* (London: Earthscan Publications).

Zammit, A. (2003) *Development at Risk: Reconsidering UN–Business Relations* (Geneva: United Nations Research Institute for Social Development [UNRISD]).

Abbreviations

AA1000	AccountAbility Standard 1000
AAJ	American Association of Jurists
ACFTU	All-China Federation of Trade Unions
AI	Amnesty International
AIDS	acquired immuno-deficiency syndrome
APEC	Asia–Pacific Economic Co-operation
ATS	Alien Tort Statute
BIAC	Business and Industry Advisory Committee
BSE	bovine spongiform encephalopathy
BSR	Business for Social Responsibility
BT	British Telecommunications
CEC	Commission of the European Communities
CEO	chief executive officer
CEPAA	Council on Economic Priorities Accreditation Agency
CERES	Coalition for Environmentally Responsible Economies
CETIM	Centre Europe tiers-monde (Third World Centre Europe)
CIME	Committee on International Investment and Multilateral Enterprises
CIP	Corporate Involvement Programme
CSM	*Christian Science Monitor*
CSR	corporate social responsibility
CTC	Commission for Transnational Corporations
DJSI	Dow Jones Sustainability Index
DKK	Danish krone
DRC	Democratic Republic of the Congo
DTCI	Division on Transnational Corporations and Investment
DTIE	Division of Technology, Industry and Economics
EBIT	earnings before interest and tax
ECOSOC	Economic and Social Council
EFTA	European Free Trade Association
ETI	Ethical Trading Initiative
EU	European Union

EUR	euro
FDI	foreign direct investment
FTSE	Financial Times Stock Exchange
GAN	global action network
GATS	General Agreement on Trade in Services
GATT	General Agreement on Tariffs and Trade
GEL	*Gallon Environment Letter*
GeSI	Global *e*-Sustainability Initiative
GPF	Global Policy Forum
GPPN	global public policy network
GRI	Global Reporting Initiative
GSP	Global Sullivan Principles
GUF	global union federation
HBS	Harvard Business School
HIV	human immunodeficiency virus
HRW	Human Rights Watch
IAPAC	International Association of Physicians in AIDS Care
IBFAN	International Baby Food Action Network
IBLF	Prince of Wales International Business Leaders Forum
ICC	International Chamber of Commerce
ICEM	International Federation of Chemical, Energy, Mine and General Workers' Unions
ICFTU	International Confederation of Free Trade Unions
ICHRP	International Council on Human Rights Policy
ICT	information and communications technology
ICTR	International Criminal Tribunal for Rwanda
ICTU	Irish Congress of Trade Unions
IFG	International Forum on Globalisation
IHT	*International Herald Tribune*
ILD	Institute for Leadership Development
ILO	International Labour Organisation
IMEC	International Maritime Employers' Council
IMF	International Monetary Fund
INGO	international non-governmental organisation
IOE	International Organisation of Employers
ION	inter-organisational network
ISO	International Organisation for Standardisation
IT	information technology
ITF	International Transport Workers' Federation
ITU	International Telecommunications Union
JIM	Judge Institute of Management
LCHR	Lawyers' Committee on Human Rights
LDC	least-developed country
MAI	Multilateral Agreement on Investment
MNC	multinational company/multinational corporation
MNE	multinational enterprise
MSC	Marine Stewardship Council
MSCI	Morgan Stanley Capital Index
MSD	multi-stakeholder dialogue
NFSD	Novartis Foundation for Sustainable Development
NGLS	Non-Governmental Liaison Service
NGO	non-governmental organisation
NPC	national contact point
OECD	Organisation for Economic Co-operation and Development

OHCHR	Office of the High Commissioner for Human Rights
PP10	Partnership for Principle 10
R&D	research and development
RCC	responsible corporate citizenship
RING	Regional and International Networking Group
RSPB	Royal Society for the Protection of Birds
SA8000	Social Accountability 8000
SAI	Social Accountability International
SAM	Sustainable Asset Management
SARS	severe acute respiratory syndrome
SMART	sustainable, measurable, achievable, realistic and timely
SME	small or medium-sized enterprise
SRI	socially responsible investment
SWHD	Sourcing with Human Dignity
TADB	Trade and Development Board
TB	tuberculosis
TBL	triple bottom line
TNC	transnational corporation
TQM	total quality management
TRIPs	Trade-Related Aspects of Intellectual Property Rights
TRM	total responsibility management
TUAC	Trade Union Advisory Committee
UDHR	Universal Declaration of Human Rights
UN	United Nations
UNCED	UN Conference on the Environment and Development
UNCHR	UN Commission for Human Rights
UNCTAD	UN Conference on Trade and Development
UNDP	UN Development Programme
UNEP	UN Environment Programme
UNESCO	UN Educational, Scientific and Cultural Organisation
UNGA	UN General Assembly
UNHCHR	UN High Commission for Human Rights
UNICEF	UN Children's Fund
UNIDO	UN Industrial Development Organisation
UNPD	UN Population Division
UNRISD	UN Research Institute for Social Development
WBCSD	World Business Council for Sustainable Development
WEED	World Economy, Ecology and Development
WHO	World Health Organisation
WSSD	World Summit on Sustainable Development
WTO	World Trade Organisation

Biographies

Jim Baker is Director of the Department of Multinational Enterprises at the International Confederation of Free Trade Unions (ICFTU) in Brussels, an organisation representing member trade union confederations with 158 million members. His department works with Global Union Federations (representing workers by sector and occupation) on global social dialogue, campaigns, and other activities related to MNEs.

Baker previously held several positions in the American Federation of Labor–Congress of Industrial Organizations (AFL–CIO), including Executive Assistant to the President and Regional Director for the nine Western States. He was European Representative of the AFL–CIO and was based in Paris for nine years. He served on the Governing Body of the International Labour Organisation from 1986 to 1991.

Before becoming a trade union official, Baker was an autoworker employed by the Ford Motor Company and a member of the United Automobile, Aerospace and Agricultural Implement Workers' International Union (UAW).

jim.baker@laposte.net

Jem Bendell is a visiting fellow in the International Centre for Corporate Social Responsibility, Nottingham University Business School, UK. With a doctorate in international policy, Jem Bendell has consulted for the private, voluntary and intergovernmental sectors on globalisation and sustainable development issues for nine years, including work for four UN agencies. An author of two books on relations between the voluntary and corporate sectors, and a columnist on corporate responsibility, he is particularly involved in the international development dimensions to these issues. His latest book, *In Our Power: The Civilisation of Globalisation*, is published by Greenleaf Publishing in late 2004.

www.jembendell.com

Tanja D. Carroll recently finished her MBA at Boston University, where she also graduated with an MA in international relations. Her research interest in corporate social responsibility has brought her to CERES (Coalition for Environmentally Responsible Economies), where she

is doing a one-year fellowship. Her work at CERES has focused on promoting better understanding of the risks of climate change among institutional investors.
carroll@ceres.org

Dr **Gill Coleman** works with the Centre for Action Research and Professional Practice at Bath University School of Management, focusing on corporate social responsibility and change. She was director of the New Academy of Business until 2001, and helped establish the MSc in Responsibility and Business Practice at Bath University, with which she continues to be a core tutor. Gill has co-authored two books on corporate social responsibility: *Corporate Citizenship* (Financial Times Pitman, 1998) and *Living Corporate Citizenship* (Financial Times Prentice Hall 2002).
gillc@blueyonder.co.uk

Thomas Donaldson is the Mark O. Winkelman Professor at the Wharton School of the University of Pennsylvania, where he is director of the Wharton PhD programme in ethics and law. He is the associate editor of the *Academy of Management Review* and a member of the editorial boards of other journals, including the *Business Ethics Quarterly*. Books that he has authored or edited include: *The Ties that Bind: A Social Contract Approach to Business Ethics* (Harvard University Business School Press, 1999), co-authored with Thomas W. Dunfee; *Ethical Issues in Business*, 7th edition (Prentice-Hall, 2002), co-edited with Patricia Werhane; *Ethics in Business and Economics*, a two-volume set (Ashgate Publishing, 1998), co-edited with Thomas W. Dunfee; *Ethics in International Business* (Oxford University Press, 1989); and *Corporations and Morality* (Prentice-Hall, 1982). He has consulted and lectured at many organisations, including Goldman Sachs, Walt Disney, Microsoft, Motorola, JP Morgan, Johnson & Johnson, Los Alamos National Laboratory, Shell International, IBM, Pfizer, the AMA, the IMF, Bankers Trust, the United Nations and the World Bank. In the summer of 2002, he testified in the US Senate about the Sarbanes–Oxley corporate reform legislation.
donaldst@Wharton.upenn.edu

Claude Fussler is a director of the World Business Council for Sustainable Development. He principally acts as special advisor to the UN Global Compact. In 2002 he co-ordinated the business input to the World Summit on Sustainable Development in Johannesburg and produced the business book *Walking the Talk* (Greenleaf Publishing, 2002) in which prominent business executives demonstrated the opportunities and responsibilities to found in globalisation. As a vice president of Dow Chemical in Europe, where he worked for more than 30 years, Claude managed a number of international business assignments. He often speaks at top-management briefings. He also is becoming more involved in local issues in Provence, where he runs a farm and vineyard with his wife, Martina.
fussler@wbcsd.org

Mara Hernandez is a PhD student at MIT's Sloan School of Management; she has a master's degree in public administration from Harvard University and a bachelor's degree in economics in Mexico. Her fields of concentration are labour and negotiations, and her research focuses on the relationship between freedom of association (or lack thereof), competitiveness and democratic governance. She also works in Mexico with non-governmental organisations and academic institutions to increase negotiation and consensus-building skills.
marah@mit.edu

Georg Kell was born in 1954. He studied economics and engineering at the Technical University of Berlin. Following his postgraduate studies at the Fraunhofer Institute, he spent two years in Tanzania where he helped establish an industrial research institute. He has

worked as a financial analyst in developing countries in Asia and Africa. In 1987 he began his career at the United Nations: from 1987 to 1990 he worked at the UN Conference on Trade and Development (UNCTAD), Geneva; in 1990 he joined the New York office of UNCTAD, and from 1993 to 1997 he was head of the office; in 1997 he became senior officer at the executive office of the Secretary-General, responsible for fostering co-operation with the private sector. Since 2000 he has worked as executive head of the Global Compact, United Nations, New York.
kell@un.org

Deborah Leipziger is a consultant in the field of corporate social responsibility. Her clients have included the UN Global Compact, the Global Reporting Initiative, Social Accountability International and Warwick University. She has also advised a wide range of companies on CSR in the retail, manufacturing, cement and beverage industries. Ms Leipziger played a key role in the development of the standard Social Accountability 8000 and its guidance document. She is the author of *The Corporate Responsibility Code Book* (Greenleaf Publishing, 2003); *SA8000: The Definitive Guide to the New Social Standard* (Financial Times, 2001) and co-author of *Living Corporate Citizenship* (Financial Times Prentice Hall, 2002) and *Corporate Citizenship: Successful Strategies of Responsible Companies* (Financial Times Pitman, 1998). Deborah serves as an advisor to Morley Fund Management, advising it on its socially responsible investment. A native of Brazil, Ms Leipziger resides in The Hague, with her husband and three daughters.
thehague@wanadoo.nl

Klaus M. Leisinger is the president and executive director of the Novartis Foundation for Sustainable Development (www.novartisfoundation.com). In addition to his position at Novartis, he teaches and conducts research as professor of sociology at the University of Basel. Focus themes include business ethics and globalisation, health policy for poor countries, sustainable development as well as human rights and business. He has contributed to the debates with a significant number of publications in several languages. Dr Leisinger has served as an invited lecturer at several European and US universities and serves in several advisory functions in different national and international organisations dealing with corporate social responsibility and sustainable development issues. He is a member of the Board of Trustees of the German Network Business Ethics (Deutsches Netzwerk Wirtschaftsethik) and of the Advisory Council of Mary Robinson's Ethical Globalization Initiative.
klaus_m.leisinger@group.novartis.com

David Levin holds an MBA from the Wharton School, University of Pennsylvania. He is a Zicklin Center for Business Ethics Research Fellow at the Global Compact, where he serves as a strategy consultant. David was also a co-founder and Director of the Wharton Social Impact Management Initiative, and graduated as a Siebel Scholar, Thouron Scholar and Rotary Ambassadorial Scholar. He has authored work on socially responsible investment with Wharton finance professors, as well as a study on corporate citizenship in Argentina with the IAE School of Management and Business. David received a BS in Economics and a BA in International Studies from the University of Pennsylvania, where he was elected to Phi Beta Kappa and graduated summa cum laude.
dalevin@wharton.upenn.edu

Malcolm McIntosh is a writer, teacher and consultant on corporate responsibility and sustainability. He divides his time between advising global corporations and international organisations and teaching in universities around the world. He is a special advisor to the UN Global Compact and has worked on various aspects of this corporate citizenship initiative for a number of years, including representing the UN at conferences. He is adjunct professor at Waikato Management School, University of Waikato, New Zealand, and visiting professor at

the Universities of Bath and Nottingham, UK. He also teaches at the Universities of Stellenbosch, South Africa, and Bristol, UK. He was the founding editor of the quarterly peer-reviewed *Journal of Corporate Citizenship* (Greenleaf Publishing) and remains on the editorial board. He was editor of *Visions of Ethical Business* from 1998 to 2002 (FT and Pricewaterhouse-Coopers) and is the author of many books and articles on corporate citizenship. He has held the posts of director of the Corporate Citizenship Unit at Warwick Business School, and European director of the Council on Economic Priorities (Social Accountability International). He has served as a member of the governing council of the Institute of Social and Ethical Accountability and currently serves on the Conference Board's European Working Group on Corporate Citizenship.
malcolm.mcintosh@btinternet.com

Errol Mendes is a professor of law at the University of Ottawa, Canada. His work focuses on globalisation, corporate ethics and international law. He is an advisor to the UN Global Compact and is also an advisor to the Canadian federal government and several Canadian multinationals on corporate integrity, diversity and human rights issues. He co-chaired the Global Compact working group that developed the *Business Guide to Conflict Impact Risk Assessment*. He is co-author of the multidisciplinary text on human rights, corporate ethics and the global economy titled *Global Governance, Economy and Law: Waiting for Justice* (Routledge, 2003).
emendes@uottawa.ca

Nancy Nielsen is senior director of corporate citizenship for Pfizer Inc. and is leading the company's global cross-divisional effort on corporate citizenship. She applies her public-sector and private-sector experience to Pfizer's focus on sustainable health. Previously, she led a project at Harvard University on globalisation and backlash, she was vice president of corporate communications at The New York Times Company, she was director of communications at ABC-TV and was a consultant at McKinsey & Company. Concurrently, she did *pro bono* work in international stakeholder relations at the UN, the World Bank, and a Carnegie Commission. She is a member of the Council on Foreign Relations, serving on its Public Diplomacy committee, and is a trustee of the HealthCare Chaplaincy. She serves on Transparency International's Steering Committee on Business Principles for Countering Bribery. She graduated from the University of California at Berkeley with a BA in journalism and Yale University with an MBA.
Nancy.Nielsen@pfizer.com

Michael Hougård Pedersen is an advisor on corporate social responsibility at Novozymes Sustainability Development Centre in Copenhagen, Denmark. Prior to that, he was an advisor on stakeholder issues at VKR Holding (VELUX) in Copenhagen, Denmark. Michael holds an MSc in political science from Aarhus University, Denmark, and is currently enrolled in the MSc in responsibility and business practice at the University of Bath, UK. During an assignment to the Policy Planning Unit of the Department of Political Affairs at the UN Headquarters, Michael was engaged in preparing and attending the inaugural Global Compact High-Level Meeting in July 2000.
mail@mhpedersen.dk

James E. Post is professor of management at Boston University and has written extensively on corporate responsibility, public affairs management and business ethics. He is co-author, with Lee E. Preston and Sybille Sachs, of *Redefining the Corporation: Stakeholder Management and Organizational Wealth* (Stanford University Press, 2002). He is also co-author, with Anne T. Lawrence and James Weber, of *Business and Society: Stakeholders, Ethics, Public Policy*, 11th

edition (McGraw–Hill, 2004). His current research addresses institutional integrity and the relationship of corporate citizenship strategies to business strategies among companies with global brand identities.
jepost@bu.edu

John Gerard Ruggie is Kirkpatrick Professor of International Affairs and Weil Director, Center for Business and Government, at Harvard University's John F. Kennedy School of Government. From 1997 to 2001 he was Assistant Secretary-General of the United Nations, serving as senior advisor for strategic planning to UN Secretary-General Kofi Annan. His portfolio included positioning the United Nations *vis-à-vis* key global challenges and constituencies, including institutional reforms and priorities, UN–US relations and UN relations with the global business community. Ruggie remains the Secretary-General's special advisor on the Global Compact, of which he and Georg Kell were the principal architects.
john_ruggie@harvard.edu

Annette Stube is advisor, social responsibility, and project manager in stakeholder relations at Novo Nordisk. The Stakeholder Relations strategic unit reports directly to the executive management. Annette has been working with Novo Nordisk since 1997 and has been part of the team that has developed the triple-bottom-line approach on social responsibility. With an MA in organisational psychology Annette has previously worked as a human resource consultant, freelance as well as in Novo Nordisk. She started her career working for SOS-International, a Nordic alarm centre, as a manager for psychological crisis intervention teams and as manager of supplier relations in Eastern Europe and Africa.
astu@novonordisk.com

David Teller is deputy director of the Committee for Melbourne, a private, not-for-profit network of leaders drawn from Melbourne's business, scientific, academic, community and government sectors. He is keenly interested in urbanism and urbanisation-related issues and is the author of the Melbourne Model—a new mechanism to tackle intractable social, economic and environmental urban problems by facilitating partnerships between business, government and civil society. David is also the international programme co-ordinator of the Global Compact Cities Pilot Programme.
dteller@melbourne.org.au

Ruth Thomas is now a Senior Sustainability and Environmental Advisor with Defence Estates, part of the UK Ministry of Defence. Previously she worked as an independent researcher and writer on corporate citizenship. Dr Thomas has degrees from University College London and Bath University, and is an associate membership assessor for the Institute of Environmental Management and Assessment (IEMA).
ruth.andy@btinternet.com

Chris Tuppen co-ordinates development of British Telecommunications (BT)'s global strategy across the social, environmental and economic dimensions of sustainable development. He is also responsible for producing the company's corporate accountability reports and for communicating BT's business case for corporate social responsibility. He previously led BT's environmental issues unit. He is chair of the Global e-Sustainability Initiative in association with the United Nations Environment Programme and the International Telecommunications Union, sits on the Council of the Institute of Social and Ethical Accountability, the Boards of CSR Europe and the US-based Business for Social Responsibility, and the Social and Environmental Committee of the Association of Chartered Certified Accountants. He co-

chaired the Global Reporting Initiative measurement working group, chaired the ETNO (European Telecommunication Network Operators' Association) environmental working group and has advised many institutions, including the Commission of the European Communities, the Organisation for Economic Co-operation and Development and the Advisory Committee on Business and the Environment.
chris.tuppen@bt.com

Cornelis Theunis van der Lugt was born in Port Elizabeth, South Africa, in 1967. He studied and taught political science and political philosophy at the University of Stellenbosch, South Africa, from 1986 to 1992. Over the past 15 years he has done extensive research in the field of international relations, focusing on the environment. In a professional capacity he also gained personal experience of international environmental diplomacy, as multilateral diplomat in the South African Foreign Ministry. He received his PhD in international relations at the University of Stellenbosch in 1998. His doctoral studies involved research at the Albert-Ludwigs-Universität Freiburg (Germany) and the Rijksuniversiteit Leiden (Netherlands) from 1993 to 1996. Since then he has been involved in various international conferences and negotiations at multilateral meetings in the environmental field, in particular those of the United Nations agreements on climate change and ozone depletion. Since January 2000 he has been based in Paris at the Division of Technology, Industry and Economics (DTIE) of the United Nations Environment Programme (UNEP), where he is responsible for the Global Compact of the UN Secretary-General and the Global Reporting Initiative. His responsibilities over the past three years have included representing UNEP at international conferences on corporate environmental and social responsibility.
cornis.lugt@unep.fr

Steve Waddell supports large systems change. The issues may be as broad as issues of trade, poverty and sustainable development, or as specific as road-building, youth employment, development of specific communities and banking. Usually, the change strategy involves creating business–government–civil society collaborations and networks; these collaborations may be local, national or global. Steve brings organisational, network and societal development and change expertise to work as a consultant and researcher with two core concepts: societal learning and change, and global action networks. He has a PhD and an MBA, is widely published and he has led the formation of several leading organisations (see www.gan-net.net; www.strategic-clarity.com; www.thecollaborationworks.com).
www.strategic-clarity.com

Sandra Waddock is professor of management at Boston College's Carroll School of Management and Senior Research Fellow at Boston College's Center for Corporate Citizenship. She has published extensively on corporate responsibility, corporate citizenship and inter-sector collaboration in journals such as *The Academy of Management Journal, Academy of Management Executive, Strategic Management Journal, The Journal of Corporate Citizenship, Human Relations,* and *Business and Society.* She is author of *Leading Corporate Citizens: Vision, Values, Value Added* (McGraw–Hill, 2002) and co-editor of the two-volume series *Unfolding Stakeholder Thinking* (Greenleaf Publishing, 2002-2003). She is a founding faculty member of the Leadership for Change Programme at Boston College and currently edits *The Journal of Corporate Citizenship.*
waddock@bc.edu

Index